Forgiveness *and*
Reconciliation

Forgiveness *and* Reconciliation

Theory and Application

Everett L. Worthington, Jr.

Routledge
Taylor & Francis Group
New York   London

Routledge is an imprint of the
Taylor & Francis Group, an informa business

Published in 2006 by
Routledge
Taylor & Francis Group
270 Madison Avenue
New York, NY 10016

Published in Great Britain by
Routledge
Taylor & Francis Group
2 Park Square
Milton Park, Abingdon
Oxon OX14 4RN

Printed in the United States of America on acid-free paper
10 9 8 7 6 5 4 3 2 1

International Standard Book Number-10: 1-58391-333-5 (Hardcover)
International Standard Book Number-13: 978-1-58391-333-8 (Hardcover)
Library of Congress Card Number 2005033905

Library of Congress Cataloging-in-Publication Data

Worthington, Everett L., 1946-
    Forgiveness and reconciliation : theory and application / Everett L. Worthington, Jr.
        p. cm.
    Includes bibliographical references (p.   ) and index.
    ISBN 1-58391-333-5 (hb : alk. paper)
    1. Forgiveness. 2. Reconciliation. I. Title.

BF637.F67W68 2006
155.9'2--dc22   2005033905

---

informa
Taylor & Francis Group
is the Academic Division of Informa plc.

Visit the Taylor & Francis Web site at
http://www.taylorandfrancis.com

and the Routledge Web site at
http://www.routledge-ny.com

To John M. (Jack) Templeton, Jr., MD—man of God,
friend, leader, philanthropist, and visionary—who
has done more to promote a scientific understanding
of forgiveness than anyone I know.

Contents

Preface

You can transform your world. Help others forgive. Change one relationship at a time. Transformation can spread from your personal life, to your clinical relationships, to society. I believe this theory of forgiveness will help bring about that transformation.

Within the existing research literature on forgiveness, there are many *models* of how people forgive. There are also many clinical models of how to help people forgive. In this book, I describe a *theory* relating biological, psychological, and social aspects of both forgiving and helping people forgive. The theory draws on general stress-and-coping theory (see Lazarus, 1999). Perhaps "theory" is too pretentious for what I have written. A model describes how concepts fit together. A theory weaves models into a larger biopsychosocial fabric by intertwining threads of ways to understand people. I try to weave several scientific models into a story: the biology of stress, the justice motive, coping theory, positive psychology, emotion-motivation models, the social psychology of predicaments and accounts, intergroup relations, and societal interactions. I relate those basic scientific models to clinical science. By drawing from psychodynamic theories, emotion-focused therapy, integrative behavior therapy, hope-focused relationship enhancement, and solution-focused therapy, I describe interventions to promote forgiving. Those interventions derive from and inform the basic-science models.

To the extent that I succeed in creating a stress-and-coping theory of unforgiveness and forgiveness, you should expect to see literatures woven together into a seamless fabric. You should develop an understanding of the driving concepts within the theory, and you should ask questions you were not asking before.

Inevitably, I will fail at producing a forgiveness "theory." But perhaps I can move our thinking along. If you are not a psychological scientist or a clinician, you can enrich your world by entering this theoretical journey. But, this book is aimed at researchers and clinicians. If you are a psychological scientist—perhaps even an accomplished forgiveness researcher—I hope this will take you on a stimulating new journey. I hope you will tweak your own theorizing and find new concepts to study. If you are a clinician, I hope you will see new ways to help clients who are dealing with transgressions without them feeling that forgiveness is coerced.

I am convinced of the usefulness of the theory. I have used it in research. I have tested the basic ideas in counseling with groups, couples, and individuals. I have applied it in my own life. For example, on January 2, 1996, in the wee hours of the morning, I encountered the most difficult transgression I ever had to wrestle with. I forgave the youths who had murdered my mother less than two days before.

I had studied forgiveness in the lab since 1989 and done marriage, family, individual, and group counseling for almost 20 years. Yet I was not prepared to deal with horrific personal loss. We never are. These life tests are too big, too unexpected.

My mom was alone on that New Year's Eve night. She puttered around the house waiting for New Year's. At age 78, though, she cared more about dropping off to sleep than about the ball dropping in Times Square. She may have thought about her physical restrictions. She often felt ill. She was prone to worry. Would lung cancer, which had claimed Dad, get her? Her legs bothered her. Her blood pressure was high. Her hearing had begun to fail. "What will this new year hold?" she might have thought as she pulled on the sheer pale-blue nightgown. Settling in, she switched off the light.

Later, a youth armed with a crowbar smashed the window in the back door. He and his buddy began to search for valuables. In the darkness, there were gentle scrapes of drawers pulled out, paper thrown to the floor, cushions tossed about. They were pirates, and there was treasure to be found.

The youth with the crowbar went into the hallway, pulling the contents from an old, refinished glass-doored bookcase. Suddenly, behind him he heard something that set his nerves on edge. A voice, quivering with fear: "What are you doing in here?!" My mother had at last awakened. She stepped into the hallway behind the youth.

The youth whirled, taking a defensive pose automatically. Some primitive thought may have flooded his brain. A whining voice might have buzzed inside his head, "This is not the way it's supposed to be! This was supposed to be a perfect crime! This old woman is destroying my perfect crime!" He felt the heft of the crowbar in his hand and looked down, thinking, "Even worse. I'm going to go to jail! This old woman has seen my face! She's looking directly at me. She can put the finger on me."

Without thinking, he may have taken a step forward, drawn back the crowbar. As my mother threw up her hands, he struck down over the top of her hands, hitting her in the face. She fell. He shifted his grip—two hands now. He struck her on the back. He grabbed her by the hair and rolled her over. Then in a final surge of adrenaline, he smashed her in the left temple.

"Man, what have you done?!" his buddy might have shouted from the doorway. "You killed her!"

"She would have sent us both to jail! I didn't have any choice!"

As the murderer wrestled with his own actions, he became angrier. He began to smash mirrors in every room. He looked down at her bleeding body. He ran to the case he had been rifling when he was interrupted. He smashed the mirror into thousands of pieces. Then he sprinted to the kitchen, bashing things with the crowbar.

He snatched a wine bottle. My mother was unconscious. She was probably breathing irregularly and weakly. Her negligee made her look as defenseless as a frumpy old granny. All the worse. She had the power to put them in prison.

He jerked up the negligee. He thrust the bottle hard up under the negligee, twisting and punching. Blood began to ooze from beneath her hips.

The youths fled. One carried a crowbar. The other carried a few dollars in coins. Both carried the weight of guilt.

Within 30 hours, I was able to forgive the youths who had committed this horrible crime. How could I forgive such a crime in a mere 30 hours? Was this merely a flight into forgiveness? Not genuine? Forgiveness done out of obligation or duty? Or was I able to forgive this murder because I was so practiced at forgiveness that this was not really much of a challenge? Did I think rationally about this act and then decide to forgive? What if this youth were to be caught? Would my forgiveness, granted alone in the middle of the night, allow me to meet him and tell him I forgave?

In this book, you will learn not only how you can promote forgiveness but also what forgiveness is, why it does and does not happen, and how to understand its complexities. You will learn the theory and its research support. You should see justice, forgiveness, and coping in a new light. You will also learn practically how to help people who wish to forgive to do so. As a clinician, I developed a program to promote forgiveness. It was informed by the basic research. I teach people five steps to REACH forgiveness, and because much forgiveness occurs within relationships, I expanded the program to deal with both forgiveness and reconciliation. It is called Forgiving and Reconciling through Experiencing Empathy

(FREE). Both REACH and FREE have been studied empirically and used by counselors throughout the world. You will learn these interventions. You can apply them to transform your world, one relationship at a time, and to help others transform their worlds.

What This Book Will Not Do

I want to be clear. I will not try to convince you that forgiveness is the only way or always the best way people should deal with interpersonal transgressions. People deal with transgressions using many ways that do not involve forgiveness. I value many alternatives to forgiveness. I believe that forgiveness is often the best way to deal with transgressions. But, forgiveness must fit the belief system of the person employing it. If not, forgiveness can be a blunt instrument, not a tool.

What This Book Will Do

This book will teach you evidence-based interventions to promote forgiveness. The reliance on scientific evidence is a product of medical science. In the early 1900s, the world of medicine was changed forever when John D. Rockefeller left millions of dollars to fund the scientific study of health and medicine. Until that time, medical practitioners treated illness through intuition and clinical experience. After Rockefeller's generosity, people began to study biology, health, and medicine scientifically. The creativity, experience, and intuition of the practitioner remains medicine's most highly valued commodity, but science systematized that experience and intuition. Mistakes were culled out of the medical practice through the scientific method. Research found basic processes, which led to new medical treatments. Psychopharmacology was born. Other treatments of diseases were developed. Even better, their use was not based on the charisma of the developer nor word-of-mouth testimonial. Medical interventions were based on controlled scientific studies. Medical scientists found which interventions were effective and which were not for what type of problem.

In the same way, understanding of forgiveness and its promotion have also benefited by science. People forgave others for centuries. Peacemakers, religious leaders, and helpful friends advocated forgiveness. But we did not know the social, personality, and developmental processes underlying forgiving and not forgiving. We could not describe the interpersonal interactions around transgressions despite millennia of experience in human conflict. The fledgling field of scientific research known as forgiveness studies, involving both basic and clinical science, is transforming our understanding of forgiveness just as the understanding of medicine was transformed by medical research. When Rockefeller began to fund research on health and medicine in the early 1900s, many people thought he was crazy: "Why give away money to egghead scientists to do laboratory studies when there are a lot of sick people who could be helped?" they asked. People have said the same about basic research in forgiving. But basic research and theory are needed. In this book, I digest the research from this new field of forgiveness studies and present it as a theory. I hope it proves useful to you.

Acknowledgments

I am indebted to numerous people for their support. My wife (Kirby) and children have encouraged and supported me. Without that support, my writing and my life would be fruitless. Their love keeps me going.

I am grateful for those who have contributed monetary support for my research and writing of this book. Funding for my research has come from the John Templeton Foundation (Grant #239), *A Campaign for Forgiveness Research,* the Fetzer Institute (Grant #1653.3), Virginia Commonwealth University's (VCU) Center for the Study and Prevention of Youth Violence (Award #2003-11, under a grant from the Centers for Disease Control and Prevention), the VCU General Clinic Research Center (NIH #5M01RR1000065), and an internal grant from Virginia Commonwealth University. The Center for Advanced Religious and Theological Societies (CARTS) at the University of Cambridge and its Cambridge Centre for Science and Religion—under the direction of Sir John Polkinghorne and Fraser Watts—also supported me financially and provided a stimulating environment that enhanced the revision of this manuscript, and VCU provided half salary during a year of scholarly research leave, during which the book was completed.

I also am greatly indebted to my students, former students, and colleagues. Although they are too many to mention, I hope they know that I have always, and do now, depend on them for ideas, energy, hard work, social support, friendship, and (you guessed it) forgiveness. The Positive Psychology Research Group has done research upon which much of this book depends. Mary Ann Ryan and Michael Scherer, my assistants at VCU, and Guy Brandon, my assistant at Cambridge, have been particularly helpful on this book manuscript. Michael typed it many times. Although I have at times disappointed all of my coworkers, I believe we have had a great run together.

I must thank the bright and energetic researchers who study forgiveness worldwide. My interactions with them through e-mail, personal contact, collaboration, working with them on a campaign-funded project, hearing them at the Scientific Conference on Forgiveness in Atlanta in 2003, and working shoulder to shoulder with many to bring about the *Handbook of forgiveness* (Brunner-Routledge, 2005) have informed me about the research in the field.

Finally, I thank George Zimmar, Dana Bliss, and the team at Routledge. They believed in this project. They kept supporting me (and prodding me for needed change) even though this book took far longer than I originally predicted.

Introduction

I was pumped up. I was going to have my first interview with one of the six major newspapers in the country. The occasion for the interview was the announcement that A Campaign for Forgiveness Research had just been formed. The Campaign aimed to raise money to support additional research beyond the studies already funded by the $3 million that the John Templeton Foundation had provided to study forgiveness.

Beginning of the Forgiveness Movement

Forgiveness studies had begun after the publication of Lewis Smedes's (1984) book, *Forgive and Forget: Healing the Hurts We Don't Deserve*. Its premise was that forgiveness benefited the forgiver. Smedes suggested that people could be their own therapist by forgiving those who harmed them. That appealed to psychotherapists. They began to write articles in the professional literature.

The topic of forgiveness also caught the eye of a developmental psychologist at the University of Wisconsin-Madison, Robert D. Enright. He had studied the moral development in children in his early career. He became convinced that reasoning about justice, as Kohlberg (1984) had held to be the basis of moral thought, needed to be tempered by reasoning about mercy or forgiveness. Enright courageously launched a research program to study how reasoning about forgiveness developed as children aged.

About 1989, we began to study forgiveness in my lab at Virginia Commonwealth University (VCU). From then through the mid-1990s, Michael McCullough, Steve Sandage, and I conducted reviews of the literature and early studies in forgiveness. We developed the basis of our empathy-based treatment of forgiveness and investigated its efficacy. By 1997, we had published a book, summarizing the state of the field: *To Forgive Is Human: How to Put Your Past in the Past.*

At the end of 1997, the John Templeton Foundation announced a research competition through a worldwide request for proposals (RFP). Scientists all over the world submitted research proposals to study forgiveness scientifically. I cochaired that RFP with David G. Myers. A panel of eight eminent scholars adjudicated the 135 submitted research proposals based on evaluations from over 70 reviewer-scholars. In early 1998, the panel identified about 26 for funding by the Foundation with the $3 million and worked with the John Fetzer Institute, which funded two more. Many excellent proposals could not be funded. We formed A Campaign for Forgiveness Research. Its goal was to raise money to fund unfunded proposals that had been ranked highest by the panel. The announcement of the Campaign was accompanied by press releases, which attracted the attention of journalists. This was my first major interview.

A Challenging Interview

The phone rang and the reporter identified herself. She immediately jumped into the interview, "This Templeton initiative and forgiveness Campaign are just thinly disguised excuses for a religious agenda, wouldn't you say?" said Lottie Hostility. (Okay, you caught me. That was not her real name.)

I have to admit, that was not exactly the opening gambit I had anticipated. I guess unconsciously I was hoping for more, like, sustained applause. "Actually," I said, "the Campaign is far removed from a religious agenda. About one-fourth of our investigators do profess to personal religious faith, but only three studies purport to study religious forgiveness. Instead, we have some high-caliber scientists who will study forgiveness. Some of their methods might not even be acceptable to some religious people."

"Name a couple."

"Robert Sapolsky at Stanford University is studying peacemaking in primates in the wild. He hopes to see how a baboon troupe that lost its aggressive members passes on its culture of peace to future generations. Frans de Waal of Emory's Yerkes Primate Center is studying reconciliation in chimpanzees in captivity. Lyndon Eaves at the Behavioral Genetics Institute at Virginia Commonwealth University is using a twin registry to look into gene expression of forgiveness.

"Four investigations are studying transgressions in other countries. Irwin Staub at the University of Massachusetts-Amherst is studying the Rwanda massacres. Audrey Chapman, an officer at the American Association for the Advancement of Science in Washington, DC, is collaborating with South African scientists to study the Truth and Reconciliation

Commission hearings, as is Jeffrey Sonis at the University of Michigan. Ed Cairns in Ulster is studying the Northern Ireland conflict.

"Neuroscientists Thomas Farrow and Peter Woodruff are studying brain functioning using functional MRIs in England. Social psychologists, including Roy Baumeister and Caryl Rusbult, are studying social interactions. Clinical and social psychologists like C. R. Snyder are studying personality and social interactions. June Tangney at George Mason University is looking at forgiving the self and forgiveness in children. Frank Fincham is studying marriage. Sociologist David Williams is using a national probability sample to see if forgiveness and health are related. You can see, this is not a religious subterfuge. It really is an opportunity for major scientists to try to discover what is going on when people do and don't forgive."

"What's going on is this: forgiveness is very dangerous," said Lottie Hostility. "Women are told to forgive batterers. They get back into the relationship. They get beaten worse—or killed. This is irresponsible. What do you have to say to that?"

"You raise a good issue. Certainly, we would not encourage someone to rush to reconcile an abusive relationship. Forgiveness is fairly independent of whether a person decides to reconcile. Forgiveness occurs inside an individual. Reconciliation is restoring damage in a relationship, not inside an individual. Trust can't be restored unless people are trustworthy. So, if an abuser continues to harm, no clinical psychologist would suggest that a woman return to an abusive relationship, regardless of whether she had forgiven. Forgiveness is not dangerous, but *misunderstanding forgiveness* is. Using it improperly can be just as dangerous as misusing any sort of medication. Through research, we hope to clear up some common misunderstandings about forgiveness and to identify its limitations."

"Well," said Lottie, "forgiveness doesn't hold wrongdoers accountable. It lets them off the hook."

"As far as letting the offender off the hook, usually the offender isn't on the hook. The offender is usually free to offend again. Whether a person does or doesn't forgive, the offender might still offend. Forgiveness is an internal experience. Rightly understood, it should not be confused with holding an offender accountable. Those are different issues. One has to do with justice. The other, with mercy."

Lottie was undaunted, "When people forgive, don't they quit seeking justice?"

"Forgiveness is at the individual, internal level. It does not determine whether a person will pursue social, civil, or societal justice. Justice is at the social level."

Lottie said, "Well, I have a friend who was betrayed by her husband. She was a Christian. Her Christianity dictated that she had to forgive. So she announced to everybody that she had forgiven her husband, but it was clear to her friends that she had in fact not forgiven. Every word about her husband dripped with venom. She was resentful, hostile, and hateful. Eventually, it made her sick. She developed stress-related disorders because she said she had forgiven and couldn't admit that she really hadn't."

"You're hitting a very important distinction," I said. "How people talk about whether they have forgiven and even what their intentions are toward the person who offended them don't determine their emotional forgiveness. There does seem to be a difference in a person's intent not to act in hostility toward an offender and the person's experience of positive feelings toward the offender. As you say, sometimes people feel coerced to say they have forgiven when in fact they are merely giving in to social pressure. Or they might maintain a façade of forgiveness when they may in fact even be plotting revenge."

Lottie paused. "Well, my friend went to a therapist. He convinced her that she needed to work toward real forgiveness. He said that she was experiencing pseudo-forgiveness. He told her that she was making herself sick and miserable by her hateful attitudes. He said it was good for her to forgive. Do you think he did the right thing?"

"It's hard for me to say whether he did the right thing without talking to your friend. People can forgive for their own benefit. My own research shows that some other motivations for forgiving can help people be even more successful at forgiving. But it sounds as if her therapist believes that your friend did the right thing. That therapist was seeing your friend, not me."

"Well, I was appalled that he brought up forgiving. Forgiveness is religious. The therapist ought to have waited until, or if, it came up naturally in therapy," said Lottie.

"Forgiveness is found throughout our culture. It is the theme in *Les Misérables*. It is the subject of country and pop music songs. It doesn't seem to be fully identified with religion any longer. For most therapists, whether or when to promote forgiveness is dependent on the client's value system. If forgiveness fits, the therapist can pose the possibility of forgiveness tentatively. Few would suggest that someone ought to forgive. I suspect that your friend's therapist probably either picked up on a cue from your friend, or posed a question about whether she might consider forgiveness."

"You're a clinical psychologist, right? Has forgiveness therapy worked in your practice?"

"Let me give you an example. I'll call this woman Heddy Hardwick, even though that isn't their real name. For ethical reasons, I'll disguise some of the characteristics of her case. Heddy had been abused and battered by her husband for many years. After she left home, he went to groups on anger management. They didn't seem to take. She was hurt badly. She saw me for counseling after having separated from her husband again."

Lottie said, "So you counseled her to forgive?"

"We began by talking about her safety. We reviewed the times that she had been battered. We talked about whether she might ever decide to move back with her husband. I'll call him Bart. Heddy and I talked about how to make a decision as to when it might be safe to move back with Bart. By that time, Bart had often failed to control his temper. So Heddy decided that she would only return if he successfully completed counseling and Bart's therapist recommended that he could control his temper. She invited Bart to come to therapy first to work on anger, and second, if that was successful, to work on marriage counseling. Bart agreed. He stuck with the treatment of anger with a different therapist. After almost 6 months of weekly therapy, the therapist agreed that Bart had anger control strategies in place. Bart and Heddy came to me for marriage counseling. Whether he and Heddy would reconcile was still up in the air."

"You're not going to give me some Cinderella fairy tale about them living happily ever after, are you?"

"Actually, no. Bart could not seem to control his anger when the two of them were together. He lost his temper with Heddy during two sessions. It did not seem likely that he could control his temper better at home. Eventually, Heddy simply decided that she couldn't be married safely. She filed for a divorce. It was granted quickly because they had not lived together in almost nine months."

"Thank you for talking with me, Dr. Worthington. I hope you don't mind my direct frontal assault. You're doing some good work in funding the scientific studies of forgiveness. I had to ask hard questions so that I could write a balanced article."

We disconnected. At the end of the week, I saw the website version of the completed feature article. It turned out to be a sympathetic account of the scientific studies of forgiveness.

Most of us have questions about forgiveness. Not all of our questions are as in-your-face as Lottie Hostility's queries. But we harbor reservations. Is forgiveness appropriate? Under what conditions? Most of us—truth be known—also have the nagging problem that we sometimes cannot forgive a wound to our body or spirit even when we think we ought to forgive.

Let me be clear from the outset. Forgiveness is not called for in all situations, for all transgressions, by all people. Sometimes, it can be especially difficult.

South African Experience

I can imagine few cases when that central idea of this book has been put to a more stringent test than in the experience of Pumla Gobodo-Madikizela. She was a commissioner of the Truth and Reconciliation Commission (TRC) in South Africa. As a young clinical psychologist, she interviewed Eugene deKock, perhaps the most notorious perpetrator of evil within the apartheid Nationalist government. DeKock was so notorious for heading the apartheid government's killing machine that he was labeled "Prime Evil." He was imprisoned for crimes that he had committed as a policeman in the apartheid government.

One such incident involved three black policemen at the Motherwell police station in Port Elizabeth, South Africa. They had threatened to expose white policemen's involvement in deaths of four black activists. General Nick van Rensberg, commander of the police, asked deKock to silence the Motherwell policemen. DeKock sent them on a false mission. A bomb in their car was detonated by remote control. It blew to pieces the three policemen and a fourth man who happened to be in the car with them.

After Nelson Mandela was elected president and the new government took over, deKock was convicted and sentenced to serve hundreds of years in prison for those and other killings. Gobodo-Madikizela interviewed him many times. She usually met with him in C-Max—C-section of the Pretoria maximum-security prison. They sat with a table between them. DeKock wore prison orange.

DeKock's mind was compartmentalized. He justified his killings. He believed that he was trying to keep communism under control, fighting terrorism, preventing needless deaths by preemptive killing, and only doing what the other side was doing. He could kill men and women without batting an eye. But he would not let anyone harm a child. He threatened his killing squads: if they killed a child, he would personally execute them.

In one interview, Gobodo-Madikizela asked deKock to talk about a meeting he had with Darlene Mgoduka and Pearl Faku, widows of two of the policemen killed in Motherwell. DeKock became upset. His eyes teared, his voice broke, and he appeared to be remorseful. As he related the story of his meeting with the widows, he lamented his inability to bring back their husbands. He concluded, "I just have to live with it" (p. 32).

His hand was shaking. Gobodo-Madikizela compassionately touched his hand. She said it was "clinched, cold, and rigid as if he were holding back. As if he were holding on to some withering but still vital form of his old self" (p. 32). She recoiled, shaken. The interview soon ended.

The next morning, the arm of her hand that had touched deKock in his moment of vulnerability was numb. DeKock had touched her emotionally, and she had touched his hand. That in itself was a violation of social norms. In South Africa, a black woman did not touch a white man. But the unexpected coldness of deKock's hand had jarred her. It triggered the paralysis the next morning.

The next time that Gobodo-Madikizela met with deKock, they found that both had been wrestling with what it had meant to touch and be touched. DeKock thanked Gobodo-Madikizela for the previous conversation, which had taken almost four hours. Then he got an expression on his face of "genuine amazement" (p. 39), and he said, "You know, Pumla, that was my trigger hand you touched" (p. 39). DeKock spoke those words, as Gobodo-Madikizela recollected, "in the tones of a self-shaming confessional, the cry of a leper in ancient times shouting, 'Unclean, unclean'" (pp. 39–40).

Gobodo-Madikizela interpreted deKock's comment as trying to tear down the boundary between her as interviewer and himself as subject. The comment made her feel "invaded, naked, angry" (p. 40).

Others might question deKock's motives. It is easy to interpret deKock's act as an attempt to restore his sense of power over this black woman. He had shown vulnerability in the previous interview, which Gobodo-Madikizela had drawn attention to by a dramatic norm-violating touch. His sense of power must have been greatly damaged. By calling attention to her touch and associating it with the hand that committed murder, he made her feel vulnerable and weak.

Between September 1997 and April 1998, Gobodo-Madikizela met with deKock for 42 hours. In September 2002, she met with deKock at Pretoria prison. By then, as a result of his cooperation with the TRC, deKock had received amnesty for all his political crimes except two, for which he was serving two life sentences. He was hoping to have those reversed by presidential pardon. DeKock had committed the most heinous of crimes in his position as the head of the killing squads in South Africa, but he also laid bare his soul both publicly and in less public conversations with Gobodo-Madikizela. Under the TRC's mandate, complete cooperation and truthfulness with the TRC could result in amnesty. That amnesty had largely been granted. This series of interactions around deKock's crimes illustrates many of the things that you will learn in the book.

The Importance of the Injustice Gap

After a transgression has occurred, people sense that an injustice has been done and not resolved. I call that difference between the way a person would ideally like to have an injustice resolved and the perceived current status of the events the *injustice gap* (Worthington, 2003). People experience threat, stress, unforgiving feelings and motivations, fixation on ways of coping, and degree of difficulty forgiving in direct proportion to the magnitude of the injustice gap. The size of the injustice gap can lead people to experience poor mental, physical, relational, and spiritual health.

DeKock had inflicted so many awful transgressions on people throughout South Africa that many people had huge injustice gaps because of his acts. The populace was unforgiving of deKock. They were threatened by his presence and by his merely being alive. They felt stress when they considered the possibility that other deKocks might ever obtain power. Many people were terrified of him. Many felt vengeful.

Gobodo-Madikizela experienced her own injustice gaps. She had herself experienced discrimination. She felt the collective wrongs that were inflicted on black and white people alike. DeKock was a symbol of those injustices. Yet when deKock said that she had touched his trigger hand, she felt personally vulnerable and disempowered. The gentle assault numbed her arm merely by knowing she had touched him. "I have touched evil," she might have thought. It affected her emotions. It hurt her relationships with others due to that threat. She ruminated about deKock. Was he evil? Or had he merely done evil? She questioned human nature. She read philosophers like Hannah Arendt. If her negative interactions with deKock had persisted long enough, she might have experienced stress disorders or perhaps even long-term chronic problems.

Forgiveness Is One of Many Good Ways to Cope With Injustice

Gobodo-Madikizela never admitted to whole-heartedly forgiving deKock. She came to understand him, to empathize and sympathize with him, to feel compassion for him. As he began to seem less powerfully Evil and more fraily human, her emotions became less negative and more positive toward him.

In the final chapter of her book, she recommended that society embrace and perhaps pardon deKock because of his vulnerability and cooperativeness. Gobodo-Madikizela had not made a decision to grant forgiveness explicitly to deKock. But her experience and empathy with him indicated some emotional and motivational change. She also had, through her interviews with him, constructed a different picture of him. No longer was he the dark, evil, unknown, all-powerful inflictor of suffering. Instead, he was a human being who had been caught up in a corrupt and evil political system, which had indeed corrupted him. Through deKock's sincere expressions of remorse and contrition, that part grew in Gobodo-Madikizela's mind, and the evil part dwindled.

Forgiveness Can Change Our Experience in Relationships Dramatically

Forgiveness can change personal outcomes, such as appraisals and rumination, directly. Forgiveness can also change relationships. Those changed relationships can feed back and make personal experiences, in turn, become more positive.

Gobodo-Madikizela gradually became less negative and more understanding. Such gradual transformations often happen. It is like a person walking up one side of a teeter-totter. There might come a tipping point (Gladwell, 2002). That tipping point suddenly changes things dramatically, like flipping a light switch brings a dark room to light. After a protracted period of unforgiveness, forgiveness might suddenly transcend the injustice gap, shut off rumination, provide a sudden steadying of emotions, or switch from negative to positive emotions. Appraisals of the relationship can suddenly change from threat to challenge—an appraisal that makes all the difference in the world with how we cope with relationship problems.

People Practice Patterns of Dealing With Transgressions

Most people have a limited repertoire of ways they deal with transgressions. Some people hold grudges. Some seek vengeance. Some forgive. Most people are someplace in the middle of that triangle (see Figure I.1). They flutter back and forth depending on circumstances. But if they practice one set of responses often, they lock in their personality and simultaneously shape their interpersonal world. They also influence their mental, physical, relational, and spiritual health by the patterns they practice.

Gobodo-Madikizela grew up as a black child in South Africa. Living in the black community, she experienced being a bystander in a massacre. She also was swept along in mob violence in which a man was killed. Her history made her one type of person, but her doctoral education at

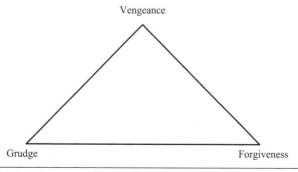

Figure I.1 Response-to-transgression triangle.

Harvard and her return to South Africa in June 1994 changed her. "[I] became aware for the first time, that in my past travels I could not describe myself as a South African. I could only say that I was *from* South Africa. I remember thinking in Cape Town that this is *my* country, *my* home" (pp. 6-7). Gobodo-Madikizela passed the tipping point. That tipping point set her on the road that allowed her to be able to participate in the Truth and Reconciliation Commission, to interview Eugene deKock, and to write a book, *A Human Being Died That Night: A South African Story of Forgiveness*, about her experiences.

Overview of the Book

Forgiveness is a complex of internal experiences. Beyond that, social interactions feed back and affect the internal experiences. Even societal events can affect whether forgiveness does or does not happen. A complete theory of forgiveness would need to consider the social interactions around transgressions and the societal contexts in depth. In this book, though, I admittedly make only passing references to societal contexts—mostly in chapter 14. I concentrate on the individual experiences of forgiveness. My goal is to articulate a theory of forgiveness and sketch its connections with the social and societal aspects so that those connections will be mapped for future expansion. I hope to create a theory that will inform scientific research but also usefully inform intervention.

Transgressions are stressful and demand to be coped with (Part I). Making life changes, however, is more than dealing with stress as it arises. It involves transformation of personality, which I discuss in Part II. Having laid the theoretical foundation, I describe ways a clinician can promote forgiveness of others and of the self and aid reconciliation and some small role they can play in societal issues (Part III).

Let us look briefly chapter by chapter. In chapter 1, I summarize models of forgiveness from interpersonal and intrapersonal points of view. In chapter 2, I describe the stress-and-coping theory of forgiveness. I talk the reader through each of the steps in the theory. In chapter 3, I present evidence that unforgiveness is indeed stressful—a key premise of the theory. In chapter 4, I go to the heart of the theory—the role of emotion in emotional forgiveness. In chapter 5, I explain the concept of forgiveness as emotional replacement—the heart of hearts. I also array evidence from many sources that bear on the correctness of the theorizing and particularly the emotional replacement hypothesis.

In chapter 6, I examine the Big Five personality traits and dispositions that are central to the theory. In chapter 7, other important personality traits and dispositions are discussed. Those are more modifiable within the therapeutic approach (in Part III) than are the Big Five. Life changes—whether stimulated by therapy, personal introspection, religious transformation, or adjusting to suffering and life circumstances—is often about helping people to transform their personalities. Thus, in chapter 8, I consider forgiving as a change in personality, laying the groundwork for an approach to therapy that will maximize the promotion of forgiveness.

For many, Parts I and II of the book will be the focus of attention. Those parts outline the science of forgiving. For others, though, Part III will be the meat and Parts I and II will have been the starter course. Part III describes my approach to helping people become more forgiving through learning to effectively and quickly forgive the transgressions they experience daily. Intervention programs are based on client choice. Forgiveness is not something to be demanded, coerced, or manipulated. Yet, clinical science has told us about how forgiveness can be effectively promoted. In chapter 9, I lay out the principles of psychotherapy aimed at promoting forgiveness, or more generally dealing with transgressions. In chapter 10, I summarize the five steps to REACH forgiving (REACH is an acrostic for the first word in each step). In chapter 11, I discuss the particularly difficult problems of forgiving the self and in clinically helping people deal with self-condemnation. In chapter 12, I describe and give numerous examples of interventions as a method to promote reconciliation, Forgiveness and Reconciliation through Experiencing Empathy (FREE). In chapter 13, I summarize the research support for the REACH and FREE clinical models. In chapter 14, I consider forgiveness in society. I consider only three situations—forgiveness within the family as children develop, within the justice system, and within societies in which groups with long-standing differences must reconcile or continue to breed conflict, hatred, and sometimes war.

I conclude with a statement of the limitations of forgiveness. Yet, I also suggest that forgiveness, while not a panacea, offers a sense of hope for making real transformations in our world.

PART I

A Stress-and-Coping Theory of Forgiveness and Relevant Evidence

CHAPTER 1

Models of Forgiveness

One of the questions I am most frequently asked is, "How do I know if I have really forgiven someone?" Usually, that question is motivated when a person notices he or she is acting inconsistently.

How Can We Know?

For example, Diana might have worked through forgiving her ex-spouse and believes herself to have completely gotten over the difficulties that resulted in the divorce. Years later, she sees her ex-spouse and negative feelings flood her. She is angry, afraid, and sad. "I thought I'd forgiven him," she thinks, "but obviously I haven't."

Other inconsistencies motivate us, as observers, friends, or therapists, to ask the same question. Gertrude was hurt by a romantic betrayal. She is gritting her teeth, clenching her jaws, crossing her arms, and muttering, "Of course I forgive him," without seeming to move her lips. Do we believe her? Has she really forgiven?

What about Bob? He says, "Yesterday my boss fired me. He said I took too much time to go to the doctor to deal with my neck injury that I received in an auto crash. He said the company just did not get enough work from me to make it worthwhile to continue my employment. It's so unfair." Then he continues. "However, I forgive him for that unfair treatment."

Bob showed no hostility in his voice or his manner. So I asked, "What prompted you to forgive him so quickly?"

Bob said, "The Scripture says that if I don't forgive someone who wrongs me, then I won't be forgiven by God. So, by will, I simply chose to forgive him." Did he really forgive? Is it really so easy? Can one simply choose to forgive and by willpower affect full forgiveness?

Such inconsistencies make us question whether the forgiveness is real. Contrast divorced Diana, teeth-gritting Gertrude, and Bible-responding Bob with the following cases. Sally lost a promotion to vice president of a corporation because she had an enemy within the management team. "I was the subject of a smear campaign. My enemy told things about me that were true, yet she twisted them. It sounded as if I was not working hard and was doing things that were marginally ethical. I have had the opportunity to get even with her before, but I swore not to take revenge on her. So I never have. I have forgiven her. I no longer feel resentment."

Abigail, a middle-aged woman, had struggled for years to forgive her father for his physical abuse of her and her siblings. After two years of psychotherapy, she felt that her forgiveness was complete. Finally, she initiated contact with her father after being away from home for over 10 years. "He started right in on me," she said. "It was as if I have never been away. He was insulting, demeaning, and ugly. I think he would have attacked me physically, but I yelled that I would call the police and have him put away. Now, I don't know what to think. Did I forgive him? He was able to push my buttons so easily. Of course, he installed those buttons. Still, if I had really forgiven, I should be above being provoked. Shouldn't I?"

Sid, an elderly man who was embezzled of ten thousand dollars, said, "The guy who swindled me was a friend. I trusted him. When he asked me to loan him $10,000, I didn't hesitate. Then he skipped town. It took a while, but I got over it. I don't miss the money now, and I don't really hold any hard feelings toward him. In fact, I hope he gets some use out of that money."

"Have you forgiven him?"

"I suppose so," he said. "Never really thought about it as forgiving him. I sorta accepted it and got a kind of peace. I guess you could say I forgave."

Ellie, an elderly woman, was really ill. As she talked to a hospice care worker, the woman said, "I used to have so much resentment of my daughter Marie. But as I have gotten nearer to seeing my Maker, I have simply determined in my spirit not to be resentful against Marie for the harm she did to me. It's difficult. I struggle every day. I think about her, but I'm determined not to let resentment cloud my last days on this earth. I think I've succeeded. I still get upset, but I honestly think my resentment and hate are totally gone."

Suzanne, a middle-aged woman, was talking with a reporter. She was reacting to the death of her mother. She said, "I believe I have completely forgiven the youth who killed Mama. I have had peace about this since I was able to forgive. I still remember my mother and miss her. Yet I do not feel that this young man should be sentenced to a death penalty for what he did. I'll testify to that in my victim impact statement next week. Still,

I don't believe he should be let off. He is responsible for his crime, and society says that he should pay. It wouldn't be right to simply let him walk scot-free. Forgiveness has nothing to do with whether he is required to pay for his crime under the law."

So, What Is Forgiveness?

What forgiveness is and what makes people forgive are highly complex, as these case summaries illustrate. I have repeated these eight cases in Appendix A, and there I discuss each in light of the theory I will develop. I invite you to delay looking at Appendix A until after you complete chapter 5. Then, see whether you would respond as I have.

Philosophers, theologians, psychological researchers, and lay people can develop their own views about the essence of forgiveness. Like blind men feeling the proverbial elephant, they can be adamant that they have the truth and can adduce evidence to support their views. I am no different. I have my own blind spots and theoretical biases. Over the years, I have tried to listen to the other voices and synthesize a big picture. Whether I have succeeded, or to what degree, you judge. Have I fairly accounted for the complexities of forgiveness and used the voices fairly?

At the center of this stress-and-coping theory of forgiveness rest several concepts. First, there are different types of forgiving. Instead of treating forgiveness as an all-or-none, think of it as different processes. They occur differently in different types of relationships—we forgive strangers and acquaintances differently than we do loved ones who violate a trust. Our decisions to forgive have different effects than our emotional experiences of forgiving. Therefore, our common notion of complete consistency as the indication of forgiveness is not productive. Second, forgiveness is a global term that suggests changes over time. Because all sorts of events happen over time, it is often difficult to say whether we have "fully forgiven" once and for all time. Third, forgiveness is related to perceived injustice. Fourth, despite this complexity, one aspect of forgiving is the major barometer of change over time—emotional forgiveness. Fifth, I propose *the emotional replacement hypothesis* (Worthington & Wade, 1999; Worthington & Scherer, 2004) as a centerpiece of emotional forgiveness: Emotional forgiveness occurs due to replacing negative, unforgiving stressful emotions with positive, other-oriented emotions.

Before I describe the stress-and-coping theory and discuss the emotional replacement hypothesis, I will describe other researchers' models of forgiving. First, let us look at interpersonal models.

Interpersonal Models of Forgiveness

Baumeister

Baumeister, Exline, and Sommer (1998) have identified two components to forgiving: an intrapersonal and interpersonal component. The intrapersonal component can reflect either an internal forgiveness or a lack of it. The interpersonal component involves the *expression* of forgiveness to the person toward whom one is unforgiving. The victim could either express or not express forgiveness. This results in four possibilities.

In the first possibility—no intrapersonal forgiveness and no interpersonal forgiveness—the person is simply *unforgiving*. The transgressor is never told otherwise. However, if the person feels forgiveness toward the transgressor but does not say so, *silent forgiveness* has occurred. Silent forgiveness has many benefits for the victim, who can feel peace but can nonetheless hold the transgression over the head of the transgressor and perhaps extract concessions. If the victim does not feel forgiving but tells the transgressor he or she is forgiving, this is *hollow forgiveness*. Hollow forgiveness is given when victims feel that social norms require forgiveness. It can be the most costly to the victim. It expresses that one has let the transgressor off the hook, yet negative feelings remain. So the victim gets little benefit other than the adherence to social norms and relief from social pressure for not adhering to those norms. In *full forgiveness*, internal forgiveness is expressed to the perpetrator. Both victim and perpetrator benefit.

Sapolsky and de Waal's Reconciliation-Based Models

Sapolsky (Sapolsky & Share, 2004) and de Waal (de Waal & Pokorny, 2005) draw heavily from evolutionary theory to understand reconciliation. Some rituals are necessary in animal troupes that live in close social proximity so that disagreements can be patched up. Reconciliation rituals are hypothesized to lower arousal and foster repair of closer social relationships. One can see how this would provide a selection advantage. With lower emotional arousal, animals within the troupe could more easily defend the troupe, cooperate to achieve survival tasks, and mate. Lowered arousal that accompanies reconciliation rituals could thus be considered a precursor to forgiveness, which is thought to have developed later in humans.

McCullough's two-system model. McCullough (2001a) has extended evolutionary theory-based reasoning to a two-system *opponent-process* model. An attachment-empathy system competes with a rumination system to govern social processes. Sometimes forgiveness is at the fore. At other times, rumination, justice, or revenge are more dominant. Whereas McCullough's two-tier system model is more a model of intrapersonal than interpersonal forgiveness, it is derived from evolutionary theory and is considered here as an extension of reconciliation theory.

Hargrave's Four Stations of Forgiveness

Hargrave and Sells (1997) posited an interpersonal theory of forgiveness that was based largely on Boszormenyi-Nagy's (Boszormenyi-Nagy & Spark, 1973) theory of family therapy. Hargrave and Sells identified both exoneration and entitlement as the driving forces of forgiveness. They identified four stations of forgiveness. Each station can be a starting point for forgiveness, but it is not a sequential process (Hargrave, 2001). *Insight* (station 1) involves recognition of the dynamics of the transgression. *Understanding* (station 2) grasps why the transgression occurred. Together, Hargrave calls the first two stations *exoneration*. Within the context of a family systems theory, the system is responsible for problems. Thus, when one has insight and understanding, one may declare that no individual is *guilty of the way the system responds,* thus the individual is exonerated. In the third and fourth stations, *allowing for compensation* and *explicit forgiving*, Hargrave and Sells describe the interpersonal aspects of forgiving. Allowing for compensation permits a consideration of responses of the offender. Explicit forgiving considers the expression of forgiveness from victim to offender as well as the responses of the offender.

An Interdependence Theory Model of Forgiveness

Rusbult and her colleagues (Rusbult, Hannon, Stocker, & Finkel, 2005) advocate an interpersonal view of forgiveness. They describe forgiveness as entailing an immediate gut response to wrongdoing, which is characterized by a vengeance motive and angry emotions. Most people restrain the gut response within a few seconds. People then may experience cognition, emotion, and motivation that move them toward pro- or antirelationship behavior. The third aspect of forgiving involves acting to actively or passively affect the relationship positively or negatively. These acts are called *voice* (positive active), *loyalty* (positive passive), *exit* (negative active), and *neglect* (negative passive) responses.

Critique of Interpersonal Models of Forgiveness

The foregoing models not only describe forgiveness proper but include the interpersonal context within which forgiveness is often considered. Forgiveness occurs in a clear interpersonal context when it involves transactions between parent and child, romantic partners, or others in ongoing intimate relations. However, when one is robbed on the street, run off the road in an act of road rage, or offended by a stranger on the subway, then any consideration of forgiveness is not well described as interdependent. The consideration of forgiveness is interpersonal only in a highly abstract sense. The victim usually does not interact with the stranger again, and whether the victim decides to forgive has little impact on the victim's friends, family, and greater society. Certainly, the *transgression* occurred in interpersonal context, but not considerations of nor experience of forgiveness.

Even in intimate relationships, forgiveness does not occur in a relationship. It occurs within the forgiver. Models of interpersonal forgiveness—to be precise—are better termed models of interpersonal interaction surrounding transgressions. As such, they are valuable in themselves. They affect whether, how, and how fast forgiveness might be experienced. But strictly speaking, they are not forgiveness. We must look to intrapersonal models to describe the experiences of forgiveness.

Intrapersonal Models of Forgiveness

Most other theorists separate the interpersonal aspects of interacting around transgressions from the intrapersonal aspects of forgiveness. Following are important intrapersonal models of forgiveness.

A Classical Conditioning Model

In Worthington (1998a) I suggested an emotional conditioning model of forgiveness. I likened a transgression to a stimulus that triggers pain (and thus fear and anger). The transgression and aspects of the situation surrounding the stimulus could become classically conditioned to anger or fear. I examined usual responses to classical conditioning of emotional responses. An animal could freeze, attempt to withdraw, and, avoidance failing, fight. Those responses might then be paired with angry or fearful responses to a transgression.

Pushing the model further, I likened extinction to forgiving. Extinction might yield to spontaneous recovery of the fearful or angry response even after "forgiving" if the animal was (1) placed in a similar situation again, (2) subjected to another pairing of conditioned stimulus (e.g., if the animal was hurt again), (3) reminded of the original harm, or (4) hurt similarly by another situation.

Critique. The classical conditioning model is of limited utility. It focused on fear more than anger as one's response to a transgression. It also did not account for (a) exercises of willpower and (b) the richness of cognitive complexity and the nuances in construing situations.

Decision-Based Model

Addressing one weakness in a conditioning model of unforgiveness and forgiveness, DiBlasio (1998) emphasizes willful decision-making. DiBlasio draws on his clinical experience to develop his model of decision-based forgiveness. "Decision-based forgiveness is defined as the cognitive letting go of resentment and bitterness and need for vengeance. However, it is not always the end of emotional pain and hurt. Forgiveness here is viewed as an act of the will, a choice to let go or to hold. People can separate their thoughts of resentment and bitterness from their feelings of hurt" (p. 76).

DiBlasio (1998) draws on theorizing by family therapists including Ivan Boszormenyi-Nagy (Boszormenyi-Nagy & Spark, 1973), Murray Bowen (1985), James Framo (1982), and Madanes (1990). DiBlasio presented a description of the use of an intervention in family therapy modeled from Worthington and DiBlasio (1990) for couples therapy.

Critique. DiBlasio (1998) emphasizes willful decision, which is a cognitive act but is in sharp distinction from cognitive therapy with its systematic attack on cognitive structures and processes. DiBlasio ignores emotional forgiveness as less important than the decision to forgive.

Cognitive Models

Some theorists of forgiveness, such as Gordon, Baucom, and Snyder (2000), have posited a cognitive theory of forgiveness (Gordon, Baucom, & Snyder, 2000; Gordon, Baucom, & Snyder, 2004; Gordon, Baucom, & Snyder, 2005; Snyder, Gordon, & Baucom, 2004). In their cognitive theory, they believe that forgiveness becomes necessary when one has had one's cognitive structures violated or damaged. These cognitive structures may involve assumptions, beliefs, standards, or perceptions. Thus, Gordon et al. (2005) employ standard cognitive therapy and psychodynamic therapy interventions to help people change their cognition.

Thompson, Snyder, Hoffman, and Rasmussen et al. (2005) have proposed a cognitive model of forgiving. They define forgiveness as "The framing of a perceived transgression such that one's responses to the transgressor, transgression, and sequelae of the transgression are transformed from negative to neutral or positive. The source of the transgression, therefore the object of forgiveness, may be oneself, another person or persons, or a situation that one views as being beyond anybody's control (i.e., an illness, 'fate,' or a natural disaster)" (p. 8). Thompson et al. draw on cognitive interventions such as Thoresen (2001), which discussed a reframing process as constructing a new narrative about the transgression, transgressor, and forgiver. They cite Malcolm and Greenberg (2000), who describe the forgiving person as being able to "see the offender in a more complex way" (p. 181). Because Thompson et al. adopt a cognitive perspective, they include situations as being a potential source of transgressions and target for forgiveness. Many people could not agree that situations are an appropriate source of hurt, because no moral wrong can be done by the situations (e.g., Enright & Zell, 1989). However, within the cognitive perspectives of Thompson, Snyder, and their colleagues, a person could attribute causality to situations. It is one's perception that is thought to matter.

Critique. Cognitive theories draw heavily on cognitive therapy approaches. In therapy, the therapist leads clients to intentionally change thoughts, which presumably change emotions and behaviors. During normal living, not all emotions and behaviors are caused by conscious cognition.

Process Models

Enright's cognitive affective behavioral process model. Enright has long written about the psychology of forgiveness. His early work studied the way that children and adults developed their reasoning about forgiving situations (see Enright & the Human Development Study Group, 1994). He paralleled his stages of development of reasoning about forgiveness on Kohlberg's (1984) stages of development of reasoning about justice. Cognitive roots permeate Enright's theory. However, as he articulated his process model more thoroughly as an intervention to promote forgiveness, Enright clearly combined affective and behavioral aspects into his understanding of forgiveness (see Enright & Fitzgibbons, 2000). He believes that all three aspects—cognitive, affective, and behavioral—need to change if a person is to forgive. In addition, the person must have an emotional readiness to forgive before the person is likely to be receptive to forgiving. Enright and Fitzgibbons provide the best overview of the process model to date. Freedman, Enright, and Knutson (2005) update the research on the intervention model.

Critique. Enright's model is comprehensive and thorough. Its weaknesses are a failure to connect basic research with the clinical theory, a failure to articulate a theory of change on which the intervention is based, and generally assuming too much power and universality in the clinical application of the model. Nevertheless, Enright's is the current gold standard against which other research models and clinical models must be measured.

McCullough's model of changing forgiveness over time. McCullough, Fincham, and Tsang (2003) articulated a theoretical description of the process of how forgiveness might be thought to change over time. They described three related concepts. If we imagine two people who have been offended by the same event—perhaps a teacher scolds both of them for talking in class—we can see differences in forgiveness-related concepts depending on how people respond to an objectively similar event.

If we measured people's negative revenge and avoidance motivations and their benevolent motivations soon after the scolding, it would not be surprising to find that the two people had different levels of negative motivations. McCullough et al. (2003) describe the difference as *forbearance*. The assumption is that the difference in different starting reactions is due to people being able to forbear responding with negative motivations.

Over time, people change their motives toward the person who has committed the transgression. The amount of decrease over time represented by the best straight line connecting all the measurement points is called *trend forgiveness*. A steep slope would represent high trend forgiveness. A shallow slope would represent low trend forgiveness. Thus, if two people had equal amounts of forbearance at the beginning, but after 3 weeks Person A is lower in unforgiving motivation and higher in positive motivation than Person B, then Person A has higher trend forgiveness.

It is likely that the person's forgiveness will not decrease smoothly, with every measurement point falling on a straight line between the starting and ending points. Positive or negative life events, moods, or differences in judgment (as well as simple measurement error) cause the deviation. McCullough et al. (2003) called this deviation from the straight line decrease of trend forgiveness, *temporary forgiveness*.

Critique. McCullough et al.'s (2003) technical definition of forbearance might not accord with what other people believe forbearance to be. For example, the initial level of negative motivations might be influenced by the person's personality, self-confidence, perception of the teacher, prior experience with the teacher, mood, or perceptual set. Many people see forbearing as trying actively to control one's negative motivations. Furthermore, as McCullough acknowledges, temporary forgiveness cannot separate measurement error and other causes for daily fluctuation.

Emotion-Centered Models

Malcolm and Greenberg (2000) articulated a model of forgiveness that derived from emotion-focused therapy. They identified five components necessary for forgiveness to occur. These are (1) the acceptance into awareness of strong emotions such as anger and sadness; (2) letting go of previously unmet interpersonal needs; (3) a shift in the forgiving person's view of the offender; (4) development of empathy for the offender; and (5) the construction of a new narrative of self and other.

Emotion-related events are seen as the impetus for later cognitive changes. Malcolm and Greenberg (2000) draw heavily on Greenberg's previous work (Greenberg, Rice, & Elliott, 1993) on unfinished business. Greenberg had previously found that unfinished business could be resolved by what he calls self-validation, self-assertion, and holding the significant other accountable. Unfinished business might also be resolved by gaining a new view of the other person. Forgiving the other person falls under developing a new view of the other person.

This transformation, however, is seen to occur not typically by cognitive insight, but by emotional insight. In psychotherapy, blame and complaining are often met with an invitation to participate in an empty-chair technique. This enacts imaginary conversations with the transgressor and allows an expression of anger, fear, sadness, or vulnerable feelings. The admission into awareness of those feelings and emotions allows the person to express needs from the offender. The enactment in the empty chair allows the view of the other person to become more affiliative. Empathy is developed for the other person. Finally, a resolution might be reached through forgiveness. Malcolm, Warwar, and Greenberg (2005) report on recent advances in counseling techniques and research relevant to forgiveness.

Critique. Whereas emotional events might stimulate later understanding and behavior, emotional events are not always the impetus for change. Also, some people have an aversion to emotional expressiveness, on which the therapeutic method of emotion-focused therapy rests.

McCullough, Sandage, and Worthington's (1997) empathy-centered model. We developed a model of promoting forgiveness based on empathizing with the offender. That model and the importance of empathy were argued in McCullough et al. (1997). We claimed that empathy was not sufficient to promote forgiveness, but it might well be necessary to promote forgiveness. We showed the importance of empathy in mediating between apologies and the experience of forgiveness (McCullough, Worthington, & Rachal, 1997; McCullough et al., 1998).

Critique. When empathy has been investigated experimentally, it usually has been related to forgiveness. However, the variance accounted for has not always supported McCullough et al.'s (1997) claims that empathy is necessary for forgiveness to occur. Other emotions might replace empathy in promoting forgiveness.

Worthington and Wade's (1999) emotional juxtaposition hypothesis. In a review of the existing literature in 1999, Worthington and Wade described a dynamic model in which people could respond to a transgression by juxtaposing positive other-oriented emotions against negative unforgiving emotions. The conflict of opposing emotions was hypothesized to result in a gradual replacement of negative emotions with positive emotions. This formulated the emotional replacement hypothesis.

That work resulted in three modifications to McCullough et al. (1997). It shifted emphasis from earlier versions that focused more on motivational transformation to a focus on emotional transformation. It broadened the replacement emotions beyond empathy to other positive other-oriented emotions. Third, it hypothesized a mechanism for how emotional forgiveness might occur.

The Unfolding Story

We have taken a brief look at existing models purporting to describe forgiveness. Each seems to contribute one or a few pieces to the puzzle. What we need is a comprehensive theory that relates the models. Not surprisingly, I have found the seeds to this model in Worthington and Wade (1999). Clinical research and personal experiences have led me to modify the Worthington and Wade (1999) model over the past seven years. I will briefly give a development of the major modifications that occurred and why each occurred.

Incorporation of Both Decisional Forgiveness and Emotional Forgiveness

In my earliest thinking about forgiveness, I conceptualized forgiveness as being a decision people could make (Worthington, 1989; Worthington & DiBlasio, 1990). I would now call this decisional forgiveness. DiBlasio and I focused on changing people's motivations, usually within couples therapy. The therapist could change motivations by allowing partners to interact with each other, to confess misdeeds to each other, and to see each other's contrition.

About 1993, under McCullough's lead, he and I began to talk about forgiveness as parallel to Batson's empathy-altruism hypothesis. This linked emotion (i.e., empathy) with altruistic motivation. My focus began to shift away from the decision to forgive toward the emotional-motivational experience of forgiving.

Eventually, I began to see these not as points in a continuous process but as two separate processes. People could decide to forgive and not experience emotional forgiveness. They also could experience sudden compassion for a transgressor—perhaps upon hearing of a misfortune having befallen the person—and realize that unforgiveness had disappeared even though no decision had been made to forgive. I separated the concepts in 2003 (Worthington, 2003).

Return to More Emphasis on Motives

Emotions are connected to motivations. For years, McCullough, Sandage, and I had posited that emotional forgiveness led to motivational transformation. I emphasized the emotions (subsequent to Worthington, 1998a). McCullough has continued to emphasize motivations. We had theorized little about the specifics of motivational transformation. In 2006, with a nod to McCullough's (2001a) opponent process idea, I and my coauthors described possible mechanisms of motivational change, incorporating mercy, grace, benevolence, and conciliation as motives that countered revenge, grudge-holding, and avoidance (Worthington, Sharp, Lerner, & Sharp, 2006). These positive motives arise from positive emotional experiences, which might in turn arise from a variety of stimuli.

Justice and the Injustice Gap

Since the mid-1990s, I have considered how justice and forgiveness interact with each other. This grew from my personal experiences. These include, since 1995, having been a victim of burglary three times, robbery once, and vandalism twice, and most significantly by having my mother murdered. In February 2000, at Fordham Law School, I first addressed forgiveness and justice conceptually. The idea of the injustice gap arose as we began to study justice in the laboratory. Most of those studies were done in collaboration with Nathaniel Wade, Charlotte Witvliet, Rebecca Kiefer, and Jack Berry. A review paper by Exline, Worthington, Hill, and McCullough (2003) surveyed the research on forgiveness and justice. We proposed our current understanding of the injustice gap and its relationship to unforgiveness and forgiving.

Biological Considerations in Forgiving and Unforgiveness

In 1996, I received a grant from the John Templeton Foundation to study forgiveness in couples. I used salivary cortisol as a measure of relational unforgiveness. We received a subaward from the NIH-funded Virginia Commonwealth University's General Research Center to conduct the cortisol studies. We developed a cortisol test to measure relational unforgiveness (Berry & Worthington, 2001). We also have studied peripheral psychophysiological reactions to a variety of transgression scenarios (Witvliet, Wade, Worthington, & Berry, 2005; Witvliet et al., 2005). We summarized the status of the field in forgiveness and health in an article in *Psychology and Health* (Worthington & Scherer, 2004) and in Forgiveness in Medicine (Worthington, Witvliet, Lerner, & Scherer, 2005).

Threat Appraisal

We first published on forgiveness as coping in 2001 (Berry & Worthington, 2001). Scherer and I concluded that evidence supported viewing forgiveness as an emotion-focused coping strategy (Worthington & Scherer, 2004). Thinking about forgiveness as a coping strategy suggests immediately that challenge or threat appraisals are important in how people respond to stressors.

Transgressions within Continuing and Noncontinuing Interactions

Unilateral forgiveness is forgiveness of someone unavailable to interact with. Interpersonal forgiveness is forgiving someone with whom one is having ongoing interactions. Even though we previously observed (McCullough & Worthington, 1994) and studied (McCullough et al., 1998; McCullough et al., 1997) that interpersonal and unilateral forgiveness differed, I only recently realized the importance of that distinction. It might clarify many of the definitional controversies (Worthington, 2005a).

Social Aspects of Forgiveness

Forgiveness takes place within a person's skin. However, a person is forgiving *someone*. Thus, in interpersonal forgiveness, the social context is usually important. McCullough and I, and other colleagues, began to look at interpersonal processes over 10 years ago (McCullough et al., 1997). We continue to examine the social-psychological aspects of forgiveness.

Forgiving Personality

In our clinical research and practice, it became apparent that people were not always interested in simply forgiving one big transgression. In many cases, they were interested in forgiving a marriage partner for years of transgressions. Some even wanted to be more forgiving people—to cleanse their personality. I began to examine forgiving personality dispositions in my work with my colleague Jack Berry (Berry & Worthington, 2001; Berry, Worthington, O'Connor, Parrott, & Wade, 2005; Berry, Worthington, Parrott, O'Connor, & Wade, 2001), a personality psychologist. We have examined how a forgiving personality develops in children, looking at development from an emotional replacement point of view (Worthington, 2005c). We have also looked at religion and forgiveness in a variety of contexts (Lampton, Oliver, Worthington, & Berry, 2005; McCullough & Worthington, 1999; Worthington, 2003; Worthington, Berry, & Parrott, 2001). In addition, we have been interested in cultural influences on forgiveness and have looked at the development of ethnic unforgiveness (Jones, 2004).

Theoretical Synthesis

We began with Worthington and Wade (1999). Based on this rapidly changing field of studies, I have made updates, which have drawn from models by other researchers and from our own studies. The base for the models has broadened. Biological, social, and psychological processes have been integrated into a biopsychosocial theory of forgiveness. I will describe it in chapter 2.

A Biopsychosocial Stress-and-Coping
Theory of Forgiveness

In this chapter, I describe the elements of a stress-and-coping theory of forgiveness. Stress-and-coping theory (Lazarus, 1999) is well established. Thus, my tasks are threefold. First, I must describe how the process, from transgression to forgiveness, parallels the stress-and-coping theory. Second, I must elaborate the parallel process to show how unforgiveness-forgiveness requires specific nuanced modifications. I will do both in this chapter. Third, I must provide evidence that unforgiveness is indeed a stress reaction. I will do that in chapter 3.

Transgressions are interpersonal stressors. People must cope with those stressors or give in to the stress reactions that inevitably and repeatedly occur. The theory is given schematically in Figure 2.1. This adapts Lazarus and Folkman's (1984) stress-and-coping theory to a forgiveness context. Let us take a bird's eye view.

Transgressions lead to perceived injustice gaps. Depending on how much injustice and what size transgression people experience, they will appraise the interpersonal stressor as either a threat or a challenge. If they perceive the transgression to be a threat, they will ruminate, feel unforgiving emotions, and be motivated to seek justice, get revenge, or avoid transgressors. If they appraise the interpersonal stressor as a challenge, they will problem-solve, regulate their emotions, and try to find meaning in the event. That can trigger justice and conciliatory or altruistic (i.e., mercy, grace, love) motivations. People will thus cope with the transgression by resolving threats or challenges to their competence, to their relationship,

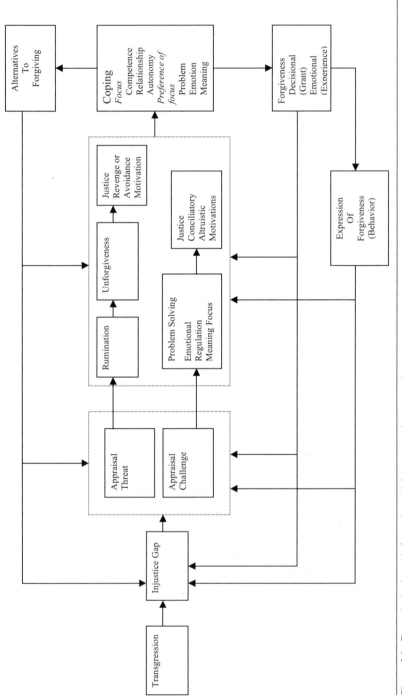

Figure 2.1 Theoretical schematic for coping with interpersonal transgressions.

or to their autonomy. They will try to cope by employing problem-focused coping, emotion-focused coping, or meaning-focused coping strategies. They will thus either (1) engage in some of the alternatives to forgiveness, which will affect the different steps in the process, or (2) forgive, which can also affect the steps. Privately, the person does or does not forgive. Publicly, the person might express the forgiveness or lack of forgiveness to the offender (or might not express either), which will also affect the different steps in the process.

In Figure 2.2, I have shown a schematic of a model that explains how transgressions accumulate. People respond over time to those transgressions, emotionally, cognitively, and behaviorally. They therefore solidify their personality characteristics and social relationships on the basis of the most habitual responses. That will, therefore, lead to mental, physical, relational, and spiritual consequences.

In this biopsychosocial stress-and-coping theory, I tie together basic scientific findings into a web of understanding of forgiveness at individual (primarily), dyadic, and societal levels. I try to integrate and apply basic research into interventions to help others therapeutically or through psychoeducation. If I am successful, you should put down this completed book with an integrated theoretical understanding.

Transgressions

Transgressions Defined and Illustrated

Transgressions are of two basic types: hurts and offenses. Hurts violate our physical or psychological boundaries. When my mother was murdered, the youths physically violated her boundaries. They hurt her. They also took a loved one from my family and me. That hurt us. Offenses or "wrongs" violate moral boundaries. The murder certainly was such a violation of moral boundaries.

Sam and Natalie. Sam and Natalie had been married for 15 years. They had never had significant marriage problems, even though Natalie's whining and complaining often aggravated Sam. "It seems incessant," said Sam to their marriage counselor. "It grates on me the way that running your fingernails down a blackboard would. She always focused on herself. Never on me. I needed someone to affirm me. Someone who could get past herself long enough to see that the world is bigger than her own petty life."

Sam wasn't the only disgruntled spouse. Natalie complained about Sam's ego. "He thinks he is the center of the universe. The world revolves around him. The facts are clear. He avoided work around the house. He shirked responsibilities at raising the kids from both our families. His first wife divorced him because of his arrogance, too. He always wanted people

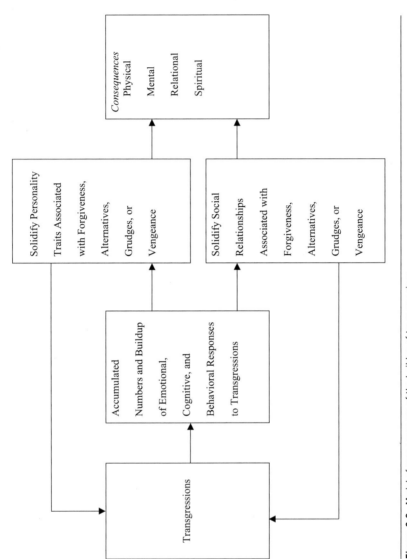

Figure 2.2 Model of consequences of the buildup of transgressions.

to admire and worship him. That's why he had those affairs during his first marriage. But I thought that he had gotten over that."

Sam had not gotten over that. At work, he flirted with a married woman who was in the operations department. She had separated from her husband and lived alone near the workplace. Sam and she shared sexual innuendos as if they were sharing e-mail jokes. After a while, they shared lunch, then a bed. The affair came to light when Natalie was running an errand that took her near Sam's work. She saw Sam and his lover slipping into a house, holding hands. Natalie slipped into despair, anger, rage, and fear.

The next day, she confronted Sam: "I saw you and that woman last night." Sam was uncharacteristically quiet. "Who was she? Are you screwing her?"

"What? Are you spying on me?" said Sam.

"Spying? I was driving home. I saw the two of you kissing and playing. I saw you go into that apartment together. Admit it. You're screwing her, aren't you?"

"What if I am?"

"You amaze me. You're in the wrong, yet you say I'm spying. You arrogant...."

"Well, it's not just 'screwing' like you delicately put it. We love each other. At least she cares about me. And she doesn't just lay there. She shows me she loves me."

Sam didn't apologize. Worse. He blamed Natalie.

But two months after the affair was discovered, Sam had a change of heart. He expressed remorse and contrition and begged Natalie to take him back. She refused.

"He had multiple affairs when he was married to his previous wife. Now he has done it again. He expects me to let bygones be bygones. Well, I said 'Bye' and he's gone. He wants us to pick up our life as if nothing had happened? That's ridiculous. He's so conceited. He thinks because *he* wants to come back, that I should take him back. All I have to say is 'Bye bye, Sam.'"

The more Sam begged for forgiveness, the more Natalie refused to grant it. The whole relationship turned negative. They could not recall any positive times in their marriage. Their thoughts and talk revolved around the affair and its aftermath. They went to marriage counseling. After six months of counseling, they had still not reconciled. But at least things were tolerable. Sam moved back into the house. Separate beds.

After Sam had his affair, he eventually apologized and asked Natalie for forgiveness. For Natalie, though, his apologies were too little, too late. Natalie let Sam's pleading fall on deaf ears. Sam in turn became unforgiving of her lack of mercy. They tried to put the marriage back together, but in the end, they ended it.

Bob and Randi. This was not the case for Bob and Randi. Randi was a physician who had worked hard, won scholarships, and battled the odds. She was the only woman to successfully complete medical school in her class. Upon graduation, she married Bob. Bob was a high-school teacher who loved English literature and loved to impart that knowledge to his students. People described Bob as gentle and nice.

In some ways, Randi and Bob had some gender stereotypes reversed. Randi was hard-driving, unemotional, and calculating. She set her sights on goals and pursued them doggedly. Bob was nurturing. He kept up with correspondence with the in-laws and his own family, planned meals, and did most of the cooking and household work. In the summer, he was content to call himself a househusband.

As their marriage progressed, Bob became more self-confident and assured. Randi became consumed by her work at a major hospital. In their seventh year of marriage, Randi fell for a male nurse who worked on the ward that she attended. It lasted for one month. Randi broke off the affair, but the nurse was not unhappy that it had ended.

Full of remorse, Randi confessed the affair to Bob. He was wounded and thought that they needed marital counseling. After a while in marital counseling, he forgave Randi and told her so. The turning point came suddenly. In the beginning of the session, Randi was not very engaged. She began talking about the damage she had done to the relationship and the things she was afraid she would lose. Without warning she broke down into weeping. She was not consolable. After 5 minutes, she asked to take a recess from the session. Before she could leave, though, Bob granted forgiveness. "Until that moment," he said, "I didn't know how deeply you cared about our marriage." In the weeks ahead, they worked out a plan describing how they would stay in closer contact.

When Sam and Randi each had their affairs, they not only hurt their partners by betrayal of their marriage bonds, but they also wronged and offended their partners. They violated the partner's moral boundaries. Hurt and offense were blended together.

Sociometer Theory

Sociometer theory described. Psychologists Mark Leary and Roy Baumeister (2000) identified people's attachments and their need to belong as among the most basic human motivations. They suggested that people had an internal "sociometer," which monitors the quality of relationships with others. According to sociometer theory, people scan their social environment to detect possible cues of disapproval, rejection, or exclusion. When the sociometer detects such cues, it automatically and unconsciously alerts the person that something is wrong. Negative moods and emotions are the sociometer's alarms. They motivate people to try to minimize the likelihood that they will be judged, rejected, or betrayed. The sociometer is preattentive. People do not usually pay conscious attention to it. But when the emotional alarms go off, people are quick to react. How they react depends on their personal disposition and learning history.

Scientists who have studied emotions (e.g., Damasio, 1999) have suggested that negative emotions serve at least three functions with helping people deal with threats to their well-being. First, negative emotions alert people when undesired changes occur in the body or environment. People then can respond to the environment. Second, negative emotions interrupt ongoing behavior so people can assess the situation. Perhaps one may decide to act, perhaps not. Third, a decrease in negative emotions signals that a motive is being dealt with. For example, a hungry man feels cross. When he finds food, the decrease in negative emotion rewards him for seeking the food.

The sociometer is a psychological way of talking about how people attend to their social world. It helps people maintain social attachments that they value. It helps them recognize when relationships are endangered. Of course, some people are more sensitive to social cues than are others. Some people can articulate what they are feeling better than others, even though another person might actually be more sensitive to the cues.

Sociometer theory applied to transgressions. The sociometer detects that one has been hurt or offended. Fear, anger, or both are stimulated. If the person has been hurt, he or she usually feels both fear and anger. When a person has been offended by a violation of his or her moral boundaries, the sociometer triggers a feeling of anger. The injustice generates a sense of righteous indignation.

A Psychological Study of Hurt Feelings

Leary and his colleagues (1998) conducted a study of 164 undergraduates. Half were men. Half of the participants were assigned to think of a time they hurt someone else's feelings. The other half were instructed to think of a time when someone else hurt their feelings. Participants described the event and the events that led up to it, exactly what each party did or said that was hurtful, how they felt if they were victims, how they thought the victim felt if they were perpetrators, and also what happened afterwards. Then, the students answered questions about the event.

Types and Degree of Hurts

Raters sorted the accounts of transgressions into one of seven types. The most common type—in one third of all participants—was *hurt feelings*. Being *criticized* seemed to hurt the participants the least of any act except for teasing, and by far, it generated the least perception of rejection. *Betrayals* were reported by 20% of the people. Betrayals hurt more than any criticism except being unappreciated. Betrayals made people feel rejected and usually happened between close friends or romantic partners. *Active dissociation* consisted of acts such as explicitly rejecting the person, ostracizing the person from a group, or abandoning the person in a time of need. Of the participants, 18% reported active dissociation. The hurt feelings were almost as high as in betrayal, and the amount of perceived rejection was even higher. *Passive dissociation* included things like being ignored, not being included in other's activities, or other incidents that were interpreted as rejection, but were not clearly rejection. Passive dissociation was reported by 17% of people. The hurt feelings were little worse than criticism but not as bad as betrayal or active dissociation. The rejection was less than in active dissociation. *Being unappreciated* was reported by only 5% of participants. However, when people felt unappreciated, the results were devastating. The highest degree of hurt feelings and of perceived rejection was reported for those who felt unappreciated.

Who Hurts Our Feelings?

The people who are the closest to us seem to be the ones who can inflict the most damage on us. In this group of undergraduates, the episodes reported by the victims involved close friends (about 40%), romantic or dating partners (about 30%), acquaintances (12%), family members (about 10%), and bosses (4%). The amount of hurt feelings experienced at the hands of romantic partners or family members was much higher than at the hands of close friends, acquaintances, or bosses. The same was true in rejection. Strangers hurt people's feelings in about 16% of the episodes reported. Remember, the participants were students. Clearly, a group of adults working 9 to 5 and participating in family and community life would have a widely different profile of offenders.

How Do People React to Hurt Feelings?

About 80% of people who had been hurt said they expressed their anger to the offender. About 75% said that they argued and defended themselves. About two thirds said they told the offender that their feelings had been hurt. Three in every five said they countered with a critical or nasty remark. Distress was a major reaction. A third cried in front of the offender. About 42% said they cried later when they were alone. The emotions people felt were strongly related to the way they reacted. For example, when people felt hostile, they usually said something critical or nasty or expressed their anger. Feeling hostile was not related to whether they told the other person their feelings had been hurt, or whether they cried. When people felt anxious, they often cried. When people's self-confidence was damaged, distress and tears were the order of the day.

The consequences of having one's feelings hurt included consequences to the relationship and to oneself. The relationship was weakened according to two thirds of the victims. In 42%, the victims said that the relationship was weakened permanently. In only 5% of the cases did the victims indicate that the relationship was not affected.

What Are the Lasting Effects of Having Our Feelings Hurt?

In addition, people's personal feelings about the offender were affected by the event. Sixty percent said they trusted the offender less than before the incident. Almost half (44%) said they disliked the person more afterwards. Victims also reported that the event affected them psychologically in the long term. Hurt feelings lowered their self-esteem (22%), made them worry more about what others thought of them (23%), made them worry more about being hurt again (46%), and undermined their self-confidence in similar situations (45%). Even long after the event, 93% said the event still brought up negative feelings for them, and 33% said those feelings were either strongly or painfully negative.

What Conclusions Do People Draw When Their Feelings Are Hurt?

Victims draw conclusions about the reasons why offenders hurt their feelings. These are called attributions of cause. People's attributions were strongly related to the effects they believed the acts had. For example, let us take four conclusions victims might make. They could attribute the hurtful act to an accident, to retaliation, to offender insensitivity, or to trying to help the victim.

If victims thought that the offender had accidentally hurt their feelings, they usually did not see much effect on the relationship. They just lost a little self-confidence in the situation. But when victims thought the offender had been trying to hurt them or get back at them, they usually believed that either permanent or temporary damage to the relationship was caused. They highly distrusted and disliked the offender, but they did not suffer lowered self-esteem or self-confidence. When victims thought the offender was insensitive or inconsiderate, the relationship was not damaged, but victims distrusted and disliked the offender more. When victims thought that the offender had hurt their feelings while trying to help, the relationship was not damaged. But being "helped" by being criticized undermined victims' self-esteem.

How Do Victims and Offenders See Things Differently?

The victims and the perpetrators saw the situation differently. Leary and his colleagues (1998) compared the different perceptions of the offender and victim when they rated the same topic. When asked how the victim behaved after the victim's feelings had been hurt, there were no differences in the accounts given by victims and perpetrators. The victims and perpetrators rated the reasons for the events quite differently. Perpetrators saw the events as more accidental and less intentional, and more often the result of something the victim had done first. In rating the victims' feelings after their feelings were hurt, victims described themselves as more hostile than the perpetrators thought they were. Victims also thought the perpetrators liked them less than the perpetrators reported liking the victims. Victims also felt more rejected than the perpetrators were actually rejecting.

Victims and perpetrators also gave different accounts about how the perpetrator reacted to the event. The perpetrators thought that they apologized (42%) more than the victims thought they did (20%). The victims tended more often to think that the perpetrator did nothing, as if the perpetrator did not care much. Both victim and perpetrator rated the perpetrators' blame of the victim and asking the victims' forgiveness approximately equally.

Lessons From This Study

We can draw several lessons from this study by Leary and his colleagues (1998). First, perception is very important about what a transgression is. The emotions that victims feel when their feelings are hurt differ, depending on whether they believe that the hurt was accidental, deliberate, or retaliatory. When people are offended, they usually feel angry. When they are hurt, anxiety, fear, and distress are more common.

Victims simply do not see things through the same lens that offenders do. The offense seems much worse when one is a victim of it. The hurt seems bigger, the intentions more malevolent, the relationship more damaged, the liking for the perpetrator suffers more, and the person's self-esteem is damaged more than the perpetrator believes to be the case. Perpetrators minimize the effects of the transgressions or see aspects that are more self-serving (Baumeister, Stillwell, & Wotman, 1990).

Leary and Baumeister's (2000) sociometer theory seems to be supported. When transgressions happen, people respond with negative emotions, which are cues to ways that people organize their responses to the transgression. Does the person feel anxiety? He or she feels threatened. Does the person feel anger? He or she might retaliate. Are the feelings interpreted as a challenge to the relationship or the self? The person might mobilize to respond to that challenge. Transgressions, thus, are injustices that are perceived differently by victims, offenders, and probably even observers (see Figure 2.2). A counselor, impartial observer, or even a family member on one party's side cannot expect that he or she has the truth about a transgression. When emotions get involved, perceptions, attributions, reactions, and sense of justice are all affected.

Injustice Gap

Forgiveness must be seen within the context of justice. Thus, as an example, let us examine a person's perceived *injustice gap* (Exline, Worthington, Hill, & McCullough, 2003; Worthington, 2003; Worthington & Scherer, 2004) after a crime. A person has a *desired outcome* for ultimate resolution of the crime. In Figure 2.3, assume that the Desired Outcome can be represented by a bar at 100 units.

A lower level, say 80 units, is what a person realistically expects the outcome to be if fair procedures are followed (called the Realistic Outcome). Most people believe that some departure from the ideal will result. At any time after a transgression, there is a Current Outcome, which sums the social, material, and emotional costs and benefits to the person. Shortly after the crime, the person might be at 20 units. Thus, in Figure 2.3, the first column represents the initial status.

Assume the crime were a burglary. Now assume that police were intrusive and required much time of the victim. They blundered about and asked insensitive questions. The victim's Current Outcome might dip to 10. The difference between the Current Outcome (10) and the Desired (100) or the

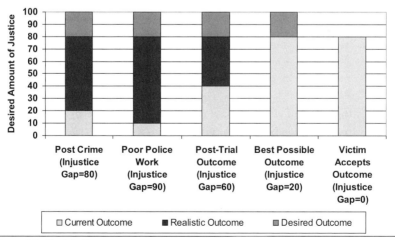

Figure 2.3 The injustice gap.

Realistic Outcome (80) is filled with dissatisfaction and anxiety. Dissatisfaction is easily converted to unforgiveness if the victim is inclined to ruminate about the offense (Berry, Worthington, O'Connor, Parrott, & Wade, 2005). The injustice gap is 90 (see the second column).

Assume, now, that the perpetrator was apprehended. The perpetrator goes to trial and is convicted. The victim's Current Outcome might be raised to 40 units. The size of the injustice gap, therefore, would have been reduced as a result of the enactment of justice from 90 (100 - 10) to 60 (100 - 40). This is shown by the third column.

Assume now that the perpetrator agrees to replace all stolen goods, repair the damage caused by the break-in, and pay the victim restitution of $1,000. The victim's Current Outcome might increase to 80 units. The injustice gap would be 20 units (100 - 80; see the fourth column). However, suppose the victim eventually resigns himself to accept that nothing can improve the outcome. With the acceptance of the Realistic Outcome, the victim lowers his Desired Outcome from 100 to 80. The injustice gap would then be 0 (80 - 80), which is depicted in the fifth column.

Because our legal system is a three-party system, and crimes are typically seen as crimes against the state rather than crimes against a victim, victims are rarely fully satisfied with the outcome of a legal case. So, usually the victim experiences an injustice gap between the Desired Outcome and the final Current Outcome even under the best circumstances (from the point of view of the victim). Even if the Realistic Outcome were achieved, net injustices remain. In this case, the injustice gap, even under the best conditions, would be 20 units, which would be the case if the person believed the Current Outcome was equal to the Realistic Outcome.

Interlocking Injustice Gaps

Multiple people are involved in any transgression. In some way, we must consider the amount of injustice each person has experienced. Each person will have a personal injustice gap. The size of that injustice gap will be informed by not only the amount of injustice he or she experienced, but also injustices affecting others, society, and God. I have been careful not to say that the personal injustice gap equals the sum of the private injustice gap + other injustice gaps + the divine injustice gap + society's injustice gap (divided by the number of gaps being considered to get an average). Rather, these various injustice gaps inform the personal injustice gap. This process of informing the personal injustice gap is more subjective than merely adding the gaps together to come up with a sum or taking the mean of the injustice gaps.

A perpetrator might also feel wronged by the victim's response or by judgment from others. If a perpetrator feels wronged, he or she will not likely respond with contrition or remorse over the crime, with apology, or with an offer of restitution.

Appraisal of Threat or Challenge

Look for the Tipping Point

Another important judgment takes place as people try to make sense out of the transgression. People appraise the transgression as a stressor that is making demands on them to adjust. They ask themselves two questions (Lazarus & Folkman, 1984): Might this harm me? Can I cope? If the person feels able to cope, the stressor is appraised as a challenge. If not, the stressor is appraised as a threat. The appraisals of challenge or threat strongly influence ways that people will attempt to cope.

In the marriages of Sam and Natalie and Bob and Randi, the affairs tossed both couples into threat. In Sam and Natalie's case, Sam was self-confident. Natalie wasn't. She whined and complained. Sam's infidelity further threatened her sense of competence. When her attitude hardened, though, Sam could not get his way, and he became threatened. For Bob and Randi, Randi's tears lessened Bob's sense of threat. It freed him to forgive, and tipped the relationship into a more positive state.

Finding that tipping point is what marital counseling is usually about. The counselor is always looking for some event, intervention, or incident that will allow the couple to experience and articulate a new perspective on the marriage relationship. This tipping point sometimes occurs gradually. But in my counseling experience I have observed that, even if there is a gradual growth toward the tipping point, in most cases, couples look back to a particular incident, homework assignment, or intervention that tipped the balance.

Integrative-behavioral couples therapists look for interventions that help the couple either accept their limitations and move on, or change from the negativity of problem focus into the positivity of skill building. Emotion-focused couples therapists look for interventions that reinvigorate the attachment bond and provide often-startling emotional insight into each partner's behavior. Solution-focused therapists try to uncover little changes that make a big difference. Instead of focusing on the problem, they try to get the couple to find a small solution and amplify its effects. Insight-oriented therapists are trying to find insights into personal dynamics that allow couples to break out of negative patterns. All couples therapists look for ways that threat appraisals can be converted to challenge appraisals. Threats paralyze. Challenges motivate action.

Types of Appraisals to Stressors

Stressors can challenge or threaten different targets: (1) a person's confidence and competence, (2) attachment bonds, or (3) autonomy and self-determination. For example, Leary, Springer, Negel, Ansell, and Evans (1998) found that people often had their feelings hurt when a friend tried to "help" by criticizing or expressing no confidence in them. Expressions of nonconfidence, when seen as a threat, can erode people's competence. But some people take such criticism as a challenge.

An affair can threaten or challenge the romantic relationship but also the person's competence and confidence. For example, in Sam and Natalie's case, Sam was self-confident. Natalie was not. She whined and complained. Sam's infidelity threatened her sense of competence. On the other hand, for Bob and Randi, Bob had come into his own in self-confidence. So Randi's affair, while being a blow to Bob's self-confidence, challenged but did not threaten him.

An example of a challenge or threat to one's autonomy or self-determination might arise at work. Suppose Suzanne were working on a report. Her supervisor loses patience with her, steps in, and takes the report away from her. That could challenge her sense of self-determination. She might respond with hurt and anger, but she could soon put her emotions behind her and bounce back. If Suzanne were less confident, though, her boss's interference may heighten her sense of lack of control.

Tipping From Challenge to Threat and Back Again

Malcolm Gladwell (2002) describes tipping points—sudden changes in state that stimulate sudden change. Miller and C'de Baca (2001) calls those "quantum changes." Three characteristics affect whether a tipping point will occur: qualities of the messenger, the message, and the context.

What can tip the teeter-totter from challenge to threat appraisals, making forgiveness more likely as a response to an interpersonal transgression? Of course, there are the usual suspects. An overstressed victim perceives almost any transgression as a threat. Reducing one's stress makes forgiving more likely. If the offender shows no sensitivity toward the victim, that lack of caring will threaten the victim's competence, relatedness, or autonomy or self-determination. Forgiveness would be less likely.

The victim's spiritual life also makes a difference. The victim will be likely to interpret transgressions as threatening rather than challenging if the victim concludes that "God hates me," or "God is trying to punish me." When the sacred is brought in on the side of the transgression, this ups the threat, especially if a person feels separated from God anyway. When God is brought in on the side of forgiveness—"God is loving and merciful and wants me to be the same"—then challenge appraisals more often prevail.

There are also message characteristics. If the severity or number of transgressions is particularly high, then additional transgressions are more threatening than they would be alone. We saw with Leary et al.'s (1998) research that several types of messages—betrayals, active dissociation, and not being appreciated—were particularly harmful.

The context is important. If the relationship is at a vulnerable time, then any transgression is likely to be interpreted as a threat. Often, this is indicated by a low ratio of positive to negative interactions (Gottman, 1994). The relationship does not automatically become troubled, but the relationship is vulnerable. Each negative interaction is likely to pose more of a challenge until a particularly severe interaction or a symbolic interaction tips the relationship into being a troubled relationship. Appraisals of transgressions shift suddenly from mostly challenge to almost exclusively threatening.

The injustice gap is a person's summary response to a relationship that has experienced a major transgression. High stress, poor relationship with God, a hostile offender, and a low ratio of positive to negative interactions conspire to convert a transgression into a wide injustice gap. When that gap is wide, threat appraisals are likely. The sociometer (Leary & Baumeister, 2000) reacts quickly to fire up negative emotions with each perceived new transgression. And transgressions not only multiply but also create more stress and less productive coping.

Responses to Threat

Freeze, Flight, or Fight

Most people are familiar with the three major responses to threat. Typically, the first reaction to a sudden stressor is to freeze. After initially freezing, animals that are kept under stress will seek to escape from the stressful situation and avoid it in the future. They flee. If they are cornered, they will fight.

People also freeze, flee, or fight when threatened. Their brain seems to lock up and they cannot think (freeze). They try to escape or avoid stress and hope it will disappear (flee). They attack the source of stress and become hostile or surly (fight).

Tend and Befriend

Recently, Taylor et al. (2000) have suggested two additional responses to threat: tend and befriend. The model for the freeze, flight, or fight responses describes how a lone animal on the savanna behaves when it suddenly encounters a hostile creature. However, humans (and many other animals) live in social groups. Some responses to threat, then, involve use of their social instincts. For example, if a predator is sighted, some animals will bunch together in a herd, befriending each other and making the survival chances greatest for the entire herd even though one animal might be picked off. Meanwhile, the animal might also be maximizing its own response to threat internally. This is called tending to itself. The animal might monitor itself, calm its emotions, or solve practical problems for escaping or dealing with the threat.

Humans use the same type of coping responses. They befriend each other, seeking social support when under stress. They also tend to themselves, handling problems so they can most effectively deal with the stressor.

Rumination

A Model for Rumination and Aggression

Whether people forgive depends on their emotional responses to transgressions, which are shaped by the injustice gap and their appraisals. Some people are particularly vulnerable to stewing, ruminating, feeling unforgiveness, and holding grudges. Those people tend to replay the event over repeatedly in their minds, elaborating on it, exploring the negative consequences for themselves or their relationships, and worrying. Rumination has pernicious effects on people's mental and physical health.

Rumination has been studied extensively in the last 15 years. Much of the study derived from our interest in post-traumatic stress disorder (PTSD), which received high attention in the mid-1970s after Vietnam veterans returned. Susan Nolen-Hoeksema also boosted interest in rumination. She demonstrated a link between rumination and depression and described it within the Response Style Theory of Depression (Nolen-Hoeksema, 1987). She also associated ruminative thoughts with anxiety (Nolen-Hoeksema, 1991; Segerstrom, Tsao, Alden, & Craske, 2000).

In 1993, Leonard Berkowitz proposed a cognitive-neoassociationistic model of rumination and aggression. In 2003, Miller, Pedersen, Earlywine, and Pollock elaborated on that model by describing triggered displaced aggression. In short, the model, which is summarized in Figure 2.4, suggests that rumination produces negative emotion. Negative emotion triggers associative, cognitive, motivational, and emotional networks. Those networks can arouse motives, which then affect people's appraisals and behavior. We might think of this as the mechanism behind Leary and Baumeister's (2000) sociometer theory. Let us walk through the five steps of this neoassociationistic network model.

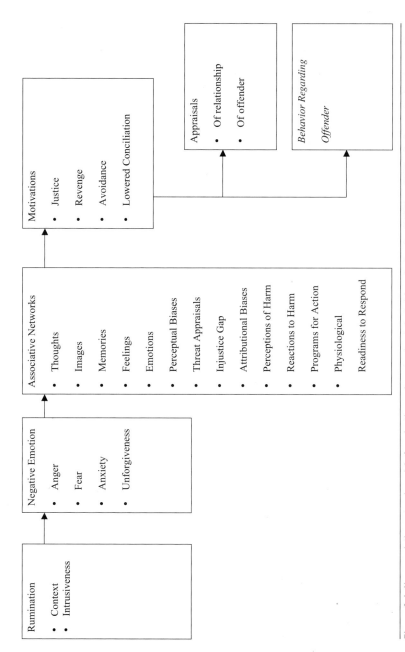

Figure 2.4 Neoassociation network model of rumination and aggression (adapted from Berkowitz, [1993], and Miller, Pedersen, Earleywine, and Pollock [2003] and applied to unforgiveness and negative interpersonal motives).

Rumination Triggers Emotion

Rumination triggers the emotion. The content of the rumination strongly affects the negative emotion (see Berry et al., 2005). As people ruminate about sad aspects of a situation, they may become depressed. If they ruminate about injustice and frustrated goals, they may become angry. If they ruminate about potential harm, they may become fearful and anxious. If they have unforgiving ruminations, they may experience unforgiveness. Unforgiving emotion will trigger unforgiving associationistic networks.

The degree of intrusiveness of rumination is important. Sometimes rumination is unbidden. Other times, we invite it. If rumination occurs mostly under people's control, its power is decreased. But if rumination occurs spontaneously and cannot be stopped, then the negative emotions aroused are higher.

Negative Emotions

The key step in this model is the generation of negative emotion by the rumination. If rumination is not emotionally involving, the associative networks are not triggered. But if negative emotions such as anger, fear, anxiety, depression, or unforgiveness are generated, then the stronger the emotion, the more the emotion activates associative networks.

Associative Networks

Associative networks are combinations of related mental and physical activities. These can operate smoothly, flashing from one aspect to the other in a coordinated slideshow. Or associations can flit about, herky-jerky like freeze-frames caught by a strobe light in a crowded dance hall. Thoughts about the event and its consequences might be triggered. Negative emotions might flood the body. Images may flash before the mind's eye. Memories from past events might leap to mind. People can elaborate those into full-blown memories. Feelings can be associated with those memories, and if the associative networks remain activated, full-blown emotions can be experienced. Perceptual biases can be triggered. Namely, an offender about whom one is ruminating in an unforgiving scenario can be perceived as evil. The person sees the offender in a Darth Vader suit. Threat appraisals are activated.

When ruminating, an unforgiving person can experience threats to the relationship, to their competence, and to their own self-determination or autonomy. The injustice gap is recalled and reviewed. By ruminating about how unjust or offensive an act was, perceptions of the amount and seriousness of the harm can be highlighted. Reactions to harm—like vengeance or retaliation—can also be rehearsed. Even if the victim believes he or she would not succumb, the mental programs for action can be rehearsed.

Finally, rumination can arouse the person physiologically, increasing the blood pressure, activating the sympathetic nervous system (SNS), and turning on the proprioceptive nervous system.

As the person bounces back and forth among the associations, the person becomes more and more motivated to carry out some of the action programs. These might be automatic (i.e., lash out in rage) or may be more thoughtful coping strategies like seeking justice, accepting, or perhaps forgiving. A woman was a self-proclaimed ruminator. She seemed focused on the past and kept the past on the front burner by talking about it often with her sister. She confessed to me that her father had made her "feel uncomfortable" as a child. She had awakened at times and saw him "watching her sleep." She did not believe that any abuse had ever occurred, but she resented feeling nervous and afraid around her father. When her father divorced her mother and remarried, she informed her vengeful and vindictive sister about the address of the father and his new wife. The sister phoned the new wife and made accusations against the father that created a conflict between him and his wife. The woman had stirred up resentment, which led to her coping mechanisms: get support from her sister and manipulate her sister into doing the dirty work—a skill she had perfected in childhood and still used today.

Appraisals Motivate Behavior

Association networks motivate actions. The motivation changes the way people appraise ongoing relationships or potential future relationships. It also changes appraisals about the offender as a person. Finally, threat appraisals can be activated.

Behavior in Regard to the Offender

The negative motivations also may lead to new behavior toward the offender. The ruminating victim could be aggressive or could act out thoughts, images, and programs for actions that had aroused justice, revenge, or avoidance motives. Or the rumination could lead to a rumbling, grumbling grudge.

What Causes Rumination to Begin?

Many external triggers can set off a ruminative sequence. These could include the mere sight of the transgressor, reminders of the transgression, being hurt similarly (by the person or even by someone else), or even being under a lot of stress. Internal triggers can set off rumination, too. When people get in negative moods, they tend to ruminate, even in the absence of external triggers. Memories or intrusive images sometimes seem to pop up spontaneously. Once an emotion-loaded memory of a transgression occurs, a train of thought might lead to rehearsing other grudges. When thoughts are triggered, negative emotions like anger and unforgiveness usually are not far behind.

Effects of Rumination

Once rumination begins, it can lead to a number of effects. I have already mentioned at the beginning of the chapter how depression can be a product of rumination (Nolen-Hoeksema, 1987, 1991). All sorts of other negative effects can result from rumination (Mor & Winquist, 2002). Anger can be a frequent product of angry rumination. This has been shown in research by Rusting and Nolen-Hoeksema (1998). Angry people who ruminate become angrier than those who do not. When people ruminate angrily, they prolong their angry states relative to those who do not ruminate. Bushman (2002) recently showed that if people ruminate angrily while hitting a punching bag, they tend to be more aggressive toward the person they are ruminating about than if they do not ruminate while hitting the punching bag.

Under most cases, angry rumination is associated with an increased likelihood for anger, aggression, and displaced aggression (Miller, Pederesen, Earleywine, & Pollack, 2003). It is not surprising, then, that studies have looked at whether forgiveness or unforgiveness is related to rumination. This hypothesis was proposed early in forgiveness studies (McCullough & Worthington, 1994; Worthington & Wade, 1999). Quelling rumination is necessary for lasting forgiveness to occur.

Experimental studies of forgiveness and rumination began with McCullough et al. (1998). They showed that forgiveness was predicted by a decrease in rumination. McCullough et al. (2001) examined the connection between rumination about a transgression and lack of forgiveness of it. Rumination was correlated with both revenge and avoidance after a transgression. In addition, McCullough et al. (2001) showed that changes in rumination were associated with changes in scores on revenge and avoidance. Others have found connections between rumination and unforgiveness at the trait level. For example, Berry et al. (2001), Thompson et al. (2005), and Walker and Gorsuch (2002) have all found connections between trait measures of rumination and trait measures of unforgiveness. Berry et al. (2005) showed that the content of rumination affected the amount of unforgiveness that a person felt. Finally, McCullough and Bono (2004) found that when people ruminate about transgressions that fluctuate from day to day, they are more unforgiving on days they ruminate more, and less unforgiving on days they ruminate less. Over 2 to 3 months, McCullough and Bono found that to the extent that rumination decreased over that time, rumination also decreased.

Back to Our Stress-and-Coping Model of Unforgiveness and Forgiveness

If we examine Figure 2.1 again, we can see that we are developing a picture of how a person becomes unforgiving. Transgressions are perceived as hurtful or offensive. People respond in anger, fear, or perhaps sadness. Overall, several theories can be brought together to explain the role of unforgiveness in transgressions. Sociometer theory (Leary & Baumeister, 2000) suggests that the emotions of unforgiveness might be the emotions triggering the sociometer. The injustice gap stimulates unforgiveness and awakens the justice motive and triggers the neoassociationistic network (Berkowitz, 1993; Miller et al., 2003). Unforgiveness can also be seen as part of the stress reaction. It is this aspect of unforgiveness to which we now turn.

Unforgiveness

Unforgiveness Defined

Unforgiveness is a stress reaction in response to an appraisal of threat, or sometimes challenge, which is brought about by transgression. More specifically, *emotional unforgiveness* is defined as a complex of emotions experienced at some time later than a transgression (Worthington & Wade, 1999). Those emotions involve resentment, bitterness, hostility, hatred, anger, and fear. They arise from perceiving that one has experienced a transgression.

Immediate negative emotions in response to a transgression include anger, fear, or both. Anger is typically thought to be an emotional state that arises due to a threat, frustration, or perceived transgression (Spielberger & Moscoso, 1999). Unforgiveness is a more limited, nuanced, and delayed response to a perceived transgression. It also includes unforgiving motivations, like revenge or avoidance.

Not everyone will develop unforgiveness when transgressed against. Only people who ruminate angrily (and perhaps anxiously and depressively) will likely develop unforgiveness. People try to reduce negatively experienced unforgiveness by dealing with the transgression to rectify it (thereby leading to a narrowed injustice gap and less unforgiveness) or by dealing with the emotion directly.

Unforgiveness is a stress reaction, and because that is a pivotal point, I will discuss the evidence supporting that statement in the following chapter. For the moment, let us take this at face value and complete the discussion of the theory. Unforgiving emotions motivate people to cope with the unforgiveness, which they do in many ways.

Coping

How people appraise stressors is related to how they cope with those stressors. Skinner, Edge, Altman, and Hayley (2003) summarized how people cope. They analyzed over 100 measures of coping. At the most basic level are what Skinner et al. called instances of coping. These are simple reports of what people do to deal with stressors. Skinner et al. identified from these 100-plus instruments over 400 separate instances of coping. Even for the most intrepid researcher, that is TMI—too much information.

So Skinner et al. (2003) collapsed the list into fewer more general categories that they called ways of coping. Each way of coping typically divides types of coping into categories. For example, one helpful system is Lazarus and Folkman's (1984) emotion-focused coping versus problem-focused coping. *Emotion-focused coping* intends primarily to control one's emotions. For example, the person says, "I'm feeling anxious over this exam. It is stressing me. I will calm my anxiety by deep breathing or meditation." Deep breathing is not aimed at solving the problem of lack of study or doing well on the test. It is aimed at reducing the person's anxiety. Note, however, that if it is successful, the person will score better on the test, too. *Problem-focused coping* is aimed primarily at solving the problem. For example, if the person studies all night, that is aimed at making a better score on the exam. Note, however, that to the extent that the person is successful at studying, the person probably will become calmer. This illustrates the problem with almost every category system for different ways of coping: Categories are not always mutually exclusive.

Other classifications of ways of coping divide them into assimilating versus accommodating ways of coping. *Assimilating coping* finds an existing method that one can apply to the problem. *Accommodating coping* finds a new method that one can use to crack the problem. In another classification system, *approach coping* is when the person approaches the problem and deals with it. An approach strategy might be aggression toward the person causing the stress. In *avoidance coping*, the person tries to avoid the problem—perhaps by socially withdrawing or distracting oneself. Yet another classification groups coping into prosocial, antisocial, or asocial ways of coping. *Prosocial coping* seeks support from others. *Antisocial coping* opposes a person causing a roadblock. *Asocial coping* cognitively reconstructs one's understanding of an event. Ways of coping can also be classified as effortful or involuntary. *Effortful coping* requires energy. *Involuntary coping* is automatic. One might merely distract oneself from stress by watching television, without consciously planning such a distraction.

Skinner et al. (2003) called even more general subdivisions, families of coping. Examples include good-news versus bad-news coping strategies.

Some strategies such as helplessness are bad news in many ways (physically, emotionally, relationally). Others are good news if engaged in over a period of time. By analyzing category systems, from bottom-up and from top-down, Skinner et al. arrive at 13 categories that they call families of coping strategies. These are problem solving, seeking social support, avoidance or escape, distraction, positive cognitive restructuring, rumination, helplessness, social withdrawal, emotion regulation, information seeking, negotiation, opposition, and delegation.

At the highest level of generality is what Skinner et al. (2003) call basic adaptive processes. Adaptive processes are ways people seek to match their personal capabilities to the environment. More about those follows in just a moment.

Coping With the Stress of Unforgiveness

An Anecdote

When I was in high school, in the early 1960s, we had a pep rally before a big football game. You can tell this is a long time ago because the centerpiece of the pep rally was a big bonfire. Free hot dogs and marshmallows were distributed to students. We slipped as close to the fire as we dared without being incinerated and plunged the wiener on a stick into the flames. This produced a 1-inch-thick corndog-looking wiener covered in ashes. Or we thrust the stick-impaled marshmallows near the fire and watched them burst into flame as we moved them into the same postal code as the fire. I was having a great time. Blowing up marshmallows.

Someone whirled around and smashed a flaming marshmallow into my left hand. You can imagine what happened. The marshmallow was melted on the inside and flaming on the outside. It adhered to my finger.

At age 15, I was a macho-macho man and did not cry. I did run (like the wind) to the entrance of the nearest building and plunged my hand into sink full of cold water. It was the most excruciating pain I have felt in my life. To make it worse, the pain would not go away. I could not peel the burnt marshmallow off of my hand. Finally, I pried it off, leaving a bloody scorched trail down to the bone. That ended my revelry for the night. I hopped on my bicycle and rode the mile and a half home. There, I got the wound dressed by my mother, who was a nurse.

Drawing an Analogy

A transgression can often hurt people as much as that burning, bubbling marshmallow attached to my skin. It can be as stubborn to get rid of as the marshmallow was. Trying to dislodge a serious transgression can feel like people are ripping out parts of their hearts along with the sticky hurt.

Victims try to deal with the pain, but they often do not know how. Running, crying, trying to ignore the hurt, or feeling sorry for oneself does not help. Perhaps getting sympathy from friends or succor from mother could ease the suffering, but the pain within is still just as strong. Even finding the bully who carelessly marshmallowed me with his stick and pounding a little politeness into his head (with my other hand) would not help. (But tempting.)

I tried several of those coping mechanisms—anything to get away from the pain. Only three things seemed to help. First, shoving my hand beneath icy water briefly neutralized the heat. Second, I got the marshmallow off. In transgressions, empathy detaches the marshmallow. Sometimes it detaches the skin, too, but we know there will be no healing if we do not get the marshmallow off. Third, getting empathy, social support, and meager medical attention from my mother encouraged me to persevere—as if I really had a choice.

I threw away the marshmallow. It was irrelevant to how fast I healed. In the same way, once people can throw off the hurt, they unstick it from themselves. When they forgive, they unstick it from the person who transgressed against them. Then, that hurt can become irrelevant to their reaction to that person again. This anecdote was about coping with the stress of injury. Below, I describe a plan for coping with unforgiveness.

Matching Personal Qualities to Environment

Skinner et al. (2003) described different levels of categorizing coping processes. At the most general level, they identify three *adaptive* processes. First, people try to *match their actions to the environmental contingencies*. That is, people want to perform behaviors to deal with their unforgiveness that will be rewarded and not punished. Importantly, people match based on long-term outcomes. For example, I wanted to go beat some sense into the boy who burned me. This might have been rewarding for me in the short-term (although he might actually have given me a lesson in manners). But picking a fight as a result of an accidental burn is not to my long-term advantage. That coping strategy would be much more costly in loss of friends, potential damage to myself, or getting in trouble with the boy himself, his parents, or his parents' lawyers. Altogether, my coping mechanism needs to be likely to reward me and not likely to result in additional punishment or pain.

Second, people *match their personal reliance on others to the social resources available in the environment*. For example, I needed care for the physical wound. My mother was a nurse. So I did not hang around and hope I would be able to find someone to treat my injury at school. I rode home and within 10 minutes I was receiving her nursing care.

Third, people want to *match their personal preferences with the options that the environment provides*. For example, my personal preferences to end the pain as quickly as possible was matched with quickly finding a restroom that had sinks. I took advantage of the option available in the environment. Had there been a tub of ice housing soft drinks, I would have used that option.

Problem-, Emotion-, and Meaning-Focused Coping

Berry and Worthington (2001) conceptualized unforgiveness as a stress reaction to appraisals of interpersonal stressors that include transgressions, betrayals, offenses, and wrongs. Using Lazarus and Folkman's (1984) schema, the transgression is considered a stressor. People appraise stressors. The appraisals create physiological, cognitive, motivational, behavioral, and emotional stress reactions. Unforgiveness is one emotion within the stress reaction.

People cope. Their attempts to reduce the injustice gap (Exline et al., 2003) and unforgiveness (Worthington, 2001) are coping strategies. Some are problem-focused. People might seek to bring about justice. Others are emotion-focused. People try to regulate their emotional experience (see Thayer & Lane, 2000). They might self-soothe or avoid even the thought of the transgression. My definition of emotional forgiveness, an emotional replacement of negative emotion (unforgiveness) by positive other-oriented emotions, seems to place it within Lazarus and Folkman's (1984) model as an emotion-focused coping strategy (see Folkman & Moskowitz, 2000b; McCullough, 2001b; Park & Folkman, 1997). Worthington and Scherer (2004) have made that case and arrayed evidence to support it. Still others are meaning-focused coping strategies. People might renarrate the event, excusing or justifying the transgression.

Research on coping has shown that neither problem-focused nor emotion-focused coping strategies per se are superior for dealing with stress (Park, Folkman, & Bostrom, 2001). When direct action is possible, problem-focused coping has often been found to be superior (Lazarus, 1999). When direct action to remove stressors is hampered, emotion-focused coping has often been found to be superior (Lazarus).

By extension, this suggests that unforgiveness might be reduced most effectively by using several different strategies. Sometimes, in the spirit of problem-focused coping, a person might seek redress for injustice. Sometimes, in the sprit of handling negative emotions, a person might emotionally forgive. Both strategies might be simultaneously or sequentially employed at still other times. In addition, a person might use meaning-focused coping (Park & Folkman, 1997).

Worthington and Scherer (2004) have argued that emotional forgiveness is usually an emotion-focused coping effort. In the present book, however, I am retreating from that position. Decisional forgiveness can, at times, be a result of problem-, emotion-, or meaning-focused coping—though it usually is associated with problem-focused coping. Similarly, even though emotional forgiveness occurs through an emotional replacement mechanism, it may be pursued as a problem-focused coping effort or meaning-focused effort as well as an emotion-focused coping effort.

To Deal With a Transgression, One Tries to Change What One Can Possibly Change

After a transgression has occurred, people cannot undo that transgression. They must change what they can. They perceive the transgression as a hurt or offense and respond to it with anger or fear. Perhaps they can control some of their anger and fear. If they can self-soothe, they might lessen any subsequent unforgiveness. Self-soothing can give a sense of control, but it can also help convince one that he or she is not all that unforgiving. This is based on Daryl Bem's (1967) self-perception theory. Bem argued that we observe our own behavior and infer our internal states from our observed behavior. If we do not seem to be upset, then we will not become more upset. So, to reduce emotional unforgiveness, people can try not to react strongly. Do not say, "I'm furious." Do not scream, cry, or storm about in rage. Express emotion in measured doses.

Of course, trying to suppress emotional reactions can backfire. The more one tries to keep a lid on one's emotions, the more force can build up behind them. As a therapist, or in our own lives, we often walk a tightrope. We need to know ourselves and our clients before trying to suppress emotional reaction.

People might try to change the magnitude of the injustice gap through two strategies. Look back at Figure 2.3. A victim can introduce more justice, raising the bottom bar (how one perceives things currently are). Or a victim can lower expectations about the ideal outcome, lowering the top bar. Usually, one cannot fully exact justice. One can try to seek redress from the person who hurt them, but it is unclear how he or she will respond. The offender might even exacerbate the situation by rejecting one's overtures. It seems at first blush that lowering our expectations is easier. Yet even there, change requires hard work. Modifying the injustice gap, though difficult, is something people can change.

If one has appraised the situation as threatening, usually that appraisal was not rational. Trying to force oneself to view a situation as a challenge rather than a threat usually only partially succeeds. People can mouth the words that a situation is merely challenging, but threat appraisals are notoriously unresponsive to willful changes.

Seek the Ray of Hope That Tips the Appraisal From Threat to Challenge

Take a tip from the solution-focused therapists. Find what might be working, even to a small degree. Try to magnify that positive action. People who are mired in unforgiveness are caught in a repetitive cycle. They feel they have no ability to escape. But sometimes, if they make one tiny change, it gives them a glimmer of hope in what had seemed like a hopeless battle with unforgiveness. It provides the tipping point that helps transform those appraisals from threat, danger, and destruction to challenge.

Of all areas, perhaps people have the most control over their coping strategies. Perhaps, simply not seeing the person would reduce unforgiveness. Maybe a person goes to a restaurant weekly and runs into the person. The person might ask, "How much did I like that food anyway? Did I like it enough to put myself through feeling renewed hostility each week?" Making a small change can sometimes tip the balance.

Calm or Short-Circuit Rumination

Rumination that triggers negative emotions activates neoassociationistic networks. If one spots rumination quickly, he or she can usually short-circuit the rumination before it gets revved up. Catching oneself worrying or replaying scenes in one's head should serve as an alarm bell that alerts one to do something else.

If a ruminator misses early warning signs, then he or she can still catch rumination in the initial stage. The first hint of feeling bitter or resentful, seeing oneself make hostile statements, thinking hostile thoughts toward a transgressor, or hearing oneself use the word "hate" can be a second set of alarm bells. These are sirens that scream, "Get out of this rumination immediately."

Decisional and Emotional Forgiveness as Mechanisms for Coping With Unforgiveness

Researchers who study forgiveness have used many theoretical understandings of the construct. Most agree that forgiveness is complex (Enright & Fitzgibbons, 2000). It involves cognitive (Flanigan, 1992), affective (Malcolm & Greenberg, 2000), behavioral (Gordon, Baucom, & Snyder, 2000), motivational (McCullough et al., 1997), decisional (DiBlasio, 1998), and interpersonal (e.g., Baumeister, Exline, & Sommer, 1998) aspects. Researchers do not agree about which aspects are most important.

Types of Forgiveness Differentiated

Decisional forgiveness is a behavioral intention statement that one will seek to behave toward the transgressor like one did prior to a transgression. One decides to release the transgressor from the debt (Baumeister et al., 1998; DiBlasio, 1998). One might grant decisional forgiveness and still be emotionally upset; cognitively oriented toward angry, anxious, or depressive rumination; and motivationally oriented toward revenge or avoidance. However, in some cases, decisional forgiveness could trigger emotional forgiveness.

The second type of forgiveness, *emotional forgiveness*, is rooted in emotions (Worthington, 2000, 2001, 2003; Worthington, Berry, & Parrott, 2001; Worthington & Wade, 1999) that affect motivations. Magnitude of the injustice gap is hypothesized to be inversely proportional to ease of forgiving and directly proportional to emotional unforgiveness.

Some Indirect Support for This Distinction

Huang and Enright (2000) studied physiological responses to unforgiveness. They differentiated two types of forgiveness. One they called "anger-related forgiveness" (ARF) due to obligation, and they compared this with "unconditional love forgiveness" (ULF). They found that people who experienced ARF had significantly more masking smiles, more downcast eyes, and higher blood pressure at 1 minute than did people who had experienced ULF. This study provides indirect support for a distinction between decisional and emotional forgiveness.

Decisional Forgiveness as a Coping Mechanism

Decisional forgiveness can be based in rational logic or will. Typically, when one says that one wills to make a decision, it is because the intent to control behavior goes against how the person would like to behave. Therefore, the decision seems to require willpower or self-control to bring it about. People will often then say that they have decided to forgive the person even though they do not feel like forgiving the person. People may decide to grant decisional forgiveness not because they rationally believe that forgiveness matches their motivations, but because forgiveness might be consistent with their belief system.

Decisions to forgive can occur before emotional forgiveness is experienced. In fact, that is the usual sequence of events. People decide to forgive, and as their emotions change, they experience emotional forgiveness. Decisional forgiveness usually leads to emotional forgiveness in time.

This is not always the case. Sometimes, a person can experience a change in feelings toward the perpetrator and then, upon reflection, label it as having decided to forgive. For example, suppose that a person offends me, and then some horrible catastrophe befalls the person. Feeling compassion and sympathy for that person elicited by those events will drown the small feelings of unforgiveness for the person. At some point later, then, someone might ask whether I had forgiven the person for offending me. If I at that time assay my current emotional state, I will realize that my feelings are positive toward the person, so I say that I have emotionally forgiven. Decisional forgiveness would have come after the emotional forgiveness was experienced.

Decisional Forgiveness Will Have Sequelae

Changes will likely follow a decision to forgive. The decisional forgiver's motivations will usually become less negative and more positive. Motivations are drives to behave in certain ways. If a person has made a decision to change his or her behavioral intentions, it is likely that he or she will report lowered revenge, avoidance, and grudge-holding motivations. The decisional forgiver's behavior is also likely to change if he or she is brought back into contact with the offender. To the extent that a forgiver is able to control his or her behavior in line with his or her behavioral intentions, behavior will indeed change as one of the sequelae of making the decision to forgive.

Once a decision to forgive is made, it is likely that a forgiver's emotions can change. The person who has decided to forgive might act more benevolently. When that happens, the forgiver sees himself or herself behaving with forgiveness while still feeling unforgiveness. This creates a dissonance, which leads the forgiver to change his or her emotional experience.

The decisional forgiver might become more open to trying emotional forgiveness techniques in response to counseling after making a decision to forgive. Once the person believes that he or she should act on the changed intentions and control his or her behavior, the decisional forgiver typically wants to bring his or her emotions in line with that decision. Thus, if a therapist offers to employ emotional forgiveness interventions, or if the person has the opportunity to participate in a psychoeducational group, then the decisional forgiver is often open to making emotional changes.

The decisional forgiver may get a sense of peace from deciding to forgive. The person might feel that the matter is settled once the decision is made. He or she might expect his or her emotions to fall into line eventually. Having made the decision, then, the person begins to experience a sense of closure and peace. That sense of peace is not a foregone conclusion. In fact, making a decision to forgive when one feels unforgiving can cause the person to suppress his or her emotional expression of negative emotion. Emotional expression has typically been studied in terms of its effects on the person's continuing emotions. Emotional suppression can frustrate or magnify those emotions.

James J. Gross (2002) has studied the effect of efforts to suppress emotions on people's recall of emotional situations. In a typical experiment, Gross and his colleagues invite couples into the laboratories to discuss topics that were likely to produce disagreements. Each partner might be given an instruction either to suppress all emotions, or to reinterpret the situation differently (such as remembering that disagreements are likely to occur in normal couples), or they might be given no instructions about regulating emotion.

Partners who tried to suppress their emotions had worse recall of what was said in the conversation with their partner than did people who reappraised the situation or were given no instructions. People who suppressed their emotions recalled less than 70% of what was said in the conversation. People who appraised the situation recalled over 80% of what was said. Gross (2002) explained that suppressing emotions is difficult and requires that we pay attention to not showing emotion. The more attention we pay to controlling our emotion, the less we are able to listen to what the person actually says. The tragedy of that is that it will likely lead to additional misunderstandings, hurts, and transgressions.

Decisional forgiveness is different from emotional forgiveness, but they are clearly related to each other. In Table 2.1, I have compared some of the major attributes of decisional and emotional forgiveness.

Emotional Forgiveness and the Emotional Juxtaposition Hypothesis

Worthington and Wade (1999) defined emotional forgiveness as the emotional juxtaposition of positive other-oriented emotions against negative unforgiveness, which eventually results in neutralization or replacement of all or part of those negative emotions with positive emotions. The positive emotions that lead to emotional forgiveness have been identified as empathy, sympathy, compassion, romantic love, and altruistic love (Wade & Worthington, 2003; Worthington et al., 2001).

Whereas the experience of some positive emotion is necessary to neutralize unforgiveness, the person may or may not have a *net final positive emotion* toward the transgressor. To some degree that depends on (a) whether the relationship is expected to continue and (b) whether other affectively charged events intervene. The forgiveness might be partial (reduced unforgiveness) or complete (resulting in a net neutral or even net positive emotion toward the transgressor).

Table 2.1 Comparison of Decisional and Emotional Forgiveness.

Decisional Forgiveness

a. Arrived at rationally or by will
b. May come before or after emotional forgiveness
c. May occur without emotional forgiveness
d. Aimed at controlling future behavior (not motives or emotions)
e. May make person feel "settled," calming emotion and motivation (i.e., might lead to emotional forgiveness or at least reduce emotional unforgiveness)
f. May give new meaning to situation
g. Changes behavior
h. May improve interactions by de-escalating or promoting reconciliation

Emotional Forgiveness

a. Arrived at by emotional replacement
b. Necessarily reduces unforgiving emotions
c. May come before or after decisional forgiveness (but usually after)
d. May occur without decisional forgiveness on rare occasions
e. Aimed at changing emotional climate but inevitably triggers neoassociationistic networks leading to changes in motives, thoughts, and other associations
f. May give new meaning to situation
g. May change behavior
h. Will change motivation
i. Makes person feel less negative emotionally and perhaps more positive
j. May improve interactions and promote reconciliation
k. May reduce the injustice gap
l. May reduce the justice motive

I Make No Claims About What Initiates Forgiveness

Note that in this emotional replacement hypothesis, I am making no claims about what might initiate forgiveness. Forgiveness, at times, can be initiated by changes in cognition, the offender's behavior, the victim's behavior, willful decision, emotional experience or expression, spiritual experience, or any combination of those. My concern is not what initiates emotional replacement. Rather, my contention is that when emotional forgiveness is occurring, it is because emotional replacement is occurring. When emotional forgiveness is complete, the person will have replaced the negative emotion of unforgiveness by the positive emotions associated with empathy, sympathy, compassion, and romantic or altruistic love. The change in emotional forgiveness—as it begins and moves toward completion—will be reflected most accurately by changes in emotions, not by changes in thoughts, other cognition, motivations, or behavior, though each might occur. Before emotional forgiveness is complete, if a person is actively attempting to forgive, some measure of positive emotion would be experienced for a person in a cherished ongoing relationship but not for an offender in a noncontinuing relationship, and a reduction in unforgiveness will have occurred.

Recall the examples that began the chapter. Both the marriages of Sam and Natalie and of Bob and Randi were characterized by sincere apologies, expressions of regret and contrition, and promises of fidelity. Yet Bob and Randi's relationship tipped from a troubled marriage characterized by instability and problems to a stable relationship with promise for enduring. Sam and Natalie's never could get over that tipping point. Why? Sam and Natalie continued to show a hard face to each other. That kept them focused on justice. When Randi broke down in tears, though, her suffering was evident. That not only reduced the magnitude of Bob's injustice gap, but it also triggered empathy, sympathy, compassion, and love in Bob. Emotional forgiveness followed, and Bob quickly expressed decisional forgiveness.

Let Us Take Stock

I began this chapter setting an agenda of two tasks. First, I paralleled the stress-and-coping theory of forgiveness to general stress-and-coping theory. In Figure 2.1, we see the process described. Second, I described modifications of the general theory to create a specific stress-and-coping theory of unforgiveness and forgiveness. Finally, I briefly discussed two types of forgiveness—decisional and emotional.

In chapter 3, I will address a third crucial point. I will evaluate the evidence bearing on whether unforgiveness is a type of stress reaction.

CHAPTER 3

Evidence That Unforgiveness
Is a Stress Reaction

Eric Lomax (1996) was a British soldier in World War II who had the misfortune of being captured in Burma. His Japanese captors forced him to work on the Burma–Thailand railway through the jungle. Few survived that experience. During Lomax's internment, the prisoners were mistreated. At one point, Lomax was part of a small rebellion. He was interrogated. The interrogator used physical punishment for Lomax's noncooperation. Strangely, it was not the interrogator that Lomax focused on. It was the translator, a small Japanese man who reacted with almost no emotion regardless of what was said or done to Lomax.

Liberation day came, and Lomax was repatriated to Great Britain. However, his life was forever different. For 20 years, he suffered flashbacks, intrusive thoughts, and fantasies of the face of the nameless interrogator. He became easily upset and angered. Lomax was a troubled man who could not stop ruminating, nor get the injustice out of his mind. His spiritual life was in turmoil, his relationships troubled. Disoriented by his prison-camp experience, Lomax felt his life was unbearable. He had to do something about the terrible resentment, bitterness, hatred, hostility, anger, and fear that he felt for this nameless Japanese translator.

The Importance of Unforgiveness Being a Stress Reaction

I have claimed that forgiveness can be described by a stress-and-coping theory. One cornerstone in this argument is whether unforgiveness truly is stressful. In this chapter, I have arrayed the evidence to support this case.

61

Unforgiveness Feels Stressful

Eric Lomax was a classic example of someone experiencing chronic emotional unforgiveness. His experience parallels the experience of stress.

Unforgiveness feels stressful. People who are mired in unforgiveness will often report that they cannot stand the tension. They complain that they hate to go home because of their hatred for their partner or their resentment of their children. Some people cannot stand to go to work because of their unforgiveness toward either coworkers or supervisors. In short, unforgiveness seems to feel similar to the experience of stress whether we experience it in marriage, family, or workplace. Unforgiveness feels stressful.

Unforgiveness Creates Similar Physiological States to Stress

Let us look at the evidence to see whether unforgiveness could lead to physical changes similar to those produced in other stress reactions.

A Brief Summary of the Biology of Stress

Sapolsky (2005) has provided a thorough summary of the physiology of chronic and acute stress. Stress involves decreases in prefrontal activity and associated increases in limbic-system activity and later changes in cortisol-mediated areas of the hippocampus and amygdala. Basically, stress turns off rational thoughts to some degree and tosses one into emotional responding. Of course, emotions include some thought, so this is not all-or-none.

Stress also involves (a) release of the vagal "brake," (b) engagement of the visceral afferent system (i.e., gut responses), (c) stimulation of the direct pathway from hypothalamus to adrenals with subsequent release of epinephrine, (d) activation of the sympathetic nervous system (SNS), and (e) stimulation of the hormonally mediated hypothalamus-pituitary-adrenal (HPA) axis.

These five body systems are ways we prepare physically to deal with stress. The fastest system is the release of the vagal brake. The vagus nerve wanders throughout the body—like a vagabond. It is part of the parasympathetic (i.e., calming) nervous system and keeps the sympathetic nervous system under control. It is like a brake of a car. Even though the accelerator may be revving up the motor, the brake keeps the car from moving. When a sudden event occurs (like a loud noise or like seeing a hated foe)—even before the mind can appraise the situation as threat or challenge—the body releases the vagal brake and the SNS is activated. This happens in tenths of a second.

The visceral afferent system—gut feelings—often responds before the brain can get into gear. Those nerves send alert-alert, danger-danger messages to the brain. The hypothalamus, a small organ within the limbic system of the inner brain, has a direct link to adrenals. It cranks up the adrenaline within seconds. The SNS can also be activated quickly. Systems turn on in sympathy with (at the same time as) each other. The hormonal route to bodily activation is the slowest. The hypothalamus secretes a hormone (pituitary stimulating hormone), which stimulates the pituitary to release another hormone (adrenocortico-stimulating hormone, ACH), which releases glucocorticoids (like cortisol) and adrenaline from the adrenal gland.

Each of these (and all in conjunction) lead to allostasis (McEwen, 2002). Allostasis is characterized by increases in respiration, blood pressure, heart rate, and energy release and by decreases in digestion, growth hormone, and sexual hormones. Allostasis is a type of equilibrium. In homeostasis, a body system comes back to the same state after arousal ends—like body temperature always returning to 98.6°. In allostasis, the stable point changes, like heart rate, depending on conditions.

Evidence That Unforgiveness Is Physically Stressful

There are four lines of evidence that unforgiveness is stressful and arouses corresponding negative emotions. First, activity in the brain during unforgiveness is consistent with activity in brain structures involved in stress and other negative emotions. Pietrini, Guazzelli, Basso, Jaffe, and Grafman (2000) have examined anger using positron emission tomography (PET) scanning with 15 participants who imagined neutral and angry scenarios. Pietrini et al. showed that when people become angry, cognitive activity in the ventromedial prefrontal cortex diminishes and limbic-system activity increases. Unforgiveness, which has been shown to correlate highly with anger (Berry & Worthington, 2001; Berry, Worthington, Parrott, O'Conner, & Wade, 2001; McCullough, Bellah, Kilpatrick, & Johnson, 2001), might thus have a neurophysical basis that identifies it as an emotion.

Second, hormonal patterns—notably glucocorticoid secretion—in unforgiveness are consistent with hormonal patterns from negative emotions associated with stress. Berry and Worthington (2001) assessed self-reports and measured salivary cortisol for 39 people involved in romantic relationships. They selected people who had happy ongoing versus either unhappy ongoing or recently ended romantic relationships. Baseline levels of cortisol were moderately negatively correlated with the trait forgivingness. Also, a modest change in salivary cortisol level, when thinking about a typical interaction with the relationship partner, was related to both relationship satisfaction and self-reported unforgiveness toward the partner.

Third, cardiovascular, sympathetic nervous system activity and EMG tension in facial muscles are similar to patterns obtained with stress and negative emotion. Witvliet, Ludwig, and Vander Laan (2001) assessed 71 undergraduates using subjective ratings and measures of physical responses. Undergraduates imagined four ways of responding to a single transgressor: (a) reliving the hurt (ruminating), (b) holding a grudge, (c) generating empathy, or (d) granting forgiveness. Participants' heart rate and mean arterial pressure during periods of imagination as well as skin conductance were measured. EMG in three facial locations was recorded during participants' imagery. Mean arterial pressure, heart rate, and skin conductance all showed higher levels of reactivity when imagining the transgression or the person against whom one held a grudge. Facial muscle EMG was consistent with the expression of anger, fear, and subtle secondary emotions that include both. These findings are consonant with research by other emotion researchers (Ekman, Levenson, & Friesen, 1983).

Witvliet, Ludwig, and Bauer (2002) presented three studies that examined students' reactions to an imaginal crime. The three studies will be discussed later in the book. For now, note that in Witvliet et al.'s Study 3, participants were assessed physiologically using the same measures as in Witvliet et al. (2001). People who imagined that they were robbery victims responded similarly to people in Witvliet et al. (2001) who had imagined being unforgiving or holding a grudge. Thus, Witvliet et al. (2001) was replicated.

Fourth, measures of blood chemistry reveal a similarity between unforgiveness and both stress and negative emotion. Seybold, Hill, Neuman, and Chi (2001) conducted a correlational study of forgivingness disposition and physical markers in 68 patients at a Veteran's Administration Medical Center. They measured corrugator EMG, blood pressure, heart rate, plasma protein, cholesterol (LDL and HDL), nonestisfied fatty acids, triglicerides, total lymphocytes, neutrophils, T-cells, and T-activated cells. People who were unforgiving chronically had blood chemistry assays that were similar to those of people under stress. The evidence was weak: Only 3 of 16 correlations were significant. Dispositional forgivingness was correlated negatively with blood viscosity and positively with toxicity-preventive activity. Forgiving the self was positively correlated with the T-helper-to-T-cytotoxic ratio.

Temoshok and Wald (2005) have reported their progress in several studies that examine similar physical indicators in people living with HIV/AIDS. These results seem, at this point, even more congruent with the unforgiveness-as-stress hypothesis than were those of Seybold et al. (2001); however, Temoshok and Wald's findings have not yet undergone full scientific review.

In general, research evidence to date suggests that unforgiveness is stressful. Numerous experiments and studies using a variety of methods converge to support this proposition.

Levels of Unforgiveness and Forgiveness

Thus far, I have considered unforgiveness at two different levels of generality. In some cases, I spoke of *emotional unforgiveness for a particular transgression*, but in other instances, I discussed *chronic emotional unforgiveness* that generalized across situations and over time. Chronic unforgiveness has been labeled *dispositional unforgivingness* to distinguish it as a personality disposition relative to unforgiveness for a particular transgression (Berry & Worthington, 2001; Berry et al., 2001).

There are other levels of generality, however, for unforgiveness (McCullough, Hoyt, & Rachal, 2000). For example, a person might be forgiving dispositionally and might not be fixated on any particular transgression, yet he or she might be unforgiving toward their spouse. The level of unforgiveness has transcended individual transgressions and become generalized. If asked, the person could recall numerous transgressions. But the problem is not simply forgiving 150 individual transgressions. It is *forgiving a person*.

At a higher level of generality, people might hold *racial, ethnic, or social class unforgiveness*. This racial, ethnic, or social class unforgiveness is distinguished from prejudice. Prejudice is a general *attitude* of discrimination toward a racial, ethnic, or social class, but no transgressions necessarily have been experienced. Discrimination might not (or might) proceed from prejudicial attitudes. Racial, ethnic, or class unforgiveness involves the experience of transgressions at the hand of members of different groups. Those transgressions have been generalized to other members of the groups.

Let us take ethnic unforgiveness, for example. Suppose an African-American woman has been hurt and offended by individual Euro-American transgressors. In addition, she might perceive "the system" as having inflicted offenses or hurts on her. Because the system is not identifiable with any particular individual, the unforgiveness is particularly difficult to deal with. She recalls four times Euro-Americans hurt her family members. She can also name historic injustices perpetrated by Euro-Americans against African Americans. She is experiencing ethnic unforgiveness (Jones, 2004).

Taken together, a definition of forgiveness depends on the level of generality from temporary fluctuations day by day to trend forgiveness (over time; this also involves decisional and emotional forgiveness in which a person implicitly compares his or her current state with a previous state), to forgiveness of a person, ethnic forgiveness, and trait forgiveness.

Unforgiveness Can Create Moods and Mental States Similar to People Under Stress

When people are under stress, they commonly feel one or more of three moods. First, people under stress often feel hostile. This hostility is a generalized floating hostility that is aimed at whoever gets in their target zone. Note that hostility is one of the core emotions that make up unforgiveness.

Second, a feeling of lack of control can arise out of stress, especially excessive stress. Physiologists Meier (Meier, Brigham, Ward, & Myers, 1995) and Drugan (Drugan, Paul, & Crawley, 1993) have separately shown that there are numerous physiological and biochemical markers that indicate stressfulness. This is especially true in people who are depressed, feel a lack of control, and feel helpless. Let us loop back to Eric Lomax. He felt completely unable to control his life. He could not undo the trauma. Nor could he control his rumination, PTSD flashbacks, or unforgiveness.

People under stress often are angry and desire to act on that anger by lashing out at the sources of stress. Again, Lomax was a classic example. His unforgiveness toward the translator drew him continually to ruminate about the translator, and he fantasized acting out his anger.

Unforgiveness Puts Relationships Under Strain

Stress tends to focus people's attention on themselves. This is especially true during threat appraisal. People must deal with the threat to survive. The body is hardwired physically to respond to stress.

Unforgiveness also focuses attention on oneself. Relationships require time if they are to flourish. They seem to do best when partners have a sense of commitment to each other, trust of each other, and a willingness to sacrifice for each other. Stress undermines those capabilities through focusing the attention on the self. When Lomax was so consumed by his unforgiveness, his relationships were troubled. He was self-absorbed and focused on his own pain and internal experience. In the matter of focusing attention, unforgiveness also acts like stress.

Unforgiveness, Like Stress, Can Challenge People's Spiritual Well-Being

Numerous studies of people under stress have shown that spiritual coping is a common response to stress. However, religious and spiritual coping is complex. Pargament (1997) has devoted his career to unlocking the intricacies of how people cope with stress through religious and spiritual means. For many people, stressful situations provoke spiritual struggles (Pargament, Murray-Swank, & Magyar, 2005). When people struggle spiritually, they may question long-term faith commitments. The faithful may become shaken in their faith. But, sometimes committed atheists or firm agnostics have those spiritual beliefs shaken as well.

Lomax reports that his faith was virtually nonexistent after going through his internment during World War II. Unforgiveness rattled his belief system. He was confused and struggled with his worldview.

Unforgiveness Triggers Similar Coping Responses to Stress

Skinner, Edge, Altman, and Hayley (2003) completed the taxonomy of coping responses that I discussed in chapter 2. Virtually all of the coping responses to unforgiveness map directly onto the coping responses to stress.

Unforgiveness May Be Responsive to the Same Interventions as Stress

Stress has been particularly well treated with relaxation techniques and meditation. A large literature shows that the relaxation response (see Benson & Klipper, 1975) can be generated through meditative-like imagery, deep muscle relaxation, or progressive relaxation. The relaxation response can calm people and reduce stress. One hypothesis might be that not all of these interventions that promote positive responses to stress will necessarily promote positive responses to unforgiveness. Unforgiveness is a type of interpersonal stress. To the extent that it is one particular subtype of interpersonal stress, it may require separate interventions.

On the other hand, some dissertations have investigated relaxation as a treatment for unforgiveness. Humphrey (1999) found that relaxation effectively reduced unforgiveness. Wade (2002) used a 6-hour relaxation intervention aimed at reducing unforgiveness and producing forgiveness. His participants reduced their unforgiveness comparably to those using my REACH model.

Unforgiveness Is Stressful

Most of those lines of evidence converge on a common conclusion. Unforgiveness is stressful. It is one form of interpersonal stress. Thus, we may see its conceptualization within a broad stress-and-coping framework, which can suggest new ideas to test directly concerning unforgiveness.

Conclusion

Unforgiveness reveals itself at different levels of generality: from minor unforgiveness of a transient transgression to chronic unforgiveness of a difficult transgression such as Eric Lomax experienced, to ethnic unforgiveness, to traits of dispositional unforgivingness. Evidence supports a conceptualization that unforgiveness, in each of its levels of generality, can be considered an interpersonal stress reaction.

CHAPTER 4

Emotion in the Stress-and-Coping Theory of Forgiveness

I hypothesize that emotional forgiveness occurs when positive other-oriented emotions replace negative unforgiving emotions in whole or in part. In this chapter, I examine the evidence for the hypothesis.

Understanding Theories of Emotion That Inform This Biopsychosocial Theory of Forgiveness

Feeling Versus Cognitive Theory of Emotion

Newberry (2001) has discussed theories of emotion that have derived from philosophy. He identifies the reigning theory of emotion 2 centuries ago as being a feeling theory of emotion. That is, feelings were said to arise in a person who has been wronged. For example, the person might feel resentment. Feelings were seen as uncontrollable. We were thought not to be able to muzzle our desires and our resentful feelings by will, and we could not change our desires by reason. Therefore, we were not morally responsible for our feelings.

We were considered to be morally responsible for beliefs. Newberry (2001) identifies a cognitive theory of emotion as deriving from Descartes' writings. Descartes believed that we could change our beliefs. Therefore, we could affect the *expression* of our emotion of resentment that arose from being offended. Newberry believes that most philosophers today embrace a cognitive theory of emotion. Nevertheless, after surveying philosophical writings about forgiveness, Newberry commented as follows:

"But much of our current concerns about forgiveness seem to be more directed toward our emotional lives; virtually every definition put forward in the philosophical literature during the last three decades has defined forgiveness in terms of our emotional change on the part of the forgiver. Whether forgiveness is defined as the overcoming of resentment or another emotion, a process during which certain emotions must be overcome, or even when forgiveness is defined as a speech act, emotions always have a central role, if not the central role in the definition." (p. 242)

Embodied Emotion

The theory of emotion that I hold throughout this book is aligned with a recent theory of emotion that was put forth by Damasio (1994, 1999). Damasio has argued that *feelings* are the labels that people place on the experiences that are taking place within their bodies. The working memory in the neocortex integrates information that is being derived from sites throughout the body and the mind into a summary experience that we call a feeling. We might say, "I am feeling angry," or "I am feeling resentful," or "I am feeling unforgiving toward that person."

Emotions involve thoughts, memories, associations, brain pathways within various brain structures, information from neurochemical patterns in the brain, hormone types and levels within the bloodstream, gut or proprioceptive feelings, tension in facial musculature, tension in gross body musculature, and self-observed and interpreted acts of emotional expression. A social aspect of feelings comes from observing reactions of others and inferring their interpretation of our feelings.

Working memory integrates many sources of information to label bodily and mental experiences with a summary label, a feeling word. Damasio has argued that people have at least two types of emotional experiences (Damasio, 1994, 1999): primary and "as-if" emotional experiences. *Primary emotional experiences* are activated by real-life situations or visual imagery. The bodily and neural circuitries are triggered by primary emotional experiences.

"As-if" emotional experiences are more cognitive, verbal, and reasoned than are primary emotional experiences. It is as if the primary emotion is actually experienced when, in fact, it is not. Through beliefs, reasoning, or logic, one has triggered the same neural and bodily circuitry and created the same pattern of information flow to the working memory. In as-if experiences, however, the stimulation is less intense than in primary emotional experiences. The embodied emotion is the same for an as-if experience of an emotion as for a weak real-life experience of the emotion. In fact, sometimes as-if emotions can be powerful emotional experiences.

Note that in the embodied emotion paradigm, emotion is not as simple as earlier emotion theories suggested. Namely, the James-Lange, Cannon-Bard, and Schachter-Singer models implied that perceptions of the environment, appraisals, and internal arousal interacted in different ways to produce emotion. However, Damasio suggests that our conscious experiences are nuanced—from conscious thoughts to flitting associations not even in awareness—and our internal body states are similarly nuanced and usually not in our conscious awareness.

A few speculations about sensing emotion without conscious awareness. I hypothesize that when rumination takes place, a person has numerous as-if experiences. Recalling transgressions and their emotional concomitants strengthens those experiences through repetition. When a person thinks about a past event, such as a transgression, the person will activate centers in the association cortex that bring to mind memories and other associations that are related to the transgression. Edelman (2004) has argued that consciousness and memory do not depend on restimulation of precise neuronal patterns. Rather, similar memories and mental experiences can trigger a weak remembrance of a prior experience. Thus, there may not be specific pathways to memories that are related to a specific memory of a transgression. But similar memories can trigger virtually the same emotional memory. Thus, the working memory might be informed nonverbally and nonsymbolically about the emotions one is experiencing in the body.

Gut feelings communicate without conscious awareness. Damasio (1994) has found that simulations within the gut, or what he calls gut feelings, may actually precede cognition. He has examined patients who have problems with damage to a specific portion of their brain. This portion of the brain has been thought, since the famous case of Phineas Gage, to be a center of the brain in which moral reasoning occurred. Gage was a foreman on a railroad work crew who had a tamping iron blown through his skull. He lived. Gage had been a moral and upright person, but after this accident, he seemed to lose his moral functioning. He made bad decisions and poor judgments throughout the rest of his life.

Hanna Damasio reconstructed from Gage's skull the portion of the brain that appeared to be damaged when Gage suffered the accident. Antonio Damasio then began to study people with damage to that brain region.

To investigate the difference between gut feeling and moral judgment, Damasio (1994) created a mock gambling task. In this task, people drew win-or-lose-money cards from high-risk or low-risk decks. Prizes for winning money were given, making the game have real consequences. Damasio measured people's physiological responses during a task requiring them to draw numerous cards from the stack of their choosing. He particularly monitored people's gut responses.

After a few trials, people's guts began to be strongly activated as they started to draw from a high-risk pile. If the person was asked why he or she was drawing from that pile, the person would answer, "I'm just testing. I don't have a reason." Nevertheless, the person's gut was responding strongly to risk even if they did not consciously know why.

The people who had damage in the area in which Gage had sustained damage could not stop themselves from making the risky choices, even after their gut feelings warned them that they were likely to lose money if they made such a choice. People without damaged brains quickly inhibited risky choices. Damasio's research thus showed that the gut feelings were actually sending a warning message to the brain even before they consciously realized they were about to make a risky decision.

Hormones can be sensed without conscious awareness. Likewise, hormones convey information to the brain. Early theories of emotion posited a nonspecific arousal that occurred in any emotional state. More recent research, though, has shown that different hormone patterns of subtle emotions might be detectable by our brains.

Neuromuscular feedback can communicate our emotions to working memory without conscious awareness. Musculature has long been associated with emotion. Ekman (2003) has investigated the expression of emotion for many years, as have others (Matsumoto, 1992; Izard, 1990a, 1990b). Gross musculature, such as clenching one's fist, is easily associated with emotion such as anger, or putting one's hands up is associated with surprise or fear. But the most telling musculature is facial musculature (Izard, 1990a, 1990b). Placing one's face in the shape of musculature contractions similar to an emotion will generate that emotional experience. For example, Izard (1990b) had college students complete questionnaires holding pencils in their teeth in such a way as to stimulate the same muscles that were stimulated in either smiling or frowning. When the students were queried midway through the study about their emotional state, those whose muscles were flexed in a smile reported happier emotions than did those whose muscles were flexed in a frown. Presumably, the facial musculature is sending a message to the brain that informed the working memory that a particular emotion must be being expressed. The working memory labeled the message.

The working memory integrates sources of information. As a consequence of these many channels of embodied emotion—often from channels not in conscious awareness—the working memory is being informed about an emotional state through numerous channels. It integrates the information and places a feeling-label on the experience. The person might conclude, "I am feeling unforgiving toward a transgressor," as the person has as-if experiences remembering the person, or as the person sees the transgressor in real life even though he or she is not thinking about the transgression.

Complex Secondary and Tertiary Emotions
Blend Similar Primary Emotions

Plutchik (2002) identified primary emotions, which are differentiated from secondary emotions. Primary emotions are thought to be basic to human functioning and universal across cultures (Matsumoto, 1992). Typically, the complex emotions are combinations of similar primary emotions. Plutchik uses an emotion wheel to show emotions that are affectively similar to each other as being physically close on the wheel. Dissimilar emotions are far away from each other on the wheel. Those similar emotions combine into secondary emotions at a deeper level. Depending on the intensity of the experience, the wheel of emotions is converted into a parabola. *Similar emotional states blend. Emotions on the opposite sides of the wheel compete with each other.*

For most theorists who are not physiologists or neuroscientists and do not consult that literature, unforgiveness and forgiveness are conceptualized as being on a continuum. The stress-and-coping theory is based on the supposition that unforgiveness is a complex, tertiary negative emotion in which one can be high or low. It is on the opposite side of the emotion wheel from empathy, sympathy, compassion, and love. Emotional forgiveness is a complex, tertiary positive emotion on which one can be high or low, and is the product of the competition. Substantial evidence supports this proposition. It will be summarized in the following chapter.

Unforgiveness: A Complex of Negative Emotions

Offenses and hurts result in anger and fear usually in immediate response to the transgression. After rumination, angry and fearful emotions are blended with resentment, bitterness, hostility, and hatred to produce unforgiveness. Resentment is low-level anger that is derived from an injury or offense. Bitterness is a sense of negativity and sourness that is experienced during disgust for a person. It is associated with cynicism about the possibility of any positive outcome. Hostility is an attitude of negativity toward a person, especially wishing a person to come to harm or ill. Hatred is deep dislike with strong negative affect associated with any thought, sight, or reminder of the person.

Positive Other-Oriented Emotions Juxtaposed
Against Unforgiveness, Which Might Replace It

Let us briefly examine the emotions that can commonly replace unforgiveness. These include empathy, sympathy, compassion, and altruistic love.

Empathy

Empathy is being able to determine and respond to the emotions of another person. It is presumed to have evolved as social systems evolved (Brothers, 1989). Levenson and Ruef (1991) identified three types of definitions of empathy. They referred to the qualities of (a) knowing what another person is feeling, (b) feeling what another person is feeling, and (c) responding compassionately to another person's distress. Levenson and Ruef settled on a definition of empathy as involving the ability to detect accurately the emotional information being transmitted by another person. Empathy has been conceptualized both as a trait (Davis, 1996) and as a state (Batson, O'Quin, Fultz, Vanderplas, & Isen, 1983).

A variety of theorists have identified empathy as being important in forgiving. The victim is presumed to be most likely to forgive if he or she can accurately identify the perspective and especially the emotions felt by the offender and respond with sympathy, compassion, or love to those emotions. Importantly, empathic accuracy is not necessary to forgiving in cases where an offender is truly malevolent and hateful. Furthermore, empathy is not always a natural response. If one is observing another person, one is likely to empathize with a person to the degree to which one possesses that empathic trait. However, if one is involved in an altercation with the person, one is likely to respond to the provocation instead empathizing. If one is to forgive, one must not only empathize but also mix that empathy with other positive emotions such as compassion, sympathy, gratitude, or some other positive emotion.

Through a series of studies, Levenson and Ruef (1991) demonstrated that people tend to empathize more with negative emotions observed in the other person than with positive emotions. If the transgressor experiences and shows remorse, distress, contrition, and regret, the victim's empathy (and thus forgiveness) will be enhanced.

The fact is that people usually harm others not because they are seeking to do evil, but because they believe they have been provoked or threatened (Baumeister, 1997). Thus, when a victim empathizes with an offender, the accuracy of the victim at discerning the true processes and motives that went on in the offender will usually lead the victim to see that the offender thought himself or herself to be attacked, threatened, or provoked. If the victim has empathic capacity, the victim can then experience some of those emotions and can develop a sense of compassion, sympathy, or unselfish love toward the offender.

A side benefit occurs when one accurately empathizes with an offender. Rowe et al. (1989) identified this benefit: "One sees the other as having acted in a way as human beings do, out of his or her own perceptions; there may even be the recognition that what he or she did is something one has done or could well do" (p. 242). Thus, even if the offender acts maliciously or evilly, by accurately empathizing, the victim might still derive an amount of sympathy toward the offender. Rowe et al. observed that an injured person is likely to perceive the transgressor negatively. However, as the person experiences forgiveness, the victim usually experiences a shift in his or her view of the offender. Rowe et al. observed that this often involves seeing the offender "as distinct and separate from one's own needs and desires" (p. 242).

Sympathy

Studies in sympathy began over 50 years ago. Wispé (1986) and Gruen and Mendelsohn (1986) have distinguished between sympathy and empathy. Observing a person in distress can produce signs of emotional arousal, autonomic nervous system, facial expression, and subjective responding in the observer (Eisenberg, Schaller, and Fabes, 1988; Eisenberg, Miller et al., 1989). Empathy is a more neutral term than sympathy and has more to do with understanding the emotions and experiencing the emotions of the person with whom one is empathizing. Sympathy involves generating positive emotions toward the person. Eisenberg has studied sympathy in some detail (Eisenberg, Miller et al., 1989; Eisenberg et al., 1988).

Eisenberg, Miller, et al. (1989) studied the role of sympathy and altruistic personality traits. People (37 females and 41 males) completed questionnaires and were randomly assigned to either an experimental or a control group. Participants saw a fictitious news report about a single mother who is struggling to help her two children who were hospitalized due to an auto accident. Participants were given the opportunity to volunteer to help the mother by running errands, doing yardwork, or offering other help. People who scored high on measures of dispositional emotional empathy, fantasy empathy, and perspective-taking saw the mother's need as greater than participants who scored lower on those measures. They expressed more sympathy. Both empathic concern and perspective-taking were positively correlated with amount of time volunteered to help the mother. Self-reports of situationally induced sympathy were also positively related to helping. Dispositional empathy was related to situational sympathy and helping, both directly and indirectly, through a moderating path of fear of negative evaluation.

Fabes, Eisenberg, and Miller (1990) investigated mothers of 59 second-graders and 58 fifth-graders. They found that mothers who were more sympathetic and better perspective takers had girls who reported feeling more sympathy and more negative affect and less happiness after being exposed to needy others. For boys, there was little relationship between a mother's sympathy and vicarious emotional responses and the boys' helpfulness or emotional responses to needy people. In this study, Fabes et al. found a link between the verbal reports of emotion, independently judged facial expressions, and heart rate, providing some convergent validity data for indications that children showed dispositional empathy.

Compassion

Compassion is seen as a virtue and is recommended by virtually all of the leading religions. Psychologists have investigated compassion as well (see Gilbert, 2005). Worthington et al. (2005) have shown how compassion can play a role in forgiving during psychotherapy. They showed both helpful and unhelpful roles of compassion.

Batson, Klein, and Highberger (1995) investigated the effects of compassion relative to justice. This provides some insight into the emotional juxtaposition hypothesis. In Study 1, 60 female subjects were randomly assigned to one of three conditions: no communication, communication with low empathy, or communication with high empathy. In the communication conditions, subjects received a fictional account of a recent relationship breakup from 1 of 2 other participants in the study. (These other participants actually were fictitious.) In the high-empathy condition, participants were asked to imagine how the fellow student felt about the breakup. In the low-empathy condition, participants tried to take an objective view of the breakup. The participant had to assign the two fellow students to tasks that had positive or negative consequences. The subjects had to weigh whether they thought the task was morally right, the degree to which they were concerned with fairness in making the decision, and the degree to which they were concerned with the welfare of the participant who received the communication.

Task assignment was evenly distributed in both the no-communication and low-empathy condition. In the high-empathy condition, however, the subjects more often assigned the saddened student to receive positive rather than negative consequences. Subjects in the no-communication and the no-empathy conditions rated fairness as more important than did subjects in the high-empathy communication condition.

In Study 2, 30 male and 30 female subjects were assigned to low- and high-empathy conditions. All participants listened to an audiotape of a radio commercial for a local child-welfare charity. Some listened objectively (i.e., low empathy) and others with compassion (i.e., high empathy) for an affected child who could benefit from an expensive drug treatment but had been put on a waiting list due to unavailable funds. Participants indicated whether the needy child should be moved from the waiting list to the immediate list, ahead of other children higher on that list. Participants were asked to what extent fairness and sympathy for the child played a role in making their decision. Participants were then placed into two groups depending on whether they rated fairness higher than sympathy, which was called the justice-dominant group, or vice versa, which was called the altruism-dominant group.

Participants in the high-empathy condition were twice as likely to help the needy child than were participants in the low-empathy condition. Neither fairness nor sympathy for the needy child differed according to condition. In the high-empathy condition, participants were more altruism-dominant, by a ratio of almost 2 to 1. In the low-empathy group, participants were more justice-dominant. Overall, altruism-dominant participants (95%) were more likely than justice-dominant participants (30%) to help the needy child.

Batson et al. (1995) suggested that empathy-induced altruism and justice are independent, prosocial motives. Each has its unique ultimate goal. In resource allocation situations in which these two motives conflict, empathy-induced altruism can lead to immoral justice. Thus, Batson et al. showed that if people can be induced to experience compassionate empathy, the empathy edged out their justice motives, which is precisely the claim of the emotional replacement hypothesis.

Altruistic Love

Researchers have studied altruistic love for many years, and recently several compendia of that research have been created (see Post, Underwood, Schloss, & Hurlbut, 2002, for a thorough summary). Altruistic love has the well-being of another person as its objective. Some people, from an evolutionary standpoint, have argued that there is no such thing as true altruistic love. They argue that all love either is self-interested or is motivated by kinship ties or closeness to a person. Others argue that there is pure altruistic love. Batson has been the most consistent proponent for the pure-altruism position. In research spanning 20 years, Batson has attempted systematically to eliminate alternative explanations for altruistic behaviors and show that people engage in altruistic behaviors to the extent that they empathize with a person who is exhibiting some need.

Rushton, Fulker, Neale, Nias, and Eysenck (1986) measured the inheritability of various traits in 573 monozygotic and dizygotic twin pairs from the University of London Institute of Psychiatry Volunteer Twin Registry. They found that altruism increased over the age range from 19 to 60. Women had higher scores than men in altruism and lower scores on aggression. The estimates of inheritability were 56% for altruism, 68% for empathy, and 70% for nurturance. In a follow-up study, Rushton, Fulker, Neale, Nias, and Eysenck (1989), using the same sample, found that altruism was related to assertiveness, nurturance, empathy, and extroversion, and negatively related to aggressiveness.

Facilitating Positive Emotions (but Not Replacement Emotions)

Several positive emotions are hypothesized to facilitate the emotional replacement process as people forgive. The facilitative emotions do not neutralize unforgiveness, but they set the emotional stage for empathy, sympathy, compassion, and love. The major facilitative emotions are those that focus a person on warmth-based virtues rather than conscientiousness-based virtues. These facilitative emotions include gratitude, humility, contrition, and hope.

Gratitude

People might experience gratitude, which contrasts with unforgiveness. Gratitude might be felt toward the offender for trying to make the relationship better, toward other people for having forgiven the victim for when the victim had transgressed, or toward God for bestowing forgiveness to the victim for his or her own offenses. Gratitude may be an emotional state or a disposition.

Emmons and McCullough have been most active in writing about gratitude. Emmons and Crumpler (2000) reviewed the literature, to that time, about gratitude. They described the theological foundations of gratitude in the major religions and summarized the empirical research that was available at that time. Emmons described his study in which students recorded instances of gratitude and thanksgiving for 10 weeks. Those people's responses were compared with a group of people who attended to other events, such as hassles (in one condition) or events that affected them throughout the week (in the third condition). Students who wrote about events for which they were grateful tended to report positive effects on their physical, emotional, and mental health and physical vitality by the end of the 10 weeks. They also reported more progress toward their goals than did the other groups.

McCullough, Kilpatrick, Emmons, and Larson (2001) reviewed the literature related to a grateful disposition. Gratitude was described as a moral affective trait, like empathy, sympathy, guilt, and shame. Gratitude was likened to a moral barometer that is a response to others' generosity. In addition, gratitude acts like a moral motive. It motivates benefactors to act prosocially and beneficently. It also, when expressed, acts as a moral reinforcer. Gratitude varies in intensity (i.e., how much), frequency (i.e., how often), span (i.e., how long-lasting), and density (i.e., how widespread).

McCullough, Emmons, and Tsang (2002) developed a six-item measure of dispositional gratitude and validated that measure against a number of criteria. They showed that people high in dispositional gratitude differed from those lower in dispositional gratitude in terms of emotional well-being, prosociality, spirituality, and religiousness. Dispositionally grateful people were reliably found to be more agreeable and extroverted, and lower in neuroticism than were less grateful people. They also were more empathic and forgiving.

Emmons and McCullough (2003) and McCullough, Tsang, and Emmons (2004) conducted studies to investigate dispositional and state gratitude. Emmons and McCullough found that people who focused on gratitude reported higher well-being and more positive affect. People who focused on their hassles or daily events rated themselves lower on well-being and reported less positive affect. McCullough et al. found that strongly dispositionally grateful people tend to have moods characterized by gratitude irrespective of the number of events for which they are grateful or their moods. However, people who are not dispositionally strong in gratitude are influenced more by daily events regardless of whether they are in a grateful mood.

Gratitude is not a positive other-oriented emotion that might replace unforgiveness. However, Emmons and McCullough's (2004) work shows clearly that gratitude is influenced by a similar constellation of dispositions and personality traits as is forgiveness. In addition, they have shown conclusively that gratitude is a positive other-oriented emotion and that gratitude can affect people's affective mood as well as serve as discrete emotional experiences. I consider it a primary facilitative emotion.

Humility

Humility is hypothesized to promote forgiveness (Worthington, 2003). A humble person is not a person with low self-esteem. Rather, it is a person who realistically esteems the self but who counts others as worthy of sacrificing for. Measuring humility has been found to be difficult (Tangney, 2000). Exline and her colleagues (Exline & Martin, 2005) have begun to show that humility can facilitate forgiveness.

Contrition

Contrition is a sense of one's own moral imperfection coupled with both a distress over one's moral failings and a motivation to avoid moral failures and to thus act virtuously (Roberts, 2005). Contrition is an emotion that motivates one to empathize, refrain from judgment, and act in love and compassion—thus promoting forgiveness.

Hope

Hope is an emotion that is associated with beliefs about a positive outcome. Without hope, one might find conciliatory motives to be short-circuited. With hope, forgiveness might be undertaken to promote a better relationship. Without hope for better mental, physical, or spiritual health, a person might not forgive because he or she expects forgiveness to be beneficial. With hope, forgiveness is undertaken. Without hope, one might not pursue forgiveness to please God. With hope, such forgiveness is practiced.

Transformation of Motives

When emotional replacement begins, neoassociationistic networks are triggered by the changing emotions. Motives are thus linked closely to the changing emotions. The motives for justice, vengeance, and self-protective and anger-controlling avoidance are transformed into more positive motives (Worthington, Sharp, Lerner, & Sharp, 2006). These are of a conciliatory or benevolent nature. Conciliatory motives are relationship-enhancing motives. They move people to repair damaged emotional bonds or to move into closer relationships.

Benevolent motives seek good for the other person—the person who has harmed one. The primary benevolent motives active when forgiveness occurs are mercy, grace, and altruistic love. *Mercy* is restraint at applying deserved punishment. Mercy holds back at giving a person his or her just desserts. *Grace* is treating a person to an undeserved benefit. Whereas mercy is a motive not to punish a wrongdoer to the extent deserved, grace seeks to give the wrongdoer a blessing. *Altruistic love* is doing beneficial acts, feeling loving emotions, and thinking positive thoughts about another without considerations of self-benefit. Whereas grace gives undeserved gifts, one may be gracious for self-interested reasons. One may want approval, recognition, or awards (such as a peerage), or later "return on investment." Altruism is grace without substantive consideration of self-benefit.

As emotional replacement occurs, changing emotions are thought to trigger a transformation of motives. Importantly, motives might be transformed without behavior actually changing (say, for example, the perpetrator died or moved to another country). Different behavior, and even different behavioral intentions, would not be possible.

Conclusion

I have argued that people can decide to forgive, thereby controlling future behavioral intentions. However, the experience of emotional forgiveness is characterized at its root by emotional change, which triggers neoassociationistic networks and brings along other changes. I have put forth the emotional replacement hypothesis as the major mechanism by which emotional forgiveness occurs. The emotional replacement hypothesis is the centerpiece of the biopsychosocial stress-and-coping theory of forgiveness. In this chapter, I have tried to build a case that makes this hypothesis seem plausible. However, the theory must, in the end, rest on empirical evidence. Let us, in the next chapter, consider some of the evidence that will support aspects of the emotional replacement hypothesis.

CHAPTER 5

Evidence Supporting the Emotional Replacement Hypothesis

Let me begin to answer the question posed in this chapter with the bad news. There has been very little direct experimental evidence that can suggest how forgiveness takes place. We can say for sure that when people completely forgive, their thoughts, emotions, motivations, and sometimes behavior will change. Almost every existing study that directly investigated forgiveness has shown that these changes are correlated with forgiveness. The causal ordering of changes has not been investigated, nor has the essence of forgiveness been experimentally determined.

With this disclaimer, though, I will argue that substantial indirect evidence supports the hypothesis that emotional forgiveness occurs by emotional replacement. I considered six propositions—four primary hypotheses and two more peripheral—that constitute the emotional replacement hypothesis. (Actually, I would include an initial proposition—that emotion is an embodied experience [see Damasio, 1994], but Damasio has already arrayed substantial evidence on behalf of that proposition. I will not include it here.) I will examine each of these four primary propositions and evaluate the evidence for each.

Negative Emotions and Positive Emotions Act in Contradistinction to Each Other (Proposition 1)

A Brief Journey Into Semantics

My claim in the emotional-replacement hypothesis is that unforgiveness, which is a complex negative emotion, is replaced systematically or all at once by positive other-oriented emotions. Whichever emotions become the replacement emotions, in which combination, varies from situation to situation. Forgiveness, then, is a process of changing emotions from something negative to something neutral, or from something negative to something neutral and then more positive. The context will determine the content of the final state.

Emotions motivate us for action. They provide physiological readiness and target action toward an object. We can measure the motives that people have toward the transgressor, both at the beginning and at the end of a transgression incident. Thus, forgiveness is a process by which unforgiving emotions are replaced by positive other-oriented emotions, producing an affectively less negative, neutral, or more positive state, and an associated change in motivations away from unforgiving motivations toward more conciliatory or reconciliatory motivations.

Psychologist James Russell at Boston College is one of the leading authorities on positive and negative affect. Russell and Carroll (1999) reviewed the research literature on whether positive and negative affect were separate systems or one bipolar system. The evidence for two systems is strong enough that Watson and Clark (1997) declared, as a "fundamental psychometric principle" that "oppositely valenced affects tend to be only weakly negatively correlated with one another" (p. 282). They suggested, then, that positive and negative moods varied largely independently of each other. Russell and Carroll summarized, saying, "Evidence has challenged the bipolar view so often that it now seems on its death bed, and independence has taken its place as the prevailing assumption" (p. 3).

Russell and Carroll (1999) argue for independence of positive and negative affect. However, they admit how difficult this is to establish. They argue that, for a positive affect to be bipolar to a negative affect, the domain of the positive affect would have to be directly opposite the domain of the negative affect. If this were the case with unforgiveness, then only forgiveness would oppose unforgiveness. There are two pieces of evidence suggesting this is not the case. First, unforgiveness can be relieved by justice, acceptance, renarration, and many processes other than forgiveness. Second, Brownstein, Worthington, Berry, and Shivy (2006) sought to determine predictors of unforgiving motivations and forgiveness using the same predictors in a regression approach. The pattern of significant predictors was different in each case. This suggests that forgiveness and unforgiveness are not the mirror images of each other. That is, they are independent of each other, and different predictors predict them. Different consequences are likely to ensue that are not mirror images of each other. Wade and Worthington (2003) showed the same finding.

Evidence From Other Systems Positing Contrary Emotions, Motivations, or Interactions

I previously reviewed two lines of reasoning that suggest independence of unforgiveness and forgiveness (i.e., Plutchik's, 2002, emotion-wheel and McCullough's, 2001a) opponent process model). I will not repeat those.

Evidence From Biology That Unforgiveness and Emotional Forgiveness Are Contrary Emotional Systems

Evidence from emotion researchers. Theories of emotion support the concept that emotions can be contrary, yet independent. Salovey, Rothman, Detweiler, and Steward (2000), in a major review of the psychology of emotional states and its relationship to health, argued that negative emotions have qualitatively different effects from positive emotions. Salovey et al. reviewed many studies on the effects of negative emotions on the cardiovascular system and on stress and immune responses. Positive emotions, while they have been less well studied, differ substantially from low- or no-negative emotions (Salovey et al.).

Despite subtle detectable differences in autonomic responding, Witvliet and Vrana (1995) observed that there were many more similarities among negative emotions than there were differences. They concluded from their data in mapping emotions onto a 2 x 2 matrix of arousal (high or low) and valence (positive or negative) that emotions tended to cluster along the diagonals. This suggested that the positive emotions seemed to be related to each other and the negative emotions were related to each other. Furthermore, those systems were different from each other. Witvliet and Vrana provided an experimental and conceptual justification considering unforgiveness and forgiveness to be along different dimensions.

Evidence from research on the biochemistry of aggression. Physiological evidence that suggests that unforgiveness and forgiveness might be different and contrary systems comes from investigations of aggression (Berkowitz, 1993). Berkowitz distinguished aggression from hostility and anger. *Anger* is defined as an emotional state of negativity toward a person, with no particular goal to resolve this state. *Hostility* is anger with a desire for ill toward a person. *Aggression* is behavior aimed at harming or injuring another person who is motivated to avoid such harm.

Berkowitz (1993) identified two types of aggression, which were distinguished by the goals. *Instrumental aggression* is essentially harmful actions that are intended to achieve a goal other than mere harm. For example, if a police officer subdues a potential bank robber and the bank robber resists arrest, the police officer might engage in harmful action, but the purpose is not harm for its own sake. *Hostile aggression* is an act intended primarily to cause harm to the person.

Two chemicals with receptor sites in the limbic system have been associated with higher or lower levels of aggression. Testosterone tends to arouse, and serotonin (5-HP) tends to calm. Testosterone has been related to high levels of aggression. For example, the onset of criminal activities in males is correlated with a surge in level of testosterone (Kreuz & Rose, 1972). The relationship between testosterone and aggression is reliable but more complex than a simple correlation might indicate (Dabbs & Ruback, 1988). Testosterone might be related to a complex of other behaviors and experiences that may themselves be related to aggression. Testosterone has been found to be related to dominance, and that relationship is moderated by socioeconomic status. For example, in examining military veterans, people with high socioeconomic status tend to engage in few acts of aggression regardless of testosterone level, whereas people of lower socioeconomic status tend to engage in more acts of aggression, depending on the level of testosterone.

Serotonin (5-HP) is related to lower aggression. Coccaro (1989) reviewed accumulated data that show that impulsive aggression has been reliably associated with lower levels of serotonin in 5-HP systems. In addition, lower levels of the metabolites of 5-HP (5-HIAA) and the level of 5-HIAA in the cerebral spinal fluid has been related to level of aggression. Because testosterone is related to increased aggression, and serotonin is related to decreased aggression, one might hypothesize that if an animal with elevated testosterone were given an increased dose of a serotonin agonist (i.e., increasing the amount of serotonin), then the level of aggression might decrease. In a series of studies by Bonson and her colleagues, such relationships have been demonstrated in rats (Bonson & Winter, 1992).

Two brain structures in the limbic system have been most commonly associated with aggression: the hypothalamus and the amygdala. The ventral medial portion of the hypothalamus controls many appetitive behaviors, such as eating, thirst, and sexuality. It might be easy to speculate that aggression and dominance, which are often linked to animals being able to procure food, water, and sexual partners, might be evolutionarily linked to areas of the brain that control aggression as well.

The amygdala, particularly the medial amygdaloid nucleus, has been found to be associated with aggression (Weiger & Bear, 1988). The amygdala is the primary structure that is associated with conditioned fear responses and many anger responses. Weiger and Bear speculate that the amygdala might pass sensory inputs to activate the hypothalamus, which turns on aggressive responses.

Numerous studies have demonstrated that the amygdala and the hypothalamus have many receptor sites for both testosterone and serotonin (for a review, see Bell & Hobson, 1994). This could suggest that aggressive behavior might be controlled through the ebb and flow of testosterone and serotonin competing with each other in these limbic system structures. One might speculate, although empirical evidence has not addressed this directly, that the emotions of unforgiveness and forgiveness are stimulated partially within the hypothalamus and the amygdala, and that the competing levels of these two biochemicals are responsible for the degree to which a person holds on to unforgiveness or is able to reduce the unforgiveness and perhaps to forgive. Positive emotions tend to calm people and produce serotonin; also, increases in serotonin levels produce calm and positive emotions. Negative emotions tend to arouse people and might produce testosterone; also, increases in testosterone tend to arouse people and produce aggression. Importantly, testosterone production and serotonin production act in opposition to each other but are separately controlled neurohormones.

Evidence from evolutionary theorists. Newberg, d'Aquili, Newberg, and deMarici (2000) have suggested that three brain processes affect the way people experience unforgiveness and forgiveness. The first is the development of a sense of self and ego. For survival, a human with an expanded sense of self that allows the person to perceive, analyze, and evaluate all the input regarding the self, would be at an evolutionary advantage. However, this does set the stage for being more likely to perceive hurts as being primarily aimed at the self.

The second development is conspecific congruence. *Conspecific congruence* is a nonhierarchical relationship between oneself and others, which exists alongside other hierarchical orderings of self to others. Thus social creatures, like humans, have group loyalties to similar creatures while living simultaneously in competitive hierarchies. A violation of conspecific congruence (i.e., an attack against an in-group member) would activate a system in the brain aimed at restoring the balance through revenge or some effort to protect the groups. Justice within society is a social formalization of this evolutionary drive.

The third development was the emergence of a long-term memory of harmful events. Long-term memory arose with the development of a hippocampal amygdala memory system, which connected the limbic system structures, especially hippocampus and amygdala with portions of the neocortex.

It is easy to see how unforgiveness might have evolved. Revenge and grudge-holding relate the person's aggrandized sense of self with the transgression of conspecific congruence and the memory of that in long-term memory. Despite the advantages to the individual of pursuing revenge, a group is likely to be destroyed if each person avenged each wrong that was committed. The group would be characterized by violence and unable to protect itself from threats from outside.

Newberg et al. (2000) hypothesized that forgiveness might have evolved in victims due to experiencing empathy and warm feelings from observers who were not involved in the initial confrontation. In addition, grudge-holding of the victim could be tempered to the extent that the victim experienced empathy and warmth toward the offender.

Escalating anger, revenge motivation, and unforgiveness would be based on an affective misperception of the importance of the self and a resulting misjudgment of the amount of revenge necessary to restore order. Thus, benefits accrue to the group, victim, and offender if positive feelings counteract the negative feelings of unforgiveness.

Evidence From Philosophy

Evidence, not just from the biological research or evolutionary theory, supports the emotional juxtaposition hypothesis. In fact, a number of philosophers and psychologists have conceptualized forgiveness in terms of both a reduction of negative emotions and a simultaneous increase of positive emotions. Because I want to emphasize scientific evidence, I have not arrayed this evidence from philosophy.

Evidence From the Experience of Positive and Negative Emotions During Times of Chronic Stress

Susan Folkman was one of the early scientists involved with Richard Lazarus in the formulation of stress-and-coping theory. By 2000, Folkman was observing regularly that much research on stress and coping had focused on how people cope with negative emotions and outcomes when under stress. She began to focus her attention on positive coping and outcomes as part of the stress process. Lazarus, Kanner, and Folkman (1980) suggested that positive emotions might have three important functions. They can (1) sustain coping efforts, (2) provide a time of restoration and emotional breathing space, and (3) restore depleted resources.

In 1997, Folkman studied male caregiving partners of men who had AIDS. The participants were 86 HIV+ caregivers, 167 HIV- caregivers, and 61 HIV+ men in relationships with healthy partners who served as controls. These caregivers were assessed for up to 5 years. The caregivers generally reported being depressed. As a group, they scored higher in depression than the general population by over one standard deviation (SD). During crisis times, they usually scored over two standard deviations higher than the general population did in similar stress periods. However, throughout the entire study, except for the weeks immediately before and after the partner's death, the caregivers reported feeling positive moods at a frequency comparable to the frequency of negative moods. How did these highly stressed caregivers have such positive moods? Folkman (1997) found that they used three classes of coping mechanisms. They positively reappraised the situation, trying to find positive aspects to it. They also engaged in goal-directed problem-focused coping, in which they searched for things that they could do to contribute to easing the partner's suffering. This included things such as making simple lists of to-do items and carrying them out. Third, they created positive events in their lives.

Folkman (1997) observed that positive reappraisal did not always lead to experiencing positive emotions. Positive appraisal gives meaning to the situations. Sometimes, the meaning did not make people happy, but gave them a sense of purpose. Also, sometimes, because of increasing limitations of the partner who had AIDS, goals had to be reappraised. Goals were continually downgraded from an ambitious goal of perhaps being a successful attorney to practicing part-time to finding one's contribution while one was working. During such reassessments of life goals, the person felt less distressed, but did not necessarily feel more positive emotion.

People found positive experiences that would create positive moods. Folkman calls these "time outs" (see Folkman & Moskowitz, 2000b, p. 116). Folkman observes that more than 99% of the caregivers in this study noted and remembered positive events that occurred in the midst of some of the most stressful circumstances that people have to deal with in life. Not only did they take note of positive events that happened in ordinary everyday life, but they also planned and created positive events.

Folkman and her colleagues have shown that within stressful situations, negative mood is not predetermined. This is, of course, what we all know. Even in our darkest hours in our lives, or in our most stressful experiences, we enjoy humor with friends; we hear a joke and feel uplifted. We experience jubilation that comes with a success. Folkman's research on stress and coping suggests that unforgiveness and the experience of positive emotions are not two ends of the same scale. If people feel unforgiveness and if the scale is bipolar, then that would mean that it would be impossible to feel positive emotions. However, positive emotions can be experienced while the person is in an unforgiving mood and reflecting on unforgiveness. Unforgiveness is an emotional system that is contrary to the emotional system that is created by positive emotions. Those two systems are disjointed from each other unless a person intentionally puts them together.

Summary of the Evidence for Proposition 1

I have brought together evidence from affect in personality psychology (e.g., Russell & Carroll, 1999); from theories of emotion, motivation, and interpersonal interaction; from the brain chemistry of aggression; from evolutionary theory; and from stress-and-coping theory (Folkman, 1997) to suggest that positive emotions and negative emotions are different systems. The systems may at times compete and neutralize each other. At other times, positive and negative emotions exist side by side. Evidence solidly supports this proposition.

When Experiencing Positive and Negative Emotions Simultaneously, They Will Compete With Each Other (Proposition 2)

Evidence From Judgments About Forgivability and Empathy Versus Judgments About Fairness

Farrow et al. (2001) used functional MRIs (fMRIs) to determine the brain structures that were active in making judgments about what one might, or might not, forgive (called *forgivability*), what one might or might not empathize with, and what judgments one might make in social situations. Participants (N = 10; 7 males, 3 females) were subjected to a number of decision-making choices while being monitored in a functional MRI unit. Among the many findings, Farrow et al. reported that the judgments about whether an act was forgivable and how empathic it was occurred primarily in a different portion of the cortex than did judgments about fairness. Presumably, to forgive one must consider the other person, which stimulates empathy. To judge whether a decision is fair, though, does not bring in the human element and promote prosocial emotions. The left front temporal region was most associated with both forgivability and empathy. The implications of Farrow et al. for our current hypothesis is that when one imagines a scenario involving judgments of fairness—as one might do in thinking about the injustice gap (as it affects oneself or others)—and one empathizes or forgives, different regions of the brain are activated.

Farrow and Woodruff (2005) reported a series of additional studies. They used the regions associated with forgivability judgments as a map to indicate that forgiveness might be occurring. Using a pre- and post-test design, they gave 13 patients who were diagnosed with post-traumatic stress disorder (PTSD) 10 weekly 1-hour sessions of forgiveness-oriented cognitive-behavior therapy. Relative to pretest patterns, post-test patterns showed evidence of increased forgiveness judgments and empathy. They also found that 14 patients with schizophrenia increased forgivability judgments relative to healthy control subjects.

Other Neuroimaging Evidence

As I mentioned briefly in chapter 3, Pietrini, Guazzelli, Basso, Jaffe, and Grafman (2000) studied anger and aggression using PET scans for 15 people (8 men, 7 women). People imagined four scenes. In each scenario, the person, his or her mother, and two men were in an elevator. In one scenario, the participant rode and talked with the mother. In the other three scenarios, the two men assaulted the participant's mother while the participant (a) watched, unable to help; (b) tried to intervene but was restrained by one man while the other continued the assault; or (c) attacked the two men with a sincere intent to injure or kill them. On a 9-point scale (1–9), people who talked reported 1.6 anger. Those who were unable to help reported 8.1. Those who were restrained reported 7.2. Patterns of ratings of frustration and anxiety paralleled the pattern of ratings of anger.

In their functional analysis of angry reactions, Pietrini et al. (2000) found that people who were instructed to imagine vividly angry situations—regardless of which of the three—began to have high activity within limbic system structures such as the amygdala and inhibited rational thinking in the orbitofrontal cortex. (The orbitofrontal cortex is considered to be the limbic portion of the frontal association cortex.) Thus, the one implication might be that negative emotion will act antagonistically toward reasoning. This does not necessarily imply that by reasoning one can change negative emotional states to more positive, but it does suggest that reasoning is disrupted by anger. Another implication is that imaginally rehearsing angry and aggressive mental scenarios (i.e., ruminating angrily) will (1) catapult one into negative emotive responding and (2) shut down calm emotions.

Pietrini and his colleagues (2000) also described preliminary data on the neuroimaging of forgiveness (reported by Farrow & Woodruff, 2005). They found that, with six healthy participants, remembering forgiven and unforgiven transgressions stimulated different brain regions and also different centers associated with emotional experience. Pietrini et al. show clearly what happens when people ruminate angrily and vengefully. They also studied actual forgiveness and unforgiveness.

Evidence From Motivational Systems

Gray's theory of motivations suggests that people have two motivational systems that underlie much behavior. One is called the Behavioral Approach System (BAS; Gray, 1982, 1994). The BAS has been shown to manage approach behavior, incentive motivation, and appetitive behaviors.

It is hypothesized to respond to stimuli associated to reward and safety. The other system is called the Behavior Inhibition System (BIS; Gray, 1982, 1994). It inhibits ongoing behaviors. The BIS responds to conditioned stimuli associated with punishment or negative experiences, and conditioned stimuli associated with the termination of reward or with the frustration at not being rewarded or novel stimuli. The BIS causes an organism to interrupt its ongoing behavior and increases arousal, which prepares the organism to deal with the situation. The BIS also increases attention toward the stimuli. It prepares for fight, flight, or freezing.

The two systems not only involve different portions of the brain, but they also are involved in generating emotions that are relevant to approaching an object (i.e., BAS) including approach for predatory purposes, and inhibiting behavior (i.e., BIS). The BAS has been hypothesized to being involved paradoxically in both euphoria and anger. The BIS has been hypothesized to be involved with experiences of anxiety.

It might seem odd that the left cortical hemisphere can be associated with both positive affect and anger. However, this becomes less confusing if we remember that the BAS motivates the organism to engage with the environment. The BAS may motivate angry and aggressive behaviors that are aimed at removing some animal or person that is aversive—the removal of which is rewarding.

Substantial research has shown that experiencing state anger is associated with relative left-frontal activity compared to right-frontal activity (Harmon-Jones, 2001; Harmon-Jones & Sigelman, 2001; Harmon-Jones, Vaughn, Mohr, Sigelman, & Harmon-Jones, 2001). Harmon-Jones and her colleagues show that when people are insulted they respond with anger and higher left-frontal activity. Anger, of course, focuses attention on the person who is provoking one.

Harmon-Jones, Vaughn-Scott, Mohr, Sigelman, and Harmon-Jones (2004) noted how left-frontal cortical activity has been repeatedly shown to be associated with approach motivation, emotion, and behavior. On the other hand, right cortical activity has been repeatedly shown to be associated with withdrawal motivation, emotion, and behavior (Coan, Allen, & Harmon-Jones, 2001). Harmon-Jones, Sigelman, Bohlig, and Harmon-Jones (2003) showed that, in anger provocation, people experienced high left-frontal cortical activity, especially when they were able to move toward the source of anger in order to try to resolve the anger-producing situation. If people did not anticipate having the chance to resolve the situation, they did not show an increase in left-frontal activity. Left-frontal activity is more associated with approaching a person and working things out when one is angry instead of simply stewing in resentment.

Harmon-Jones et al. (2004) sought to determine whether an emotion such as sympathy, which has been shown to reduce aggressive motivations, would also reduce relative left-frontal cortical activity relative to right-frontal activity. They suggested that if such a finding were to occur, it would suggest that the increase in relative left-frontal activity that has been observed after arousal to anger would be due more to approach motivations than other processes. College students (53 women, 26 men) participated. Participants' brain activity was recorded during a baseline period. Participants were then told that the study consisted of themselves and another person who would be writing an essay and then evaluating each other's essays. Participants wrote a 10-minute essay for or against a tuition increase. Participants were then told either to remain objective or try to imagine how the other person must feel while they read the other person's essay. The other person's essay described the struggle the person went through after having been diagnosed with multiple sclerosis. The experimenter then left the room and retrieved what was said to be the other person's evaluation of the participant's essay. The evaluation either contained neutral comments, called the no-insult condition, or insulting comments. Participants rated the other participant and completed an emotion questionnaire. Their EEG was also measured.

Harmon-Jones et al. (2004) predicted that the insult would result in participants having greater left-frontal activity, but sympathy would reduce the activity to the level of the no-insult condition. They found that, for ratings of sympathy, anger, positive affect, and hostile attitudes and for frontal asymmetry, the insult-low sympathy (i.e., instructions to remain objective) condition was different from both the low sympathy- and high sympathy-no insult conditions. The high sympathy-insult condition was different from either insult conditions for the frontal asymmetry. However, there were some differences in reports of hostility, anger, and sympathy. Harmon-Jones's research showed that insults did increase left-frontal activity and decrease right-frontal activity. High levels of sympathy eliminated that effect. Sympathy acted in opposition to anger arousal in decreasing brain activity in the left-frontal cortex. Hostile attitudes did not show the same effect.

This finding, which manipulated sympathy, replicated Harmon-Jones et al. (2003). In the previous study, recall that they showed that the manipulation of people's ability to cope with an angry stressor affected left-frontal activity, decreasing the activity. Harmon-Jones and his colleagues showed that manipulating coping capability and the experience of a positive other-oriented emotion both affected brain activity that was associated with unforgiveness, anger, and hostility.

These findings are consistent with my hypothesizing of different ways of coping with a transgression. That is expected to calm physiological arousal in the left hemisphere. However, self-reports did not immediately reduce either in Harmon-Jones et al. (2003) or in Harmon-Jones et al. (2004). Harmon-Jones and his colleagues have done some of the most direct tests of Proposition 2 of the emotion replacement hypothesis. The results do not fully support the proposition. They support it on the physiological, but not self-report, level.

Evidence From the Psychology of Moral Dilemmas

Greene, Sommerville, Nystrom, Darley, and Cohen (2001) studied two perplexingly similar moral dilemmas. In the first scenario, called the trolley problem, imagine yourself to be standing on a footbridge overlooking trolley tracks. A trolley is running out of control. If you do not take any action, the trolley will hit and kill five strangers. You are standing by a switch that can divert the trolley into a side track. The problem: One stranger is standing on that track and will surely be killed if the trolley is diverted. Would you choose to allow nature to take its course, resulting in the death of five people? Or would you actively intervene and cause the death of one person? In this problem, about 90% of the people chose to divert the trolley and kill one person.

Now consider a similar footbridge problem. Again there is a runaway trolley headed toward five strangers. This time, though, you are standing on a footbridge far above the switch. You see a track onto which the trolley can be diverted, and this time no people are on that track. You think, "Perhaps I could jump down on the switch," but because of your placement you would surely miss the switch. However, sitting on the footbridge directly above the switch is a stranger. You think, "That person is precariously balanced. I could easily tip the person over the edge." (Talk about a "tipping point"!) You know with certainty that he would trip the switch and save the five people from the trolley but he would die. Would you push the stranger and save the five?

This footbridge problem is seen, by most philosophers, as morally equivalent to the trolley problem. It is a question of the harm of one versus the harm of five; whether to allow nature to take its course, or to intervene and actively do harm in the intervention, albeit less harm than if nature took its course. How did your answer compare with Greene et al.'s (2001) subjects? In contrast to the 90% who would trip the switch in the (first) trolley problem, only 10% said they would tip the stranger over the edge in the (second) footbridge problem. Why the difference?

Greene et al. (2001) suggested, "Some moral dilemmas (those relevant to the footbridge dilemma) engage emotional processing to a greater extent than others (those relatively similar to the trolley dilemmas), and these differences in emotional engagement affect people's judgments" (p. 2105). The clever part of Greene et al.'s experiment was that people (N = 9) were in fMRI units as they were presented these two dilemmas. As they contemplated the unfolding story, brain activity was the same in both scenarios until, in the footbridge problem, the experimenter posed the possibility of pushing the person onto the switch. Suddenly, activity in the brain areas associated with rational thought declined and the emotional areas lit up. Greene et al. suggested that emotional processing took over.

They followed up the experiment with a second one. They reasoned that people who went against the "natural" tide would take longer to react to the dilemma than those who went with the tide. Thus, in the trolley dilemma, those who sided with the 10% (do not throw the switch) would delay their choice. In the footbridge dilemma, those who sided with the 10% (push the person) would delay their choice. They were correct. They suggested that the delay occurred because more cognition was needed to overcome the "natural" tendency.

We might speculate on Greene et al.'s (2001) research. First, we might accept Greene et al.'s circumspect interpretation, which simply noted that the footbridge dilemma "engage[d] emotional processing" (p. 2105) unusually well. But second, we might be more daring in our interpretation. In the footbridge dilemma, the participant had to imagine actually touching a person. In the trolley problem, the participant had only to touch an impersonal switch. The footbridge dilemma may have stimulated empathy, which competed against the reasoning that the trolley dilemma evoked.

Thus, this suggests the other side of the coin from Pietrini et al.'s (2000) studies. They found that anger caused rational thought to cease. Harmon-Jones et al. (2004) found that sympathy caused anger to decrease (at least left-frontal activity to decline, though not self-reports of hostility). In this case, the possibility of doing personal harm diverted people toward a more emotional, empathic reasoning rather than a strict logic. Third, we might speculate that the personal touch may have activated warmth-based virtues. The nonpersonal scenario (the trolley problem) may have activated conscientiousness-based virtues. These two studies taken together suggest more evidence that unforgiveness might be undone by emotional processes such as sympathy and empathy.

Evidence From Peripheral Nervous System Studies

As mentioned briefly in chapter 3, Witvliet and her colleagues (2001) at Hope College had undergraduate students (N = 71) complete questionnaires about experiences of unforgiveness and forgiveness. Recall that people imagined four conditions in a counterbalanced order: immediately after being hurt, holding a grudge, empathizing with the person's position, and forgiving the person. They completed questionnaires and were monitored physiologically. Typically, immediate hurt produced higher sympathetic nervous system responses than did nursing a grudge, except for the measure of skin conductance. Usually, the empathic condition produced more sympathetic nervous system reactivity than did forgiveness, except the two were equal on blood pressure. When forgiveness and empathy were compared with the two unforgiving responses, there were significant differences in indicating sympathetic nervous system activity to be greater in unforgiving versus forgiving situations for heart rate, mean arterial pressure, skin conductance, and muscle tension. Differences in self-report between unforgiveness and forgiveness showed the unforgiveness imagery to be higher in anger, sadness, perceived control, empathy, and overall arousal.

Similar findings were found by Lawler et al. (2003) in a similar set of situations but with a between-subjects design rather than a within-subjects design. That is, participants were assigned to imagine different conditions and different groups were compared. Lawler essentially replicated what Witvliet had done.

Summary of the Evidence for Proposition 2

I have considered the proposition that positive emotions compete with and, if strong enough, may subdue negative emotions. I conclude that there is considerable indirect evidence from a variety of sources to offer circumspect support of this hypothesis (see Gray, 1994; Greene et al., 2001; Harmon-Jones et al., 2004). Some research has supported the proposition when examining forgiveness directly (e.g., Farrow & Woodruff, 2005; Witvliet, 2005).

Emotions Experienced in the Present Are Generally Stronger Than "as-if" Emotions When They Compete With Each Other (Proposition 3)

Evidence From Psychotherapy

One piece of evidence for this proposition is somewhat indirect, but powerful. Psychotherapy provides corrective emotional experiences for psychotherapy patients. If one thinks of the logic of psychotherapy, it seems quite arrogant to think that meeting with a psychotherapist for 4 sessions, 6 sessions, or 100 sessions can undo the emotional damage that might have been traumatic during the formative years of the person's life. In fact, the client has likely built an entire lifetime of behaviors based on that formative emotional experience. Yet, psychotherapists provide strong experiences in therapy and juxtapose those against the weaker remembered "as-if" emotional experiences that the person recalls and talks about during therapy.

Because the patient discusses these early emotional experiences in weak doses, yet experiences strong present emotional experiences, emotional corrective experiences occur and the person is changed.

This is true even when the therapist does not embrace a psychodynamically informed perspective on psychotherapy. The cognitive behavior therapist and the cognitive therapist provide present experiences that change the person's cognition and behavior as well as emotional experience to overcome a past that has an enormous amount of accumulated emotional experience driving it.

In helping people forgive, especially when they forgive an offense that is very powerful, we are drawing on the same tradition as psychotherapy. We rely on creating present healing emotions (i.e., positive, other-oriented emotions) that are stronger than "as-if" emotions (i.e., the person's memory of transgression—even a traumatic transgression).

Evidence From the Relaxation Response

Benson (Benson & Klipper, 1975) has studied the relaxation response for over 20 years. Relaxation involves a positive relaxed and calm physical state as well as positive associated moods. This relaxation response can be stimulated through deep breathing, meditation, positive imagery, and the like. The relaxation response has been associated with positive health effects. Bensen advocates using powerful relaxation-response inducing exercises, such as meditation, deep breathing, meditative prayer, or progressive relaxation, to oppose daily tension and stress. He finds that brief relaxation responses of only a few minutes can overcome negative physical and mental health effects of negative stressors.

Evidence From Research on Emotional Expression

Pennebaker (2004) has studied the effects of emotional expression on physical health. Typically, Pennebaker has people reflect on negative emotional life events and write about them for 15 minutes per day for 2 weeks. Thus, Pennebaker is asking people to experience negative emotions temporarily as they write about those events. This is similar to forgiveness. Whether forgiveness is attained through natural reflection about a transgression and its aftermath or through therapeutically guided reflection on the transgression, the person will undoubtedly remember the negative event and experience negative emotion. Yet the person experiences the emotion weakly in a context that is presumably "healing." This is similar to weak "as-if" emotions (Damasio, 1994).

One might expect that such an experience of negative emotion might create negative health effects. Indeed, in Pennebaker's (2004) paradigm, such effects have been discovered in the short term. Yet the reverse is true for long-term effects. Kelley, Lumley, and Leisen (1997) found that patients who had rheumatoid arthritis and talked about the stressful life events they were experiencing nevertheless had better physical functioning 3 months after the disclosure than those who did not talk about such stressful events. Strangely, the degree of improvement was also related to the degree that the discussion of the stressful events generated negative mood states. That is, better health benefits were obtained by people who were able to emotionally get into the experience of the stress and talk about the events while expressing the emotion.

The expression of the emotion, however, is not the only thing that occurs as the person talks about stressful events, or writes about stressful events as with Pennebaker's (2004) studies. In fact, the person often reframes the events. The person sometimes writes about finding meaning in the events. Thus, the deep processing of events, which generates manageable emotional experience but also allows for rethinking the meaning of the events, may be responsible for the improvement in physical health. A similar finding has been found in Pennebaker's writing task. Pennebaker's teams counted the number of negative emotion words that were used in the expression of the event, and also rated the amount of insightful thinking that occurred during the writing (Pennebaker & Francis, 1996; Pennebaker, Mayne, & Francis, 1997). To the extent that disclosure helped people work through their traumatic experiences, and re-experience those events emotionally, people reported fewer physical symptoms.

This same process of re-experiencing emotional events, thinking through them to insightful conclusions, and speculating about the cause of the events has also been reported in the way people try to regulate their emotions in natural ongoing living (Gross, 1998; Salovey, Mayer, Goldman, Turvey, & Palfai, 1995).

Salovey et al. (2000) suggest that an interaction is at work here. Obviously, it is not the mere experience of negative emotions that produces health consequences, but the experience of healthy emotions and subsequently working through those emotions to a different understanding of them.

If a person is perplexed and distressed over a transgression, that person will likely maintain negative mood states as he or she ruminates about the events. That rumination will make things worse. However, if the person writes or speaks differently about the events and is able to come to a different understanding of the event, the person will also simultaneously usually experience different emotions about the event: More relief; greater feelings of control; less anxiety, anger, and hostility; and perhaps less depression or sadness are likely to occur. These changes in cognition and changes in emotion are likely to occur at virtually the same time. It is impossible to disentangle, which (if either) is more causal of a positive health impact.

In general, writing about emotional experiences has been found to result in substantial improvements in health. These have included fewer self-reported health problems (Greenberg, Wortman, & Stone, 1996; Pennebaker, Barger, & Tiebout, 1989), less frequent use of health services (Pennebaker, Kiecolt-Glaser, & Glaser, 1988), and enhanced immune system activity (Esterling, Kiecolt-Glaser, Bodnar, & Glaser, 1994).

Pennebaker has found that writing is not mere catharsis—the release of negative emotions or the simple expression of negative feelings. The ability of the writing to influence positive health depends on the person's capability of expressing negative emotion and working through the traumatic negative events to arrive at a more positive place (Pennebaker & Francis, 1996; Pennebaker, Mayne, & Francis, 1997). Salovey et al. (2000) suggest that this process of writing to work through the negative feelings might be similar to the process that people typically use in coping with negative feelings (Gross, 1998; Salovey et al, 1995).

The implication of this for forgiving is that forgiveness should not involve an attempt to squelch expression of negative feelings. The attempt to suppress negative feelings will probably result in negative health outcomes (Gross & Levinson, 1997). Rather, the person should be allowed to express negative feelings to an extent that allows appropriate emotional catharsis. Yet, the person should eventually be encouraged to move past mere expression of negative feelings and strive for some type of insightful thinking beyond the expression of the negative emotion.

A Word in Response to an Objection

Let us raise an issue here. How can a momentary emotional experience do away with a lifetime of psychological problems (as we claimed in psychotherapy), a full day of stress (as we claimed for the relaxation response), or a traumatic emotional experience (as we claimed in Pennebaker's [2004] emotional writing studies)? Folkman & Moskowitz, (2000a) raised this very issue. They showed that caregivers of dying people who had AIDS could experience positive and negative emotions during the same days or weeks, yet overall their mood remained negative. Clearly, a person can experience transitory positive feelings while experiencing a persistent negative mood. That positive feeling does not overwhelm that negative mood. Emotions are more transient than our moods. A look on the bright side of things, an uplift, a breather, may each erode a small amount of the negative mood. Why did Folkman et al. not find a change in stable mood for her patients?

There are several possible reasons. First, in Folkman and Moskowitz's (2000a) case, the negative experiences were continuing to occur at a higher rate than were the positive experiences. Second, the negative experiences were not "as-if" experiences at all. They were present (and very negative) experiences. Third, in Folkman and Moskowitz's case, a potential competition between the positive and negative experiences was not set up. Whereas the person might feel depressed and watch a television comedy show and feel a little better, there was not a systematic intent to change the negative mood; rather, the attempt was to gain some relief from a mood that was expected to continue because the person is dealing with a dying significant other.

In the situations that we will work with, of trying to systematically and intentionally juxtapose positive other-oriented emotional experiences against weakened negative, unforgiving experiences, we will not usually be working with situations that are parallel to the research of Folkman and Moskowitz's (2000a). (I say "not usually" because there are relationships that are characterized by frequent ongoing transgressions and general negative expectations.) Nor is trying to promote forgiveness parallel to a natural process in which we unsystematically and occasionally try to think something positive about a transgressor and hope that will result in forgiveness. We usually will focus concentrated energy on forgiving.

Summary of the Evidence for Proposition 3

Overall, from a variety of sources, it appears that actual experienced emotion is stronger in most cases than recalled emotion. However, in conditions such as PTSD or highly meaningful emotionally charged events, a web of meaning keeps the emotional connection in place. Only strong pairings and repeated efforts to change the connections can break the emotional patterns.

The Specific Positive Emotions Will Oppose Unforgiveness and Result in Emotional Forgiveness (Proposition 4)

Evidence From Research on Empathy and Forgiveness

Let us begin by looking at some specific research that has dealt with the role of empathy in forgiving.

First, empathy facilitates a number of prosocial phenomena. This includes altruism and the inhibition of aggression (Batson, 1990, 1991a; Batson & Oleson, 1991; Eisenberg & Fabes, 1990; Eisenberg & Miller, 1997; Rusbult, Verette, Whitney, Slovik, & Lipkus, 1991). Some theorists have included sympathy, compassion, and tenderness within the conceptualization of empathy. For example, Batson (1990) made such inclusions. Eisenberg frequently includes sympathy and empathy together, although she distinguishes between the two. Empathy does involve both cognitively taking the perspective of the other person and an affective dimension of feeling with or identifying with the person.

McCullough, Worthington, and Rachal (1997) conducted two studies to investigate the empathy model of forgiveness. In Study 1, we showed that empathy mediated partially between receiving an apology and forgiving motivations. In Study 2, we used 134 students who sought to forgive someone who hurt them by participating in one of two seminars, or being assigned to a waiting-list control condition. People in the seminar that promoted empathy forgave more than the people in the seminar aimed at forgiving for self-enhancing motives or more than the wait list. In addition, when all of the participants were examined together, those who forgave did so in direct proportion to the amount of empathy they experienced toward the transgressor.

In the first study, empathy was a partial mediator between apology and forgiving. That is, empathy accounted for most of the variance, but apology still affected forgiveness above and beyond what the empathy accounted for. McCullough et al. (1998) investigated empathy again as a mediator between apology and forgiving. In that series of four studies, the fourth study investigated a variety of structural models that explained the relationship after considering alternative structural models. The final model relating the variables began with the amount of closeness in the relationship prior to the offense. The closeness was correlated with the amount of empathy felt for the person, which was negatively correlated with avoidance motivations. Closeness before predicted whether the person would give an apology. Whether a person apologized strongly predicted how much empathy the person felt for the transgressor who gave the apology. Empathy was directly related to the final closeness, but was also indirectly and strongly related to the amount of avoidance and amount of revenge toward the person who had harmed them.

Closeness prior to the relationship was also positively related to the amount of rumination that took place. The amount of rumination was related to the amount of revenge sought, but not to the amount of avoidance of the partner. Empathy completely mediated the relationship between apology and the two unforgiving motivations associated with unforgiveness.

Evidence From Psychotherapists

A number of psychotherapists have suggested that empathy is a crucial element of whether a person can be brought to forgive a transgressor. This includes many of the early writings by psychotherapists about forgiveness (e.g., Brandsma, 1982; Cunningham, 1985; Fitzgibbons, 1986; Hope, 1988; the Human Development Study Group, 1991; McCullough, 1997).

However, even after writings about forgiveness became more than distillations of clinical experience and clinical researchers began to write about forgiveness, one important observation remained. Almost every major theory of promoting forgiveness in the clinic has targeted empathy as a key player. For example, in reviewing the role of forgiveness within individual psychotherapy, Malcolm and Greenberg (2000) identified empathy as crucial. They reviewed research from phenomenological studies, saying, "An acquired ability to empathize with the offender was also apparent in the stories of people who participated in these studies" (p. 182). They examined in their own emotion-focused approach to promoting forgiveness the role of empathy: "The third discovery also came out of an examination of the empathy component. We were intrigued by the presence of statements from the other chair indicating that the offender was imagined as taking responsibility for the offense and explicitly freeing the client from guilt and blame ... . [S]hould it be found that most successful forgiveness processes include this step, future refinements of the model will need to include a component of taking responsibility on the part of the imagined significant other" (p. 198).

Enright and Fitzgibbons (2000) in their 20-step process model have emphasized how empathy and compassion are important in promoting forgiveness: "Empathy is morally neutral." They write, "As one steps into another's shoes, one can use this new information for good or ill. Compassion, however, is one of the moral emotions because its goal is the other's good. To have compassion is to come alongside another person, be willing to help, or suffer along with him or her" (p. 82). Empathy and compassion toward the offender is considered step 13 within the work phase of Enright and Fitzgibbon's model. In Enright's book, *Forgiveness Is a Choice* (Enright, 2001), he also stresses empathy and compassion. He says, "Empathy, in turn, may generate a sense of compassion toward the other" (p. 158). He provides some exercises to promote empathy and compassion.

Luskin (2001) suggests that people often mistakenly believe that their negative experiences of the transgression are somehow more real than the positive experiences. He suggests that people can "imagine now, that each of us has a remote control to change the channel we are viewing in our mind" (p. 112). "When you tune in to the gratitude, love, beauty, or forgiveness channels, you give your body a rest. When you are focused on your problems and grievances, your body is under stress" (p. 114). Thus, Luskin encourages people to replace the negative unforgiving feelings associated with ruminating about hurts, with experiencing gratitude, love, beauty, or forgiveness.

I could march systematically through the forgiveness models and show that empathy, sympathy, compassion, and love are elements of each of these systems. There is a clinical experience at work that validates this idea of emotional replacement. But clinical validation is not the same as carefully controlled clinical scientific studies. Nevertheless, with so many therapists using so many approaches over so many years arriving at a similar practice, the sheer amount of support calls out for an explanation behind why it works. This, I believe, is the emotional replacement hypothesis.

Evidence From the Broaden and Build Model

Barbara L. Fredrickson (1998) described a Broaden and Build Model of Positive Emotions. She showed that positive emotions did not fit the existing models of emotion. Positive emotions are very few and less differentiated in comparison with the many negative emotions, such as anxiety, anger, depression, and the like. Because problems that create negative emotions demand attention, such negative emotions have received attention from investigators for years. Thus, a large body of literature exists in understanding negative emotions, but little attention was devoted to understanding positive emotions. Negative emotions point to problems that could be very costly to people. They are very specific. They are more like a rifle than a shotgun. They narrow attention to the problem at hand and focus the person's motivation to dealing with it. If an animal freezes, it attends carefully to the novel or danger stimulus that got its attention. If it can possibly escape, it flees. If not, it fights.

People have long observed that negative emotions disorganize an organism. Negative emotions disrupt business as usual. However, negative emotions are far from disorganizing. They are organizing, but they organize around dealing with the specific hurtful, stressful, or dangerous situation. In contrast, Fredrickson suggests that positive emotions share the ability to "broaden people's momentary thought-action repertoires and build their enduring personal resources ranging from physical and intellectual resources to social and psychological resources" (Fredrickson, 2001, p. 222). Fredrickson notes that while positive emotions can occur in adverse circumstances, usually they do not occur in life-threatening situations.

When positive emotions do occur, they broaden the person's momentary perspective by creating an urge to play or somehow push the limits to be creative and explore different options. In contrast to the negative emotions in which the person has to deal with a specific problem right now, the positive emotions have more long-term benefits. Broadening of perspective builds enduring personal resources.

Fredrickson (2001) examines the work of Isen and colleagues (for a review see Isen, 1999). Isen shows, in a number of ways, that when people experience positive affect, they are usually more flexible, creative, integrative, open to information, and efficient than when not experiencing the positive affect. They also show an increased preference for variety, and they accept a broader array of options as being possible (see Estrada, Isen, & Young, 1997; Isen & Labroo, 2003).

Fredrickson (2001) notes that some questions remain about her theory. She asks whether distinct positive emotions broaden the scope of attention and the scope of working memory. In addition, the neurological substrata are up for grabs. Ashby, Isen, and Turken (1999) suggested that positive emotions have their effects by changing levels of dopamine within the brain; however, the physiological mechanisms are still not clear. Answering those unanswered questions can provide new directions for the Broaden and Build Model to move.

Specific relevance to the emotional replacement hypothesis. Fredrickson (2001) suggested that positive emotions can undo lingering negative emotions. She says, "The basic observation that positive emotions (or key components of them) are somehow incompatible with negative emotions is not new and has been demonstrated in earlier work in anxiety disorders (e.g., systematic desensitization; Wolpe, 1958), motivation (e.g., opponent process theory; Solomon & Corbit, 1974), and aggression (principle of incompatible responses; Baron, 1976)" (p. 222). She observes that the way that this opponent process works is not clearly specified, but she suggests that broadening a person's momentary thought-action repertoire might loosen the "hold that a negative emotion has gained on the person's mind and body by dismantling or undoing preparation for specific action" (p. 222). When people experience negative emotions, their cardiovascular activity increases, which redistributes blood to relevant skeletal muscles for responding to stress. So, "in the context of negative emotion, then, positive emotion should speed recovery from, or undo this cardiovascular reactivity, returning the body to more midrange levels of activation" (p. 222).

Fredrickson and Levenson (1998) and Fredrickson, Mancuso, Branigan, and Tugade (2000) have tested this hypothesis. They induced high activation negative emotion. In one study, Fredrickson et al. used a time-pressured preparation for a speech. Participants were told that that the speech would be videotaped and evaluated by their peers. Fredrickson et al. randomly assigned people to view one of four films. Two films elicited mild joy or contentment. A third was a neutral control condition. A fourth elicited sadness. Fredrickson and her colleagues examined the people's arousal at the beginning of the film and looked at the amount of time it took for the people's cardiovascular reactions to return to baseline levels. The two positive emotions showed faster cardiovascular recovery than those in the neutral or sadness condition (which took the longest to promote recovery).

In addition to improving cardiovascular reactivity, Fredrickson has suggested that positive emotions might help people improve their psychological well-being and perhaps their physical health. She suggested that experiencing positive emotions to intentionally cope with negative emotions (Fredrickson, 2001) might affect physical health. Let us recall that Folkman and her colleagues made similar claims about positive affect and coping with chronic stress (Folkman, 1997; Folkman & Moskowitz, 2000a). Aspinwall, Richter, and Hoffman (2001) have described how positive affect and positive beliefs can serve as resources for people coping with a difficult or stressful situation. Fredrickson (2001) reported several studies that supported that proposition as well. To the extent that forgiveness does indeed involve emotional replacement of negative unforgiving emotions with positive other-oriented emotions, Fredrickson's research provides additional indirect evidence for promoting forgiveness interventions.

Finally, Fredrickson (2001) suggested that experiencing positive emotions builds resiliency and triggers what she calls "upward spirals toward improved emotional well-being" (p. 224). As we can see, Fredrickson's research program has been conceptualized along the same line as the emotional replacement hypothesis. She has systematically accumulated evidence that positive emotional experiences can affect negative experiences, undoing them, and promoting better ability to cope.

Summary of Evidence for Proposition 4

From a variety of trajectories, I tentatively conclude that direct evidence supports a connection between empathy and forgiveness. The Broaden and Build Model provides indirect evidence for positive emotions in general. Tests are needed to discover whether sympathy, compassion, and altruistic love can replace unforgiveness.

Two Additional Propositions

The fifth proposition is that if a relationship is expected to be noncontinuing, no residual positive emotions or motivations toward the offender will be reported if the victim reports "complete forgiveness." The sixth proposition suggests that for relationships that are expected to continue, other relational events will likely influence outcomes. (For instance, if a couple goes to a movie together or makes love, those events can promote forgiveness even though they do not address any specific transgression.) Hypothetically, though, in the absence of major positively or negatively charged events, when people report "complete forgiveness," they will be likely to report that positive emotions toward the offender have been restored, not merely that negativity has been eliminated. Note that at present there is little support for these propositions. They deserve immediate testing.

Conclusion

In this chapter, I have compiled existing evidence that forgiveness is a process of replacing the complex negative emotion of unforgiveness by any of several positive other-oriented emotions. This is a key step in this stress-and-coping theory of unforgiveness and forgiveness as well as its application to the promotion of forgiveness. So I have gone into this evidence in detail.

This stress-and-coping theory asserts that unforgiveness is stressful and people cope by various coping mechanisms, including seeking justice and cognitive reframing. Many seek to cope by forgiving, which they do via decision and replacing negative emotions by positive ones. I have arrayed the evidence to date on this stress-and-coping theory of forgiveness. My hope is that you are armed to apply these concepts in moving to a more general level of understanding personality (Part II), clinical interventions (Part III), and societal issues (Part IV).

Perhaps it is useful to pause and test yourself on your understanding. In chapter 1, I presented eight case studies to illustrate concepts surrounding forgiveness. I invite you to turn to Appendix A, read the cases, and compare your responses with mine.

PART **II**
Personality Traits of Forgivers and Nonforgivers

CHAPTER **6**
Forgiveness and the Big Five Personality Traits

In Victor Hugo's book, *Les Miserables*, Inspector Javert is obsessed with justice. For Javert, mercy does not exist. Every crime, no matter how tiny, deserves punishment. Violations of justice are personal affronts to Javert. Mercy by others enrages him and sets his bloodhound nose to the ground to root out kindness.

Javert is the nemesis of Jean Valjean, who once stole a loaf of bread and served over 19 years at hard labor. Paroled, Valjean breaks parole. Javert tracks Valjean relentlessly, seeking to bring him to justice.

Angry, fearful of new injustice, reactive to potential crimes, and obsessive, Javert is the epitome of unforgivingness. Over time, his unforgiving lifestyle is rewarded by success. He is promoted through the ranks from jail-keeper, to policeman, to inspector. When he is caught spying on rebels at the barricade, though, Javert realizes his life is over. He has been caught violating the rebels' justice, and he is resigned to death. As life's irony unfolds, Javert is handed over to Valjean, who will be Javert's executioner. Valjean, though, has experienced forgiveness. In fact, having experienced great forgiveness, Valjean has been transformed into a man whose life is characterized by forgivingness. He shows mercy to Javert. Javert stumbles through Paris, unable to comprehend mercy and forgiveness. Unwilling to live with mercy, Javert drowns himself in the Seine. Javert is a prototype of a person with an unforgiving personality. Valjean's parole-breaking offended Javert's sense of justice. Javert nursed his grudge.

Vengeful Personality

People often e-mail me and ask for advice or resources in dealing with their unforgiveness. Below, I will modify one e-mail I received in late 2004, changing the identifying characteristics to disguise the woman's identity. She wrote:

> I thought I would be married by 2000. I was 35 years old and had lived with the love of my life for 5 years. Instead of getting married, I found out about a "friendship" he had with another woman. It was more than that. He decided that I needed to move out so that I could start a life in another state…. I now know that this was a way to ease his guilt and continue his behavior. He gave me money, and off I went. No home. No address. No place for my adolescent daughter to call home….
>
> I have read about "getting even." I did things I didn't know I was capable of doing…. The other woman lost her marriage (because I informed her husband of the "friendship") and her job because of my getting even…. My ex dumped her as well, leaving her with nothing and no real employment opportunities…. My next plan was to call the IRS and let them know about a huge income that wasn't reported by my ex. I still haven't given up that idea altogether, and I know I should, I just don't know how…. I call my ex often and tell him how his thoughtless actions have made me so angry and sad. I have to move on. I just don't know how.

Forgiving Personality

Jean Valjean had an altruistic streak that got him in trouble. He stole bread for his sister's child during a time of hardship, was caught, and was sentenced to prison. After serving 19 and one half years, he was paroled. Valjean was destitute, and because he had to show his parole papers, people who employed him paid him only half as much as they paid others for the same amount of labor.

One night, he was invited into the humble cottage of Monsignor Bienvenue, who lived humbly despite his status in the Roman Catholic Church. Fed, clothed, and rested that night, Valjean took the silver that he had eaten with to finance his life. The police apprehended him, but Monsignor Bienvenue, in an act of mercy, snatched up the silver candlesticks, saying, "My friend, you forgot the silver candlesticks that I gave you. They are worth much more than the silver that you took." When the police had left, Valjean tried to return the silver. The Monsignor insisted that he keep the silver and use it to become an honest person. Valjean was overwhelmed with being forgiven and receiving grace and mercy. His life was transformed.

From that moment, Valjean was the prototype of a forgiving person. The cynicism that had worked its way into his soul in his dealings with imprisonment and prejudice was eradicated. Of course, Valjean was often put to the test. Javert hounded him. Yet when Javert was handed over to Valjean to execute justice on Javert for spying, Valjean released Javert with the full knowledge that Javert would continue to hunt Valjean and imprison him for breaking parole.

Three Types of Personality

In these three examples, we see three constellations of personality characteristics relating to forgiveness. Javert is unforgiving. He does not forgive because he is obsessed with justice and is unable to feel mercy. His heart is good but cold. Offenses stimulate grudges, which he nurtures. Second, a deeply wounded woman has also become unforgiving. Her unforgiveness is less high-minded than Javert's. She is consumed with personal attempts to get even. She is vengeful. She is willing to hurt others in order to hurt the one who has injured her. While she feels sorry for doing so and wants to quit, she continues to inflict damage because of the pain of the wound she has experienced. Third, Valjean was a consistent forgiver.

Unforgiving Disposition

When people experience unforgiveness across situations and over time, we say that they have an unforgiving disposition. If they meet this unforgiveness with forgiveness across situations and across time, we say they have a forgiving disposition. It is possible, of course, to have both unforgiving and forgiving dispositions simultaneously; however, most of the time unforgiveness and forgiveness act contrary to each other.

An unforgiving disposition—as either a grudge-holder or vengeful person—might come about primarily due to nature or to nurture. That is, a person might be genetically predisposed to react emotionally to the slightest noises or startles. The person might be sensitive to all sorts of stimuli (Aron & Aron, 1997)—noises, noxious smells, irritating touches, slights, vaguely threatening words. The person might be biologically predisposed to stress and unforgiveness. The person might react to unusual situations with fear or with anger. These are characteristic of Gray's (1982, 1994) behavioral inhibition system (BIS) (fear) and behavioral approach system (BAS) (anger), respectively (Harmon-Jones et al., 2002). Yet, a genetic predisposition to unforgiveness does not fix one's personality. People learn to deal with unforgiveness.

People can respond by grudge-holding, seeking vengeance, or forgiving (see Figure Intro-1). As they respond to different transgressions over time, they stamp into their character a disposition that governs the preponderance of their responses to transgressions. They can develop into grudge-holders, vengeance-seekers, or forgivers. Or they can respond using a mixture of styles.

Grudge-Holding Disposition

Grudge-holding is hypothesized to be characterized by rumination about one's victimization, which is highly correlated with negative affect. Three affective states dominate. Fear of being hurt, offended, and victimized again is primary. Anger—mostly the anger that is associated with pain and suffering rather than with active destruction—is a constant subcurrent. Sadness and even depression over inability to escape the grudge or to retaliate can be dominant or a subcurrent. Grudge-holding leads to unforgiving emotions, namely resentment, bitterness, hostility, hatred, anger, and fear. It is characterized more by passive resistance and nastiness than active retaliation and in-your-face opposition. It wishes harm and misfortune on the offender, but does not usually perpetrate it.

Vengeful Disposition

Typically, people are not born vengeful. They channel an unforgiving disposition toward vengeful motives. I believe that some people do so because they are hyperattuned to justice, or they suffer a narcissistic wound to their pride. Some people are frequent victims who, like cartoon-character Popeye the Sailor, say, "That's all I can stands, and I can't stands no more." They fight back. Against everyone. They become radar detectors who can zero in on hurt and punish those who are perceived as hurtful. Their own wounds might involve an early trauma that affects the memories powerfully in the hippocampus. Or their wounds might have been in a series of wrongs or hurts. Often this happens in the family, where relationships are presumed to be the safest and most supportive, yet the family becomes toxic and harmful. However, people might even have a very supportive family system and encounter hurtful experiences at school, especially during the middle school and early adolescent years. At any time during the life cycle, a person can be hurt or offended systematically and can develop an unforgiving and vengeful disposition.

Rumination again plays a key role in developing a vengeful personality. Rumination centers around getting even, striking back, evening the score, retaliating, honor, avenging oneself, and hypervigilance toward justice. The major affective state is anger and hatred. Seething calculation drives the motivation to avenge an offense. Action is highly valued. When the opportunity to exact perceived justice presents itself, it is seized and acted on decisively.

Yet, as we saw from the e-mail that the woman sent me, a sense of guilt and shame can vitiate the pure sense of vengeance. Vengeance is not met with full social approval, and an active conscience can make a vengeful person feel self-condemnation while at the same time justifying his or her vengeful acts and motives.

Forgiving Disposition

Similarly, a forgiving disposition can be facilitated by nature and nurture. If forgiveness is indeed a replacement of the negative emotion of unfor-giveness by any of several positive other-oriented emotions, a biological disposition toward forgivingness might be apparent soon after birth. The infant will use self-soothing strategies to calm itself. Temperamentally, the baby will likely be an easy baby. Thus, a person can become dispositionally forgiving by having an agreeable nature. Some children are naturally more empathic and sympathetic than other children, and these traits might be developed early in life. Similarly, some children are more predisposed to love and altruism than are other children.

Forgiveness might be developed through learning even if the child is by nature a difficult baby, unable to easily calm itself, not naturally warm. The child can learn in his or her household or social environment that unfor-giveness grudges, revenge, or generally nasty retaliation are not tolerated. Rather, the child can learn that forgiveness, acceptance, and benevolence are expected. Parents might model forgiveness and reinforce the child's forgiving behavior.

Parenthetically, based on my observations in the clinic and in my life, I suspect that another personality characteristic exists. We might call these people *nonreactive*. They simply do not respond with emotional reactions to transgressions. They are not forgiving. They do not seem to develop unfor-giveness. It takes a lot of injustice to provoke them to respond. These people are likely high in agreeableness and extremely low in neuroticism. Nonre-active personality types typically do not perceive transgressions as being severe, or do not even notice slight betrayals that others would describe as transgressions. They might be considered repressors in the perceptual sense, relative to sensitizers, who tend to make mountains out of molehills.

The Big Five Personality Traits

The Big Five personality traits are generally thought to be most funda-mental to people's character. They spell out the acrostic OCEAN. *Open-ness to experience* describes a person who is seeking new experiences and willing to accept them. *Conscientiousness* describes attention to responsibility, duty, and detail. *Extroversion* is one end of the extroversion and introversion spectrum. Extroverted people tend to seek stimulation, be energized by social conditions and social interaction, and be personally outgoing. Introverts, on the other hand, are usually more self-contained, withdrawn, and drained by social interaction. *Agreeableness* is a general quality of getting along well with people and not letting difficult situations, challenges, or stresses upset one. *Neuroticism* is a term retained for historical purposes, but it means something different than Freud's term "neurotic." Neuroticism means emotional reactivity or emotional lability. People who are high in neuroticism tend to be reactive to situations.

All of the Big Five except openness have been found to relate to an unforgiving or forgiving personality disposition. However, the two of the Big Five personality traits that are most strongly related are agreeableness and neuroticism.

Condensing Research on the Big Five and Forgivingness and Unforgivingness

Mullet, Neto, and Rivière (2005) recently summarized the research on correlations between personality dispositions and measures that assessed (a) enduring resentment and grudge-holding, (b) revenge, and (c) forgiveness of others. Also, they summarized research on the relationship between the Big Five and forgiveness of self, but that will be discussed in Chapter 10. I examined each correlation reported by Mullet et al. Arbitrarily, I selected $r >$ .25 as a correlation that I considered meaningfully large. In Table 6.1, I summarized the fraction of studies that reported correlations of $r > .25$ between each of the Big Five separately with grudge-holding, revenge, and forgiving.

Predictors of grudge-holding. Grudge-holding was strongly predicted by neuroticism. Of the 26 correlations, 73% were at $r > .25$. The emotionality and the emotional reactivity of a person scoring high in neuroticism predisposes people to ruminate about grudges. The relationship between agreeableness and neuroticism shows a strong negative correlation with each other, though they clearly are not polar opposites. The relationship between agreeableness and grudge-holding, while negatively correlated (as we might expect), was less strong than the positive correlation between neuroticism and grudge-holding. Only 57% (4 of 7 studies) found a correlation of .25 or more between agreeableness and grudge-holding.

Predictors of vengefulness. On the other hand, vengefulness was strongly predicted by low agreeableness. In 8 of 8 comparisons, $r > .25$. A vengeful person is not agreeable. (Surprised?) Substantial, but less consistently strong, correlations were found between vengefulness and neuroticism.

Table 6.1 Personality Characteristics That Predict Forgiving Based on Percentage of Studies with *r* > .25 in a Review of Research by Mullet, Neto, and Rivière (2005).

	Enduring Resentment and Grudge	Revenge	Forgiveness of Others
Agreeableness	57% (4/7, Neg.)*	100% (8/8, Neg.)**	72% (13/18, Pos.)**
Neuroticism (Emotional Instability)	73% (19/26, Pos.)**	61% (28/46, Pos.)*	61% (19/31, Neg.)*
Extraversion	8% (1/3, Neg.)	38% (3/8, Pos.)*	5% (1/20, Pos.)
Conscientiousness	0% (0/3)	57% (4/7, Pos.)*	0% (0/7)
Openness to Experience	0% (0/4)	0% (0/5)	0% (0/8)

Note: Numbers in parentheses indicate the fraction of studies reporting a correlation > .25. Underlining indicates that the percentage is based on four or fewer studies and is thus not necessarily reliable.

 * Over 1/3 but less than 2/3 of the studies found *r* > .25; reliable and moderate prediction.

 ** 2/3 or more studies found *r* > .25; reliable and strong prediction.

Only a little over half of the correlations were at *r* > .25. Vengefulness seems more related to emotional stability than instability, but the affect is negative and anger-related. Conscientiousness was as strongly related to vengefulness as was neuroticism. Because vengeful people are often concerned with getting even, paying people back for injustices, and other forms of restoring perceived justice, we might expect that conscientious attention to fairness, balancing rights and wrongs, and perceived importance of doing one's duty (or rectifying instances where someone else does not do his or her duty) would be related to vengeful behavior or motivations. Extraversion was also related to vengeance in 3 of 8 studies at *r* > .25. One might conjecture that to seek vengeance, one needs to be uninhibited enough to act vengefully. Looking at causality the other way around, a person who is vengeful might plot or carry out vengeance because he or she is generally in need of emotional stimulation—i.e., an extrovert. Conflict is interpersonally stimulating. True, the stimulation is affectively negative, but the extrovert might be willing to pay the price of interpersonal tension and conflict to increase his or her excitation to an acceptable level. An introvert, to the contrary, is typically conflict-avoidant. Whereas an introvert might be more inclined to ruminate than would an extrovert, the rumination is generally perceived to be more controllable than is interacting with another—especially if one plots vengeance against the other.

Predictors of forgivingness. Forgivingness tends to be strongly predicted by high scores in agreeableness (with 13 of 18, 72% at *r* > .25) and low scores in neuroticism (19 of 31, 61%). The forgiving person is generally agreeable and emotionally not very negatively reactive. Neither introversion nor extroversion seems to be related to a trait of forgivingness, nor is conscientiousness or openness to experience.

Specific Research Studies on the Big Five and Forgivingness and Unforgivingness

Neuroticism is interpreted as emotional lability. That is, it is a measure of emotional reactivity and instability. McCullough, Bellah, Kilpatrick, and Johnson (2001), in their Study 2, found forgivingness as measured by Mauger et al.'s (1992) scale to be correlated with neuroticism negatively and agreeableness and conscientiousness positively. Berry, Worthington, Parrott, O'Connor, and Wade (2001) conducted three personality-relevant studies on our scenario-based assessment inventory for forgivingness, called the Transgression Narrative Test of Forgivingness (TNTF). We found in each of the three studies that agreeableness was negatively correlated with neuroticism and positively correlated with forgivingness. Less consistently, we found in Study 3 only that forgivingness and conscientiousness were positively correlated. Also in Study 3 only, we found extroversion to be positively related to trait forgivingness. (Note that all correlations except agreeableness and neuroticism were modest, i.e., $r < .25$.)

Other investigators have looked at aspects of the Big Five that were assessed differently than use of the Big Five Inventory. For example, Symington, Walker, and Gorsuch (2002) analyzed a number of dimensions of the 16 TF and other instruments together and grouped them under characteristics that were most closely related to Big Five traits. Like the two previous reports, Symington et al. found that forgivingness was negatively correlated with emotional instability and emotionality but not correlated with other measures of neuroticism, anxiety, or distress in relationship. That suggested partial support for the hypothesis that forgivingness is related to neuroticism. Forgivingness, however, was found to be related to agreeableness, warmth, and sensitivity, all of which are measures of the Big Five characteristic of agreeableness. Like the other cases, Symington et al. found no significant correlations between extroversion and forgivingness (six measures) or conscientiousness and forgivingness (three measures). However, they did find that intellectual openness was correlated with trait forgivingness ($r < .25$).

Ashton, Paunonen, Helmes, and Jackson (1998) subdivided their measure of forgivingness into two types, which they called empathy-attachment and forgiveness nonretaliation. This suggested that there is a component to forgiving that perhaps is associated with Gray's Behavioral Approach

System (BAS). It also suggested a negative response or retaliation-inhibiting aspect to forgivingness associated with Gray's Behavioral Inhibition System (BIS). Consistent with this theorizing, Ashton et al. found a strong correlation between agreeableness and the empathy-attachment measure of forgivingness. They found a weaker correlation between agreeableness and the forgiving nonretaliation measure. To the contrary, they found strong negative correlations between neuroticism and the forgiving nonretaliation measure of forgivingness. They found weaker correlations between the empathy-attachment measure and neuroticism. On both measures of forgivingness, they found no significant correlations with conscientiousness, openness, or extroversion.

McCullough and Hoyt (2002) studied the Big Five in perhaps the most sophisticated way to date. They aggregated six responses to transgressions using the Transgression-Related Interpersonal of Motivations (TRIM; McCullough et al., 1998), which is a measure of revenge and avoidance motivations toward a single transgression and also benevolence motivation toward the offender. In Study 1, they found that aggregated TRIMs were positively correlated with neuroticism for avoidance motivations. For revenge motivations, agreeableness was negatively correlated with revenge. For benevolence, neuroticism was negatively correlated with benevolence. The remainder of the correlations, each of the three subscales with extroversion, conscientiousness, and openness, were not significant.

In Study 2, they used self-ratings and compared those with peer ratings. The findings were similar but slightly different in the self-ratings from Study 1 to Study 2. For the avoidance subscale, avoidance was negatively correlated with agreeableness and positively correlated with neuroticism. Revenge was negatively correlated with agreeableness and not significantly correlated with any other scale. Benevolence was positively correlated with agreeableness and negatively correlated with neuroticism. Peer ratings were of a similar pattern. For avoidance, neuroticism was positively correlated with avoidance but not with any other of the Big Five traits. For revenge, revenge was negatively correlated with agreeableness, but not with any others of the Big Five. For benevolence, benevolence was negatively correlated with neuroticism but not with any others of the Big Five.

The correlation between the aggregated self-report measures with the aggregated peer-report measures was a moderate range of correlations. This suggested that people's friends could reasonably accurately assess the way the acquaintance was reacting to a transgression. The external manifestations of unforgiveness—when aggregated over a series of transgressions—were moderately discernible by peers.

Conclusion

Overall, these investigations from Mauger's, Rye's, Gorsuch's, McCullough's, Hoyt's, and our labs suggest a consistent picture. Dispositional forgivingness is consistently related to agreeableness and negatively related to neuroticism. Inconsistently, correlations will pop up relating forgivingness to extraversion and conscientiousness, but in only one case was any measure related to openness. Unforgiving people differentiate into two types. The grudge-holder is largely an emotionally reactive person. He or she is also not very agreeable. The vengeful person is usually conscientiously vigilant to injustices. Injustices set the person off into negative emotional reactions. He or she is highly nonagreeable and may provoke the injustices he or she perceives. By keeping vigilant track of injustices, he or she is primed to pay back any injustices—often with interest.

CHAPTER 7

Dispositions Related to Unforgiveness and Forgiveness

The Big Five personality traits set the stage on which grudges, vengeance, and forgiveness are acted out. A person or the person's therapist can do little to affect the Big Five; those traits are high in genetic heritability. But specific transgression-related dispositions are better targets for modification if a person wishes to change.

To structure our discussion, let us assume that three elements are involved: the victim, offender, and transgression. In this chapter, I will examine dispositions from the viewpoint of the victim—who will or will not forgive. The victim will inevitably not only have personal dispositions but also develop dispositions related to perceiving an offender and the relationship with the offender. I have characterized this framework for considering dispositions in Figure 7.1.

First, I will discuss dispositions and traits from the point of view of the victim as they relate specifically to unforgiveness and forgiveness. These include self-oriented, affective, and cognitive-motivational dispositions of the victim. Second, I will summarize the victim's perception of dispositions of the offender. Third, I will explore dispositions associated with the victim-offender relationship.

Most people are spiritual by nature. For many, spirituality is contextualized within a formal religious belief and value system and lived out in contact with a religious community. For others, spirituality is seen within a connection to the cosmos, to nature, to life, or to humanity. Within spirituality, people find or create a sense of meaning. Thus, the victim-offender

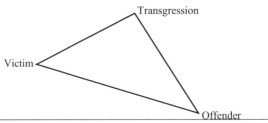

Figure 7.1 Relationships in forgiving.

interactions around the transgressions must usually be seen within a spiritual context. For some people, that spiritual context is extremely important. For others, it is less important. Michael McCullough, Steven Sandage, and I have depicted the relationships among victim, offender, and transgression as a triangular base on a horizontal plane. The spiritual dimension is shown extending horizontally, forming a pyramid with the Divine at the apex. Therefore, fourth, I will discuss one's perception of and relationship to the Divine, and, fifth, I will discuss one's perception of the offender's relationship with the Divine.

Self-Oriented Dispositions of the Victim

Adult Attachment Model of Self

Bowlby (1969) posited that infants developed a sense of attachment to their primary caregiver, usually the mother. Those attachments—considered a dispositional quality—reflect important cognitive frameworks that are likely to drive interpersonal behavior in adulthood (Kachadourian, Fincham, & Davila, 2004). Therefore, I suggest that the representational models underlying attachment security will influence an individual's forgiveness.

Bowlby (1988) suggested that humans are born with an attachment system, which motivates them to seek closeness to significant others when feeling needy. When attachment figures are not reliable or supportive, becoming close fails to relieve distress. Different coping strategies are needed (Mikulincer & Shaver, 2005). Infants interact with the caregiver and the environment and develop mental representations of the self and others. Those internal working models guide behavior throughout the lifespan (Bowlby). Ainsworth and Bell (1978) identified the usefulness of attachment in understanding romantic relationships. Hazan and Shaver (1987) and Main, Kaplan, and Cassidy (1985) described adult attachments. Bartholomew and Horowitz (1991) operationalized Bowlby's definition of internal working models by crossing two dimensions. The *model of other* portrays how the individual perceives the social world. Other people may be perceived as either trustworthy and responsive or uncaring and rejecting. The *model of self* portrays how the individual perceives and values the self. Individuals with a positive model of self do not require much external validation, feel that they are worthy of love, and feel confident in handling relationship threats. Individuals with a negative model of self are dependent on others for their sense of worth. They blame themselves for relational difficulties. When these two cognitive models are crossed, four attachment styles result: *secure* (positive model of self and a positive model of others), *preoccupied* (negative model of self and positive model of others), *fearful* (negative model of self and negative model of others), and *dismissing* (positive model of self and negative model of others).

Working models are particularly likely to be activated and influential following transgressions (Gaines et al., 1997; Shaver & Hazen, 1993; Shi, 2003). Securely attached individuals communicate better, exhibit more understanding, and are less likely to engage in withdrawal or aggression. Fearful people often blame others and are verbally aggressive. Avoidant attachment leads to withdrawal and unwillingness to compromise (Feeney, Noller, & Callan, 1994; Mikulincer & Nachshon, 1991).

Insecure individuals are often less forgiving than securely attached individuals. For example, when a close partner hurts one, individuals with insecure attachment working models do not accommodate (Gaines et al., 1997; Scharfe & Bartholomew, 1995) and report lower forgiveness (Kachadourian et al., 2004, 2005).

Rumination has been suggested as a connector between affect and ways people respond to hurts (Berry, Worthington, O'Connor, Parrott, & Wade, 2005). Insecurely attached people respond intensely to threatening events. They ruminate about the relationship (Mikulincer & Shaver, 2005). Rumination is likely to chronically prime an individual's insecure working model (Kachadourian et al., 2005), suggesting that almost any threat will activate it.

Kachadourian et al. (2004) hypothesized that model of self might be unclearly related to forgiveness. On one hand, those with a negative model of self might be more likely to forgive because of a fear of abandonment. Anxiety would maintain insecure attachment. However, people with a negative model of self might also be prone to anger and hostility, which would inhibit forgiveness. Individuals with a positive model of self might be more likely to forgive because they are not threatened by a transgression. Their self-worth is high and they do not expect partners to abandon them. In Study 1, 130 female and 54 male undergraduates who had been in a dating relationship for at least 4 months were assessed for unforgiveness, attachment, and relationship satisfaction. Only securely attached participants (positive models of self and others) were more likely to forgive partners for committing transgressions. This greater tendency to forgive was also related to relationship satisfaction. Models of self and others independently predicted relationship satisfaction. In Study 2, Kachadourian et al. studied 96 married couples from the community. They found a gender difference in married couples in the tendency to forgive. Husbands' models of self and others independently predicted forgiveness. Wives' models of self and others interacted to predict forgiveness. Models of self and others independently predicted relationship satisfaction, as in the first study. Additionally, greater forgiveness was related to marital satisfaction. Forgiveness partially mediated the relationship between model of others and satisfaction for husbands; this relationship was not found for wives; however, forgiveness partially mediated the relationship between model of self and relationship satisfaction for both husbands and wives.

Sensitivity

Aron and Aron (1997) have suggested that reactivity related to sensory stimuli is related to both introversion and emotionality. Worthington and Wade (1999) proposed this as a predictor of unforgivingness. Sensitivity to rejection seems to be an obvious personality characteristic related to sensory sensitivity and to unforgiveness. Although neither has been investigated to date by forgiveness researchers, it seems reasonable to hypothesize that people who are prone to overreact to sensory stimuli are likely to be at risk for being easily hurt or offended and thus likely to develop unforgiveness. This hypothesis deserves some testing.

Stability of Self-Esteem

In the 1980s, low self-esteem was thought to be related to almost all problems, and elevating self-esteem was the almost-universal solution. Baumeister, Campbell, Krueger, and Vohs (2003) reviewed the experimental evidence on whether high self-esteem produced such outcomes. They found no convincing evidence that higher self-esteem caused better school or work performance. Nor did they find evidence to suggest that more interpersonal success came with higher self-esteem. They found that people who had high self-esteem more often seemed happier.

Kernis, Cornell, Sun, Berry, and Harlow (1993) have shown that in many ways high self-esteem is not as important as the stability of self-esteem. Some people have fragile high self-esteem, which can change quickly under threat. Despite the high self-esteem, they often are not able to function well. People with stable high self-esteem, however, tend to be happier. Little research has examined the relationship between self-esteem and forgivingness. In fact, only two labs have studied it to date. Tangney, Boone, and Dearing (2005) found no significant relationship between forgiveness of others and self-esteem. Neto and Mullet (2004) studied 192 undergraduates in Portugal (90 females and 102 males), and they also found no significant correlation between propensity to forgive and high self-esteem.

Stability of self-esteem might be more important to forgiveness than simple high self-esteem. That has not been studied. I hypothesize that people with stable high self-esteem indeed are able to be less self-focused and more forgiving. But people with fragile high self-esteem are more easily threatened. They are more focused on the threat. They tend to appraise transgressions as threatening often. Thus, they are inclined to try to cope with the threat by more aggressive means. They are less likely to forgive. People with low self-esteem, we might hypothesize, are less likely to forgive than those with stable high self-esteem.

Ruminative Style of the Victim

There are many types of rumination. Rumination is repetitive thinking about an event and its consequence for the person. Rumination is affect-laden and is associated with some type of emotion. Furthermore, rumination occurs seemingly automatically, and intrusive thoughts interfere with the person's daily activities.

However, there are many types of negative rumination; rumination has been found to be associated with post-traumatic stress disorder (PTSD) (Horowitz, 1975), depression (Nolen-Hoeksema, 1987, 1991), obsessive-compulsive disorder (Rachman, 1997), coping with disease (Baider & De-Nour 1997), and other psychological disorders. Rumination has also been associated with unforgiveness and forgiving.

McCullough et al. (1998) found that rumination, as measured by the Impact Event Scale, mediated between the closeness of a relationship before a transgression and whether a person sought revenge. No mediation with rumination linked closeness in the relationship and whether the person avoided the transgressor.

In two studies, Thompson et al. (2005) and Brooks and Toussaint (2003) have shown that depressive rumination is related to depression or negative moods about a transgression. For example, Brooks and Toussaint studied 283 undergraduates. They found that depressive rumination was correlated with trait forgivingness, and that trait forgivingness was weakly and negatively correlated with depression. When measures of state and trait depressive rumination were statistically removed, forgivingness still predicted depression. Angry rumination was not found to be related to depression.

Some people can ruminate fretfully; they may worry about negative events happening and are afraid of what might happen if they meet the transgressor again. Fearful rumination was studied by Ashton et al. (1998); they investigated 118 undergraduate students. Students high in agreeableness were low in fretful rumination. Students high in neuroticism were high in fretful rumination. Low levels of forgivingness have also been tied to trait anxiety (Segerstrom, Tsao, Alden, & Craske, 2000).

Kachadourian et al. (2005) examined ambivalence, rumination, and forgiveness of transgressions with marriage relationship, predicting that there would be an interaction between rumination and ambivalence. The authors thought that ambivalence would serve as a priming influence in forgiveness, so that rumination and transgression would prime negative attributions and lead an individual to be less likely to forgive. Measures of attitudinal ambivalence, marital satisfaction, rumination, transgression severity, forgiveness, and depressive symptoms were given to 87 married couples who were also participating in a study with their adolescent child. Rumination about transgressions affected the relationship between the degree of ambivalence and decreased forgiveness. People who were ambivalent had decreased forgiveness. When rumination was low, there was no relationship between ambivalence and forgiveness. This study shows that ruminating about an event has a significant effect of forgiveness.

Berry, Worthington, Parrott, O'Connor, and Wade (2001) assessed vengeful angry rumination using the Caprara Dissipation Rumination Scale (DRS) in 62 undergraduates. We found that trait forgivingness was negatively correlated with the score on the DRS 8 weeks later. The Transgression Narrative Test of Forgivingness measured trait forgivingness.

In a recent follow-up study, Berry et al. (2005) studied the same 62 undergraduates but using a measure of forgivingness called the Trait Forgivingness Scale (TFS). That measure consisted of 10 Likert Scale items. The scores on the Trait Forgivingness Scale were again correlated highly with scores on the DRS. Berry et al., however, tested the hypothesis that angry vengeful rumination was a mediator between trait forgivingness and negative affective dispositions. They found that hostility and trait forgivingness was mediated to the degree that people ruminated angrily and vengefully. They found the same relationship between rumination and hostility. Berry et al. also found that responses to individual transgressions were predicted by trait forgivingness, and angry vengeful rumination mediated that relationship as well.

This suggests that it is not enough to know that a person ruminates; rather, it is necessary to find out the content of the rumination. Is the rumination fearful or simply obsessional, or does the person ruminate about getting revenge and responding angrily? The content of people's thinking will typically affect whether they will be more forgiving or more vengeful in their motivations and perhaps in their actions.

Narcissism

Emmons (2000) has written about the possible impact of narcissism on an unforgiving personality. Narcissism, of course, is drawn from the legend in Greek mythology of Narcissus, who was so obsessed with himself that upon seeing his reflection in a pool that he fell in love with himself. Emmons defines narcissism as self-admiration that is characterized by tendencies toward grandiose ideas, exhibitionism, and defensiveness in response to criticism; interpersonal relationships are characterized by entitlement, exploitiveness, and lack of empathy. Perhaps the most important aspect of a narcissistic personality is that it is highly related to problems with interpersonal relationships. If people are disdainful of others and chronically unable to get along, it is often because they have a sense of entitlement and lack an ability to empathize with people. These are two core features of narcissism. Narcissistic people believe they are entitled to special considerations regardless of whether they earn it. They demand attention and honor from others. They are selfish. They expect special consideration, but do not necessarily believe that they need to reciprocate.

Narcissism, thus, sets people up to perceive transgressions as hurts or offenses, to feel that they are acted against in a highly unjust way. Thus, they experience a high number of perceived transgressions. Emmons (2000) summarizes the few scattered findings that suggest that narcissistic traits inhibit forgiveness. For example, he reports that Millon (1998) asserted that vengeful gratification was a common response when people perceive narcissistic wounds. Often, they fantasized about revenge as an anodyne to the wound. Raskin and Novacek (1991) found that narcissism was associated with fantasies of power, success, glory, and revenge. They found that people scoring high in narcissism who were under a lot of daily stress were especially likely to fantasize about power and revenge. Bushman and Baumeister (1998) gave people with varying degrees of narcissism a chance to respond by cranking up the noise level that a person had to endure if the person had either insulted or not insulted the subject. Bushman and Baumeister interpreted their results to support their belief that threatened egotism contributes strongly to aggressive and violent behavior.

In 1993, Davidson found levels of narcissism to be negatively correlated with forgiveness in response to hypothetical and real-life hurtful situations.

Pride

People who have, as a strong personality disposition, a sense of pride or high sense of ego are hypothesized to likely provoke others to transgress against them. Baumeister, Exline, and Sommer (1998) have observed that transgressions often involve blows to a victim's self-esteem and pride. For a victim to forgive such transgressions would be to accept a loss of face. The person might feel that he or she has not stood up for his or her rights, or that others might perceive him or her as foolish.

In 1968, Brown showed that a loss of face or a blow to one's pride is a powerful stimulus to seeking revenge. In 1997, Baumeister reviewed evidence to avenge blows to self-esteem and described such blows as one of the major causes in interpersonal violence and evil. Nevertheless, at present, no one has actually investigated the effect of pride on unforgivingness or forgivingness, though the relationship would seem to indicate that it would be promising to study.

One recalls the classic movie *Casablanca*. Rick (Humphrey Bogart's character) was left at the train station in the rain by Ilse (Ingrid Bergman's character). Over time, Rick nursed his damaged pride, turning his character into an unforgiving man—angry, obsessive, vindictive, and hateful. Rick's crusty exterior had become brittle with unforgiveness. Yet beneath his public persona, Rick maintained a heart for the underdog.

Affective Traits of Victim

Self-Forgetful Dispositions

I suggested that self-forgetful emotions—humility, gratitude, generosity, and contrition—might facilitate forgiveness. Few have been studied in relation to forgiveness.

Affective dispositions of negative valence are much more strongly linked to unforgiveness. We will examine trait anger, trait fear, shame- and guilt-proneness, hostility and aggressiveness, and vengefulness.

Trait Anger and Trait Fear

Several investigators have examined the relationship between trait anger and trait fear, and forgiving others. In every instance in which investigators measured anger regardless of the measure of trait forgivingness or measure of trait anger, a significant and strong negative correlation was found between the measures (Mullet, Neto, & Rivière, 2005).

Fewer people have studied trait fear. Thompson et al. (2005) used the State Trait Anxiety Inventory, trait version (STAI-T), and found negative correlations between the STAI-T and the Heartland Forgiveness Scale (HFS), Tangney's Multidimensional Forgiveness Inventory (MFI; Tangney, Boone, & Dearing, 2005), and the forgiveness of others (FO; Mauger et al., 1992). Seybold, Hill, Neumann, and Chi (2001) measured trait anxiety and found a significant negative correlation between trait anxiety and the FO. Tangney, Boone, Dearing, and Reinsmith (2002) correlated trait anxiety with forgiveness of others, but did not find a significant negative correlation. Our conclusion then would be that there appears to be a negative relationship between trait fearfulness and trait forgivingness, but the strength of the relationship is not fully established.

Shame- and Guilt-Proneness

Tangney calls guilt and shame *self-conscious emotions* (Tangney et al., 2005). Based on clinical experience, Flanigan (1987) theorized about the role of shame and forgiveness in alcoholism. She suggested that shame involves negative feelings about the self even though no violation of a rule or actual offense might have been committed. The shamed person feels responsible and accountable for having done something wrong and morally negligent or reprehensible as a result. The shamed person probably shares a sense of guilt, contrition, and self-disgust. However, unlike guilty people, there is no sense of a clear violation of a rule. In alcoholism, there is shame because (1) no one has been able to prevent the alcoholic from the alcoholism or to stop its course, (2) everyone has endured the humiliations of alcoholism, (3) everyone in the family system has revealed himself or herself as weak and unable to react properly to the alcoholism, and (4) family members consistently break rules about drinking. Forgiveness was hypothesized to allow the alcoholic to rejoin the family and the family to begin to right itself.

Tangney has investigated shame, guilt, and other self-conscious emotions for many years (see Tangney & Dearing, 2002; Tangney, Wagner, Hill-Barlow, Marschall, & Gramzow, 1996; Tangney, Wagner, & Gramzow, 1992). Similar to Flanigan, Tangney understands guilt to be a proper and healthy emotional response to wrongdoing, but shame is an overgeneralization to one's wrongdoing in which one blames the self. People who habitually feel guilty for doing things that are wrong and try to correct their behavior to bring it more in line with the moral conditions are said to be *guilt-prone*. People who are habitually embarrassed and ashamed of their failures to live up to someone's moral code are said to be *shame-prone*. Shame and guilt are often intertwined with each other, so Tangney often reports guilt with the variance that is due to shame removed (called shame-free guilt) and shame with the variance due to guilt removed (called guilt-free shame). Correlations with forgiveness of others were small. Sandage (1997) also investigated shame- and guilt-proneness as possible predisposing personality attributes that might influence a person's acceptance of different interventions. Effects were significant but accounted for only 4% of the variance. We surmise that, despite therapeutic experience and face validity, little experimental evidence supports a connection.

Hostility and Aggressiveness

Several investigators have studied hostility and forgivingness, and most have also studied aggression and forgivingness (Berry et al., 2001; Berry et al., 2005; Seybold et al., 2001; Tangney et al., 2002; Thompson et al., 2005). The results are extremely consistent despite their using six different instruments to assess forgivingness. For hostility, small correlations were found. Sometimes they were significant. Other times not, depending mostly on size of sample. Correlations were slightly smaller for forgivingness and aggression.

Vengefulness

As I observed in chapter 6, one style of unforgiving personality that has been often validated is a vengeful personality. We examined Big Five predictors of vengeful personality and found strong and consistent predictions. In the present section, let us look at a few studies of vengeful personality.

Vengefulness can result in poor recovery from losses. Weinberg (1994) used a quasiexperimental cross-sectional survey with 200 participants selected from nonacademic employees and graduate students. All participants identified the death of a loved one as being the most difficult and distressing event they had experienced. Participants rated whether they blamed themselves or blamed another, and the degree of the desire for revenge. Deaths were either unnatural deaths such as murder, accident, or suicide or deaths from natural causes, such as illness or miscarriage. Unnatural deaths were associated with greater blame: 78% of the survivors blamed someone—40%, both themselves and another; 20%, only another; and 18%, themselves alone. For deaths due to natural causes, only 39% blamed someone—14% blamed themselves and another; 13% only another; and 12% themselves only. Self-reported recovery from the death was greater for death by natural causes than death due to unnatural causes. Furthermore, self-blame interfered with recovery from the death. Those who blamed others but did not desire revenge reported greater recovery than those who blamed others but did desire revenge.

McCullough, Kilpatrick, Emmons, and Larson (2001) studied vengeance as a disposition and its relationship with forgiveness with 91 students. They found vengefulness to be related to rumination; they also found it to be highly related to efforts to suppress thinking and to both avoidance and revenge motivations. There was a negative correlation between vengefulness and satisfaction with life and a positive correlation between vengefulness and negative affectivity. McCullough et al. followed these students for 8 weeks and then reassessed them. They found that students' changes in rumination were related to changes in thought suppression, avoidance, and revenge. Changes in rumination were not significantly correlated with changes in satisfaction with life. Vengeful personality predicted only change in revenge score when negative affectivity was controlled. Vengefulness did not predict changes in rumination, thought suppression, avoidance, or satisfaction with life if negative activity was controlled.

Emmons (1992) earlier had investigated revenge, examining a scale that measured beliefs about revenge. Emmons measured 420 undergraduate college students and adults from the local community using the Beliefs about Revenge Questionnaire (BARQ). Scores on the BARQ were correlated with three measures of rumination, one involving undifferentiated ruminative thinking, another obsessional thinking, and a third rehearsal on an emotional control questionnaire. In addition, scores on the BARQ were related to emotional expressiveness, hostility, measures of narcissism, and anger. Finally, extreme scores on the BARQ, either high revenge or low revenge, predicted attitudes towards capital punishment in general and in particular attitudes about an execution that had recently occurred in California.

Cognitive-Motivational Traits of Victims

Virtue Orientation

Not everyone believes that forgiveness is virtuous; however, most do. Even people who are personally opposed to forgiveness and more oriented toward seeking justice often admire people who are able to experience one of life's great wounds and be able to forgive. Berry and I have studied people's orientations toward virtues and classified them into conscientiousness-based and warmth-based virtues (Berry et al., 2004; Berry, Worthington, Wade, Witvliet, & Kiefer, 2005; Worthington, Berry, & Parrott, 2001; Worthington & Berry, 2005). One hypothesis might be that people who value conscientiousness-based virtues might tend to embrace decisions to forgive. Those who embrace warmth-based virtues will probably have an easier time embracing emotional forgiveness. Berry et al. (2005) found initial evidence to this effect.

Tendency to Reframe Positively, Avoid Conflict, or Deny

Transgressions can be psychologically threatening. Some people minimize the threat through employing the psychological defense of denial. Others are Pollyannas who look for the positive side and tend to renarrate stories of their life to fit more positive frames. Others will go to virtually any length to avoid conflict. These cognitive and psychological defenses likely reduce conflict and transgressions, but they might exact a psychological or relational cost.

Victim's Perception of the Offender

Victims perceive the offender. They respond on the basis of their perception. Their early experiences might affect the way they habitually perceive others (i.e., attachment). Their view of humanity, likewise, will affect their responses. Finally, some psychological defenses, like projection, directly affect the perception of the other.

Attachment Model of Other

Recall that building on work applying attachment to adult relationships (Hazan & Shaver, 1987; Main, Kaplan, & Cassidy, 1985), Bartholomew and Horowitz (1991) described working models by crossing two dimensions. We already discussed model of self. The second dimension is how the person perceives others. If a person has negative models of other, the person might perceive others in general, especially when it comes to providing nurture, as rejecting or alien. People with negative models of other will probably feel hostile and suspicious. That predisposes them to perceive transgressions even when none might have been intended. Or they might perceive the transgression as maliciously motivated when the behavior was unintentional. As with any predisposition, a negative model of self can act as a self-fulfilling prophecy. The other is likely to detect suspicion, lack of trust, and expectation of rejection, and those very behaviors might be provoked.

Perception of Humanity

Some people employ beliefs that minimize differences in humans. Examples of such belief systems are beliefs in the common personhood of humanity—people are alike under the skin. Another example is the South African belief that Nelson Mandela and Archbishop Desmond Tutu championed to help people heal from the wounds of apartheid and the struggles against it. They promoted *mbutu,* which is a belief that individuals are important only to the extent that they contribute to the community. A third example is an emphasis on unity found within Hinduism and Buddhism. These are three examples of beliefs that minimize differences that might lead to less unforgiveness and a more forgiving person.

Defense of Projection

One of the defenses leading to the most maladjustment is projection. In projection, a person feels internal conflict and projects it onto the other person. One who feels upset or angry toward an offender might project that anger onto that offender. One might even project hatred upon one toward whom one feels prejudice, transforming the person (falsely) into a transgressor. People who habitually employ projection are thus hypothesized to be at risk for frequently feeling victimized.

Victim-Offender Relationship-Oriented Dispositions

Emotional Intelligence and Relationship Skill Sets

People come equipped to relationships with personal qualities and skill sets. *Emotional intelligence* is defined as the ability to understand one's own or another person's emotional states and to actively regulate emotions in self and others. It also involves using emotions effectively in making decisions, planning, and motivating action (Salovey & Mayer, 1989–90). Worthington and Wade (1999) hypothesized that emotional intelligence was related to forgiveness, but this has yet to be tested. Similarly, over a lifetime, one has developed skills that are more or less successfully employed in relationships and certainly play a role in whether one resolves conflicts and thus mitigates transgressions. Little work has related relational skills to forgiving except that done by Fincham and his colleagues (see Fincham, Hall, & Beach, 2005, for a review) and work on accommodation by Rusbult and her colleagues (for a review, see Rusbult, Hannon, Stocker, & Finkel, 2005). Suggestions from couples therapies could easily be investigated, such as acceptance and letting go (see Jacobson & Christensen, 1996, for a review). Conflict resolution and negotiation skills are problem-solving coping mechanisms that have similarly been approached from numerous theoretical perspectives in couples and family therapies. However, in regard to forgiveness, these have not been studied. Several relationship dispositions have been studied—marital social values, commitment to relationships, willingness to sacrifice for relationships, and other-oriented emotional traits.

Marital Social Values

Ripley has spearheaded the development of an instrument to measure covenant versus contractual marital social values (Ripley, Worthington, Bromley, & Kemper, 2005). People who hold covenantal marital social values understand marriage as a sacred covenant. People who hold contractual marital values understand marriage as an agreement in which both parties have obligations. Covenantal marital social values have been associated in marital couples with stronger marital commitment, higher marital satisfaction, and other positive marital qualities. It is likely that people who embrace covenantal marital views of marriage and feel that they are together in a sacred bond until death parts them will be likely to embrace forgiveness and to decide to forgive quickly and express that decision to their partners quickly. It is unclear whether their emotional forgiveness will parallel their decision and expression to forgive. Ripley's concept is similar to distinctions that are made between individualistic and communal views of life (Triandis, 2005).

Commitment to Relationships

A strong sense of positive valence toward the relationship and a commitment to the relationship are not exactly personality dispositions. However, they are not transient states, either. They are long-standing, for the most part, evaluations that a person makes toward a relationship. Gottman (1993) has suggested that people behave toward each other in either an affiliative prosocial positive way, or a more negative way (e.g., to withdraw from each other, or to attack and engage each other). These approach or avoidance strategies are somewhat stable. Gottman (1994) has predicted them by the ratio of positive interactions the partners have with each other compared with negative interactions.

Relationship valence has been investigated by Fincham's research group in the case of close, usually married, couples, and by Rusbult's research group (involving Karremans, Van Lange, Finkel, and others). Typically, both groups have shown that, in ongoing positive committed relationships, people are motivated toward resolving relationship difficulties. That might entail accommodation practices, or forgiveness or reconciliation behaviors.

Finkel, Rusbult, Kumashiro, and Hannon (2002) have studied betrayal in close relationships. They looked at the role of commitment in promoting forgiveness. They conducted three studies. In Study 1, they used a priming procedure to momentarily activate low or high commitment in the ongoing relationship. After people were primed to think about either high or low commitment, partners indicated how they would react to hypothetical acts of betrayal. People rated the degree to which they would respond using exit reactions (e.g., seeking vengeance), neglect reactions (e.g., giving the partner the cold shoulder), voice reactions (e.g., suggesting that partners discuss it), and loyalty reactions (e.g., continuing to support the partner despite dissatisfaction). Finkel et al. found that priming people toward high commitment resulted in more forgiveness and fewer responses indicating exit or neglect.

In Study 2, Finkel et al. (2002) used a nonexperimental method and showed that highly committed partners were more likely to forgive a partner's hypothetical acts of betrayal. They tested the mediation by one's thoughts of the relationship between commitment and behaving in a way that indicated forgiving. That is, the relationship between commitment and forgiving disappeared when one considered what the partner might be thinking. Finkel et al. interpret their results as follows: "Thus, committed individuals might feel quite hurt or angry following betrayal—indeed, high commitment participants experienced more high negative immediate emotion than did low commitment participants—yet still find their way to forgiveness. In contrast, developing benevolent or malevolent cognitive interpretations to the partner's behavior appears to be a key to understanding the relationship between commitment and personal forgiveness" (p. 969). In Study 3, Finkel et al. measured reactions to betrayals using daily interaction records. They found once again that commitment was related to more tendencies to forgive.

In their second study, Finkel et al. (2002) found a result that might be related to decisional versus emotional forgiveness. When people immediately stated that they forgave their partner for betrayal, their immediate emotions were not correlated with the amount of forgiveness. When partners delayed stating forgiveness, their forgiveness was positively associated with their change in emotions. This suggests that stating forgiveness immediately might represent decisional forgiveness that is aimed at controlling their behavior and preventing reciprocal negativity. However, when forgiveness was stated only after time passed, this might indicate that emotional forgiveness had occurred and the person was conveying that emotional forgiveness to the partner.

Willingness to Sacrifice for the Relationship

If a transgression occurs in a relationship, the willingness to sacrifice for that relationship is thought to effect how one might cope with the transgression. If the threat appraisal is not exceptionally high to the self, then people may try to deal with the threat to the relationship. If there is a threat to both, then people will likely want to solve the problems within the relationship. Willingness to sacrifice for the relationship is thought to be highly predictive of how people cope. In particular, it is thought to predict if people are likely to seek, ask for, and grant forgiveness. Both seeking forgiveness and granting forgiveness are costly because they involve sacrifice. Van Lange et al. (1997) investigated the effect of the willingness to sacrifice for the relationship. Willingness to sacrifice was predicted by commitment to the relationship, relationship longevity, and relationship adjustment (Van Lange, Agnew, Harinck, & Steemers, 1997).

Other-Oriented Emotional Traits

Trait empathy, trait sympathy, trait compassion, and traits that demonstrate altruistic love are likely to be strongly associated with emotional forgiveness. These are involved in the definition of emotional forgiveness. The research has been strongest in examining trait empathy.

McCullough et al. (1997) and McCullough et al. (1998) found that state empathy mediates or partially mediates the connection between apology and forgiveness. They postulated on the basis of this that empathy was an important condition for experiencing forgiveness. If that is true, then dispositional forgivingness ought to be found to be related to dispositional empathy, and it consistently has been (see Mullet, Neto, & Rivière, 2005, for a review).

Macaskill, Maltby, and Day (2002) studied 324 British undergraduates using Mauger et al.'s (1992) scale for forgivingness of others. They found that trait empathy and trait forgivingness were correlated with forgiving others.

Victim's Perception of and Relationship to the Divine

Spiritual Strivings

Emmons (2000b) has studied people's spiritual strivings. People usually set goals for themselves spiritually and attempt to meet those goals through the way they live. People with strong spiritual strivings that include forgiving as a virtue are expected to decide to forgive when transgressed against more than those with weaker spiritual strivings.

Hope

Hope is a broadly spiritual quality. It can involve hope in life beyond physical existence—life with God. Or hope can address one's confidence in changing—that one has both the will and means to effect change in this present life. All investigations to date involving forgiveness and hope have addressed the secular side of hope, which is spiritual in the sense of pertaining to the human spirit.

Three intervention studies have shown that, when people are induced by a group leader or therapist to forgive, they also report an increase in hope. Al-Mabuk, Enright, and Cardis (1995) conducted two studies of a psychoeducational group intervention to promote forgiveness with college students who wanted to forgive their parents. The first study involved a 4-hour forgiveness intervention, which was designed not to be an effective intervention. The second study added 2 additional hours of more emotional relevance to the participants and was intended to be a powerful intervention. In those studies, people attending the intervention increased in hope and forgiveness relative to those in a control group. The first study produced small gains. The second study produced large gains.

Freedman and Enright (1996) also conducted a version of Enright's Process Forgiveness Intervention in individual psychotherapy with 12 female survivors of incest. People completing the treatment increased more in both forgiveness and hope than did the waiting control group.

Rye and Pargament (2002) tested two different group interventions to promote forgiveness against a control condition. One intervention integrated Christian theology with psychology, and the other was secular. College females who had been wronged in a romantic relationship, regardless of which intervention they attended, increased more in forgiveness and hope than did participants in the control group. Interventions, of course, do not show whether forgiveness and hope are causally related. The intervention might increase hope for different reasons that it promotes forgiveness.

Two studies have examined hope and forgiveness in the natural environment. Thompson et al. (2005) found trait hope and forgivingness to correlate .28 in the student sample and .22 and -.09 in two nonstudent samples. Sandage, Worthington, and Calvert-Minor (2000) separately investigated the ability of trait hope, shame-proneness, guilt-proneness, and subscale of the Trait Hope Scale in predicting forgiveness for a particular transgression. We found no relationship between trait hope and forgiveness.

In summary, there is some reason to believe that when people go through an intervention aimed at promoting forgiveness, they will become more hopeful. Perhaps this is because they see themselves able to overcome unforgiveness that they previously thought was intractable. However, the relationship between traits of hope and forgivingness are modest to nonexistent based on present evidence. Furthermore, both of the nonintervention studies were correlational, not experimental. For therapists or facilitators of group interventions, then, it appears unlikely that focusing hope will result in additional forgiving by the participants or clients.

Religious Beliefs and Values

People who embrace a religious view, especially in the Abrahamic traditions, value justice and mercy differentially. They also see God as more or less just and merciful. Ideally, people affirm the idea that God is wholly just and wholly merciful at the same time, but in practice because justice and mercy do bump into each other, people develop over their lives a sense of whether God is more a God of justice or one of mercy. Without implying that religious systems determine people's beliefs, we may classify Judaism and Islam as both being more in line with a God of justice and Christianity with identifying more with a God of mercy. If God is seen as a God of justice, then ultimately God is likely to exact divine justice on humans, righting accumulated human wrongdoing. For devout people of faith, that might reduce both their injustice gap and their drive to take justice into their own hands. If God is seen as a God of mercy, people of faith might look to God's ultimate mercy as absolving them of a responsibility to show mercy. On the other hand, if modeling dominates, seeing God as a God of justice or as a God of mercy might stimulate humans to copy.

Specific religious beliefs within different religious traditions might further condition believers' behavior. Many people believe that forgiving is required in Christian scripture (Matthew 6:12, 14–15; Luke 6:37–38). They believe that if they do not forgive people who transgress against them, God will not forgive them. For people who embrace that as a wholehearted life guide, deciding to forgive should be predicted strongly. Jews have a strong view that forgiveness should be embedded within a social process requiring the offender to thoroughly repent (Dorff, 1998). Thus, if thorough repentance is not evident, we might expect strong adherence to Judaism to predict unwillingness to forgive. For Muslims, forgiveness is a valued trait, but it usually is embedded within submission to God (Rye et al., 2000). If the offender is not in a relationship with the Divine that is considered properly submissive, then the obligation to forgive is less. We might expect that strong differences in forgiveness should be evident when the offender is an in-group versus an out-group member.

Religious Commitment

Religious commitment is crucial because those with high religious commitment tend to employ their religious beliefs and values across more situations and throughout a longer duration than those of moderate religious commitment (see Worthington, 1988; Worthington, Kurusu, McCullough, & Sandage, 1996). Highly committed religious people, especially people who are highly committed to Christian beliefs and communities, often value forgiveness highly. They are especially likely to forgive quickly because of the power of their beliefs and values. They are also good candidates for forgiveness therapy as an adjunct to psychotherapy. Forgiveness therapy fits easily in their worldview. As we will see in a subsequent section, research by Krause and his colleagues (i.e., Krause & Ellison, 2003; Krause & Ingersoll-Dayton, 2001) on Christians showed that just because a person has embraced the Christian faith does not mean that his or her specific beliefs are easily discernable. The wise therapist will probe the nature of beliefs about forgiveness before making assumptions about what forgiveness means to the religious person and thus adapt interventions accordingly.

For example, a Christian might believe that he or she should grant decisional forgiveness rapidly and might be troubled because emotional forgiveness does not follow immediately upon the granting of decisional forgiveness. Clinicians must help clients understand the difference in the two types of forgiving. Also, instead of applying forgiveness therapy with all people who are angry, we might consider which anger is more trait-related and which is more state-related. Trait-related anger might not yield well to a psychotherapy that is solely or primarily based on promoting forgiveness.

Religious Struggle

Religious struggle often occurs when people are transgressed against, especially when there is a high personal injustice gap. People of faith might expect that God should enact justice against a perpetrator. People who do not embrace faith might be catapulted into religious struggles if it appears that acts have occurred that are acts of divine justice or divine mercy. Religious struggle has been investigated (see Pargament et al., 1998). The strength of religious struggles is hypothesized to be strongly related to unforgiving personality dispositions.

Perception of Having Been Forgiven by God

As far back as 1952, Andras Angyal advocated helping psychotherapy clients seek and receive forgiveness from God. Guilt was seen as a primary problem underlying much psychopathology. Angyal believed that if people could confess their guilt to God, the resulting freedom would spread to other targets of psychotherapy.

Part of Christian doctrine asserts that people can forgive others because they have received forgiveness from God. Even believers in God who are not Christian often want to make things right with God as they approach the end of their lives. This might entail receiving forgiveness from God. Four studies have addressed this issue.

Meek, Albright, and McMinn (1995) in a scenario study investigated 108 undergraduate students. Meek et al. found that the likelihood of feeling forgiven by God was greater if people had intrinsic (i.e., religion for its own sake) rather than extrinsic (i.e., religion to gain external benefits such as social contacts) religious orientation. People with intrinsic religious orientation were more likely to confess wrongdoing to someone they had wronged than were those who were extrinsically oriented. Guilt mediated the relationship between religious orientation and people's feelings about their wrongdoing.

Krause and Ingersoll-Dayton (2001) studied 129 Christians (79 Caucasian, 50 African American) age 65 and over. Some Christians forgave quickly, often through imitating God, adhering to Scripture to receive forgiveness from God, or to get other benefits. Other Christians required the transgressor to do acts of contrition before being willing to grant forgiveness. These acts of contrition involved things such as (1) be aware of wrongdoing, (2) be sorry, (3) express contrition, (4) apologize, (5) ask for forgiveness, (6) offer mitigating account of the transgression, (7) say they will try not to repeat the transgression, (8) change their actual behavior, (9) make amends or restitution, (10) empathize with their suffering, (11) suffer themselves, (12) try to convince the victim that the transgressor still values the relationship, or even (13) have the transgressor keep on giving even after being forgiven. Krause and Ellison (2003) interviewed 1,316 elderly Christians, of which about half were Caucasian. They found that requiring acts of contrition resulted in higher depression, more somatic symptoms, less life satisfaction, and more death anxiety than did rapid forgiving. People who felt more forgiven by God were 2 1/2 times as likely to forgive without requiring acts of contrition.

Toussaint, Williams, Musick, and Everson (2001) surveyed 1,423 adults at ages across the lifecycle. They found that forgiveness by God was greater in older adults than in younger adults. Psychological distress was not predicted by feeling forgiven by God in any age group. Life satisfaction was predicted to be negatively related to experiencing forgiveness by God for middle-aged people, but not for other age groups. Self-rated health was not related to feeling forgiven by God.

Perception of the Relationship of the Offender to the Divine

People respond to members of an in-group much differently than they do to members of an out-group. Thus, one's perception of the offender and even one's relationship to the offender are not the only factors affecting forgiveness. One responds based on one's perception of the offender's relationship to the Divine.

Similarity or Difference of Relationship to the Divine

Recognizing whether an animal is similar or different is essential to survival. This is true across the spectrum of existence, and no less true of humans. People tend to give others who are more similar to them—through genes or social similarities—more tolerance. Members of out-groups are perceived more uniformly. They are seen with more suspicion and trusted less.

However, if a member of the in-group transgresses, the transgression is seen as all the more egregious. Thus, incest and physical or sexual abuse within the family is seen as worse than a similar abuse from outside the family. When Roman Catholic priests (i.e., "fathers") were found to have perpetrated sexual abuses on their parishioners, that was typically seen as a worse offense than similar sexual abuses among strangers.

Yet, if a member of the family—one who is similar in important ways— repents and foreswears misbehavior, one is usually quicker to forgive than in the same circumstances with a stranger. Thus, similarity of victim and offender has complicated effects on unforgiveness and forgiveness.

Karma

A belief in *karma* is a belief that justice is unremitting and inevitable. It is the religious concept that what goes around, comes around. If injustices are perpetrated by a person in this life, then a person is thought to reap the consequences in a future life. Beliefs in karma can inhibit people from being unjust. Furthermore, such beliefs can inhibit vengeful responses by victims, and it might inspire people to be more compassionate and merciful so as to attain rewards in this or a future life. Again, these ideas and their impact on forgiveness have not been studied empirically.

Conclusion

Forgiveness is affected by a huge number of dispositional qualities beyond the Big Five personality traits. Many of the dispositional qualities are related to relatively stable beliefs, values, and attitudes. If a person wants to become a more forgiving human, the person might seek to change his or her dispositional qualities. At the present, the most fruitful targets might be qualities related to the self—such as the stability of self-esteem and moderating attitudes of pride and enhancing humility. A second likely candidate for modification would be the angry, hostile, aggressive, and vengeful affective dispositions. Third, relational qualities—those that affect the affective tone of the relationship—provide another target for intervention. All of this presumes, though, that personality can be modified. Can it? Or is it virtually immutable or requires so much time that it is impractical to attempt its modification?

CHAPTER **8**

Personality Can Be Changed

In Victor Hugo's novel *Les Miserables,* Jean Valjean, a good man, was transformed into a bitter, resentful, and unforgiving man as a result of a massive injustice. But after being the recipient of forgiveness, Valjean was again transformed into a thoroughly forgiving person. For the rest of his life, he was an exemplar of forgiveness. Do such changes only happen in fiction? Or is it possible for people to change unforgiving personalities into more forgiving personalities?

Changing Our Personality

What Would It Take to Change Personality?

Psychotherapy is perhaps the most researched method of helping people change their personalities. In an atmosphere of managed care, most psychotherapies help alleviate acute emotional and psychological problems. Sometimes, it aims to help people change personality disorders and enduring lifestyle dysfunctions. As clinicians who work with personality disorders know, changing personality characteristics is a long-term, intensive, and systematic effort, even with psychotherapy.

Most people who wish to become more forgiving will find themselves somewhere in the middle of the normal distribution of trait forgivingness. Occasionally, a habitually hateful, vengeful grudge-holder wants to become more forgiving. But usually they have trouble sticking with psychotherapy because the therapist will inevitably disappoint them. On the other side of the spectrum, sometimes a person who expresses forgiveness too readily will want to become less of a doormat. For all but the extreme cases, most people can become more forgiving without 2-plus years of psychotherapy. In our research, we have seen shifts in trait forgivingness within 6 to 8 hours of intervention, though those are probably also rare cases. For most people, meaningful change in character might occur within an intensive effort to change if they continue to employ the skills they developed.

What Do Psychotherapies Have to Say About Promoting More Forgiveness?

Few therapies have specifically addressed forgiveness. Occasionally, theorists will apply theories of therapy specifically to forgiveness, such as Paul Vitz (Vitz & Mango, 1997a, 1997b), who wrote from a psychodynamic perspective, Malcolm and Greenberg (2000; Malcolm, Warwar, & Greenberg, 2005) from an emotion-focused therapy perspective, and others from a cognitive or cognitive-behavioral perspective (Gordon, Baucom, & Snyder, 2005). Enright (Enright & Fitzgibbons, 2000; Freedman & Enright, 1996) has described a forgiveness therapy that focuses specifically on the therapeutic goal of promoting forgiveness. Rather than review these scattered writings specifically about forgiveness, I will reflect on more general guidelines from therapies about helping people change their personalities.

Leona Tyler (1973) suggested that psychotherapies attempt what she called *minimal change therapy*. Therapies do not have to transform an entire personality. If a person were standing in Los Angeles, looking directly across the country at Atlanta, and the person made a 2° shift in direction, then by the time the person arrived at the East Coast, he or she would be closer to Richmond, Virginia, than to Atlanta. Tyler's point is that if a person can make a small but significant change in life direction and maintain that change over time, then the person can eventually effect a huge change in personality.

Solution-focused therapies (deShazer, 1988) also suggest that a person, couple, or family make a small but significant change in their actions and build on that change. A metaphor is often used to sport psychology. If a man consistently hooked his golf drives left, he would not need years of psychoanalysis to figure out that he was toilet-trained too early so he could correct the golf swing. Instead, he might simply shift his grip, and the problem could be solved. Solution-focused therapists suggest that change occurs through making a small but meaningful adjustment, maintaining it, and practicing it until it becomes a new habit, resulting in large changes in the person's life.

One might imagine, for instance, that a person is often rejected by potential romantic partners. The person has become angry, resentful, bitter, and grudge-holding. He or she often complains and whines. That negative affect poisons relationships resulting in (you guessed it) a vicious cycle: new rejection, new whining, new relationship, new rejection, new whining, and so on. If the person can change his or her personality such that resentment and hostility cease and the person behaves more forgivingly, agreeably, and less emotionally reactively, then fewer potential romantic partners will be driven away. This might transform the person's life because of the ripple effect of making a significant change.

When Freud first proposed psychoanalytic therapy, he described cases illustrating dramatic changes. However, once day-to-day psychoanalytic treatment began to be practiced, it became clear that those cases were infrequent. Analysis was then thought to require 5 days a week for years. No longer. Brief psychoanalytic approaches suggest that people can learn in months to exert more ego control in their lives and rid themselves of negative symptoms (Soldz & McCullough, 2000).

Cognitive therapies are also effective at helping people change. They modify the ways that people understand a phenomenon. Cognitive therapies may aim at changing worldviews, assumptions, expectations, attributions of cause, and even self-talk. Each of these levels of change in cognition can contribute to more positive psychological and emotional outcomes. Given the role that rumination often plays in resentment, grudge-holding, and vengeance, cognitive therapy might be a fruitful avenue to attempt to change people's unforgiveness into a more forgiving personality.

What Is the Point of Leverage?

Change agents seek a leverage point to shift clients from negative to positive living. Clients must change cognition to be more positive; expectations to be more hopeful; emotional experiences to be more positive; rumination to be less angry, vengeful, and bitter; and actions to be more reconciliatory. By changing people's behavior, the hope is that people in the client's social world will eventually respond more positively. It is unlikely that social changes will happen rapidly. Many people will not even notice new patterns of behavior, and even if they do, they do not trust that they will last. Eventually, people begin to treat the forgiving person differently than they did when he or she was vengeful or grudge-holding.

Why It Is Difficult to Change Personality

We experience our own personality characteristics as being stable cross-situational enduring organizations of thoughts, images, feelings, attitudes, values, beliefs, and motivations that give rise to relatively consistent behaviors. Personality is an accumulated set of experiences. It is united by a common narrative and empowered by a need to be internally consistent. Personality provides an understanding of self and the world, draws selectively on memories to support its consistency, and motivates behaviors consistent with it. Personality seems consistent and hard to change.

Yet, little things bother us with this understanding of personality. We all realize our nagging little inconsistencies. We also at times are struck by how differently we act in different situations. I do not act the same way at home with my wife as I do with my students or with colleagues in a professional meeting. We put this down to simple good sense. If I acted as formally with Kirby as I do with professors and graduate students, Kirby would not appreciate it. And if I acted as informally with those colleagues as at home, when I crack bad puns, belch out loud (I know you are shocked), and wear my tennis clothes 24-7, then the professionals would be appalled.

The Situation Side of Personality

So, we realize that the situations we live in profoundly shape our thoughts, feelings, and behaviors. Yet we usually do not admit that to ourselves.

The discipline of social psychology, though, has shown repeatedly that situations powerfully govern our behavior. Most of us will recall Phillip Zimbardo's (Haney, Banks, & Zimbardo, 1973) classic Stanford Prison experiment. He had students volunteer between terms for a couple of weeks of participation in a simulated prison exercise, with the students randomly assigned to be either guards or prisoners. On the day of the experiment's start, the police "arrested" the "prisoners" at their homes, carting them off to "prison"—the basement rooms of a hall at Stanford. The "guards" began to oversee the prisoners, dehumanizing them. The prisoners were assigned numbers instead of names. Guards wore a uniform. Zimbardo was the warden.

Within a week, prisoners and guards alike had fallen into roles that were guiding their behavior. Guards were hazing the prisoners. Prisoners were plotting escape and rebellion. Zimbardo decided to discontinue the study when his wife helped him realize that at home he was talking about crushing the rebellion of recalcitrant prisoners.

A strong situation—one with powerful norms—had transformed these normal college students into people with role-defined personalities. This is but one of the well-known instances of a strong situation almost completely prescribing behavior. Another is captured by an anecdote told by Yale psychologist Stanley Milgram after having completed his famous obedience experiments. Milgram organized a graduate seminar on the power of social norms. In the first class meeting, he asked one of the graduate students to break a simple norm—asking 20 elderly women for their seats on a Manhattan subway—and monitoring his reaction. The next week, the buzz was, "They gave up their seats." By class time, attendance in the room far exceeded the graduate students registered for the seminar.

The graduate student reported his results. "All 13 surrendered their seat without a word. It didn't matter whether the subway was empty or full, they ...."

"Wait a minute," said Milgram. "Weren't you supposed to ask 20? I thought I heard you say, '13.'"

"I'm not going back and asking any more!" the student practically shouted. "You can flunk me. I don't care. But I'm not asking any more."

"Whoooaaa, dude," (okay, you got me; Milgram probably did not say those exact words). "Violating this simple norm got quite an emotional reaction from you."

"Oh, yeah. Then you try it, Stanley."

"That's a great idea! Why don't we all try it? We'll all go to the city this weekend and each person will ask 20 elderly women for their seats. But it seems that it is difficult to carry that out in its entirety." He looked pointedly at the graduate student. "So, we'll do it in pairs, holding each other accountable. I'll join you."

The next week, excitement was still high. Milgram reported on his own experience. "I selected the first woman right off. The subway was crowded. I started over, but as I got near to her, I changed my mind—thought I'd wait another stop or so.

"'Go ahead, Stanley,' said the graduate student I was paired with.

"So, I walked right over, and boldly asked, in a voice about an octave higher than my normal voice, 'Excuse me, ma'am. May I have your seat?' She got up. I sat down. I started sweating. I felt like every eye on the entire subway system was on me. I thought I was going to throw up. So, I put my head down on my arms, and when the subway stopped, I hurried out without meeting anyone's eyes. Violating a social norm creates a powerful emotional reaction."

The Personal, Subjective, Narrative Side of Personality

We are exposed and expose ourselves to many situations in which norms guide our behavior. But there is a lot of subjectivity in deciding which situations we put ourselves in. For example, we choose our mate, and that structures millions of future situations. We choose our careers—millions more situations. We choose our avocations—millions more. These subjective choices lend consistency to experience. Because we need consistency, we use a narrative thread to tie together the experiences. We need consistency because it helps us predict responses of others and also predict and plan our own responses. It is adaptive to be able to predict what will occur. Thus, we spin a story about our consistent behavior. That story describes our Self and its relationship to others and to events we are likely to encounter in our world.

The Personality x Situation Interaction

Sometimes we stumble into more or less unusual situations. Those unusual situations cause us to do the unexpected. We do not have rehearsed moves in situations that we do not encounter frequently. When we find ourselves in an uncommon situation, we draw on familiar personality characteristics or we look around to decide what we should do (by seeing how others are reacting).

So recall Milgram's obedience experiments. Milgram had subjects, randomly placed in the role of "teacher," deliver (what they thought to be) electric shocks to a "learner" in an effort to teach the learner new paired words. In fact, the experiment was not about learning. It was about obedience of the "teacher" to the scientific authority—the "experimenter." Over half delivered over 450 volts (or would have, had the shocks been real). How could people shock a fellow human so much? Milgram concluded that the strong situation was responsible for the obedience more than people's personality. More of the variance in behavior could be predicted by how close to the "learner" the "teacher" was (further away meant more shocks were delivered) and how close to the "teacher" the "experimenter" was (closer meant more shocks) than by any personality disposition or characteristic—even stance toward violence and aggression, religion, and other dispositions.

The strong situation did not engender evil behavior. It did not transform the basically nice person into an evil one. Rather, the situation focused the "teacher's" attention and experience on two sets of virtues. Basically, the "teacher" was presented with a choice between the virtues of caring for a potentially injured helpless human (the "teacher" could hear the "learner" screaming in pain, refusing to participate, and claiming that he had heart problems) versus obeying authority, doing one's duty, contributing to science, and behaving in a way that did not ruin the "experimenter's" experiment. The "experimenter" blocked the first set of virtues by saying things like, "The experiment requires that you continue," "I'll take responsibility for what happens," "Although the shocks may be painful, they are not harmful," "Treat no response as a wrong answer," and "You can keep the money, but the experiment requires that you continue." Therefore, the "teacher" focused on the other set of virtues—duty and obedience.

We see the same phenomenon happening if we examine the transcripts of the Adolph Eichmann war-crimes trial. Hannah Arendt (1963) noted that, from Eichmann's point of view, he did not act evilly. He acted nobly. He performed difficult acts—killing millions of Jews, Russians, and others who were considered dispensable—for his country. He claimed that if Germany had won the war, he would be decorated as a hero. His crime was simply being on the losing side.

Fortunately, his argument did not win the day. Some virtues are not worth the cost in human suffering. It is good that the world established that in that public trial. We can understand Eichmann's psychology, but his behaviors were still crimes against humanity.

Changing Our Personality

General Strategy for Changing Personality

So, how is personality changed? At the most general level, one must change (1) the situations one is exposing oneself to or (2) the narrative thread that ties together experiences. Because the situations to which we usually expose ourselves are relatively stable and the stability and consistency of the narrative thread that we call the Self is tenaciously defended, it is difficult to make much headway at personality transformation. It usually requires either a powerful emotional experience or an accumulation of many emotional experiences to create a noticeable personality change.

Application to Forgiveness

Let us apply this understanding of changing personality to helping someone become a more forgiving person. Generally, one will have little success changing the Big Five (see Chapter 6). They are too deeply ingrained by nature and nurture. One will have more success helping modify the dispositions specifically related to decreasing unforgiveness or promoting forgiveness. The person presumably became either a grudge-holding or vengeful personality through having experienced transgressions in great number and eventually responding to them consistently. Rumination almost certainly played a large part. The entire stress-and-coping process becomes scripted. Acts are often interpreted as transgressions and appraised to be threats. The emotional reactions of anger and fear trigger rumination, which breeds grudges or plans for vengeance. Coping includes reacting in hostility, which leads to new transgressions.

Imagine that as a child, William was offended, reacted emotionally, and responded. Perhaps William replayed the incident mentally, seeking to understand and shape future emotional responses and behavior. Other transgressions occurred in rapid succession. After all, life is full of transgressions. As William began to develop a relatively consistent set of responses, his thoughts, feelings, and attitudes began to generalize. Perhaps, William developed a grudge against a teacher. He developed both a grudge and a tendency to seek vengeance toward Bobby, a schoolmate who bullied him. William nursed a small grudge against his mother and a large grudge against his father.

Generalization continues to occur. After being bullied by Bobby several times, William concludes, "I resent Bobby." Perhaps later, he concludes that he resents his teacher. Other grudges build up over time, and generalization can extend to William's personality. He becomes a person with a grudge-holding personality.

Generalization Is a Key to Personality Transformation

I belabor this process of generalization because the key to helping William change his personality, if he can achieve that, will involve reversing the generalization. There is no earthly way William can forgive every single transgression he experienced in every relationship throughout his entire life. So, personality change must involve changing key elements and hoping that generalization will occur. Namely, personality transformation may begin by forgiving a pivotal incident with Bobby, then another with Bobby, then another. At some point, William might conclude, "I have forgiven Bobby" (not just forgiven the important transgressions Bobby perpetrated).

Emotion Is Another Key to Personality Transformation

Emotion marks experiences as important. We do not get emotional about successfully arriving at work each morning or fixing a cup of coffee. Emotion marks events that are important. So, generalization—that helps William forgive Bobby—is aided if he forgives two or three transgressions that were emotionally important. Then he might quickly say he forgives Bobby. He might forgive seven transgressions about which he feels little emotion and still hold a grudge against Bobby.

Becoming a more forgiving person involves a generalization across relationships, too. That generalization can occur even if William grants decisional forgiveness but does not yet experience emotional forgiveness. If William declares decisional forgiveness for Bobby accompanied by an emotional insight into Bobby's background and motivations, that is a start. If William sees the same pattern in his teacher, that furthers the change to a more forgiving personality. If William then forgives his parents, that pushes generalization further. If William also works out his grudges against his therapist, the accumulation of insights into others and into his own patterns of behavior can seal the changes in William's personality.

Successful psychotherapy that produces lasting effects, though, usually does not seek merely to produce an insight and hope for personality transformation. Freud originally thought insight alone would achieve personal transformation. "Let the unconscious become conscious" was his formula for success during the early years. Rather, successful psychotherapy requires many repetitions before it makes its way into the enduring thoughts, attitudes, and behaviors of the person. Freud quickly shifted his formula for successful therapy to "Where id was, let ego be." That too required many applications. Only then did generalization occur.

A person with a grudge-holding personality usually is beset by anxious, depressed, resentful, and bitter unforgiveness. If a grudge-holding person is to change his or her personality, the person must change the pattern of emotional experience—replacing the negative with more positive other-oriented emotions. That must be done often enough and powerfully enough to allow generalization. That could be accomplished by many forms of psychotherapy, such as emotion-focused therapy, psychodynamic therapy, cognitive-behavioral or cognitive therapy, or a variety of others.

A person with a vengeful personality, similarly, will be beset by rumination, though the content will likely be flavored with more anger, rationalizations of restoring justice, and emotional unforgiveness with a mixture of the same emotions as grudge-holding but in different proportions. Again, changing the emotional experiences enough to permit generalization is the key to changing a vengeful personality.

Practical Suggestions for Changing Personality

Be Alert to Surprising Invitations to Change

Often, chronic (and even acute) suffering opens people to dramatic change. Wearied by pain, they are open to redrawing their self-concept. One of my clients was at a party. He stumbled upon his friends using cocaine and felt pressured into joining. "It didn't take much pressure, unfortunately," he said. Not only did he use coke once, but he "took several lines before the night was done."

"What happened then?" I asked.

"I woke up the next day in a fog. I couldn't seem to think clearly. I was terrified that I had burned out my brain. I did a lot of lines that night."

"So, you were afraid?"

"Not just fear. It was terror. But also a deep, deep disgust in myself. I hated myself. I cried for 3 days, on and off. I kept saying, 'That is not me. I don't do hard drugs.' Yet I had done coke. I couldn't deny it. I had to decide what the real me was. Was I a cocaine user, or not?"

"And you decided …?"

"I decided I wasn't, but because I had done so, I needed to figure out who I was. So I came to therapy to try to find out."

Psychologists William R. Miller and Janet C'de Baca (2001) have studied many people who underwent dramatic personality transformations, or "quantum changes," as they termed them. They described a man who drank alcohol a lot. Still, he maintained that he did not have a drinking problem. One day, he drove to school to pick up his child. As he waited, he decided he needed a beer. So he drove away. As he exited the pick-up area, he saw his son in his rear-view mirror.

"I just kept driving. I left him standing at the curb, calling to me as I drove off to drink beer. I had those beers, but I was disgusted with myself. So, I vowed I would quit drinking." He never had another drink.

People seek help in the midst of emotional conflicts. Often they have behaved terribly toward someone they love—or once loved. They feel guilty, ashamed, disgusted, depressed, and self-condemning. They are disillusioned with themselves. These surprising moments can strongly motivate change. People at the end of their rope are looking for a new hold on life.

Decide and Commit

First, the person must decide to change and commit to that change. Often, people say they have decided to change but are holding back, keeping their options open. For personality change to last, one needs to commit oneself and maintain the effort for at least 6 weeks, preferably 6 months. As therapist, help the person decide to become a more forgiving person. Ask, "What is keeping you from changing?" Follow up with, "Would you like to try to remove those barriers to change?" and "If you could change one thing that you believe would make a difference, what would you change first?"

Have the Person Self-Assess in Writing

Second, one needs a clear initial assessment in writing. As people change, their memory fades. Their standards shift. When a client decides to become more forgiving, he or she should make an assessment in writing of the exact nature of the problem. Direct the client to describe his or her feelings, and mention specific failures to forgive. Have the person estimate the frequency of vengeful or grudge-filled acts. This should be filed and not referred to during attempts to change. At the end of the period, a self-evaluation should again be written—not necessarily standardized testing, although that is ideal because there are norms.

Help the Person Find a Model to Emulate

Third, one needs a positive model to know what one is trying to achieve. One way to do this is to select a person who is well known and respected as a forgiving person—say, Nelson Mandela. The therapist, of course, realizes that selecting an ideal forgiver can set a perfectionistic person up for failure. Thus, this technique should be used at the therapist's discretion. The therapist can also have the person search his or her own life and select an exemplar forgiver. That puts flesh on the ideal.

Learn the Skills of Forgiving

Fourth, select a program to promote a more forgiving personality. Several programs exist to teach people how to forgive, which I have mentioned previously. People can learn essential skills of forgiving by working through books, joining psychoeducational groups, going to church-related classes, or attending community lectures. Much practical wisdom exists about forgiving, and people can systematically learn more about how to be a better forgiver. Needless to say, I believe the programs we have developed are excellent ones (and have research support to document their efficacy). You will learn practical steps to promote forgiveness and reconciliation in Part III.

Practice Forgiving

Fifth, as people learn how to forgive, they must move learning into their daily lives. They must practice the skills of forgiving. If they decide that they wish to forgive by empathizing, they must practice empathy. If they need to reduce their rumination, they should practice stopping negative thoughts and replacing them with more positive thoughts. Importantly, they must practice the component skills necessary to make up the whole process of forgiveness.

Search Out Old Grudges or Lingering Hurts

Sixth, it is important to put the skills together into examples. Most people can survey their lives and come up with numerous examples of people toward whom they probably have remaining unforgiveness. An easy way to do this is to begin to think through their development from as early as they can recall. Think about specific incidents. Visualize the person who inflicted the transgression upon them. Write a brief account of what happened. Then attempt to systematically work to forgive that person. Repeat that with at least 10 people who have harmed or wounded them. Practice systematically.

Be Alert to New Opportunities to Practice

In addition, people need to be willing to employ these skills when new transgressions beset them. They can permit themselves to react and not try to stifle all negative emotion, but when they get away from the immediacy of the transgression, they might think back to what occurred and attempt to forgive.

The Easiest Acts to Forgive Are Those Where No Unforgiveness Occurs

Obviously, one of the best ways to deal with unforgiveness is to never allow it to develop. Help people try to recognize conflicts early. They can monitor their behavior so that they do not provoke other people unnecessarily.

Find Reminders

In any systematic change, people must learn ways to cue themselves to employ desired behaviors and interrupt old patterns of harmful behavior. Thus, people must decide how they can trigger the thought that they want to be more forgiving when that thought is needed. By committing to a 6-month program and systematically practicing forgiveness, this becomes a response that more likely occurs in the heat of the moment and can short-circuit anger and unforgiveness before it gets a toehold. People will never successfully eliminate all negativity in their life. So, they will have to go back, at times, and deal with unforgiveness.

Take Stock of Progress Periodically

People need to take stock of their progress at times, preferably in writing. This can be easily done during therapy, but people need to develop ways to take stock after completing their therapy. Every year, on New Year's Day, I set goals for myself. I always look forward to New Year's. It is then that I evaluate how much I succeeded in the recently ended year. Clients can also measure themselves against their own yardstick (without being as obsessive-compulsive as I am).

Celebrate Success but Don't Expect Perfection

Finally, celebrate successes, but don't expect perfection. Some people become so intent on changing themselves that they never appreciate their accomplishments. This is one of the reasons that they might want to take stock periodically. It is unrealistic to believe that anyone ever will totally defeat unforgiveness. Progress is being unforgiving less often and, when we slip into unforgiveness, being negative for shorter times. Over time, people can change their personality if they systematically attempt to do so.

Conclusion

When people are under stress—including times when they want desperately to forgive but cannot seem to find the internal wherewithal to succeed—they often attempt to cope by coming to therapy. Therapy in which forgiveness plays a part often aims to help people deal with immediate stressors and stress (such as forgiving a troubling event). However, often people seek deeper personality transformation. They want to become more forgiving people. In the next part of the book, I will describe ways to help them achieve such a goal.

PART III

Clinical Applications to Promote Forgiveness and Reconciliation

CHAPTER 9

A General Approach to Psychotherapy

In developing a stress-and-coping theory of forgiveness and considering its application to forgiving and unforgiving personalities and their modification, we have laid the groundwork for an intervention to promote forgiveness and reconciliation. Before jumping into the midst of the specific interventions, let us lay just a bit more groundwork. I will develop a general approach to psychotherapy.

In this chapter, I will describe a general approach to psychotherapy. In chapter 10, I will apply it to promoting forgiveness and becoming a more forgiving person. Also in chapter 10, I extend it to promoting forgiveness of self. In chapter 11, I extend it to reconciliation. In chapter 12, I examine the experimental evidence for the interventions. The approach was first articulated in Worthington (1982) and subsequent revisions were made. Most recently, the approach was described in Worthington (2005d; see also Worthington, Mazzeo, and Canter, 2005; Worthington, O'Connor, Berry, Sharp, Murray, and Yi, 2005).

Personality Change

Personality change involves initiating change attempts, sustaining effort at change, and maintaining gains. To do so requires that a person modify the strong situations that govern unwanted behavior, replacing them by strong situations that will foster desired behavior. Or personality change also involves modifying the narrative threads that unify many of the person's experiences into reasonably consistent narratives.

Psychotherapy must help the person accomplish those tasks. Therapy can do so because it is, itself, a strong situation. Psychotherapy is unusual (for most people). It occurs in times of emotional upheaval and arousal and when a person is trying to solve his or her problems.

True, often the person is almost unconsciously saying, "Fix my problem, but don't change me." Master therapist Sheldon Kopp (1970) once likened change in therapy to Dorothy in *The Wizard of Oz*. Dorothy wanted to get back to Kansas. She appealed to the ostensibly powerful wizard for help. Yet, the Wizard sent her not to Kansas but on a quest in which she had to intentionally defeat the source of pain and evil in the kingdom—the Wicked Witch of the East. After the end of her successful quest, in which Dorothy discovered her heart of compassion for others and a sense of courage in the face of uncertainty and danger, she returned to the Wizard. He was revealed as a mere human, rather than as super change agent. She finds that she always had the power within her to return home, if she but used it.

Psychotherapists do not tend to think of therapy this way, but they hope that psychotherapy will be a powerfully strong situation. In fact, I personally (irrationally) hope that I can help every person I take as a client. That is, we therapists hope to create a therapeutic situation that is so strong everyone responds in the same way—changing in a direction that the client wants. Of course, that direction is different for each client. Each client's life circumstances and challenges differ. Each client requires the therapist to adjust the general plan many times, so that each counseling interaction—indeed, each moment of counseling—is in some ways unique, even if the strategy is universal.

In the same way, the therapist knows in general how to help every person before seeing the person. That is, therapists have a general strategy for therapy. That strategy has little variability from person to person. Freud always tried to promote insight into the person's psychodynamics. He sought to help the person gain ego control over his or her behavior. I doubt that there is a recorded (or unrecorded) case in which Freud said, "I can't possibly help this person with the psychoanalytic method. I need to find a behavior therapist to refer this person to." Similarly, behavior therapists know before seeing any client that they will help the person change the thoughts, manage the environmental stimuli, and change the contingencies that affect behavior. Cognitive therapists look for the locus of change in the beliefs, assumptions, concepts, values, momentary self-talk, and images—in short, the cognitive structures and processes that govern people's behavior. Whether a therapist is psychoanalytically informed, behavioral, or cognitive—or embraces any other theory—that therapist has a general strategy.

The client, as an individual, will fit the strategy more or less closely. Good theories of psychotherapy are those that can account for many people's individual life-circumstances. Good theories of psychotherapy also promote measurable change in the client to achieve the goals that the client sets in therapy.

Process of Change

All therapies first make a personal connection with the client, second move in a positive direction in which the client says he or she wants to go, third pull the client along, and fourth separate from the client, leaving the client capable of sustaining the new direction. This is accomplished in six distinct steps: (1) connecting, (2) rethinking, (3) acting, (4) following and supporting, (5) maintaining, and (5) terminating.

Connecting (Step 1)

The therapist connects with the client through listening, understanding, and communicating their understanding to the client. The technology of accomplishing this is common knowledge among therapists and is woven into training from day one. Therapists use active listening skills, show empathy for the client, and actively communicate that empathy and understanding to the client.

Reflecting one's understanding, though, is not a matter of parroting back what the client says or naming the feelings that the client demonstrates. As Meichenbaum (1977) showed in his cognitive-behavior modification, a therapist has many choices in what to reflect, what to express curiosity about, and what to ask the client to talk more about. Whatever the therapist pays attention to, the client will talk about. The client will soon adduce evidence from his or her own life that the problem (and solution) lies in the topics that are receiving the most attention from the therapist and the client. If the therapist attends to client thoughts, the client will soon see how thoughts play a pivotal role in the problem. If the therapist attends to client emotions, the client will soon see how important emotions are.

So, when a client begins to identify unforgiveness as a focal problem, the therapist should listen, reflect, and inquire curiously about several things. Let us listen to a digested version of this conversation between the therapist (T) and client (let us call her Clara, abbreviated Cl), who began talking about her unwillingness to forgive her father for his alcoholism, his resulting neglect of her and her mother, their family's economic hardships (due to losing his job repeatedly and eventually getting into an expensive treatment program), and his unpredictability in providing emotional support.

Cl-1:   I hate myself because I can't forgive my father. Rationally, I know that I ought to forgive. It isn't hurting him that I can't get over the harms his alcoholism did. But it isn't rational. It's emotional. I feel unforgiving and it bothers me to no end. I want to forgive.

T-1:   You say you are having trouble forgiving your father, and you want to be more forgiving of him. What kinds of emotions do you experience when you're unforgiving? [**Comment: I have to begin with her emotional experience of unforgiveness if I am going to understand her.**]

Cl-2:   I don't think about it all the time, but when I do, if I dwell on it, I get in an absolute rage. I want to hit and scream and tell him off. I want to hurt him, and get back at him.

T-2:   You sound angry. But you said you didn't think about it much. Yet you do think about it?

Cl-3:   Yes, many times a day. Anytime I'm sad, or feel like I can't act in a *normal* way.

T-3:   Normal?

Cl-4:   You know. If I can't connect with someone emotionally. If I can't get over a slight. If I get to feeling sorry for myself. That isn't *normal*. I don't want to be that way.

T-4:   But you feel upset, angry, and full of rage at your father several times a day.

Cl-5:   I spend a lot of my time outside of work alone. That's the worst. I start getting into a mood. Lay around the house. Eat things I shouldn't. Watch DVD movies to keep my mind occupied. Otherwise, I brood.

T-5:   What's brooding like for you?

Cl-6:   Sulking, and—you know, I'm embarrassed to admit it, but—even kind of plotting pay-back. I want to hurt him, make him suffer like my mother and I have. Because of *him*.

    [**Comment: We have been talking around the experience, but the essence of good psychotherapy is not in general description but in powerful immediate experience. I need to get her to talk more immediately about her experience.**]

T-6:   I know it's embarrassing, but would you just pretend that you are alone. You are brooding about your father and his drinking and all the pain that has caused. Would you just narrate your thoughts aloud?

Cl-7:   Well, that's different—with you here and all. And I don't think organized, really. I just think things, you know. But I'll try. Okay, so, like yesterday, I had a bad interaction with my boss, and I went home and brooded about it. I was puttering around the kitchen and thinking, *She's such a jerk. I hate her. She never understands me, and she's just not a nice person to work for. It makes me feel the same as getting scolded by Dad. How did he have the right to scold me? He never did a thing good after he started drinking. He just raged around and called us names and blamed us and put us down and treated us like pieces of dung. I hate what he did. Why couldn't he just have seen he was killing us, and stopped drinking? Why did he have to keep on with his drinking and irresponsibility until he wrecked his life and did a pretty good job of wrecking ours? I wish he knew how much damage he caused. If only I could, I'd call him up and let him have it. Maybe I'd tell him that he was the one that caused Mom to commit suicide. Yeah, he'd deny it, because she blamed her losing a job in her note. But it'd sting him. It'd give him things to think about at night when he's alone.* [Tears begin to fall down Clara's cheeks.] *I'd like to see him just skewered, like a piece of meat, turning over the coals. Damn, it makes me mad to think about him!* [Slams her fist onto her leg.] *I feel so frustrated! I know I can't really do anything. But dammit, I want to or I'll scream!* [She stops talking, wipes at her running nose, takes a broken breath.] I hate to do this. I really do. This is exactly like it happens. I get mad at him. Mad at Mom for suiciding. Mad at myself. I didn't think this would get to me, but just getting into it gets me so riled up. So *pissed.*

T-7:   It seems terribly stressful and painful for you.

Cl-8:   It is stressful. And it is very painful. It's painful because I hate myself so much that he still gets to me. So often. Knowing that I get wound up like this is a constant source of stress. I can't get away from it. It's depressing.

T-8:   You seem to have a tender heart. You are stressed and pained, and try to cope with it by thinking about it. But thinking and "brooding" moves you toward a side of yourself that you don't like—the angry side.

Cl-9:   It's not just anger. It's frustration, resentment, and, well, like you said, stress. I hear myself, and I hear bitterness just pouring out of me. I hate what he did to us, and I hate that it's still bothering me—maybe even more now than when he was living in our house. And it affects my whole life.

T-9:   It sounds as if you feel a lot of unforgiveness, and you can't control it at all.

Cl-10:   Well, if I nip it in the bud. [**Comment: At this point, Clara takes the conversation toward coping. If she had continued to talk about her feelings of lack of control and depression— which actually I was hoping she'd do—I would follow her. But because she headed toward coping, I followed her there.**] You know, if I keep distracting myself and don't get into this mood or into the brooding, then I can control it some.

The first step, connecting, and the second, helping the client rethink the situation, go hand-in-glove. By directing reflections or questions, even when following the client, the therapist helps the client begin to rethink the problem.

Rethink the Problem (Step 2)

People are meaning-making creatures. They try to understand how their life fits together. When they enter therapy, they have a conceptualization of their problems. But it is not helping them solve the problems. So, therapists must guide the client toward some different understanding of the problem. Furthermore, the understanding leads the person to change the situations of his or her life or the personal narrative connecting the strands of experiences. This, of course, is where the personal theory of psychotherapy of the therapist enters the equation. A psychodynamic therapist will help the client see (and later change) the psychodynamics dominating behavior. The behavior therapist will help the client see (and later change) the roles of thoughts, situations, rewards, and punishments. The emotion-focused therapist will help the person process the relevant emotional conflicts that disturb adult attachment relationships and integrate emotional experience and later adjust differently to those.

Concerning our client (Clara), if I want to help her rethink her unforgiveness in a way that helps her change, then I must get across the main points derived from the stress-and-coping theory of forgiveness—scattered throughout therapy as they become relevant. These include

- Forgiveness is one way of coping with the stress of unforgiveness (see T-7 and Cl-8 and Cl-9). If it eventually does not work for her, there are other ways—such as accepting and letting go. Because she has already said she wants to forgive, we will go with that first.
- The magnitude of the injustice gap is generally proportional to the amount of unforgiveness felt and to the difficulty of forgiving. So, she can make forgiveness easier if she can reduce the injustice gap.
- There are two types of forgiveness: decisional forgiveness and emotional forgiveness. She can decide to forgive. But she must

deliberately try to experience emotional forgiveness; it will not magically occur if she decides to forgive.

- Emotional forgiveness occurs through the mechanism of emotional replacement of unforgiveness with positive other-oriented emotions toward her father. She must see her father differently—with empathy or compassion—if she is to forgive.

- She can be her own therapist, actively shaping situations and intentionally changing her behavior, thoughts, and emotions. The therapist helps her become her own independent change agent. Part of being her own therapist involves not trying to change alone but consulting the resources in her environment to help her forgive. Those resources provide stable situations that reinforce her personal behavior, and thus personality. Those resources might include (a) her religious beliefs, values, and community or (b) a trusted friend or spouse.

- Becoming a more forgiving person involves forgiving specific transgressions by her father, eventually generalizing to forgiving her father, and then forgiving other people in her life until her personality is more forgiving.

Obviously, helping a client rethink a problem is not a matter of direct instruction, as it can be in portions of psychoeducational interventions. Rather, helping rethink the problem blends intimately with understanding the client and communicating that understanding to the client (Connecting, Step 1). For Clara, we have already laid the groundwork for treating unforgiveness as a stress reaction to transgressions (T-7 and Cl-8) and for treating forgiveness as a coping mechanism (T-8). Let us see how I might help the client rethink her problem with her father. Let us repeat the last interchange with Clara. Recall that I am following Clara's lead, not initiating an abrupt change and expecting her to follow my lead.

T-9:   It sounds as if you feel a lot of unforgiveness, and you can't control it at all.

Cl-10:   Well, if I nip it in the bud. You know, if I keep distracting myself and don't get into this mood or into the brooding, then I can control it some.

T-10:   So, you have a few ways to cope with this stress of your unforgiveness and desire to get even. But they aren't really fully effective. [**I repeat the idea of coping.**]

Cl-11:   Not at all.

T-11:   So, once your "moods" get started, how do they end? How do you get out of one of your moods or one of your broods?

Cl-12:   Sometimes, like just a few minutes ago, I just get so upset that I wind down, angry, depressed, and wounded. I hate that.

T-12:   I could see how wounded you were.

Cl-13:   Sometimes, I just kind of grumble around and then my mind moves to something else. Not very often, I recognize that I'm about to flame out, and I stop myself.

T-13:   How do you do that?

Cl-14:   I think something like, "Don't go there." Or, "You know where this'll lead."

T-14:   And that helps?

Cl-15:   Sometimes. Mostly, though, I don't recognize until I'm too far into raging.

T-15:   Let me ask you to estimate about how many times out of 10 you can either stop or head off your thoughts before they get you into a rage or a brooding mood?

Cl-16:   I don't know. Maybe not even 1 in 10. More like 1 out of 20 I suppose?

T-16:   I wonder. You seem pretty resourceful. Is there anything that you might do to increase this to 2 out of 20?

Cl-17:   Sure. I think just paying attention to it could probably up it to 5 out of 20.

T-17:   Yes, but paying attention to our thinking is something we get used to very quickly. Then we don't pay attention, and we slide back. Is there anything you could change to remind you not to "go there," or could take you to a different place? I just want you to change from 1 in 20 to 2 in 20. But I wonder if you can come up with something that would make it likely that the small improvement lasts?

Cl-18:   Maybe physically moving. Like if I'm brooding in the kitchen, I could move outside or go do the laundry. That might work.

Later, we pick up the conversation at a different topic.

Cl-24:   So, I want to forgive him. But I've wanted to forgive for years, and I can't make myself. Every time I try to forgive, I get angry all over again within a day or two.

T-24:   What would it mean if you forgave him? What would be different about your life?

Cl-25:   I would be less bitter all the time. And I would not get into these moods. I suppose that if I forgave, I'd just be free from the hate I've felt for so many years.

T-25:   So, you'd feel differently? You'd experience less negative emotion?

Cl-26: Yes. I'd be free of the hate and anger.

T-26: You said that you had tried to forgive him many times. How did you try to forgive?

Cl-27: You know, I just said I forgave him.

T-27: Hummm.

Cl-28: What do you mean, "Hummm?"

T-28: Just putting together what you were saying—you'd just say you forgave him and then you'd suddenly feel completely free of hate and anger.

Cl-29: [Laughs] Yeah, I guess it doesn't make sense now that I think of it. It sounds a little unrealistic that I ought to feel so free of the hate just because I said I forgave him.

T-29: I think it is important to decide you want to forgive. So you are on the right track. I also think it is important that you get rid of your hatred and anger toward your dad. That is a part of forgiving. But maybe those two parts of forgiving are not joined at the hip.

Cl-30: So, I don't get it. So, you mean, do each separately. How can I feel less hate and anger if I haven't decided to forgive?

T-30: I'm not sure you can. You have to decide to forgive. But just because you decided to forgive doesn't mean you'll automatically feel emotional forgiveness.

Cl-31: So, I need to do something special to experience less hate and anger?

T-31: Yes. What do you think you could do to change your feelings from negative to more positive?

Cl-32: Maybe if he would come and get down on his knees and grovel in front of me and beg me to forgive him, I might—just might— feel a little more positively toward him. Maybe that would make it easier to forgive him. If I thought he meant it. Oh, yeah, and if he gave me about a million dollars. That'd help.

T-32: So you feel that he did such injustices that there is this huge amount of injustice that has to be taken care of before you could feel forgiveness for him?

Cl-33: Right. He needs to pay and pay big time.

T-33: So you said, if he gave you a million dollars, you'd forgive him? [She nods.] What if he gave you $999,999? Could you forgive him then?

Cl-34: Well, yes. Okay, I see where you are heading. You'll keep saying one less dollar each time. Well, I don't think there is anything magical about a million dollars, but I just want to see him get his just desserts.

T-34: And that makes a lot of sense. The more justice that you see done—or the more you get revenge, or the more he might make some kind of apology and restitution—then the less the amount of injustice you have to forgive. So, the easier it is to feel more emotionally forgiving. But if you are to forgive, you must, in the end, forgive something that justice couldn't pay for.

Cl-35: That makes sense. If I could really pay him back, even-Steven, there wouldn't be anything to forgive. But how could I change my feelings? I've tried. How could I forgive?

T-35: You tell me. How could you neutralize the negative unforgiving emotions you feel?

Cl-36: Well, his apology would make me feel better toward him, so I guess anything that made me feel better toward him might work the same way.

T-36: Great thinking! But you think of him as such a jerk now. You seem to think that he absolutely didn't care for you or your mother. So, there might not be any way to think differently of him.

Cl-37: Well, he's not all bad, I guess. In fact, he's really more piti-ful than evil. I mean, really, I hate what he did, but as I think about it, I know he didn't want to ruin his life, Mom's life, and mine. It hurt him, too. He couldn't stop himself from drink-ing. [**Comment: She has worked with me to develop an idea of forgiveness, but the idea developed during the ebb and flow of conversation, so I need to put it all together.**]

T-37: Okay. Hummm, okay. So, let's stop a minute and see if I under-stand what you're telling me. It's a lot. Let's see if I have it all. You said, just making a decision isn't enough by itself to make you feel more forgiving. You need to do something (or he does) that would make you feel more positive and therefore would neutral-ize the negativity of unforgiveness. You could wait around for him to come grovel at your feet.

Cl-38: Not in this lifetime.

T-38: And you obviously don't want to stake the family ranch on that. Or you could try to understand his weakness, rather than just treat it as if he had set out with single-minded purpose to destroy you.

Cl-39: Whether that was his purpose or not, I feel that he did a pretty good job. But yes, that wasn't what he wanted to do. He is weak more than evil.

T-39: So, if I understand you correctly, if you put your mind to under-standing, empathizing, pitying him, maybe someday feeling compassion toward him and for his weaknesses, then that might combat the negative unforgiving feelings. That might help you feel forgiveness, not just decide to forgive. Did I get it right?

Cl-40:   Right. Yeah. I hear you. But, I've hated for so long. How can I change?

T-40:   Well, if you're right in your "theory"—that you need to empathize more or pity him more, and that will help you forgive—then I think I can work with you to develop some practical plans to try and see whether it works.

Make Action Plans Based on the New Conceptualization (Step 3)

Rethinking alone will rarely help a person experience emotional forgiveness. The person must carry out action plans, in session or out of session, to change his or her experience. Good action plans must make change seem possible, make it count, make it sensible, make an emotional impact, make change last, and allow it to spread.

Make change seem possible. By the time people get to therapy, they are usually discouraged about the possibility of change (see Cl-4, Cl-5, Cl-6, and Cl-7). They lack hope. They lack the willpower to change and the waypower to change (Snyder, 1994). That is, they might have lost the motivation to try to change, or they might believe that they have exhausted all the ways possible to bring about change. The therapist's task is to restore both willpower and waypower to change. Willpower can be restored by calling the person to a high challenge. The therapist can attribute positive motives or personal attributes (see T-8) to the person when the therapist detects those motives. (Insincerely or falsely attributing positive motives to a person will boomerang.) The therapist can also attribute the desire to change to the client, when appropriate. The therapist can share the past successes to promote hope for success. This includes mentioning empirical support in psychoeducational formats and with couples enrichment. I have taught the approach, supervised clinicians using the approach, and used it myself in psychotherapy.

Make change count. All changes are not created equal. When clients make some changes, those changes redirect the course of their life. Other changes have virtually no effect on the client. Forgiveness is difficult. When a client works hard to forgive someone who is hard to forgive, the event makes a big impression. The struggle can result in a battle that turns the course of the war toward virtue and away from a slide into self-destruction. A therapist and client can work on only a limited number of transgressions over the course of psychotherapy. So, it is important to choose wisely which transgressions are to be targeted. In learning the method I describe in Chapter 10, a transgression of moderate difficulty should be addressed first. That should prepare the person to try to forgive a difficult, personally meaningful transgression.

Make change sensible. People often learn better when they manipulate concrete objects rather than mere words, or when they turn concepts into something measurable. (For instance, see what happened when I had Clara translate her ability to control her thoughts into numbers; see T-15 through T-17.) I have argued that in couples and family counseling, it is essential to employ tangible objects and activities rather than merely talking about concepts (Worthington, 2005d). Activities should, as often as possible, be sensed—hence "sensible." In individual psychotherapy, many of the exercises that form the basis of the action plans involve manipulating physical objects. People complete written assessments rather than merely report how they feel. People build empathy through an empty-chair experience. People make up a written certificate to signify that they have forgiven.

Make change emotional. Emotion marks important events. Thus, emotion is at the core of almost every psychotherapy. It is thought to play a different role in each. In psychoanalytically informed therapy, emotion-near experiences are the grist for the psychotherapeutic mill. Abreaction involves an emotional working through of conflicts. In emotion-focused therapy, emotions reveal and conceal inner values. Thus, displayed anger may conceal fear. Displayed anxiety might conceal anger. People learn to identify the opposite pole of their emotional experience to get in touch with the full range of their emotional experience. In rational emotive therapy (RET), cognition mediates the connection between situations and emotion rather than situations directly affecting emotions. In traditional behavior therapy, rewards arouse positive emotions, which often form the basis for change.

In my approach to therapy, the heart of emotional forgiveness is emotional replacement of negative unforgiving emotions with positive other-oriented emotions (see T-35 and Cl-36). The therapeutic route by which it occurs is not prescribed. Therapies tend to be either emotionally evocative or emotionally calming. For example, emotion-focused therapy is emotionally evocative, as are psychodynamic approaches. They arouse emotion, and if they do not do so, success is thought to be hard to come by. For example, if a client in psychodynamic therapy does not resist, the resistance cannot be interpreted. RET is emotionally evocative. If it does not arouse emotions, the rational refutation of the maladaptive cognition is obscured. On the other hand, many therapies are emotionally calming. Behavior therapy does not seek to promote resistance, but to promote cooperation. Thus, emotion is calmed. Cognitive behavior therapy is typically emotionally calming. It seeks to promote cooperation and keep the emotions low. In my therapy, the therapist will not stifle emotional expression (see Cl-7). However, therapeutic progress in emotional replacement is most likely when the unforgiving emotions are experienced at a low level (see T-36 and Cl-37). It is then—when they are "as-if" emotional experiences—that they are most susceptible to replacement. If a person is highly aroused in expressing unforgiveness, a large amount of positive emotional experience is needed to neutralize the negative emotion.

Make changes last. To make changes last, it is necessary to make the therapeutic events memorable, use ceremonies and symbols, and repeat the basic forgiveness activities often. Memorable events are punctuated. They stand apart from the normal flow of conversation. In therapy, the therapist can punctuate events by making them unusual or by designating them as important. For example, in the dialogue above, when I asked the client to narrate her thoughts (see T-6), that was an unusual event. It triggered deep involvement, which she punctuated by emotion (see Cl-7). Another way to set a therapeutic event apart is to ask the client to do an exercise. I provide many forgiveness exercises in chapters 10, 11, and 12.

Ceremonies and symbolic activities also will make the effects of an intervention last. When a person works through the five steps of my model to REACH forgiveness, then the person can make a certificate attesting to him or her that forgiveness has been granted and experienced. One of the exercises I use to help people signify successfully forgiving is to have them write a short version of the transgression on their hand using permanent black ink—the original shorthand. Then, the person washes the transgression from their hand. Usually, though, the ink will not come completely off, which allows me to note that repetition is often needed before forgiveness is complete.

Make forgiveness spread. To help a client forgive a person or become a more forgiving person, forgiveness must generalize. Generalization will happen mostly through repeating interventions. A person can move through the REACH acrostic with a moderate transgression, then repeat the REACH acrostic with a severe transgression, and repeat it again with another important transgression. The repetitions continue as long as the client has not fully forgiven the person. A second person can be forgiven in a similar way—using multiple transgressions. Additional people are added, with each helping the client to generalize and become a more forgiving person.

The client must carry out the plans. Action plans are formulated piecemeal, perhaps one or two exercises or spontaneous enactments during a session and another as homework. The essential part of change, though, is creating experiences for the client. Homework is essential. Therapy is usually limited to one of the 168 hours in the week. If change is to occur and to last, it must extend into the other 167 nontherapy hours. It is essential, then, that the therapist seeks to insure that the client is carrying out attempts to become more forgiving in his or her nontherapy hours.

Follow Up on Action Plans and Support Change Attempts (Step 4)

Clients often stop doing homework because therapists fail to ask whether the client actually did the homework as it was assigned and what the client got out of it. Client compliance is essential. If the therapist does not take the homework seriously enough to spend time talking about it, then the client also will not.

Plan for Maintenance (Step 5)

Maintenance of gains will occur if the client has changed structures in his or her life. The structures could be cognitive or behavioral structures—the narrative threads linking meaningful experiences, memories, and associations and associated behavioral habits—or other structures like relationships, situations to which people expose themselves, or people with whom they interact.

Termination (Step 6)

Rarely is forgiveness the total focus of psychotherapy. Other issues must be dealt with before termination.

Conclusion

I have described a general approach to psychotherapy that does not presume whether the theory is psychodynamic, cognitive, or behavioral, or is identified with an established school of therapy. It is a process approach. Armed with a general conception of the flow of therapy, we are ready to consider specifically how to promote forgiveness.

CHAPTER **10**

Intervening Specifically to Promote Forgiveness

Within psychotherapy, there is room for guiding a client through specific steps to forgiving. Importantly, this is not a "program" that a client is run through. If therapy works as it should, the therapist will find a natural opening. Let us recall the conversation with Clara in chapter 9. The therapist has just paused and summarized where the conversation has led:

T-39:   So, if I understand you correctly, if you put your mind to understanding, empathizing, pitying him, maybe someday feeling compassion toward him and for his weaknesses, then that might combat the negative unforgiving feelings. That might help you feel forgiveness, not just decide to forgive. Did I get it right?

Cl-40:   Right. Yeah. I hear you. But, I've hated for so long. How can I change?

T-40:   Well, if you're right in your "theory"—that you need to empathize more or pity him more, and that will help you forgive— then I think I can work with you to develop some practical plans to try and see whether it works.

The client might express interest in this method, as Clara did.

Cl-41:   I'd like to work on forgiving. I've wanted to, but never seemed to know exactly how to go about it.

169

T-41:   This seems to fit exactly what you've described as your difficulty. It is a method that has been studied through controlled experiments, so lots of people have benefited from using the method. It is summarized in the word REACH—as in REACH forgiveness. Each of the letters stands for a step you go through. How do you feel about it?

Cl-42:   It sounds awfully simple. I've been trying for years to forgive. I can't believe that five steps and a puff of dust are going to help me forgive.

T-42:   You're right. The steps are easy to summarize, but aren't magic. They'll take a LOT of work from you. The nice thing is that others have walked down that road, too.

Cl-43:   Okay, we can try.

Bird's Eye View of Five Steps to REACH Forgiveness

The acrostic allows clients to remember the process. But the model begins even before the first step. Forgiveness must be defined. The client can often be led to derive the definition for him or her. Forgiveness is defined as being of two types—decisional and emotional forgiveness (see Worthington, 2003).

In the first step, R = Recall the Hurt, people recall the hurt in helpful ways. Usually, clients are very emotional as they begin to relate the harm to the therapist. The therapist allows and encourages such emotional expression. At that point, assessment should occur. Assessment is part of listening to the client's story. Some standardized instruments might supplement conversation.

At E = Empathize with the Person Who Hurt You, empathy is not the sole content of that step. Rather, at the E step, the client is led to experience empathy, sympathy, compassion, or love for the person. Through those other-oriented positive emotions, the client replaces the unforgiving emotions. Developing these positive other-oriented emotions is part of helping the client rethink the problem (harkening back to the general model of psychotherapy I presented in chapter 9). However, exercises to promote empathy are also action plans. It is necessary to follow up and support client attempts to develop positive feelings toward the transgressor.

In the next step, A = Give an Altruistic Gift of Forgiveness, the person is led to forgive not because it is good for their physical health, mental health, relationships, or spiritual health if they forgive. Rather, they are helped to forgive because they can bless the person who hurt them. Again, this involves helping clients rethink the problem, develop action plans to promote altruistic attitudes, and carry out the plans. Thinking altruistically toward a transgressor is difficult. But it is a valuable distinction that produces real differences in the ultimate effectiveness of the forgiveness effort.

In C = Commit to the Emotional Forgiveness That Was Experienced, the person makes a public commitment to the progress made. Often, that commitment is just to the therapist and to the client himself or herself.

The final step of REACH is to H = Hold on to Forgiveness When Doubts Arise. Both the C and H steps strengthen maintenance.

Each step in REACH is applied to a target transgression that the client is trying to change. Finally, becoming a more forgiving person is focused on. The REACH model is applied to several other key transgressions. The client is helped to grant decisional forgiveness and to experience emotional forgiveness for each transgression and for each person.

The Elements of Groups to REACH Forgiveness Are Consistent With the Biopsychosocial Stress-and-Coping Theory

Five Essential Elements of REACHing Forgiveness

Not every part of my five-step model to REACH forgiveness is equally important. A meta-analysis by Wade, Worthington, and Meyer (2005) identified three elements that were common among all effective forgiveness interventions, irrespective of whose intervention model or what theory the methods were based on. These three components were (1) use of multiple methods to reduce unforgiveness, (2) committing to forgiveness, and (3) empathizing or experiencing positive other-oriented emotions as an antidote to unforgiveness. I would add two additional crucial elements: promoting an altruistic attitude and generalizing until the person becomes more forgiving. These crucial elements of my model to REACH forgiveness are consistent with the stress-and-coping theory of forgiveness.

Multiple methods. First, the use of many methods to reduce unforgiveness suggests that the injustice gap can be narrowed by a variety of methods. These include stress reduction, seeking justice in some form, seeking an apology or restitution, changing one's thinking and understanding of the event, and searching for other alternative interactions between the people who are involved in the transgression. Each of these narrows the injustice gap, making unforgiveness less likely, and reducing threat appraisal. When threat appraisal is reduced, that helps people employ coping mechanisms that are more likely to be effective.

Commitment or decision. Second, committing to forgive or committing to the forgiveness that one has experienced is a willful decision to forgive the other person. This decision to forgive is compatible with cognitive interventions (like those used by Luskin, 2001), as well as interventions such as DiBlasio's (1998) decision-based forgiveness, my decisional forgiveness

(Worthington, 2003), and Enright's decision to try to forgive (see Enright & Fitzgibbons, 2000). Commitment may be seen as a meaning-focused coping strategy that attempts to change the meaning of a situation by making an intentional decision. It might lead to a solution for some interpersonal problems, thus possibly being a problem-focused coping strategy as well. Decision paves the way for experiencing emotional forgiveness.

Replacement emotions. Third, it is important to help the client experience more positive emotions of empathy, sympathy, compassion, or love for the transgressor. That emotional replacement, then, broadens and builds positive aspects into the person's experience and perhaps into the damaged relationship. Emotional forgiveness can be understood as emotion-focused coping (Worthington & Scherer, 2004). It will bring about a variety of positive effects (for a review, see Worthington & Scherer, 2004).

Altruistic motives. There is a fourth important element. Developing or bringing out altruistic motives helps promote emotional forgiveness. This was shown in three studies that compared altruistic motives with self-enhancement motives (McCullough & Worthington, 1995; McCullough, Worthington, & Rachal, 1997; Sandage, 1997). As we showed in two meta-analyses (Worthington et al., 2000; Worthington, Sandage, & Berry, 2000), forgiving by employing altruistic motives takes time. It is unnatural for a person to want to be altruistic to a person who has harmed them. A willingness to engage in altruistic motives to grant forgiveness for the benefit of the transgressor takes time to develop. Nevertheless, the effects that can accrue when a person is altruistic toward the transgressor far outstretch those that occur with self-enhancement motives.

Becoming more forgiving. Fifth, in our later attempts to promote forgiveness, we have gone beyond teaching people how to REACH forgiveness for a specific transgression. We try to help them generalize so that they can become more forgiving by nature. People practice forgiving several transgressions under different situations, enhancing motivations to be a more forgiving person, and (when done in Christian settings) drawing on the person's religious faith or philosophy to strengthen that motivation. Our program to promote a more forgiving personality has yet to be thoroughly tested.

Each of these five essential elements—narrowing of the injustice gap, decisional forgiveness, experiencing emotional forgiveness, having altruistic motives for forgiveness, and attempting to generalize the experience to promote a more forgiving personality—should be attended to in promoting effective forgiveness. Rethinking and formulating action plans will likely recur as each step unfolds. As Wade et al. (2005) pointed out, the strongest interventions are possible when a *specific type of transgression is targeted.* That occurs naturally in psychotherapy. Furthermore, the amount of time the person spends trying sincerely to forgive is directly correlated with their reported amount of forgiveness.

Exercises to REACH Forgiveness

Arriving at a Working Definition of Forgiveness

Let us return to Clara. She has just agreed to participate in a program that might help her forgive.

T-44: So, tell me, what do you think forgiveness is?

Cl-45: It's giving up my hate and not feeling angry any longer.

T-45: So, if you gave up all hate and anger, you'd say you forgave?

Cl-46: Well, I guess it's a little more than that. I wouldn't have any negative feelings about his drinking at all.

T-46: Wow. That would be quite a change!

Cl-47: Yeah, it would. But the more I think about it, it doesn't seem possible. Is it possible to not hate his drinking?

T-47: What do you think?

Cl-48: Hummm. No, I think I always want to hate the drinking, and I will never give all of those negative feelings up.

T-48: Then, if it isn't not feeling negative about his drinking, what is forgiving?

Cl-49: Well, I think it's something I decide to do. I have to decide not to blame him and not to keep holding this against him and not to keep plotting and hoping for his pain and suffering. But even if I decide I won't blame him and hope he suffers, I can't just stop doing those things. I've tried. I've tried a lot, and that doesn't work.

T-49: So, you seem to think several things are important. It seems important to you that a definite decision is involved. You don't want to drift into forgiving.

Cl-50: Right. I want to make a definite statement, but it should change things. Making a decision hasn't changed anything in the past— at least, not for more than a day.

T-50: So, besides deciding that you forgive, you also want to stop feeling the pressure to hate or blame or feel angry. Where do you think that pressure comes from?

Cl-51: From all the harm he did to me, to us. It gets me furious just thinking about it.

T-51: So, you seem to have a two-part understanding of forgiving. It's a decision about how you are going to act. But it's more. It's also changing your emotions.

R = Recall the Hurt

People plagued with unforgiveness usually recall the hurt in a resentful, bitter, hostile, hateful way. They nurture a grudge and rehearse the fantasies about the perpetrator that might include seeing the perpetrator get what he or she deserves or be harmed. In other cases, people might recall the hurt vengefully. They plot ways to get even or even how to harm the offender or make him or her suffer. Think back to Clara's recollected rumination about her father (Cl-7, chapter 9). She became very angry just thinking about her father's alcoholism. Before trying to promote forgiveness, two tasks are necessary. First, the therapist should conduct a strong assessment of unforgiveness. Second, the client will need to be helped to recall the hurt more objectively or more compassionately.

Assess Explicitly Before Beginning Attempts to Change Unforgiveness

Some conceptual clarity. Measurements of forgiveness and unforgiveness are ideally tied to the definitions that investigators use. Some issues in the measurement of constructs related to forgiveness have been discussed in Hoyt and McCullough (2005) and McCullough and Root (2005). Until recently, few researchers have made distinctions between reducing unforgiveness and forgiving (see Worthington & Wade, 1999, for an earlier distinction). Forgiveness was treated by many as the way of reducing unforgiveness. However, it is possible to reduce unforgiveness in other ways. Therefore, the reduction of unforgiveness should not be considered the same thing as forgiving (see Harris & Thoresen, 2005; Worthington & Scherer, 2004).

Assess informally and more formally. Much insight into the level of a client's unforgiveness and amount of forgiveness already experienced is possible through interviewing. While that benefits the clinician, it usually deprives the client of realizing—by the end of therapy—the amount of change that he or she has experienced. It is useful, then, to use standardized instruments to supplement interview assessment of forgiveness.

Assessing unforgiving motives. One frequently used measure of unforgiveness is the 12-item Transgression-Related Interpersonal of Motivations Inventory (TRIM; McCullough et al., 1998). The TRIM has two subscales that measure unforgiveness motivations: motivations to avoid or to exact revenge on the transgressor. The TRIM also includes a 6-item scale to assess conciliatory or benevolent motivations. The Wade Forgiveness Scale (Wade, 1989) was the forerunner of the TRIM (Hill et al.).

Assessing forgiveness of an event. The Enright Forgiveness Inventory (EFI) is an 80-item multidimensional measure of forgiveness that assesses positive and negative cognitive, emotional, and behavioral aspects of forgiveness (Subkoviak et al., 1995). Even though many of the items again equate the reduction of unforgiveness with the experiences of forgiveness, the EFI is the most comprehensive and best psychometrically supported measure of forgiveness. Because of its length and cost, some may opt for measures in the public domain. Many investigators have used single items to measure forgiveness, relying on participants to know what is meant by "forgiveness" (e.g., McCullough et al., 1998; McCullough, Worthington, & Rachal, 1997; Subkoviak et al., 1995; Worthington et al., 2000). However, I now use a differentiated pair of items—one to measure decisional forgiveness and the other to measure emotional forgiveness (see Table 10.1).

Assessing Dispositional Forgiveness. Mauger et al. (1992) created a measure of dispositional forgivingness that has dubious psychometric strength. Berry et al. (2005) developed a 10-item Likert Scale measure, called the Trait Forgivingness Scale (TFS), which is strong psychometrically. Thompson et al. (2005) developed the Heartland Forgiveness Scale (HFS). The HFS measures use three subscales: dispositional forgiveness of others (FO), forgiveness of self (FS), and forgiveness of situations (FSit). The psychometrics for FO and FS are good.

Table 10.1 Two Single-Item Measures of Decisional and Emotional Forgiveness.

Single Items to Measure Decisional and Emotional Forgiveness

Note: We want you to rate two types of forgiveness. For example, a person might perhaps decide to grant complete forgiveness but still feel very unforgiving toward a person.

Granting forgiveness is defined as deciding (even if you don't say aloud) that you will not seek revenge against the person and not avoid but will try to put the relationship (if any) back on the preoffense footing. This describes how you intend to act toward the person. Using the scale below (from 0 = No forgiveness granted to 4 = Complete forgiveness granted), estimate the current level to which you have granted forgiveness.

0	1	2	3	4
No forgiveness				Complete forgiveness

Experiencing emotional forgiveness is defined as the degree to which you actually feel that your emotions have become less negative and (perhaps) more positive toward the person who offended or harmed you. If 0 = No forgiveness experienced and 4 = Complete forgiveness experienced (that is, if you have experienced complete emotional forgiveness, you have no negative feelings and perhaps even some positive feelings toward the person who offended or harmed you), then use the scale below to indicate to what degree you have experienced emotional forgiveness.

0	1	2	3	4
No forgiveness				Complete forgiveness

R = Recall the Hurt More Objectively or Compassionately

Let us go back to the dialogue in chapter 9 and look at one of the ways the therapist helped Clara think more objectively or compassionately about her father.

T-36:   Great thinking! But you think of him as such a jerk now. You seem to think that he absolutely didn't care for you or your mother. So, there might not be any way to think differently of him. [**Comment: The therapist takes an even more extreme position than Clara has stated. She wants to correct the misperception, so she focuses on compassion rather than judgment.**]

Cl-37: Well, he's not all bad, I guess. In fact, he's really more pitiful than evil. I mean, really, I hate what he did, but as I think about it, I know he didn't want to ruin his life, Mom's life, and mine. It hurt him, too. He couldn't stop himself from drinking.

T-37:   Okay. Hummm, okay. So, let's stop a minute and see if I understand what you're telling me. It's a lot. Let's see if I have it all. You said, just making a decision isn't enough by itself to make you feel more forgiving. You need to do something (or he does) that would make you feel more positive and therefore would neutralize the negativity of unforgiveness. You could wait around for him to come grovel at your feet.

Cl-38: Not in this lifetime.

T-38:   And you obviously don't want to stake the family ranch on that. Or you could try to understand his weakness, rather than just treat it as if he had set out with single-minded purpose to destroy you. [**Comment: The therapist rephrases what Clara said to highlight the pity she expressed.**]

Cl-39: Whether that was his purpose or not, I feel that he did a pretty good job. But yes, that wasn't what he wanted to do. He is weak more than evil.

T-39:   So, if I understand you correctly, if you put your mind to understanding, empathizing, pitying him, maybe someday feeling compassion toward him and for his weaknesses, then that might combat the negative unforgiving feelings. That might help you feel forgiveness, not just decide to forgive. Did I get it right?

Cl-40: Right. Yeah. I hear you. But, I've hated for so long. How can I change?

T-40:   Well, if you're right in your "theory"—that you need to empathize more or pity him more, and that will help you forgive—

then I think I can work with you to develop some practical plans to try and see whether it works. [**Comment: The therapist again labels Clara's feeling as empathy or pity.**]

I have provided several exercises that might contribute to a client seeing the hurt more objectively or more compassionately.

Exercise 1. If the person wishes to forgive, the person needs to recall the hurt differently. Instead of dwelling on how much he or she was hurt or on hoped-for acts of justice or vengeance, the person should recall the hurt from the point of view of the perpetrator, trying to be as objective as possible.

Exercise 2. Sometimes, it is helpful to have the person relax and imagine the event. After the person has generated an accurate image (even though the image might involve negative emotion), ask, "Can you describe what is happening?" After the description has unfolded, ask, "Is this the usual sequence of events you recall when you think back to when you were hurt?"

Exercise 3. Process the answer. Then say, "Someone once defined insanity as 'doing the same thing again and again, but expecting a different outcome.' So, it seems that you need to change things. If you continue to ruminate resentfully or vengefully, you'll get the same outcome that has been occurring. Namely, you'll feel resentful or vengeful." The person needs to try to recall the hurt differently. This can help motivate a new approach.

Exercise 4. Suggest that understanding things from the point of view of the offender is likely to help in this recall. So, ask the client to imagine the same event again, but this time to try to imagine what the offender might have been thinking, feeling, seeing, and experiencing. This obviously blends with promoting empathy.

Exercise 5. After the client completes the mental imagery, he or she should describe what was experienced. In cases in which the person has done mental imagery work before, the person can narrate the image aloud as he or she imagines it. This, of course, is another transition that helps promote empathy.

Exercise 6. The client can be told that imagining the event from the other person's point of view creates a new sort of experience, but the client needs to get some distance and objectivity into imagining his or her own response, too. Thus, he or she is invited to imagine the event as if he or she were an objective news reporter, reporting the interaction between two people, both of whom have individual motives.

Exercise 7. People who have been harmed and understand themselves as victims often remember events quite differently than people who have been involved as the offender. The victim usually believes that he or she remembers the event accurately, as do offenders. The therapist can give a brief summary of studies by Baumeister, Stillwell, and Wotman (1990).

They have shown that when a person listens to a story as if he or she were the victim, an offender, or an objective person, the person will remember different things. Victims tend to remember more about the pain and suffering that the victim incurred. They conveniently forget that the offender made any efforts to repair the damage or to mitigate the harm. People listening as offenders remember well their attempts to mitigate the harm and events, and the victims saying, "It's okay," or "No problem." But they tend to think that the situation is closed and finished, whereas the victims remember their suffering and think of the situation as if it were still open.

Exercise 8. The person could even be invited to make up a fantasy *that did not actually occur.* Such a fantasy might involve recalling the hurt, and imagining that afterward an offender had apologized with deep regret, remorse, and contrition. Research at Canada's York University by Leslie Greenberg and Wanda Malcolm (2002) has demonstrated that people who can generate such fantasies and vividly imagine the offender apologizing and being deeply remorseful are ones who are mostly likely able to forgive successfully. Those who cannot imagine such fantasies are often unable to forgive without some form of justice actually being involved, or without a large amount of work to promote experiences of empathy, sympathy, compassion, or love.

E = Empathize With the Person Who Harmed You

A person does not have to empathize with the offender for emotional forgiveness to occur. However, if the person does empathize, forgiveness probably will occur. For example, to hear a person apologize for wrongdoing generally helps a person forgive. However, in research we have shown the apology effects forgiveness only to the extent that it helps the person empathize with the offender. As Greenberg and Malcolm have shown, true apology is not even necessary for this effect to occur. All the person has to do is vividly imagine the offender apologizing.

It is difficult for a wounded person to want to try to empathize with a transgressor. Understanding why an offender might have offended or why a harm-doer might have hurt someone is probably the last thing that a victim wants to do. The offense or harm created a strong justice motive. People fixate on justice, not empathy. If the person was hurt long ago, he or she has probably sought justice and is not likely to get more. He or she might be ready to try forgiveness. The event is no longer a hot event on the front burner. Following are some exercises to promote empathy or other emotions that can replace unforgiveness:

Exercise 1. The client is invited to try to empathize with the other person as an experiment, just to see how it works.

Exercise 2. Ask the client to talk about the transgression. After he or she has done so, ask *what* questions, such as, "*What* do you think the person might have been feeling when he said those hurtful things to you? *What* do you think the person was feeling toward you? Was he or she completely hostile to you? If not, then *what* was the intent?" If the person were here right now explaining to me what happened, *what* do you think that person would say?"

Exercise 3. To induce an empathic point of view, ask the person to describe the event again as if he or she were running a movie through his or her head, and the movie was being narrated from the point of view of the other person.

Exercise 4. A key to helping a person develop empathy for the transgressor is to help the client take the perspective of the other person. To assist the client, use five prompts: (1) Pressures: What were the situational pressures that made the person behave the way he or she did? (2) Past: What were the background factors contributing to the person acting the way he or she did? (3) Personality: What are the events in the person's life that lead to the person having the personality that he or she does? (4) Provocations: What were my own provocative behaviors? Alternatively, might the other person, from his or her point of view, perceive something I did as a provocation? (5) Plans: What were the person's good intentions? Did the person want to help me, correct me, or have in mind that he or she thought would be good for me, but his or her behavior did not have that effect? In fact, it had just the opposite effect. Write the five Ps on a sheet of paper as a cue to the client.

Exercise 5. Try to explore whether the client experiences sympathy, compassion, or love for the offender. Ask *to-what-degree* or *how-much* questions: "*To what degree* can you experience any sense of sympathy [or compassion, or love] for the person? *To what degree* can you identify with the person as another fallible human and thereby have a sense of mercy toward the person? *To what degree* can you believe that the person is in some distress over his or her behavior? *How* distressed did he or she seem? Remember, most people feel more distress than they show. *How much* guilt or remorse does the person feel over what he or she has done? *To what degree* do you think he or she feels embarrassed over losing control?"

Exercise 6. To help the client discern the emotions of the offender, ask, "What emotions did the person experience when he or she faced the pressures or provocations that were present in the situation? Which emotions did the person feel? How strongly did the person feel those emotions?"

Exercise 7. One of the most effective ways to help a client experience empathy is to use the empty-chair technique. The client imagines sitting across from the offender, who is imagined to be in an empty chair. The client describes his or her complaint as if the offender were there. The client then moves to the empty chair and responds from the point of view of the offender. The conversation proceeds with the client moving back and forth between chairs. The objective is to allow the person to express both sides of the conversation personally, and thus experience empathy. In doing so, the person might imagine an apology or at least an acknowledgment of the hurt that was inflicted.

Exercise 8. Homework can further the empathic exercise. The client can write a letter as if he or she were the offender. Therapist and client read and discuss it at the next session. The letter explains, from the offender's point of view, what occurred. This letter can be used as homework prior to using the empty-chair dialogs. Or it can be used after the empty-chair dialogs to reaffirm and reinforce what was learned.

Exercise 9. A related homework assignment is to write a letter of apology from the offender's viewpoint. The helper might acknowledge that the true offender might never write such a letter. The apology letter would admit blame, admit the harm done, and then express deep remorse and regret from the offender.

The therapist can structure the sessions on empathy as follows. In the first empathy-related session, get the client to talk about the issue from the transgressor's point of view. Discuss the transgression. Assign the letter of explanation (i.e., Exercise 8) as homework. In the following session, use the empty-chair dialogues and other discussions. Then at the end of that session, assign the apology letter. The following session would process the learning from these experiences.

Exercise 10. Some people simply find it impossible to empathize with the transgressor. Often, this usually occurs in severe, unexpected betrayals or heinous harms. In those cases, sympathy is a legitimate goal. The client can be invited to speculate about ways and reasons that he or she feels sorry for the person who harmed the victim. The client could be asked, "What kind of help might this offender be given? Are there nice things that people could do to help this person?" The intent is to stimulate thoughts of compassion toward the person who has been hurt.

Exercise 11. Sometimes, Christians will embrace Jesus' teaching that Christians love their enemies. If people accept that idea, then the therapist can ask the client how he or she might love his or her enemy.

Because experiencing emotional forgiveness is a result of replacing negative emotions with positive ones, the therapist should focus on promoting positive other-oriented emotions and lowering the amount of unforgiveness. But the therapist cannot suppress the client's expression of the negative. Clients react against attempts to suppress their negative feelings.

A = Altruistic Gift of Forgiveness

Replacing negative unforgiving emotions gradually with positive other-oriented emotions is facilitated by experiencing other self-forgetful positive emotions. The therapist facilitates emotional replacement by helping the client give an altruistically motivated gift of forgiveness. Use a memory described by the client to motivate altruism through (1) humility in realizing that the client too has offended, (2) contrition over his or her wrongdoing, (3) gratitude for having been forgiven, and (4) hope from the expectation that we can all do something good for others, even those who have hurt us, and that blessing will come back to us.

Clients are directed to reflect on their past to recall times in which they offended another but were forgiven. These times can be difficult to recall. The helper can give prompts to think of whether the client offended a parent, teacher, romantic partner, friend, or coworker. Usually, with these prompts, people can recall many experiences where they wronged someone and were forgiven.

Once a salient event is selected, the client thinks through the event, the acts, and the consequences. Especially, he or she is asked to concentrate on what happened when forgiveness was granted for the wrong that he or she had done. How did the client feel? Typically, he or she will report feeling grateful for having been forgiven, free of the weight of condemnation and self-condemnation, light, and unburdened by carrying around guilt.

After the client contemplates these situations of contrition felt for wronging someone, the gratitude for having been forgiven, the therapist can pose the key question (see T-63 below). Picking up the conversation with Clara:

T-60:   You have struggled but now have empathized with your father.

Cl-61:   I can see the pressures he was under. But even more, I feel sorry for him. His life was such a waste, and he really suffered from the alcoholism and what it did to his self-esteem.

T-61:   So, you can feel sympathy toward him for having gotten to the place where he could offend you. You might even feel compassion and love for your father.

Cl-62:   Compassion, yes. I do feel some compassion for him. Love? Well, only in the sense that he is, after all, my biological father. He did act like a real father early in my childhood. I should feel grateful for that, I suppose. So, I feel some love for him.

T-62:   Also, you have seen how you have felt when you were forgiven. You felt free, light, grateful to your friend Marni for giving you that gift of forgiveness when you ignored her during your courtship with Mark.

Cl-63: And mostly I felt unburdened. I'd carried that guilt around for years, and now I feel like I got out from under its weight. I'm thankful for that.

T-63: Putting both of these feelings together, *would you like to forgive your father, who hurt you?* Can you release your negative feelings and replace them with positive feelings for him?

The therapist should pause and wait for the person's response. If the client responds that some change in emotion is possible, the therapist can say, "You seem like you have experienced some changes. Can you estimate how much forgiveness you experienced? Have you forgiven three fourths of the negative feelings?" When the person says how much he or she has experienced, this actually is the first step to committing to the forgiveness the person has experienced.

C = Commit to the Forgiveness You Experienced

Commitment is multilayered. A commitment to forgive is based on the relationship with the therapist. If the therapeutic bond is damaged, the client will not risk revealing his or her vulnerabilities. The client may complain. Sometimes, complaints are a shield against revealing self-doubts. So, a tipping point of therapy can be a commitment by the client to try to forgive.

That commitment is far different than crying about one's problems. The client stands on the edge between light and darkness. It is like dawn—or is it like twilight? The client is unsure: "If I take a step, will I plunge into deeper darkness, or will a new day appear?" Committing to try to forgive is scary.

When people are threatened and scared, they defend themselves. They may fall back into complaints or find reasons why they cannot come to therapy. They put one foot forward into the unknown, but are afraid to put any weight on it, merely dangling a toe over the possibility of forgiving. To take the plunge, clients need support and encouragement. The therapeutic relationship bears the weight.

This drama of threat and courage plays itself out at every step of commitment. Entering therapy required courage, and that courage needs to be recognized and honored. Suggesting the possibility of forgiveness for the first time can be a big step—especially if it is suggested by the therapist. It is easier for the therapist to wait for the client to bring it up. But sometimes in their wounded state, clients do not have the heart to do so. If the therapist senses that forgiveness might help and that the client might be open to it, the therapist should invite the client to consider it. Deciding to work on forgiving is a big commitment for clients. Granting decisional forgiveness is another. When the therapist asks for a statement of the amount of emotional forgiveness experienced (as in T-63), that too is a big step. There is thus cause for celebration at the many acts of courage by the client. I suggest surrounding this recognition with a ceremony. Here are four exercises that solidify commitment:

Exercise 1. The client is invited to complete a Certificate of Forgiveness. That certificate will serve as a reminder of their changed emotions. The certificate might state that the decision to forgive has been made and the client intends to act differently toward the offender henceforth. In addition, though, it says that the client has experienced emotional forgiveness in which [blank] percent of the negative emotions have been replaced with more positive feelings toward the transgressor. Therapists can feel self-conscious asking the client to create such a certificate, but when they see how seriously the client takes the written statement, they quickly see its value.

Exercise 2. The client can solidify this commitment to forgive by writing a letter of forgiveness. The person should not send such a letter. When letters of forgiveness are unsolicited, they are often taken as an accusation rather than a granting of forgiveness. The letter is important for the forgiver.

Exercise 3. Another way to reinforce the commitment to forgive is to have a person write in black ink a brief account of the offense on his or her hand—like "betrayal" or "lying." The person then washes off as much of the ink as possible, symbolizing his or her forgiveness. If traces of ink are still visible after washing, the therapist can suggest that working through experiences of emotional forgiveness one time might not sufficiently cleanse the client's negative feelings.

Exercise 4. Other rituals and symbols can be employed to mark the experience of forgiveness. For example, a client can carry a rock throughout a counseling session, with the rock signifying the burden of unforgiving feelings. When the person is ready to let go of these unforgiving feelings, the person can put down the rock.

During therapy, the therapist must help the client maintain commitment. The therapist should strive to keep the work novel. If therapy turns humdrum, clients lose their commitment to work. The therapist should encourage the client to involve others in the program or should at least work with the client to plan what the client can do to affect others. For change to be lasting, structures must be modified.

H = Hold Onto the Forgiveness When Doubts Arise

It is natural for a person later to doubt whether he or she has experienced emotional forgiveness and even whether he or she has granted decisional forgiveness. Doubts occur because decisions and emotional experiences are internal and subjective. It is difficult to know whether one has completely replaced negative emotions. Even more so, however, the experiences of doubt occur because other negative emotions arise to confuse the person. For example, suppose a person sees someone who has harmed him or her previously. The person might feel no unforgiveness for the offender, yet he or she might still feel an immediate surge of anger, which recalls the transgression. This surge of anger does not indicate that the person has not forgiven. The surge of anger suggests that the person's body is responding as it should to a situation in which injury or offense has occurred in the past. The body was designed to protect people against re-exposing themselves to danger. So, when an offender is seen, the fear and anger will spontaneously arise.

The therapist has four tasks to help the person deal with doubts about whether he or she has forgiven. Convincing the person that immediate anger or fear is not lingering unforgiveness is often the biggest task. The second task is to help the person reduce negative feelings when they occur. The third task is to help the person interrupt negative rumination if it develops. The final task is to help the client think more positively toward the person when not aroused by negative reactions:

Exercise 1. Use this analogy: If a person burns his or her hand on a stove, the person will feel anger or fear associated with that injury. After healing occurs, if the person gets a hand near the stove, those negative feelings of fear and anger might recur. It is not as though the person does not forgive the stove. Rather, it is the body's protection. It recognizes the danger and fires up the emotions as a warning signal.

Exercise 2. When a client encounters a forgiven offender unexpectedly, the client will feel negative emotions rise up quickly. The client must control those emotions. This can best be done through self-instruction, reminding oneself of the stove analogy, or self-soothing through deep breathing. Practice imagining meeting the offender. Rehearse how the client will maintain his or her forgiveness.

Exercise 3. When a person begins to ruminate about the negative event and its consequences, he or she should interrupt that rumination. Suggest a person not think about white bears (Wegner, 1994). It quickly becomes obvious that the person will think more of white bears than previously. Conclude that a person cannot interrupt rumination by instructing himself or herself not to ruminate. Rather, the person could prevent white bear fantasies by distraction or by moving to a different activity.

Exercise 4. Finally, the person is told that a particular challenge, but an important one, is to think more positively about the transgressor. Planning how this should, or can, be done is a task that a therapist and client can work on together. This might involve imaginal rehearsal. It could involve carefully planning safe activities to do with the transgressor. For example, if a coworker has offended someone and must be talked to daily, the person can plan positive experiences that will eventually overshadow some of the negative feelings of the offense.

If only working through five steps to REACH forgiveness could result in complete peace. But because we all are human, we all at times fail at our goals. The client will hope never to experience unforgiveness again. But that is not realistic. Especially if the client continues to interact with the forgiven person, new transgressions will almost inevitably occur. This is not an indication of defeat. It is merely a challenge to use the five steps to REACH forgiveness to deal with new transgressions as they might occur.

Becoming a More Forgiving Person

As I discussed personality in chapter 8, and a general approach to psychotherapy in chapter 9, I reiterate: Repetition is the hallmark of effective therapy. Through repetition, people generalize. If working through the five steps once helps forgive a transgression, then working through it three or four times might result in complete forgiveness for the transgression. Repeating with other transgressions can help a client forgive a person. Working on repeated transgressions with different transgressors can move the person to become a more forgiving person.

Before ending therapy, it is helpful for maintenance of personality change to have the client create an ongoing plan about living as a more forgiving person. That could involve choosing forgiveness models, doing a morning inventory of the previous day, and settling unforgiven hurts within 24 hours. Planning one's day each morning could help anticipate difficult interactions and thus head off unforgiveness before it occurs.

Many psychotherapies use a technique that George Kelly (1991) called consigning the old person to impermeability. He noticed that psychodynamic therapy often led clients to an insight like this. "Yes, I reacted defensively to my father's control because I felt a strong threat to self. That was appropriate for a child. That is not appropriate now as an adult—either with my father or with other authority figures." The client is validated for his or her behavior, but the behavior is assigned to a dungeon of the past and the key is thrown away. Similarly, a client might be led to conclude, "Yes, I used to be unforgiving. I was especially vengeful. That was more appropriate when my spirit was wounded and I felt vulnerable. Now, though, after successful therapy, I no longer need to react with vengefulness to protect a fragile sense of self-esteem."

Conclusion

Unforgiveness is indeed stressful and threatens clients' personalities. With a general process approach to therapy supplemented by five steps to REACH forgiveness, the therapist is equipped to help deal with unforgiveness within therapy or as part of a group that can be an adjunct to therapy.

CHAPTER 11
Intervening to Promote Forgiveness of Self

Jim sat in my office and tears brimmed in his eyes: "I can forgive others for almost anything that they have done to me. I never blame God for what happens. But I can't forgive myself." Jim had just been confronted by his wife of 20 years for his third affair. He and his wife had three children. Now, his wife had announced that he had finally stepped over the line. She was taking the children and seeking a divorce.

What could I say to Jim? He seemed so sincere. So hurt. Yet with his other two affairs, he had also seemed hurt. He was so remorseful that Nicole had taken him back twice. Over the next 2 hours, Jim described his weakness in being attracted to women. He was an attorney and seemed to have a particular attraction to younger attorneys or legal aides. In the fourth session, he admitted that this was not, in fact, his third affair. It was only the third affair that Nicole knew about.

Jim wanted me to help him deal with his self-condemnation, his pain, and his guilt. This time, he said, the consequences had caught up with him and he was in more pain than ever before. Not the least of his pain was his own self-blame. He had become depressed soon after the confrontation. I sympathized with Jim. I knew self-forgiveness was difficult and could lead to some of the most painful feelings people encounter—feelings one could not get away from.

On the other hand, I was not eager to help Jim forgive himself. I had recently read Gobodo-Madikizela's book (2003) about her interactions with Eugene deKock, which I discussed earlier. As I read of horrid murders deKock committed, I realized that he should not merely forgive himself and have everything be okay. Someone who perpetrates evil should not be allowed to simply declare himself forgiven. What could ever make deKock's statement of self-forgiveness meaningful? It would take a lot more than crying a few tears and wrestling with self-forgiveness.

Why Is It So Hard to Forgive Ourselves?

Dealing with self-condemnation is often harder than with condemnation from one we wronged. Self-forgiveness is harder than forgiving someone else. There are many reasons that self-forgiveness is difficult.

First, when people try to forgive themselves, they play two roles at the same time. They are simultaneously wrongdoer and forgiver. It requires mental gymnastics to jump back and forth between roles. Most people are not particularly agile. When one forgives a stranger who has harmed one, one is only a victim. When one forgives a loved one, one might be victim and offender, but we usually focus on one role at a time—usually, how we have been the victim.

Second, self-condemnation often seems incessant. When we betray a loved one, we have to listen to them accuse us. Jim certainly had to listen to Nicole dwell on his failures. Yet, Jim could not get away from the voices in his head, but he could get away from Nicole. When he was not with Nicole, he did not have to listen to her. But Jim's self-condemnation was always there, chattering accusations.

Third, self-forgiveness can be difficult because we have insider information. We know the many times that we have erred or disappointed ourselves. We often see ourselves as the unrepentant people that we really are. Regardless of how close our relationship with someone is, we do not see all of that person's failures, and he or she cannot see all of ours. When we disappoint ourselves, we see our deep flaws.

Fourth, when we condemn ourselves, our voice is usually not the only voice that is condemning us. We usually have harmed others. They, and those who observed the wrongdoing, can join the condemnation. Our voice then becomes part of a chorus.

Fifth, we often have a sense that we not only harmed someone else and thus failed ourselves, but we have also sinned against God, nature, or humanity. The sense that we have let down others who are more important than we—those who have spiritual significance to us—adds to our guilt and shame.

Sixth, people often put pressure on themselves to forgive themselves. Some people believe that they must forgive themselves before they can be mentally healthy. They feel that they cannot carry around guilt and function as productive members of society. That pressure to forgive the self adds weight to the self-condemnation.

Seventh, when we have been wronged by another, we might not feel that we must forgive him or her. We might feel that the burden is on the wrong-doer, not the victim. But when we fail ourselves, we feel a burden.

Self-forgiveness—hard as it is—is the tip of the iceberg. Suppose a man loses his temper and strikes his 6-year-old child. He is immediately overwhelmed by guilt and remorse, and he apologizes to his child and even prays for forgiveness from God. Even if he can forgive himself for his loss of temper, he may still be wracked with negative feelings. Why? Through his act of wrongdoing, he changed his entire conception of himself. Before he struck his child, he was not "the type of father who would strike his child." Immediately afterwards, he was. His understanding of who he was was fundamentally altered. When challenges to the self-concept arise because a person's acts are discrepant from their self-concept, the person must work the new information into a modified self-concept. That takes time, effort, and discomfort.

What Does One Have to Do to Forgive Oneself?
Practical Steps to Dealing With Self-Condemnation

Because a self-condemning person is usually truly a transgressor, the first thing that the person must do is accept that. Many people accept that easily. They are *guilt-prone self-forgivers*. To deal with their self-condemnation, first, they must try to make things right with the person who was harmed. Thus, the father who struck his son would have to try to make amends for harming his son. He might confess his error to his son and apologize. He might go beyond that and apologize to his wife. He might make restitution.

If the person believes that he or she has sinned against God, the person must do what his or her religion prescribes to make things right with God. For the Roman Catholic, this might be to partake of the sacrament of reconciliation, which involves confession to a priest and penance. For any Christian, Muslim, or Jew, this might involve prayer. For other religions, prescribed acts of reconciliation with the Divine or the person harmed might be needed. After a person has done what can be done to close the victim's injustice gap, then the person might be ready to deal with the harm that he or she has done to himself or herself through the transgression.

The person can make a decision to forgive himself or herself. This requires that one accept that he or she can perhaps never do all that is necessary to completely close the injustice gap. If the person believes that he or she can "make it up" to the harmed party, efforts will continue toward restoring justice rather than seeking to forgive the self. Decisional forgiveness of the self is undertaken only after one has done all that one reasonably can—but not persevering beyond what is reasonable.

Deciding to forgive the self does not mean that emotional forgiveness will necessarily quickly follow. The person might apply the steps to REACH for emotional forgiveness for the act or acts done. Perhaps he or she can experience emotional forgiveness in that way.

As we saw, however, merely forgiving oneself for an act does not necessarily eliminate all negative feelings toward the self. The person might have experienced a distortion in his or her self-concept. He or she needs to integrate the new information into the revised self-concept. The need to rethink the boundaries of the self might threaten his or her self-esteem. If the person has fragile high self-esteem, this threat can be severe, and the person can expect more difficulty with self-condemnation. Eventually, he or she might be able to repair damage to the self.

Psychotherapists have developed many ways to help people change their self-concept, self-image, and self-esteem. Often, the defenses that are used to protect the self against threats to self-esteem are evaluated, and the person learns to recognize the threat and cope with it. Sometimes by experiencing acceptance from the therapist, the person can come to better accept himself or herself.

Most psychotherapies that seek to treat problems in self-concept, self-image, and self-esteem tend to be relatively long-term processes. Thus, if the person believes that he or she can work for a few hours and eliminate all negative feelings about the self that arise from self-condemnation, he or she is in for a big disappointment.

Finally, one should resolve to live virtuously. Throughout the process of dealing with self-condemnation, an implicit assumption is that the person admits that he or she has done wrong and wishes to repair the damage and henceforth live better. In the last step to dealing with self-forgiveness, the person commits himself or herself to trying to live more virtuously with the full knowledge of his or her imperfections.

A Special Case

I have assumed that the person wishes to forgive the self because he or she did an objective wrong. That is not always the case. Some people cannot forgive themselves for being who they are. They are *shame-prone self-condemners*. They feel defective. In that case, no amount of contrition, making amends, seeking a return to favor with the Divine, or working through the REACH steps will help them feel forgiven. The work needed is on reshaping the self to be more self-accepting and less reflexively self-critical. That precedes work on actual self-condemnation.

Types of Self-Forgiveness

I have assumed that people who feel self-condemnation wish to forgive themselves and that people who do wrong to others will feel a sense of guilt, or perhaps shame, and self-condemnation. This, of course, is a tenuous assumption.

Tangney, Boone, and Dearing (2005) identified two types of people with regard to forgiveness of self. Some struggle with forgiveness of self and manage eventually to resolve their issues. These people are likely to be *guilt-prone self-forgivers.*

Other people simply let self-condemnation roll off of them. Those people do not struggle with self-forgiveness. They have high degrees of narcissism, self-involvement, and a sense of entitlement, and are low in shame- and guilt-proneness. Those people tend to let themselves off of the hook easily. They do not spend much effort wrestling with self-condemnation. Let us call these people *self-absorbed non-self-condemners.*

I might suggest a few additional types of people to this taxonomy. Some people may not easily recognize that they have done wrong. They are low in empathy and tend to be self-involved. They do not ruminate; they dissipate condemnation. Furthermore, they are not emotionally reactive. Things that bother others do not bother them. They have a high threshold for defining any act as worthy of self-condemnation. Let us call these people *nonreactive non-self-condemners.*

Still other people might have a sensitive spirit and be radar beacons for detecting self-condemnation—looking for times to condemn themselves. They either have low self-esteem or fragile high self-esteem that collapses easily under pressure. They are highly shame- and guilt-prone. They may wrestle with self-condemnation but seem unable to resolve those issues and be able to forgive themselves. We will call these people *reactive self-condemners.*

Therapeutic Considerations to Promote Self-Forgiveness

There are important clinical considerations prior to attempting to work with a client about forgiving the self.

1. Is there an objective reason for the lack of forgiveness of the self? Has the person really done something harmful that needs to be repaired? Is the person still actively engaged in harmful behaviors? Have you asked the person? For example, a person might be ashamed or guilty because he or she is embezzling funds, abusing a spouse or child, or continuing to perpetrate some harmful behavior.
2. Is the person depressed? Depression is often a partner of unforgiveness toward the self. Have you assessed for depression and suicide potential?
3. Is the person prone by personality to self-condemnation and conversely likely to have difficulty forgiving the self? Mullet, Neto, and Riviere (2005) reviewed the literature on the personality attributes related to measures of forgiveness of the self. Agreeableness, introversion–extroversion, and openness to experience were virtually unrelated to forgiving (see Table 11.1). Measures of religion, spirituality, and hope were slightly related to self-forgiveness, as was the trait of conscientiousness. The big predictor of forgiveness of self was neuroticism (emotional reactivity or emotional instability). In three fourths of the studies, high scores on measures of neuroticism were related to low ability to forgive the self.

Clinically, the important point is that several variables confound issues of self-blame, self-condemnation, and lack of self-forgiveness. Thus, accurate and sensitive assessment is paramount. The person could be merely introspective, reactive to stimuli or to his or her own moods, ruminative, and judgmental by personality. These factors might make brief psychotherapy aimed at self-forgiveness likely to fail. Longer-term therapy would

Table 11.1 Personality Characteristics That Predict Forgiveness of Self Based on Percentage of Studies With $r > .25$ in a Review of Research by Mullet, Neto, and Rivière (2005)

Trait	Percentage of Studies With $r > .25$ (Number/ Total, Valence of Relationship)
Agreeableness	0% (0/9)
Neuroticism (Emotional Instability)	76% (29/38, Negative)**
Extroversion	0% (0/9)
Conscientiousness	25% (1/4, Positive)
Openness to Experience	0% (0/5)
Religion, Spirituality, Hope	17% (1/6, Positive)

Note: Numbers in parentheses indicate the fraction of studies reporting a correlation > .25. Underlining indicates that the percentage is based on four studies and is thus not necessarily reliable.
** 2/3 or more studies found $r > .25$; reliable and strong prediction

be indicated. But also the person might be depressed, and self-condemnation and self-blame are mere symptoms of the depression. Again, treatment would best be concentrated on alleviating the depression and only afterwards, if there is lingering self-condemnation, should self-forgiveness be the primary focus. Yet, sometimes, the self-condemnation is a symptom that in itself is herding the person toward self-injurious behavior. In that case, the clinician must deal with the self-condemnation as a matter of priority. The analogy is obvious. If a person has a 105° fever, the physician must first bring down the fever to protect the person's life, and only then put the person on medication to treat the cause.

Exercises to Promote Self-Forgiveness

Exercise 1: Assess the Extent of the Problem

Like any clinical problem, the first questions to answer involve the severity and duration of the self-condemnation. There are few psychometrically sound assessment instruments for measuring self-forgiveness or self-condemnation. Thompson et al. (2005) has created a dispositional self-forgiveness scale as part of the Heartland Forgiveness Scale. It is unclear whether dispositional self-forgiveness is actually affected by states of self-condemnation. Data to that effect are not provided on the Thompson et al. measure. A person might be dispositionally not prone to self-condemnation, but be depressed. The depression could be a trigger for dangerous levels of self-condemnation, which might not be detected on the instrument. As in all clinical work, clinical judgment in interviews must be combined with results from standard batteries of clinically useful assessments (such as the Beck Depression Inventory, Minnesota Multiphasic Personality Inventory [MMPI], or other instruments).

Exercise 2: Identify Expectations and Goals and Evaluate Their Realism

After severity and duration are assessed, the clinician should assess why a person might be condemning the self and what level of success has attended the person's coping methods. One of those methods might be self-forgiveness; however, the person might be trying to cope with self-condemnation through self-medicating, overcompensating to win approval through relationships or work performance, or other coping methods.

A person can experience self-condemnation because he or she has failed to live up to a personal standard, or because the person has done wrong to someone. An important step in promoting forgiving the self, then, is to make a careful assay of why one is feeling self-condemnation. If a person is falling short of his or her goals or expectations, the person needs to evaluate those goals and expectations to see whether they are realistic. If the difficulty has stemmed from a wrong done to someone, the clinician needs to inquire about the wrong. If the problem is more dispositional—such as with a reactive self-condemner or shame-prone self-condemner—then longer-term psychotherapy might be indicated.

Exercise 3: Take a Moral Inventory

Assess the degree to which the person ruminates about the self-condemnation. What is the content of the rumination? Ask questions such as these: "Did you do something objectively wrong? If you did something wrong, can it be repaired? What do you need to do to make restitution? Have you apologized to the person that you harmed? Have you expressed a sincere sense of remorse or contrition for your acts?"

Exercise 4: Apply the Five Steps to REACH Forgiveness

Get the person to recall the hurt (R). You can initiate such recall by saying things like, "Try to imagine objectively what you did that disappointed you or made you feel self-condemnation. Try not to blame yourself as much as you try to remember precisely what was done and what the other person might have done."

The key step is the E step in REACHing self-forgiveness, just as it is in forgiving others. Before you try to promote emotional self-forgiveness through stimulating empathy (or sympathy, compassion, or self-love), you will want to ask the following: "Are you aware of having done wrong to someone?" If the person is religious: "What have you done to make this right with God?"

Ask, "Do you think that your self-condemnation comes more from not feeling good about who you are or about things you have done that you feel guilty for or ashamed of? What have you done to right the wrongs you think you might have done?"

Ask questions like, "Can you empathize with yourself? Can you give yourself a break and see the mitigating circumstances that might have pressured you to behave as you did?" On one hand, you do not want to let yourself off of the hook easily if you have done wrong, but on the other hand, you do not want to apply standards to yourself that you would not apply to other people. If you can empathize with yourself or even grant yourself a sense of compassion, you will be likely to experience positive emotions that can counteract some of your feelings of self-condemnation.

The A—altruistic gift of forgiveness—in REACHing forgiveness involves being compassionate toward the self. You can ask, "If you have done all you can to make things right with the person you harmed and with God (if that is in the person's belief system), and you can understand and empathize or be compassionate toward yourself, then can you grant yourself an altruistic gift of forgiveness? Can you declare decisional forgiveness to yourself and allow yourself to experience a more positive sense of self?"

To solidify change, use the C step in REACHing self-forgiveness. You might direct the person to acknowledge any gains by saying something like, "If you have experienced some decisional forgiveness and some sense of emotional forgiveness, then you might write a statement or certificate attesting or committing to the forgiveness you have experienced."

To promote maintenance, you can give some practical guidance: "You have an uphill battle at not condemning yourself if the act has harmed your sense of self, or sense of self-esteem. Nevertheless, you can hold on to this sense of self-forgiveness [H = hold on] by reviewing the five steps and by reviewing your commitment to the forgiveness you have experienced."

Exercise 5: Accepting the Self

Accepting the self often takes a long time and requires many iterations before one can experience acceptance of the self. It is a good general rule to try multiple methods to promote the client's accepting the self when he or she is unhappy with something that he or she did or an inability to live up to his or her standards.

This might involve employing the imagination. Have the person imagine himself or herself as embodying the characteristics that he or she would like to embody. Or the person could be directed to imagine himself or herself making restitution. Another modality is to try to change the concept of self to accept that he or she is not perfect. This is not something one can do by repetition, but involves being able to see the good that one does despite the imperfections.

A person might be assigned to behave in a way that would be consistent with being more like his or her ideal. Sometimes behaving as one would like to be helps one to more often reach that standard of behavior.

Conclusion

In summary, then, self-forgiveness involves multiple threats to the self-system, through one's own wrongdoing or disappointment in one's achievement of personal standards. Shame- and guilt-proneness play a big part in experiencing self-condemnation, and feelings of entitlement or self-involvement seem to promote a sense of self-condemnation instead of a willingness to let oneself off of the hook or simply be insensitive to harms.

The person needs to be responsive first to any wrong that he or she has done. Then, he or she needs to try to forgive self for a particular behavior and adjust his or her self-concept based on having done that undesirable act.

CHAPTER 12

Intervening to Promote Reconciliation

Forgiveness is imbedded in a social context. Reconciliation is restoring trust. Talking about transgression is both the road to reconciliation and the social context within which people express and often experience forgiveness. Clinically, Forgiveness and Reconciliation through Experiencing Empathy (FREE) is the intervention I use with couples to promote reconciliation and facilitate the experience of forgiveness. Let us take a bird's eye view of this method.

Overview of FREE

People do not have to discuss transgressions. They can simply cut off interactions or ignore, avoid, or even move away from the person. However, often when we are involved in an ongoing relationship, we have invested in it and want to maintain that investment. We do not have to reconcile. So, reconciliation involves a decision and the cooperation of the other person. People decide whether, how, and when to do so. Partners work to collaborate so that both partners also want to reconcile. Unlike for forgiveness, reconciliation requires the cooperation of both parties.

If partners are willing to take the risk, they then enter into discussions about the transgression. As they talk about transgressions, they affect the magnitude of the injustice gap by offering or seeking explanations and reacting to those explanations for what happened. At the end, other decisions are needed. People need to decide whether to forgive and whether to express that forgiveness to the offender. That person must then either accept or not accept forgiveness.

Talking about the transgression may not heal all of the damage done by the transgression. A period of detoxifying the relationship from the transgression, its effects, or the aftermath is needed by both parties. During that period, people plan for inevitable human failures and decide on strategies for continued interaction with each other despite these failures.

The transgressions disrupted people's lives together. Even when they have detoxified the relationship of the negative, most people with ongoing relationships want to build devotion into the relationship, making it stronger in the places that were broken.

FREE involves the four processes of decision, discussion, detoxification, and devotion. It is an intervention I initially developed in working with couples in marital therapy, but it can be applied with any two partners—friends, supervisor-worker, parent-child, or teacher-student. In the psychoeducational use of the FREE intervention, we use structured exercises. Couples are involved in discussion at each phase of the intervention. Their input into shaping their own experience is an important part of FREE. In this chapter, I will describe the program and provide exercises that you can adapt to therapy or use in psychoeducation.

Reconciliation is not always desirable. Sometimes it is not possible to reconcile because the offender is dead or unavailable. At other times, it is not wise to reconcile. The relationship may be too explosive or potentially dangerous for one or both parties for the two people to even move toward reconciliation. Sometimes the safety or the simple preference of one party can make reconciliation not desirable or possible.

John Paul Lederac, an international peace-worker, has said about reconciliation, "You do not build a bridge starting in the middle. You start with a strong foundation on on each shore, build toward the middle. When it is solid, others can walk across it" (Lederac, 2001, p. 186). Let us expand on Lederac's bridge-building model. People might proceed at different rates from their side of the issue, and the bridge might not always meet in the middle, but more toward one person's edge than the other's. Importantly, though, a bridge is established, and both people can walk over it and benefit.

Decision (Plank 1 in the Bridge): Should I Discuss Transgressions?

Much of the first step might be made by virtue of a person seeking counseling. If a couple or family present for counseling, the assumption is that reconciliation is desired. That, of course, is not always the case. Many seek counseling as a way of proving that the relationship is a failure, thus disinhibiting divorce. If an individual approaches a therapist with the presenting problem of deciding whether to seek to reconcile, many considerations are necessary. People must decide whether, how, and when to reconcile.

Decide Whether to Reconcile

This is an emotional decision. Deciding whether to reconcile is not merely tabulating a pro versus con ledger, totaling the columns, and rationally deciding that one column is longer than the other. Analysis of the cost and benefits about reconciling or not is indeed important and should not be cast aside. But remember that I have made distinctions throughout about emotional and rational decision-making. Reconciliation is an emotional decision.

Analysis is important in these decisions, but there are many intangibles. First, because reconciliation involves two people, we cannot control the behavior of the other person. We cannot always rationally control our own behavior. Second, we cannot see the future. Not only can we not see how the person is going to act, but we can also not see future events that might influence outcomes. Third, our gut reactions often warn us of high risk. This does not mean that risky acts should be avoided, but it does mean that decision-making will likely be occurring differently in risky decisions as opposed to low-risk decisions.

Why might we want to reconcile? A number of reasons might exist that make us want to reconcile. We may simply not want to fail in a relationship. Or, we might want to reconcile because we value the other person and do not want to lose a relationship with him or her. Perhaps they think reconciliation will be less painful. They might not want to let behavior slide. Or people might want to reconcile because they are not willing to simply return to the status quo. Finally, they might want to forgive and reconcile because they realize that they would be lonelier if they did not resolve the transgression and reconcile. To avoid the pain of loneliness, they take the risk of attempting to reconcile.

Costs of reconciling. But, there are a lot of costs to reconciling. The costs might occur because one cannot control the partner's behavior. If a reproach is made about a partner's transgression, the partner might not be willing to change, embarrassing the person who made the reproach. The effort may blow up into a full-scale argument, resulting in new hurts or blame upon the individual who initiates the reconciliation. Some might be unwilling to attempt to reconcile because they cannot see the future. Or strange as it seems, some people just like to hold grudges. Trying to reconcile requires effort and work. This is costly and ups the cost side of the pro and con ledger. The victim might be unwilling to initiate discussion about a transgression because the victim has his or her own unresolved issues. Perhaps the person has adjusted to being apart and has a sense of closure. Perhaps the person still wants to hold on to his or her grudges and desires for vengeance. The person might prefer the misery that he or she knows to the uncertainty of potential misery if the grudges or desires for vengeance were given up. The person might not want to enter into an attempted reconciliation because the person might have to give up the fantasy that the person will crawl back and beg forgiveness. The person may realize in his or her heart that such a fantasy is unreasonable, yet the secret pleasure of the person groveling and begging for forgiveness is too delicious to give up. The victim might not want to forgive because the victim does not want to ease the transgressor's suffering. A victim might also not want to forgive because he or she does not want to risk negative consequences to the future of the relationship. The person might believe, "If I forgive, I am not holding her accountable for what she did," or "I don't want to reconcile because he will think that I am weak and take advantage of me."

The benefits to reconciling typically reduce the victim's injustice gap. The perpetrator usually engages in costly vulnerable behaviors—like apologizing—which help the victim by bringing more of a sense of justice into the situation. This should increase the likelihood of forgiveness, but it also motivates reconciliation.

Of course, it is not just a victim who might want to reconcile. Many times, it is the offender who wants to reconcile. The offender might want to do so to alleviate his or her guilt and make amends for what he or she did. The person may be genuinely contrite and remorseful over his or her behavior, and see that he or she has placed the relationship in jeopardy because of the transgression. However, in the same way that victims might not want to reconcile, the perpetrator might also not want to reconcile. The person might be ashamed of his or her behavior and might be driven not to disclose that shame. The person might feel psychologically naked by revealing his or her vulnerability. He or she might feel guilty and not want to reconcile because it would mean having to face God and confess sinful behavior, or face the partner and confess to disappointing and hurting the partner when the person professes love. The offender might feel that admitting to his or her weaknesses will result in giving up self-sufficiency or being taken advantage of. The person might not be willing to face himself or herself and admit to being fundamentally flawed. Self-esteem, then, factors into willingness to initiate reconciliation. It is likely that if the self-esteem is threatened by admitting to wrongdoing, people with fragile high self-esteem will experience an unacceptable amount of threat and be unwilling and unable to admit to their guilt, at least to start a conversation.

A wrongdoer might be inhibited from initiating reconciliation because of the threat to the self, but the person might also recognize that by failing to try to reconcile, the injustice gap remains a gaping wound that is not narrowing and may, in fact, be widening as the wrongdoer fails to take any action to repair it. The wrongdoer may not want to reconcile because he or she feels justified in his or her behavior. The person does not really believe anything was incorrect about the behavior, and in fact, any reasonable person might act the same way. The person might even see provocations by the victim and believe that he or she was simply defending himself or herself against the victim or, in the worst case, launch a pre-emptive strike against the victim, who would be certain to attack.

Of course, initiating reconciliation is risky for the wrongdoer. The wrongdoer puts himself or herself on the line by making himself or herself vulnerable. She might think, "If I confess and he refuses to forgive, I could be letting myself in for it. My confession would be out there on the table and I would be held to blame from then on, and nothing good would come out of this except that he would be able to torture me with blame that I had admitted to." The person might believe, then, that any admission might be used against the person, or the victim might demand some huge restitution that the perpetrator might be unable or unwilling accommodate.

Some people believe that getting justice will automatically lead to reconciliation. This is not necessarily the case. One cannot count on justice producing reconciliation, to which anyone in civil lawsuits can attest. Certainly, justice is important in its own right, and doing what is right is important.

Exercises for Deciding Whether to Talk About Transgressions

Exercise 1: Make a cost-benefit balance sheet. To assess the rational reason that you might want to discuss the issue, or not discuss the issue, make up a balance sheet in which the costs of entering the discussion are listed on one side and the benefits are listed on the other side. After the balance sheet is completed, use an asterisk to designate which you think are the most important reasons, pro and con, to consider.

After examining the list, ask yourself frankly whether there are any benefits that are pre-emptive and that trump all the other reasons. For some people, religious motivations might be the most important. For other people, a marital spat will be discussed because the marriage is considered the most important relationship the person has and, in fact, an important part of the person's identity. In the same way, consider if any costs are absolutely prohibitive. For example, if the partner has been savage in every such discussion in the past, then that might be an absolute prohibition that outweighs any benefit of entering into the talk about the transgression.

Assay your net feelings about this balance sheet. Try to ignore the length of each column. The number of reasons rarely wins the day in these considerations. Instead, try to feel with the gut and consider the subjective weighting of the costs and benefits. The gut will probably tell you that reconciliation is risky. That should warn you that your decision-making is going to be emotional. That does not mean you should ignore reason, but it does mean that those subjective feelings will probably hold sway over a purely rational analysis. Nevertheless, by making the balance sheet, you identify things that you might not have thought about that might be affecting your emotions and playing strongly into the emotional decision-making.

Exercise 2: Determine whether reconciliation is unsafe, unwise, or not possible. If reconciliation is impossible because the person is dead, has moved away, or is protected by a restraining order, or because in other ways communication is impossible, then give up the idea of reconciliation unless circumstances dramatically change. If it seems unwise or unsafe to reconcile, consider what might make the reconciliation wiser or safer. Could circumstances be arranged where a safer conversation could occur?

Decide How to Reconcile

If a person decides to reconcile, the immediate question that must be dealt with is how to attempt to carry out this program. On one hand, the person knows that taking a hard position, judging the other person, is likely to cause negative consequences to the relationship. The judged person will almost certainly argue, become angry, and attempt to justify and prove why he or she is correct in what was done. This negative emotion and behavior will almost certainly distance the two parties instead of reconcile them. Thus, some care has to be given to how to reconcile.

Implicit reconciliation. There are two primary ways to reconcile. One is implicit reconciliation and the other is explicit reconciliation (Worthington & Drinkard, 2000). Implicit reconciliation often occurs in nontroubled relationships. Because we are focusing on therapy, I will not belabor the many ways to implicitly reconcile. People can reconcile through working together toward a mutual goal, through simply getting to know each other better, through having a third party intervene, or even through battling a common enemy. Romantic couples might have a spat and reconcile through making love without having talked explicitly about the conflict.

Explicit reconciliation. Most therapy works with partners to reconcile by explicitly dealing with the issues. For explicit reconciliation to occur, (1) hostilities have to be brought to an end. This is why nations declare cease-fires and truces. Only if an agreement that hostilities will cease is made, will progress be made toward reconciling. (2) Parties come together. Merely stopping hostile actions but having no interactions can result in failing to build trust. As soon as a truce violation occurs, the parties will immediately resume conflict. As such, some peaceful coming-together is needed. This may require a third party to serve as intermediary. When the parties come together, both have to act positively toward each other.

There has to be some positive interaction to continue to build trust or the parties will not consider themselves trustworthy; thus, reconciliation will not occur. Most mental health professionals tend to have little confidence in implicit reconciliation strategies. Without explicitly discussing issues, people do not always understand what the other party is attempting to do and might misinterpret it. The bridge to reconciliation is a model for explicit reconciliation.

Decide When to Reconcile

There are some clear recommendations about when not to attempt reconciliation. Most are commonsense. Usually, reconciliation should not be initiated when a person is very angry, highly stressed, frustrated, or hurt. If the person feels as if he or she must have the last word, the person is usually not willing or able to listen effectively and simply wants to tell the other person off. Beware about attempting reconciliation when one or both people have severely wounded pride. That can be explosive. It is better to put off discussion of the transgressions until things have cooled off a bit. Another time to beware of discussions that are about reconciliation is when there is a large power differential between the two parties.

If the parties have a history of being able to reconcile differences, if both feel safe with the other party, if the people trust each other, then the discussions over transgressions are more likely to be fruitful. If there is a history of mutual sacrifice in the relationship, that speaks well for the possibility of reconciling.

Summary

Many decisions need to be made about whether people enter into discussions about transgressions. Those considerations are complex, and a purely rational listing of pros and cons is unlikely to shed full light on what is likely to happen if discussions are begun. Each person needs to somehow monitor himself or herself and try to assess the likelihood of acting negatively in an unbiased and fair way. This is difficult, given that discussions about transgressions involve high risk and high emotion, and decision-making is not likely to be fully rational even though the person is glibly ticking off logical reasons.

Discussion (Plank 2): How Do People Talk About Transgressions?

Most of my attention will be directed to this second plank in the bridge to reconciliation. Because it deals with discussions, I presume that both parties are present, though in a pinch, I have coached individuals in how to discuss transgressions with their partners.

Understanding What Therapists Seek to Accomplish

Be clear on definitions. Many terms seem to get linked together and used as synonyms in most people's minds. There are, however, important differences in these terms. For example, *discussing differences* is a part of communication in which people talk about different perceptions or goals and try to describe their thoughts and feelings about the different options. *Negotiating agreement* is a way of trying to arrive at some common ground in resolving these differences, and it suggests a give and take on each side and a common objective of arriving at a common agreement. *Resolving differences* does not imply that an agreement will be reached. People may agree to disagree yet feel resolved. *Conflict management* involves ways that people who are engaged in an active and emotional disagreement attempt to communicate so that they can keep the conflict from spiraling out of control. *Conflict resolution* involves coming to an agreement about an emotional conflict. All of these issues are hot on-the-table differences. *Talking about transgressions* assumes that wrongs (or perceived wrongs) have been done by one or both parties. A person could easily win a conflict but transgress against a partner in such a way that an apology might be called for. In this case, the object is to talk about the transgressions in a way that people will handle and heal hurts and obliterate offenses.

Applying the stress-and-coping theory. In interactions around confessions, the key considerations are the same as throughout this book. Both people are well advised to attempt to reduce the threat that they are making through any perceived attack on the other person's value. This might be a straightforward attack or even a hint of an implication. Thus, the person is attempting to discuss transgressions in a way that will lead to minimal threat appraisal. Yes, transgressions do pose a challenge. They are difficult for both parties to negotiate, but threats will trigger negative emotional responses.

The size of the injustice gap also plays a major role in these transgressions. The victim attempts to keep the door open so the offender can reduce the size of the injustice gap by offering an apology, expressing remorse, and perhaps even making restitution. If the reproach is harsh, this will make the wrongdoer believe that he or she is even more correct than he or she had previously thought, and the wrongdoer's attitudes will harden in subsequent communications to be widened by additional defensiveness or attack. The wrongdoer seeks to reduce the size of the injustice gap by bringing personal justice into the situation. This is accomplished by performing costly acts such as apologies or asking for forgiveness or making restitution. This helps narrow the injustice gap that the victim is experiencing, thus making it more likely for forgiveness to take place. By offering a patient excuse or even just suggesting that there are mitigating circumstances, even if the victim does not feel the need to hear those, the ease in forgiveness is also increased.

With lowered chances of threat appraisals, and reduced injustice gaps, people will be less likely to respond with unforgiveness, and their coping responses will be widened. The more people feel threatened and perceive large amounts of injustice, the more focused they are on defensive coping mechanisms. One helpful coping strategy is forgiveness, involving granting decisional forgiveness, experiencing emotional forgiveness, and then perhaps expressing that forgiveness to the wrongdoer.

Understanding how people interact around predicaments. Erving Goffman (1969) was a sociologist who was concerned about how people deal with predicaments to maintain ongoing interactions. Goffman realized that people who wrong each other and those who react to wrongs risk losing face, that is, suffering loss of esteem of others and self. People, thus, have a need to save face through their choice of interactions with others around difficult situations. Goffman outlined a series of interactions that happen that allow conversations to continue and thus enable people to save face with each other and themselves. Later, Schönbach (1990) described how people who are wronged make a *reproach* or a *request for the explanation* for the wrongdoer's acts. Wrongdoers then provide an explanation of their acts. These *accounts* are public attributions of causality. Attribution theory, a branch of social psychology, describes how people explain causes of behavior.

Therapists are not training in skills; they are helping repair the emotional bond. It is important for a therapist to be clear on what is being attempted in talking about transgressions. Talking about transgressions and healing hurts can certainly be the product of applying interpersonal skills effectively. There are particular skills that I will discuss in this chapter that are helpful for handling hurts. However, the therapist's object is not simply to equip people with skills. While skills are necessary for handling hurts, they are usually not sufficient for handling these hurts, and certainly they are not sufficient for healing hurts. This insight has come from the field of studies of dynamics of marital relationships and couples therapy (Fincham, Hall, & Beach, 2005; Worthington, 2005d). For troubled couples, the deeper problem seems to be that the emotional bond has been disrupted. The disruption of that emotional bond has changed people's behaviors so that they communicate in ways that are harmful. They become defensive due to intrapsychic or prior interpersonal conflicts. They are out of control with their emotional expression.

When therapies tried to teach skills to repair these deficits, the therapies were somewhat successful—not merely because partners were more skilled communicators. Rather, partners valued each other and attempted to communicate that valuing by trying new helpful skills within the relationship. The restoration of the emotional bond, then, occurred because of a communication of love. This literature on marital conflict has been summarized in a review article by Fincham et al. (2005).

Preparing to repair the emotional bond. People must be readied to change. The therapist can employ four methods to ready partners to work toward strengthening the emotional bond. First, promote empathy. Empathy softens attitudes and allows the other to feel valued. When clients feel understood and valued, they are more likely to listen to the therapist's perspective and be able to emphasize with that perspective. Second, invite partners to contemplate what it would mean if one lost the present relationship by seeking to understand and feel what one would experience if the relationship ended. Third, help partners show that they really do care and want to repair the emotional bond. Thus, it is helpful for both parties to listen to the other person with empathy and compassion, delay defending his or her position, forebear from negative expression, reflect back what the other person says, be fair in his or her expectations, and decide whether he or she needs to get forgiveness or give forgiveness or, in most cases, both get and give forgiveness. Finally, before trying to talk about transgressions, each party should examine his or her own acts. Usually, misunderstandings are two-sided, not just one-sided.

Exercises for Discussing Transgressions

Entering discussions about transgressions is risky. The relationship might get better or worse. Emotion is high. Decision-making is often emotional rather than rational.

Exercise 3: Establish ground rules. As such, it is helpful, before undertaking some of the exercises in making a good reproach or making a good confession, that the partners informally establish some ground rules before launching into their discussion. For example, four agreements might be reached. It is helpful, especially for a mental health professional, to make these agreements explicit rather than implicit, but with partners, implicit agreement, at least, needs to be arrived at.

Exercise 4: Arrive at explicit agreement about what is hoped for. First, the participants need to answer the question, "Can we both agree to be responsible for and change our own behavior, and not be so concerned about the other's behavior?" Second, "Can we both agree to declare a truce and try not to hurt each other again while we are discussing these issues?" Third, "Can we agree that we value our relationship and want to work out a solution that will allow it to not only continue, but even strengthen?" Fourth, "Can we both agree to attempt to formulate a plan to rebuild or heal our relationship?"

In a counseling psychotherapy or psychoeducational setting, people can participate in structured exercises to walk through each aspect of the process of discussing transgressions.

Exercise 5: Partners are taught about good communication. That might involve at least three modules of teaching: (1) Teach active listening skills and both the experience and expression of empathy. (2) Each person describes in writing what he or she specifically thinks the transgressions against them are. (3) People can role-play the worst possible communication they have in confronting each other about these transgressions. The helper processes what makes bad communication.

Exercise 6: Teach partners how to make good reproaches. A reproach asks the wrongdoer or perceived wrongdoer to explain his or her reasons for acting as he or she did. The reproach can be clumsy. It can blame the person or imply that the person is defective in personality attributes. Or a reproach can be graceful or draw the person into a nondefensive discussion of the events. An unhelpful reproach assumes the worst of the wrongdoer and may even allude to stable, global negative personality traits that cause the behavior. For example, an unhelpful reproach might say, "You always are so insensitive! How could you say such a hurtful and unfeeling thing to me?"

Helpful reproaches generally attribute positive characteristics to the wrongdoer, but identify the act as being hurtful. Effective reproaches often will express puzzlement about why the person acted wrongly and will ask for help in understanding. For example, an effective reproach might say, "You usually are very sensitive. I was hurt by what you said and I was wondering if you could help me understand why you might have said such a thing as you did." A successful reproach does not heal the relationship. It merely helps the conversation continue without provoking the wrongdoer to respond defensively.

A person who feels wronged and wishes to craft an effective request for an explanation might be told of the elements of a good reproach. These have been tabulated below. A person can use this as a template for creating his or her own reproach.

1. Consider how sure you are that the other person was wrong. Remember that we have a tendency to justify our own behaviors and not see what is causing the other person's behaviors in the same way an objective observer would.
2. Identify specifically what you think the wrongdoing was.
3. Identify aspects of the wrongdoer's personality that are strengths that usually characterize the person, but in this case, the person behaved differently.

4. Identify situational pressures that the person might have been experiencing that might have made them do wrong.
5. Express puzzlement about why the person behaved in the hurtful or offensive way.
6. Ask for help in understanding his or her behavior in a way that does not put the wrongdoer on the offensive.

Exercise 7: Teach partners how to avoid provocative accounts. Three types of accounts have been found to stifle conversation or provoke defensiveness in the person who feels like a victim. Perhaps the most toxic of those accounts is a *denial* or *refusal.* A denial does not accept responsibility for wrongdoing. In fact, it denies that any wrongdoing has occurred and suggests that the person making the reproach was incorrect, stupid, or malicious. The denial or refusal might sound something like, "I did not say anything that should have hurt you. No sane person would ever be hurt by that innocuous comment." *Justifications* also cut off positive discussions. Justifications accept responsibility for the act, but argue that any reasonable person would have acted the same way under the circumstances. The act may be acknowledged as a wrongdoing and still be accounted for as a justifiable act. The justifier might say, "Of course, I said you made a stupid remark. That's because the remark was stupid. Anybody can see that." The *hasty excuse* also is not helpful. Excuses, in many cases, can help further conversation. An *excuse* is an acknowledgment that one did the act that one is accused of doing, but offers mitigating circumstances that provide good reasons for the act. For example, the excuser might say, "Yes, I did say that you made a stupid remark, and I probably would not have done that except that I have been under a strain at work and had just been yelled at by my boss. So I was feeling pretty hurt and defensive at the time." The problem with excuses is not that they provide mitigating circumstances, but they can be clumsy, poorly timed, or defensive. The person making the reproach does not feel that he or she has been heard and the concerns are appreciated. In addition, the tone of the response can give the impression that one is trying to weasel out of trying to accept responsibility.

Exercise 8: Teach partners how to make helpful accounts. The two types of helpful accounts identified by Schönbach (1990) have been what we might term *patient excuses* and *concessions* (or confessions). The patient excuse gives a complete apology and confession without making excuses about mitigating circumstances. Then, after the wrongdoer has asked for forgiveness, the wrongdoer might say, "Would it help you to be able to consider whether to forgive me if you knew some of the things that were going on in my life that might have led to my actions?" The concession (or confession) admits fully to responsibility. It expresses contrition and remorse over having done the act and thus includes an apology. An apology has two characteristics: sincere remorse and the acceptance of responsibility. A concession or confession might include other elements such as the suggestion of possible reparation or restitution and request for forgiveness among others. For example, a good concession might sound something like, "I am really sorry that I said that you made a stupid remark. I was wrong in saying that. I am really very sorry that I exercised so little self-control and also said something that really wasn't true. I'd like to be able to make it up to you, if there is any way that you can see that I could undo the damage to our relationship. I also want to ask that you forgive me for saying those hurtful things."

Of course, people are offended or hurt and the supposed offender does not always believe he or she has done anything wrong. In such a case, is it hypocritical to apologize? One can be truly regretful and contrite that he or she said something that hurt the relationship between the partners. The person can also feel truly remorseful that he or she expressed things provocatively and gave an occasion for the other person to be offended. The person might still wish to apologize, but might be careful about how the apology is offered. On one hand, a refusal to apologize will almost always lead to additional harms in the relationship if the victim believes that an apology is in order. The wrongdoer, then, might say something like, "I really am sorry that I said something that hurt our relationship. I don't want to hurt our relationship, and I was wrong in expressing myself in such an awkward way." In this case, the person apologizes for the things that were wrong, but does not really admit that the remark made was incorrect.

The victim might detect that the apology is not really for the event, but rather for the delivery, and might directly ask about that, saying something like, "You didn't really say that the remark was wrong, that my thinking was not stupid. Do you really feel that it is stupid?"

The person then might say, "I think that my wording was about as bad as it could possibly have been. In terms of the remark, I am thinking about it, and I think it's possible that other ways of describing your idea would be better—more in line with my thinking."

Exercise 9: Teach people a model for CONFESSing when one is wrong. I have previously (Worthington, 2003) identified eight elements of a good concession or confession (see Table 12.1). Seven of these are captured in the acrostic CONFESS, and the eighth is making an offer to tell the person mitigating circumstances (i.e., a patient excuse). A person seeking to confess wrongdoing might craft his or her own confession including each of these elements and concluding with the offer to supply a patient excuse.

Table 12.1 An Acrostic for Making a Good Confession of One's Wrongdoing [from Worthington, E. L., Jr. (2003). *Forgiving and Reconciling: Bridges to Wholeness and Hope.* Downers Grove, IL: InterVarsity Press.]

C: *Confess without excuse.* Say that you did wrong and name the wrongdoing specifically.

O: *Offer an apology.* An apology involves taking responsibility, which you have just done in Step C, and expressing remorse and contrition. Importantly, the person does not have to say, "I'm sorry," as much as the person must get across the idea that he or she is truly remorseful and contrite, ashamed, guilty, disappointed in him or herself, and possessing sadness and sorrow for having done the hurtful or offensive act.

N: *Note the other person's pain.* This is a chance to express empathy for the person as you understand the person's experience. Tell the person what you perceive of them experiencing and suffering. Do so in a way that suggests that you understand their perspective and emotional experience, and can even identify with them had you been in the same situation.

F: *Forever value.* You might state that resolving the relationship problems is more valuable to you than winning or being right in this instance and you will be glad to incur whatever sacrifices are necessary to resolve this difficulty.

E: *Equalize.* Ask the person if there is anything that can be done to make up for the wrongdoing. Be wary of simply suggesting something that you think might be restitution. People understand love in different ways. For example, if you forgot a close friend's birthday, even after that friend had hinted numerous times at it, and you decided to buy the friend a Corvette, the friend might not believe that you had made restitution for your forgetfulness because the friend might not value receiving the gift. The friend might want some evidence that you value and do remember important aspects of the friend's life. Therefore, it is best to ask the other person what you might do to make restitution. Then you must be willing to do the restitution or negotiate something comparable.

S: *Say never again.* The person wants to hear that you will never try to hurt him or her in the same way ever again.

S: *Seek forgiveness.* Ask, "Can you ever forgive me for hurting you?"

The eighth step is to offer mitigating reasons for your acts: "Would it help you to know what was going on in my life in order for you to consider forgiving me?" Give reasons.

Exercise 10: Teach clients how one should not respond to a confession. The wrongdoer has just made a good confession. Coach the victim how not to respond, teaching the person not to (1) focus on the things the confession did not accomplish or (2) respond from one's embarrassment. First, an apology and restitution, no matter how thorough and how good they are, will rarely make things 100% better. An injustice gap will remain. This response will put off the offender: "Yeah, but this doesn't take care of everything. A lot of time will be necessary before things will be put right again." The victim is, on one hand, absolutely correct. On the other hand, that response is deadly to the relationship. Instead, coach the victim to empathize with the transgressor. He or she should repeat back what he or she heard the transgressor say and then express a realization of how difficult it is to apologize and to try to make things right. Even if the person made a grossly inadequate apology and little or no offer of restitution, if anything was positive, acknowledge that and how costly it is. This focus on the small positive step, rather than the large injustice gap yawning ahead, will reinforce that first step and make a second step more likely.

Second, when an offender makes a good confession, the victim will often be embarrassed for the offender and will try to ease the offender's discomfort. A common response is to minimize the confession, saying, "Oh, it's nothing, no problem," and give all the nonverbal signs that say, "Let's not talk about this anymore. This is too uncomfortable." Or the victim might offer a counterconfession, "Yes, and I did ... ." Or similarly, "I'm certainly willing to take responsibility for my part in this misunderstanding." While these knee-jerk reactions balance justice because both parties express their remorse and contrition over their part in the breakdown of communication, either communication can also deflect the importance of the confession. It is helpful if both parties remember that a good confession does not automatically restore trust. Trust is restored over time as people behave in a trustworthy way with each other. How people respond to confessions is one way that trustworthy behavior can be shown.

Teach the victim specifically how to respond to a good confession. Once a good confession is made and initial responses of empathy and appreciation are made, the victim must consider the situation. The injustice gap has probably been reduced in magnitude, as has the threat to the relationship, but the person might, or might not, be willing to forgive. Forgiving often requires time. I have continually made distinctions between making a decision to forgive and experiencing emotional forgiveness and between expressing forgiveness and both kinds of forgiving. The victim may decide to grant decisional forgiveness, but not imply that he or she has experienced emotional forgiveness. The victim might say, "I do forgive you, but my feelings are probably going to take a while to catch up with my decision to forgive. Can you accept that I do forgive you, but will have to make an effort to have my emotions be healed? I'll need to work to change my feelings and that will take a while." That might be a good time, as well, to say something about mutually accountable behaviors. The person might continue, "Can you also appreciate that because of this hurt, we are going to need to make some changes in our relationship so these hurts will not happen again? I care about you as a friend, and I don't want these misunderstandings to destroy our friendship."

Exercise 11: Responding to an inadequate confession. A person might make a confession that is far from perfect. The immediate response to that should still be empathy and appreciation. But perhaps the step is so small that the victim cannot possibly forgive. The apology was the merest hint of the acceptance of responsibility, and no promise is made of trying to avoid similar transgressions. The wrongdoer, though, might stop and wait for a positive response from the victim, expecting forgiveness. A victim probably needs to say something like, "I am trying to forgive you. I know that I'm still upset. I think we need to each do some things differently before I can fully forgive. I appreciate your apology. I'll continue to work to forgive, but I am not quite there yet. It is important to me that you apologized for part of your role in this misunderstanding. I hope we'll both think about these events and maybe come to a fuller understanding of the parts that we each played."

When the victim feels that the explanation and confession were inadequate, he or she should consider that the wrongdoer may sincerely believe that he or she took an enormous step and full forgiveness is deserved. The victim typically recognizes his or her own suffering and feels that the perpetrator did too little. Both need to examine themselves and take the steps necessary to restore the relationship.

Work Through the Five Steps to REACH Forgiveness

The victim might grant and even express decisional forgiveness, but he or she will need to seek emotional forgiveness to help restore the relationship. The victim might thus work through the five steps to REACH forgiveness.

Discussing the transgression (Plank 2 in the bridge to reconciliation) begins a process of reconciling. Follow-through requires persistence and vigilance on both parties' parts. Both are attempting to reduce injustice and future threat within their relationship. Thus, they open the door to move further onto the next plank on the bridge to reconciliation: detoxifying the relationship of negativity.

Detoxification of Relationships (Plank 3): How Do We Repair the Damage?

Like a broken bone, most relationships will not spontaneously heal. A leg with a compound fracture needs to be set and kept in a cast. On the other hand, occasionally a small break, such as a finger or cracked rib, can heal back over time without much attention to the break other than being sensitive not to place an undue strain on the area again. Detoxification of the relationship is part of the healing of damaged relationships. Partners work to eliminate the bad aspects of the relationship that may have come about because of multiple hurts and offenses over a period of time, or especially negative responses to hurt or offenses in the relationship.

Assess the Relationship

Perhaps the partners have talked about the immediate transgressions and have granted decisional forgiveness. Yet, negative emotions still exist. Emotional forgiveness is slowly being experienced. People also might realize that numerous transgressions have occurred in the past that threaten the relationship.

Assessment of the relationship failures and poisons is therefore an essential step in formulating a plan to detoxify the relationship. To assess the relationship, it is helpful to have a systematic strategy. I have identified (Worthington, 1991, 2005d) several areas in relationships that require assessment in couples counseling. First, are there *additional wounds* in the past that need to be considered and might possibly need to be forgiven? Second, are there *negative patterns of communication* existing between the partners? For example, is there a difficulty expressing emotions such that emotions cannot be expressed, and only negative emotions are typically expressed? Is there an expression of valuing between the two participants? Is information passed clearly? Third, is there *ongoing conflict* between the two participants? What is the nature of that conflict? Is there a power struggle? Fourth, is there a problem in *closeness*? Is the relationship too distant or does one person want more closeness than the other person? Is the relationship too close so the partners' lives are intertwined and they need more independence? Fifth, what about *cognition*? Are there negative assumptions, beliefs, expectancies, and attributions that are poisoning the relationships? Sixth, do the partners feel a sense of *commitment* to each other? Seventh, are there *outside factors* such as alcoholism, drug use, job pressures, and the like that poison the relationship?

Detoxifying Negative Behaviors

When partners fall into troubled relationships, their behaviors become increasingly negative. In the final analysis, they must eliminate the negative behaviors and replace them with positive behaviors. For example, the contempt that one expresses in the tone of voice or phrasing needs to be purged. Bitterness must be removed from the voice. A person has to determine that he or she will not bring up the past and continually try to beat up the partner with that past. The person must, therefore, give up the use of the past hurt to punish the person or extract good behavior in the future. When the other person does behave hurtfully, harsh reproaches must be avoided. When one is reproached for a mistake, one has to squelch defensiveness and not attack the person to provide one's own defense.

Squabbles will continually pop up and have to be short-circuited. They must be stopped before the interactions escalate.

John Gottman (1994) has described what is called the four horsemen of the apocalypse, in which a relationship degenerates from criticism to defensiveness to contempt for the person to finally either stonewalling (which is removing all feeling and determining not to be hurt) or full-scale war. To detoxify the relationship, each partner must determine where the relationship is with regard to this cascade toward dissolution of the relationship. The person must then try to reverse the cascade. If people are at war with each other, they have to declare a cease-fire and move back up the cascade even though it is moving toward an engaged emotional position that might mean expression of contempt for the partner. Not all partners move toward war at the stage prior to dissolution of the relationship. Some move to a disengaged state that Gottman calls stonewalling. If partners have disengaged, they have to accept that they will experience pain and anger again. If people are at the stage of contempt for each other, they have to move back up to a state in which they might react defensively. They still feel that attacks will happen, but they need to determine that they will not personalize the attacks and express contempt for the partner. If people are in the stage of relationship dissolution that is characterized by criticism, they need to realize that criticism is a step toward defensiveness and essentially moves down the cascade. Thus, effort must be made to avoid expressing criticism and then to attempt to not to criticize the partner, even mentally. In both defensiveness and criticism, people need to forego making negative reactions. They must decide that they do not have to point out the other person's flaws, weaknesses, or mistakes, but rather can accept the partner, "warts and all."

When conflicts become part of the relationship, people have emergent goals (Fincham et al., 2005). Emergent goals are when positive relationship goals are supplanted by the goal of winning the argument or showing that one is superior to the partner. Moving away from defensiveness and criticism requires not letting emergent goals get a foothold. Both partners must realize that they are moving toward a normal relationship. That normal relationship is not a perfect relationship. It is one that has defeat and moments of mutual victory, but it is a relationship in which the goals of the relationship are positive and forward-looking.

Overall, a good way to summarize the detoxification of behaviors is to say that people need to cultivate an *attitude of latitude* whenever the partner does not live up to one's expectations. Furthermore, when the partner behaves well, it is easy to ignore that behavior if the focus has been on failures and negativity for a while. Instead, the person might cultivate an *attitude of gratitude*. He or she must recognize the times when the partner shows restraint or does something positive. Then he or she should express gratitude to the partner for taking positive steps. The expression of gratitude must be done positively, instead of implying that the partner has been deficient for a long time and has *finally* done something positive. Instead, a partner should merely comment on the positivity of what was done.

Detoxifying Negative Cognition

Troubled relationships are plagued by negative expectations and assumptions by the partner and the partner's behavior. Partners need to examine their assumptions. Do they anticipate nothing but negative? If so, can they place those assumptions on hold and give the person the benefit of the doubt? The person has to have an opportunity to act in a trustworthy way to restore trust to the relationship and thus bring about reconciliation. They sometimes adopt equally troublesome, unrealistically positive expectations. They believe that the partner should never hurt them. That sets the relationship up for failure. Some disappointments and hurts are inevitable in even the best relationships.

Troubled relationships are undoubtedly plagued by negatively valenced memories. Those memories cannot be eliminated, and the negative emotions associated with the memories are a vestige of the troubled relationship.

The most difficult part of detoxifying cognition is the power of the situation to elicit rehearsed negative patterns. A couple can sit in a therapist's office and decide how they hope to act, think, and feel. But when a negative interaction occurs, the response often follows automatically. Partners, therefore, should develop some way of cueing themselves to interrupt the negative cycle. A therapist might help partners use the partner's face as a cue to interrupt the negative cycle. Partners can describe times in which they automatically responded by thinking negatively. After discussing this, the therapist can say, "You can let these facial expressions continue to trigger negative thoughts. Or, now that you are aware of their effect, you can choose to let the expressions trigger more positive coping methods. So, suppose you see your partner looking angry: What could you think that would interrupt the automatic trigger response?"

Partners identify interrupters, such as thinking, "Don't get triggered. I need to think of this as a roadblock to our happiness and figure a way around the roadblock." Then, in turn, one partner looks angry and the other thinks aloud what he or she thinks will bypass the automatic trigger.

Therapists can also stage supervised discussions in session. Those discussions provide new memories, which can bring up other more positive behaviors rather than the habitual automatic negativity.

Detoxifying Negative Emotions

Even if one changes one's conscious thinking and negative memories, the person's body will be conditioned to send messages that trigger negative emotions and cause the working memory to name the way a person is feeling as a negative feeling. Partners can detoxify negative emotions by creating other associations with the partner. If the partners do positive activities together, or laugh together, this positive emotion can fight against the negativity of harmful memories.

If people try hard to promote more positive relationships through doing conspicuous acts that they have not often done previously, then the partner can observe the effort and make more positive attributions to the partner about the partner's willingness to increase the degree of effort put into change. These positive attributions can also create positive feelings for the partner that can combat some of the negative bodily sensations that have arisen from the practiced negativity.

Detoxifying Situations

One of the most consistent findings in social psychology is that situations are powerful determinants of a human's behavior. Situations, then, need to be detoxified. If couples often argue in a particular situation, then it behooves them to find a way to transform that situation. For example, suppose a work unit is having conflict. They always meet in one person's office. Perhaps by finding a different office and making changes in their behavior at the same time, the situation will be detoxified. Similarly, suppose a husband and wife have most of their arguments at nighttime just before bed. They might decide that having a discussion in the bedroom is off-limits. That simple change in situation might decrease their conflict.

Summing Up Detoxification

From our look at detoxification of relationships, we can see that poisons can build up. People who are involved in conflict, even when the relationship is basically good, have trouble letting go of the conflict. There are numerous ways that people can attempt to remove this relational poison. Detoxifying the relationship is difficult. Partners are fighting against the patterns of behavior, thought, emotional response, and familiar trigger situations. Those familiar patterns trigger emergent goals—winning arguments, besting the other person, or responding to threats—high in the person's consciousness. Those goals keep people involved in habitual conflict. Those goals must be changed, and the structures that maintain those goals must be torn down. New cooperative structures must be built back into the relationship. It is not a matter of merely going back to a time of naïve peace. It is a matter of forming new structures that make allowance for failures.

Partners must cope with the onset of patterns they have been living with. Reconciliation is a major step in relational repair.

To reconcile, trust must be rebuilt through establishing new trustworthy behaviors. The old, nontrustworthy behaviors must be detoxified. There is more, however, to building trust than simply eliminating the negative. People must pay attention to building positive devotion if the relationship is to be fully reconciled.

Exercises for Detoxifying Relationships

The fundamental tasks in detoxifying the relationship are threefold. First, the partners must assess where they need to intervene to detoxify their relationship. Second, they need to establish cues that remind them that detoxification is needed. Third, they need to plan how they can detoxify behaviors, thoughts, emotions, and situations. In this application, I will describe one exercise for each of those three areas.

Exercise 12: Assessing what needs detoxification. The most likely locus for problems with any couple—romantic couple or friendship—resides in confession, communication, and conflict resolution. In each of those, people should identify toxic or potentially toxic behaviors and situations. A partner should use a single sheet of paper and list things that he or she thinks need to be detoxified in his or her particular relationship. For example, under confession behaviors, a person might identify his or her tendency to scream and berate the partner whenever the partner does a perceived transgression. The other partner might identify behaviors such as giving the cold shoulder or refusing to have sex if the partner disappoints or hurts the person.

Exercise 13: Creating cues that cultivate consideration. Once people have identified concrete things that require detoxification, partners should each individually think of what kind of cues can be created to interrupt the habitual patterns of behavior so that a toxic pattern does not habitually occur. For example, suppose one partner screams when she gets angry. She can give permission to the other partner to simply hold up a hand in a stop sign or in a gesture to pause. The screamer can let that be a cue to interrupt her screaming.

Exercise 14. Carrying out programs. Each partner is hoping to get attention off of the old habitual way of behaving and give positive attention to new ways to behave. One way to do this is to look systematically for instances in which the person was successful and the person's partner was successful in carrying out the agenda that was planned. Recognize verbally the other person's success.

Devotion (Plank 4): How Can We Put the Positive Back Into the Relationship and Build Trust?

Love is being willing to value the other person and being unwilling to devalue the other person. The recommendations I have made in each of these planks in the bridge to reconciliation are towards valuing, and not devaluing, the other person. At Plank 4, however, explicitly valuing the partner is the focal point.

To promote devotion between the partners, the partners need to know what the other person values so that one can do more of what the person values and avoid doing what is not valued. A Christian writer, Gary Chapman (1996), identified five love languages (see Table 12.2). The premise of Chapman's work was that people communicate love in ways that they would like to have love communicated to them, rather than by doing things the partner would like to have done. Chapman's five love languages are (1) words of love and encouragement, (2) quality time together, (3) physical touch and closeness, (4) gifts, and (5) acts of service. There are obviously many additional love languages by which people know they are loved and often convey love to others (see Table 12.2).

Change the Ratio of Positive to Negative Interactions

In 1993, Gottman rocked the world of couples dynamics and counseling by suggesting that he could predict marital longevity and quality by a simple metric of the ratio of positive interactions to negative interactions as observed in videotaped discussions by couples. He claimed that five positives to every negative interaction was indicative of a likelihood of marital success 4 years later. Less than a 5:1 ratio usually clustered around one positive to every negative or more negatives than positives. There seems to be little middle ground. Gottman posited a nonlinear transformation at about the level of five to one positive to negative interactions.

Table 12.2 Languages of Love

Words of love and encouragement*
Quality time together*
Physical touch and closeness*
Gifts*
Acts of service*
Empathic understanding
Respect
Having fun/Hanging out
Sharing experience

* from Chapman, G. D. (1996). *The five languages of love: How to express heartfelt commitment to your mate.* Chicago: Northfield Publishers.

This ratio was similar to other research by Hart and Risley (1995). They monitored families at home and recorded the conversations between parents and children. Vocabulary development was highly influenced by the ratio of positive to negative communications from parents to their children. If parents had a 6:1 ratio or greater, vocabulary growth was sometimes as much as a four times the rate as parents who communicated with a lower ratio of positives to negatives.

Other behavioral investigators who study marriage have found that the ratio of positive to negative interactions was similarly important. For example, a collaborator with Gottman, Howard Markman, found that couples who were seeking to repair their relationships often required a much higher ratio of positives to negatives for progress to be enjoyed. Their ratio was sometimes as much as 15:1. All this suggested, for a time throughout the 1990s, that if therapists could help couples change the ratio of positive to negative interactions, they might be able to help couples change their relationship.

Methodologically, let us note that Gottman examined the state that couples were in and did not measure what would happen if people changed their ratio. Generalizing that people who changed the ratio to a more positive ratio would make the couple have a better relationship was really not supported by any research, but was an assumption that therapists often make.

There is a definite arithmetic to the logic that governs change under these assumptions. For example, if during the course of a day, a couple had 20 positive interactions and 20 negative interactions, then the ratio was 1:1. Presumably, that relationship was troubled. To change the ratio to a 5:1 ratio, the couple could use two extreme strategies. They could increase the number of positive interactions to have 80 more positive interactions per day at the same level of negative interaction. Obviously, that is a difficult solution to the problem. An easier way to change the ratio of positive to negative interactions is to change the number of negative interactions. If the couple maintains the 20 positive interactions, by eliminating 16 negative interactions, they could raise the ratio to 5:1. It would be much easier to eliminate 16 negatives than to find 80 opportunities to have additional positive interactions. Of course, the couple would want to employ both strategies at the same time. The arithmetic, however, suggests that more impact might be felt by reducing negative interactions.

This is somewhat oversimplified. It is not just the ratio of positive to negative interactions that affects people, but their perceptions of the balance of positive and negative interactions. If a person who habitually has 20 negative interactions each day completes the day with only 4, the other person does not know how much restraint on the part of the partner was required to reduce the negative interactions from 20 to 4. The person does not see a negative interaction that does not occur. It is hard to notice that a person has decreased negative interactions. On the other hand, if someone does something positive that he or she does not usually do, that is more likely to be noticed.

Some researchers who studied couples interactions have suggested that Gottman's claims of the power of the 5:1 ratio of positives to negatives are overstated. Fincham et al. (2005) have pointed out how it appears not to be the behaviors or interactions that are of primary importance to better couples relationships, but instead the strength of the emotional bond between people. The ratio of interactions is a good measure of the strength of the emotional bond, but the bond is the key, not the interactions. Fincham et al. present strong evidence to support this contention.

Building Trust

Trust is built through the persistence of mutually trustworthy behavior on both people's parts. Thus, each person must behave trustworthily, and each person must perceive the other person's behavior as trustworthy. Partners can plan a way of increasing positive and decreasing negative interactions. Again, while this does not guarantee that the relationship will get better, if the partners realize that they are doing this in order to repair the emotional bond, it helps them interpret the acts in the spirit of how much the partner values them rather than attribute the change in behavior to a mechanical program.

People who seek to repair their relationship will often make decisions that they feel are sacrificial. The willingness to sacrifice has been shown to be important to relationship commitment and satisfaction (Karremans, Van Lange, Ouwerkerk, & Kluwer, 2003; Van Lange, Rulbult et al., 1997). For couples to promote devotion in the relationship they should know, going in, that their actions will need to be self-sacrificial at times. Furthermore, they need to be alert to perceiving the other person's self-sacrifices. Obviously, a very sensitive person might be able to spot the effort required for a person to exercise restraint or to give up things that are important to him or her for the sake of the partner. But the fact is that the emergent goals of trying to win arguments or protect the self are triggered by negativity. Those emergent goals often focus people's attention away from the self-sacrificial acts that they or the partner does, and focus them on winning conflicts, or inflicting more harms than the partner inflicts. Thus, special attention is needed to make and spot self-sacrificial decisions. If partners gently point out when they have made a self-sacrificial decision, it will help the relationship to heal.

Finally, building trust is dependent on people persistently being trustworthy. People who have been in a relationship conflict tend to get triggered easily and habitually. Therefore, they need to identify the triggers that set them off into negative patterns that are interpreted by the partner as lack of trustworthiness and then avoid those triggers. If the triggers are situational, avoid the situation. If the triggers involve the behavior of the partner, figure out ahead of time an alternative to getting triggered by a partner's provocative behavior.

Building devotion back into a damaged relationship involves being continually willing to value the partner and being vigilant to avoid devaluing the partner. This involves not just what each person does in the relationship, although that is very important; it also involves the way people's emotional bond is affected by what is done. When partners love each other and want to repair their relationship, it is most helpful if they can talk to each other and explicitly point out ways that they are valuing and not devaluing the partner.

Exercises for Building Devotion

Exercise 15: Identify Love Languages. The partners should consider each of the love languages (Chapman, 1996) listed in Table 12.2 and identify which ones they like to receive as love, and for which they like to give love. In addition, the partners should choose the top three love languages for the partner with whom they are interested in reconciling—trying to identify both how the partner gives and receives love. After each partner chooses separately, partners can compare lists and see how accurate they are.

Exercise 16: Formulate a Plan to Increase the Ratio of Positive to Negative Interactions. Partners should specify in writing what they can each specifically do to have more positive interactions. They should particularly consider the love language of the partner. How can they behave to show the partner more that they value them and are not going to devalue that person?

Exercise 17: Love Bank. Willard Harley, Jr. (1986, 1992) has developed a metaphor to describe how people can think of having more positive and less negative interactions. Each positive act that is done for the partner is like adding a dollar into the person's love bank. Each negative act is like making a withdrawal of a dollar. I have adapted this love bank to account for Gottman's 5:1 ratio so that each positive thing one does is like adding one dollar, but each negative action withdraws five dollars. The objective is to keep a highly positive balance with the partner in the love bank. Again, the actions that are considered positive are those that the partner considers positive.

Promoting Reconciliation

Reconciliation is the process of healing a damaged relationship. Although reconciliation can occur without each partner forgiving the other, forgiveness usually makes reconciliation easier and more lasting. Therapists then must aim to FREE partners from the wounds of the past by facilitating each to decide to pursue reconciliation, then guide partners as they talk about their transactions. After partners forgive, they can try to eliminate accumulated poisons in their relationship, and finally build positive acts of love and devotion into their relationship.

CHAPTER **13**

Research Support for Helping People REACH Forgiveness

Only a few studies have applied forgiveness interventions in actual psychotherapy (e.g., Freedman & Enright, 1996; Malcolm & Greenberg, 2003). Psychotherapy usually is focused on specific behavior disorders, and if forgiveness is addressed, it is part of therapy, rarely its entire focus. So, efficacy studies on forgiveness therapy will almost inevitably be either a bit contrived or contextualized within a broader therapy. The target concerns of psychotherapy are usually focused on feeling better (i.e., with emotional disorders such as depression, anxiety, anger, or PTSD), behaving better (e.g., obsessive-compulsive disorder, dissociative disorders), or making transformations in personality (e.g., personality and other Axis II disorders). Thus, forgiveness therapy usually will occur as a modular portion of more general psychotherapy, or a psychoeducational group could be made available to people for whom forgiveness was an issue in an interpersonally oriented psychotherapy.

Many people who attend therapy do so to improve relationships—such as couples in conflict, couples in which an affair has occurred, or parents seeking therapy for a child with an emotional or behavioral disorder. Targeting forgiveness can help resolve the relationship problems. Especially for affairs (see DiBlasio, 1998; Gordon, Baucom, & Snyder, 2000, 2004, 2005) but also healing after conflict (Hargrave, 2001; Worthington, 1998a), forgiveness therapy may comprise a larger portion of therapy than it does in virtually all psychotherapy.

Consequently, in this book, I have not assumed forgiveness therapy to dominate psychotherapy, couples therapy, or family therapy. Set within a general process approach to psychotherapy, I have described the REACH model to promote forgiveness of others, its application with necessary extension to forgiveness of self, and the FREE model to promote reconciliation.

In studying forgiveness interventions using clinical science, most investigators have applied forgiveness therapy as a psychoeducational group intervention, which might be applied as an adjunct to psychotherapy. In themselves, psychoeducational interventions require study of their efficacy. They treat legitimate concerns. To date, all have been studied using participants who are not in psychotherapy. So, future research needs to test the interventions with actual therapy patients.

Nevertheless, psychoeducational interventions with "normal" volunteers and with people who attend for personal or relationship enrichment or to prevent psychological or relationship problems can reveal whether forgiveness interventions might work with therapy clients—and reveal directly their efficacy for enrichment and prevention. Finding large effect sizes in nonpsychiatrically-diagnosed samples, prevention studies, and especially enrichment studies is often more difficult than in clinical samples due to a "ceiling effect." Therapy patients have more room for improvement.

Third-party payers for psychotherapeutic services and mental health consumers who pay their own bills for psychotherapy demand accountability of therapists for the interventions that are used. In this chapter, I array the evidence bearing on the efficacy of two specific interventions to promote forgiveness (i.e., the REACH intervention) and reconciliation (i.e., the FREE intervention). The evidence pertains directly to prevention and enrichment, but only by tenuous generalization to therapy.

A Meta-Analysis of Psychoeducational Group Interventions

Many clinicians have sought to develop interventions to promote forgiveness. Since forgiveness began to be studied in the early 1990s, perhaps more than any other subfield of forgiveness studies, interventions and their investigation have drawn the most attention. Because of the vigorous research activity, reviews of the intervention literature have been published (Battle & Miller, 2005; Enright & Fitzgibbons, 2000; Freedman, Enright, & Knutson, 2005; Gordon et al., 2005; Malcolm, Warwar, & Greenberg, 2005; Wade, Worthington, & Meyer, 2005). Furthermore, quantitative meta-analysis has been applied to study interventions (Baskin & Enright, 2004; Wade et al., 2005; Worthington et al., 2000; Worthington, Sandage, & Berry, 2000). Meta-analysis calculates effect sizes, which are the number of standard deviations (SDs) people change as a result of an intervention relative to some comparison group. Wade et al. conducted the most comprehensive review and meta-analysis. They identified 35 forgiveness interventions, 10 alternative treatments, and 16 no-treatment control groups from 27 studies. They included dissertations and some unpublished studies in addition to all published studies.

Wade et al. (2005) reported calculations of two types of effect size. In Cohen's *d*, the comparison group is no-treatment or other comparison treatment, such as a placebo control group. A second type of effect size compares the treatment condition at post-test with itself as its own control at pretest. That is called the *standardized mean effect size*. Cohen's *d* is useful in comparing treatments and controls, but not all studies have comparable control groups, nor do all studies even employ a control group. Thus, the standardized mean effect size is helpful in comparing how much each treatment changes from its own baseline. To provide perspective, Cohen's *d* for psychotherapy, regardless of how long the psychotherapy takes, is usually on the order of .8. That suggests that treatments are better than control groups by .8 standard deviations.

Wade et al. (2005) reported standardized mean effect size for forgiveness intervention groups as about .60. Alternative comparison treatments, such as relaxation training, which were seriously intended to promote forgiveness and not merely act as a placebo, had effect sizes about .26. No-treatment control groups that completed questionnaires but had no contact with a helper had effect sizes of about .10. Any combination of treatment groups—whether those specifically targeted at emotional forgiveness, aimed at promoting decisional forgiveness, or directed at alternative ways of treating unforgiveness—was more effective than no-treatment controls. Those groups aimed at emotional forgiveness were more effective (but not statistically) than those aimed at promoting decisions to forgive. Forgiveness-oriented treatments (collapsing emotional and decisional forgiveness together) were more effective than alternative comparison treatments at producing forgiveness. Alternatives and decisional forgiveness did not differ from each other.

Wade et al. (2005) identified seven components that were common to all of the forgiveness and forgiveness-comparison groups to some degree. Using treatment manuals, Wade et al. estimated the time spent on each of the components and correlated that with the effect size for the group. The relationship of time spent on separate components with effect size was reported as a correlation coefficient.

Wade et al. (2005) identified seven components structured along the lines of my model to REACH forgiveness. We found two additional components—(1) defining forgiveness and (2) other methods used to overcome unforgiveness (e.g., relaxation, promoting justice, cognitive reframing).

We calculated the correlation between time spent on a component and outcome for the combined sample of all groups. This included no-treatment control groups that were coded as 0 time for each component. Such a method allows the entire range of responses to be figured into how effective each component is. All correlation coefficients, except for "hold on to forgiveness," were above .5 and were significant. This suggests that, overall, it is helpful to include each of these components within a group aimed at promoting forgiveness.

However, Wade et al. (2005) noted that not all alternative treatment groups were aimed at specifically promoting forgiveness (some were intended as placebos), and no-treatment groups were not aimed at promoting forgiveness even though we asked people to reflect on their transgressions at assessment intervals. Wade et al. therefore correlated time spent on components for only the decision-based and emotion-based forgiveness treatments. The 37 forgiveness-intervention-only effect sizes were used in this comparison as opposed to 63 effect sizes when alternatives and no-treatment controls were included. Time spent on empathy was related to effect size at .51. Time spent on commitment was related to effect size at .52. Time spent on other interventions to reduce unforgiveness was correlated to effect size at .44. Other correlations were not significant: recalling the hurt, .43; defining forgiveness, .37; promoting an altruistic gift of forgiveness, .32; and holding on to forgiveness, .29.

Closer Examination of the Components of REACH

Empathy

Almost all interventions attempted to promote empathy, and many did so in different ways. For example, Al-Mabuk, Enright, and Cardis (1995) in their second study had people discuss the situational factors that might lead an offender to hurt the participant. They called this reframing. They also had participants explore what the offender might have been feeling that provoked the offender to hurt the participant. That intervention was characteristic of Enright's intervention, such as was employed in Hebl and Enright (1993) and Enright's other studies (see Enright & Fitzgibbons, 2000).

Hart and Shapiro (2002) adapted Enright's intervention to a treatment aimed at recovering alcohol and drug addicts. They challenged participants' beliefs that the offender is better off than the participants. They asked participants to personally reflect on what empathy is and what it is not. They encouraged the participants to empathize with offenders.

In our treatments, McCullough and Worthington (1995) gave a very brief educational lecture on how empathy helps develop forgiveness and encouraged victims to put themselves into their offender's shoes. In an expanded version, McCullough, Worthington, and Rachal (1997) promoted the discussion of a story intended to introduce and encourage empathy. We educated group members on the advantages of taking another's perspective and spent substantial time discussing it. Those interventions were characteristic of other studies by our group (Ripley & Worthington, 2002; Worthington et al., 2000; for a summary of the method, see Worthington, 2003). McCullough et al. found that participants in an 8-hour empathy-based intervention forgave more than did people in an 8-hour decision-based intervention. In addition, they found that the participants who forgave the most—regardless of the intervention they received—were the ones who experienced the most powerful changes in empathy.

The intervention to promote empathy is considered to use a key part of the stress-and-coping emotional replacement theory—replacing negative emotions. Promoting empathy can be thought of as largely, but not exclusively, an emotion-focused coping strategy (Worthington & Scherer, 2004). Taking another person's perspective changes the meaning of the transgression and therefore could be employed as meaning-focused coping. People can apply emotion replacement as an attempt to solve a problem—i.e., problem-focused coping. In general, though, the emotional replacement through empathy or other positive other-oriented emotions can serve as an indication of whether forgiveness has occurred. The time spent on empathy is strongly related to the effect size of the entire intervention ($r = .51$; Wade et al., 2005).

Commit to Forgiveness

Most interventions also encourage the person to commit to forgive. This has been done variously. In Enright's model (for a summary see Enright & Fitzgibbons, 2000), people committed to try to forgive and to work to forgive. They discussed the consequences of committing to forgive and were given the opportunity to sign a contract of commitment to forgive. They were also invited to privately reflect on what it means to forgive (i.e., Al-Mabuk, Enright, & Cardis, 1995). Rye and Pargament (2002) encouraged people to decide to forgive by discussing the pros and cons of forgiveness. DiBlasio (1998) worked toward deciding to forgive as his focal point. For my group, commitment is a public statement of the emotional forgiveness one has already experienced and occurs later in the intervention than in Enright's or Rye and Pergament's interventions. In later interventions, however, we introduced decisional forgiveness earlier in the group, allowing people to make a decision to forgive (Lampton, Oliver, Worthington, & Berry, 2005), which is similar to Enright's "commitment" and to "decisions" as employed by Rye and Pargament and by DiBlasio. Time spent promoting commitment to forgiving was highly related to effect size regardless of whether the commitment was to try to forgive, to decide to grant forgiveness, or to solidify emotional forgiveness (r = .52; Wade et al., 2005).

In my theory of stress and coping, the stress reaction of emotional unforgiveness motivates attempts to cope. Those attempts are cognitive, affective, and behavioral. Making a decision to forgive engages cognition and readies the person for experiencing emotional forgiveness. By deciding that one will forgive, the expectations for eventual outcome are lowered, reducing the magnitude of the injustice gap and therefore reducing unforgiveness. Threat appraisal is therefore reduced as well.

Other Methods of Overcoming Unforgiveness

The third component that Wade et al. (2005) found to be strongly related to effect size is the time spent using other interventions to reduce unforgiveness. Rye and Pargament (2002) used cognitive reframing methods to help people stop ruminative thoughts. They discussed the pros and cons of anger and desire for revenge, and the need to avoid the offender. They therefore directly confronted the motivations for holding on to unforgiveness so that people could decide to reduce unforgiveness. Worthington et al. (2000) discussed the nature of nurturing the hurt. This also included a discussion of rumination and helped people decide to change their cognition. In Enright's model, people were encouraged to absorb others' pain. People were told that this could stop the intergenerational transmission of hurt. Luskin and his group have been the most straightforwardly cognitive in approach (Luskin & Bland, 2000, 2001; Luskin & Thoresen, 1998; Luskin et al., 2001). Luskin's program is heavily cognitive-behavioral and is aimed at promoting health as well as promoting forgiveness.

These alternatives to forgiving are related to the stress-and-coping model of forgiving by serving as meaning-focused coping strategies or, as in the case of relaxation training, emotion-focused coping strategies. They also can provide a different perspective on the transgression, which can reduce the magnitude of the injustice gap and thereby reduce unforgiveness.

Altruistic Versus Self-Enhancement Motives

In three studies of interventions to promote forgiveness, we have compared empathy-based forgiveness with a forgiveness intervention based on motivating people to declare decisional forgiveness. We appeal to self-enhancement motives by focusing on the benefits of forgiving. In the three instances that we compared the empathy-based and self-enhancement groups, we found the standardized mean gain score to be roughly equal (about .4 standard deviations) for the two shorter self-enhancement groups, and even smaller for the 8-hour self-enhancement/decisional forgiveness intervention group. On the other hand, interventions that appeal to people's altruistic motives, by promoting empathy and a focus on giving a gift of forgiveness to the perpetrator, do not produce substantial effects until 2 to 4 hours of working on forgiving. But after 4 hours, they produce much larger effects than do self-enhancement groups.

Promoting a More Forgiving Personality

Most interventions that have studied forgiveness have taught people how to forgive a transgression. They have given little attention to generalizing to other instances besides the instances being focused on in the intervention. For example, in groups that seek to forgive an ex-spouse in the case of a conflictual divorce (Rye et al., 2005), the focus is limited to transgressions in the process of divorce. In my intervention to REACH forgiveness, which does not target specific types of events, people choose a target transgression and work on forgiving that transgression. In almost all cases, the person is thought to develop skills to forgive that are assumed to generalize to other instances, but in early interventions this has not been tested.

The stress-and-coping theory of understanding and promoting forgiveness suggests that several aspects of interventions are necessary. Many of the interventions are adaptable, and people who wish to tailor those should try to promote common factors that seem to promote forgiveness regardless of whether the orientation is behavioral-cognitive, behavioral-emotion focused, or eclectic.

Review of Research Specifically on REACH

The dream of every interventionist is to develop a 10-minute intervention that produces profound, lasting, and generalizable changes in the lives of every person who participates in the intervention. Furthermore, this intervention should be subjected to countless empirical studies with comparison groups and should always produce measurable changes in any condition to which it is compared. Of course, every interventionist probably realizes that this is a fantasy induced by too much chocolate. But, the dream persists.

Below, I examine the research that I studied of psychoeducational groups to promote forgiveness with individuals. I have explored the limits of how fast change can occur and studied interventions that promote changes in dyads.

Forgiveness in Untargeted Psychoeducational Groups

The first big study that sought to promote forgiveness in psychoeducational groups was designed by McCullough during his doctoral training in counseling psychology in collaboration with me (published as McCullough,

Worthington et al., 1997) and discussed briefly in chapter 10. An 8-hour intervention was heavily focused on promoting empathy. At that time, early in our study of forgiveness interventions, we thought that empathy was the primary ingredient in promoting change, so we focused mostly on a group that promoted empathy.

People defined what forgiveness meant. They arrived at a definition that suggested that people change their motivations and feelings about the person who has harmed them. We spent most of the time recalling the hurt that people were targeting, seeking to understand the perspective of the other person, and trying to move beyond mere perspective-taking to develop emotional empathy for the person. Finally, people verbalized their forgiveness for the person. This did not include much of the work that we now use involving altruism toward the other person, developing a sense of humility that recognized the wrongdoing that people had themselves been engaged in, committing fully to the forgiveness they experienced, and holding on to that forgiveness by conscious attention to maintenance. We also did not seek to promote lasting change in the person's personality. On the other hand, we spent much more time trying to promote empathy than in any of our other interventions.

We assigned about 96 people randomly to one of three conditions: empathy-based forgiveness, self-enhancement decisional-forgiveness, and a waitlist. The intervention was 8 hours and the follow-up was 6 weeks post-test. McCullough, Worthington et al. (1997) found strong effects for forgiving and reducing unforgiveness—effect sizes larger than 1.0. The self-enhancement decisional-forgiveness group had virtually zero change in forgiveness and did not change further by follow-up testing. The no-treatment control condition did not change over the three times.

Sandage (1997) developed a theoretical perspective that the presence of humility could facilitate forgiveness. He modified McCullough's 8-hour intervention into a 6-hour intervention by de-emphasizing empathy and replacing some of that time with an induction of humility, in which people reflected on their own transgressions over time, then attempted to speculate about the feelings they had when they experienced forgiveness. Sandage hypothesized that people who were guilt-prone would respond to the empathy-humility group, whereas people who were shame-prone would respond to a self-enhancement group. He randomly assigned people to one of the two interventions or a test-retest control condition. The 6 hours of treatment happened within a single weekend, but follow-up was after 3 weeks instead of after 6 weeks. Sandage found gains using the standardized effect size of about .6 standard deviations for the empathy-humility group and about .4 standard deviations for the self-enhancement group. The test-retest group changed little across the 3 weeks. The effect of personality matching was significant but small. People who were guilt-prone had greater responsiveness to the empathy-humility forgiveness intervention than people who were shame-prone.

Wade (2002) conducted a component analysis of the 6-hour REACH model with the addition of a step for defining (D) forgiveness, making a DREACH total intervention. People also participated in groups that did not include empathy, such as DRxxCH, which emphasized decisional commitment. (The xx represented 2 hours of training and practice in deep muscle relaxation.) These were all compared with a strong alternative treatment, systematic muscle relaxation, aimed at forgiving. Humphrey (1999) had found systematic muscle relaxation to be helpful in inducing forgiveness when the muscle relaxation was applied as an active coping mechanism to cope with the stress of unforgiveness. Thus, the comparison among the empathy-loaded DREACH model and the empathy-absent (DRxxCH) decisional forgiveness model against the stress reduction model provided a strong test of three alternative treatments. The models were not significantly different from each other in efficacy, although numerically the full empathy-based model was stronger than the decisional forgiveness model. Relaxation, as a way of reducing unforgiveness, was also effective. Wade's DREACH treatment followed the same protocol as did the earlier treatments. He did not assess people at the end of treatment, but rather reassessed them 2 weeks after the treatment ended at a delayed time period that paralleled the follow-up assessment in the previous studies. The amount of change at follow-up for DREACH was on the order of .6 SD.

Full REACH Treatment Within Religiously and Culturally Adapted Contexts

By 2002, I was convinced that the model to REACH forgiveness was effective in secular groups. I thought that a religiously adapted group would be even more powerful because basic research had begun to show reliably that religious people tended to forgive more than did those who were not explicitly religious (for a review, see Mullet, Neto, & Rivière, 2005). Furthermore, Christians tend to be especially good candidates for a forgiveness intervention (Marty, 1998).

Just after we conducted the Philippines study (to follow), we found that Rye and Pargament (2002) had developed a religiously oriented intervention for college women with failed romantic relationships. That intervention was successful relative to a more secular intervention with primarily Christian students. Subsequently, Rye et al. (2005) studied 149 women who had a recent divorce. All were randomly assigned to attend a secular forgiveness group, a religiously integrated Christian forgiveness group, or a waiting-list control group. Forgiveness and depression at post-treatment were both improved in the two intervention groups relative to the waiting list. There were no differences at all in comparison of the two intervention groups. They did not report significant differences in measures of parenting.

Rye and Pargament's (2002) research encouraged me to continue to develop the religiously tailored model. In February 2002, I taught a course at Alliance Graduate School in Manila, Philippines. Graduate students in that course received 40 hours of course work on the REACH model and the research behind it. They tailored the intervention to Christians and adapted the model for Filipino culture (Gingrich et al., 2005). Three different efforts were undertaken. In two efforts, the adaptation was tested in Filipino churches. In one church, two groups were run, and in the other church, one group was run. The interventions were 8 hours and produced effect sizes on the order of .5 to .8 standard deviations on forgiveness and unforgiveness measures.

My Christian-adapted REACH intervention was further developed after the publication of *Forgiving and Reconciling* (Worthington, 2003). It included exercises to produce a more forgiving character as well as forgiving target transgressions. We conducted the study at John Brown University in Arkansas, a theologically conservative Christian university (see Lampton, Oliver, Worthington, & Berry, 2005). A systematic effort was made to intervene to promote forgiveness in the entire John Brown University student body. Newspaper articles, chapel talks, invited speakers, debates, book reviews, and a general attention to forgiveness was given for 1 month. At the end of a month, group therapy was offered to students who volunteered. Alternatively, students could volunteer to receive assessments of their forgiving personality. The groups were 6 hours, 1 hour of which was aimed at promoting a forgiving character. The assessments took place at the beginning, prior to, and after the intervention, and 2 weeks later as a follow-up. Despite the potential ceiling effects, because of the emphasis on forgiveness that had gone before, the people participating in the groups changed their forgiveness of target transgressions significantly more than did people in the assessment-only condition. People in the assessment condition did change their self-rating of their forgiveness even though they were typically already at a high level of forgiveness. Significant change was not found in a measure of trait forgivingness.

Altogether, after five studies of the model to REACH forgiveness conducted in secular and religiously adapted contexts, I conclude that forgiveness using this model typically increases with time spent learning and practicing the model. About one tenth of a standard deviation is gained for every hour devoted to attempting to forgive based on emotional replacement. This has been true consistently in our studies. In fact, even when all other interventions are plotted on a graph, the same sloped line connects the dose of forgiveness intervention with the participants' amount of response.

Is Rapid Forgiveness Possible?

We have designed several studies to attempt to explore the boundaries of how fast people might forgive, and how much forgiveness can be expected reasonably in a short period of time. This is of keen importance to the clinician, who might be able to devote only a few hours to forgiving.

McCullough and Worthington (1995) designed a 1-hour forgiveness intervention and compared it to a 1-hour intervention to promote decisional forgiveness motivated by self-enhancement. The change experienced by participants in the self-enhancement (i.e., decisional forgiveness) condition was more than in the empathy-based condition, approximately .4 SD relative to the .1 SD in the empathy-based condition.

Kurusu (1997) used a combination of the two interventions that McCullough and Worthington (1995) developed—empathy-based and self-enhancement forgiveness. Each intervention was 1 hour; the combination was 2 hours. Kurusu, in his thesis, was interested in preintervention preparation and whether that would be effective. He developed a 10-minute preintervention discussion of forgiveness. He found that it did not differ from the efficacy of the treatment groups with no preparation. In his dissertation (Kurusu, 2000), he developed videotape and live preparation modules, each of which was 10 minutes. Those preintervention-discussion modules also did not add to the acceptability of the 2-hour intervention.

Wanda Bryant, in her dissertation (1998), studied the effect of making a commitment to forgive without going through an intervention. The idea was based on Aronson's studies of hypocrisy promotion (Aronson, 1999; Fried & Aronson, 1995). If people could be made to commit to a behavior without having a justification, Fried and Aronson found that they developed the internal justification to be consistent with their behavior. Collins, therefore, wondered whether, if people simply committed to forgive, that would change their internal experience of forgiveness because they would adjust their internal experience to meet the external. She did not find support for that hypothesis. Using commitment to forgive did not promote forgiveness. Kurusu's and Collins' three studies were published as Worthington et al. (2000). Generally, these very brief interventions produced about .2 to .4 SDs of increase in forgiveness. It did not seem to matter whether the intervention was 1 or 2 hours, though 10-minute interventions seemed too weak to produce any effect.

Decisional forgiveness can be facilitated by a 1-hour clinical intervention in any motivated participant. The studies showed that about half of the forgiveness experienced could be maintained after several weeks. For the clinician, this is both good news and bad news. The good news is that a clinician can rapidly address forgiveness with a motivated client, and some decisional forgiveness will likely occur. It might result in a little emotional forgiveness as well. As little as an hour spent dealing with forgiveness might change the person's internal experience. However, the bad news is that if only a passing discussion of forgiveness is undertaken—say 10 (or perhaps 15) minutes—little change is likely.

Also, the second piece of bad news is that if a therapist hopes for a large amount of change, the therapist must devote substantial time aimed at discussing and experiencing forgiveness. For example, in one of the truly psychotherapeutic interventions, Freedman and Enright (1996) found that a mean of 60 hours of forgiveness therapy was needed for women to forgive an incest perpetrator. In my studies, I show a steady dose-response curve between amount of time spent dealing with promoting an empathy-based (or other positive-emotion-based) forgiveness. About a tenth of a SD is gained each hour. So, a therapist will usually need to place the client in a psychoeducational adjunct to therapy if large gains are hoped for.

Extension to FREE

We have also studied the forgiveness and reconciliation through experiencing empathy (FREE) model. In the first study, Ripley and Worthington (2002) invited community couples to a 6-hour Friday night and Saturday workshop in which one third received training within a couples group in communication and conflict in a program called "Handling Our Problems Effectively (HOPE)," and one third the model to REACH forgiveness coupled with discussion of transgressions (which I will call "REACH-plus," a forerunner of FREE). The other third of the couples were randomly assigned to a test-retest control group. The treatment was only 6 hours long, was done in a psychoeducational format, and used a 2-week follow-up. Neither HOPE nor REACH-plus significantly affected self-report measures of marital quality, communication, or forgiveness; but the HOPE intervention did involve improvements in the couples' communication.

In a follow-up study, Burchard et al. (2003) conducted a pilot study with 20 newlywed couples recruited from the community. Couples were either assigned to an individual 9-hour consultation using FREE, an individual 9-hour consultation using HOPE, or a matched test-retest control group. Both interventions improved participants' quality of life post-treatment. The control group had a decreased quality of life, which is often the case with early married couples. The FREE intervention did not differ from the HOPE intervention in the degree to which quality of life improved at post-intervention or 3-week follow-up.

Worthington et al. (2003) reported preliminary results from a large prevention study from early married couples. We used the method of Burchard et al. (2003), but used a 9-month follow-up instead of a short follow-up. Worthington et al. reported that both HOPE and FREE were superior to the controls at the end of post-treatment, which was generally 3 to 6 weeks after the initial assessment. In some measures, HOPE reflected more improvement than did FREE. At 9 months, post-treatment FREE was superior to HOPE and both were superior to the assessment-only control group on most measures. Only self-report measures were analyzed in the initial report.

Kiefer et al. (2005) conducted psychoeducational groups with parents. Only one parent from each parent dyad attended the groups. Four groups were conducted using a waiting-list design. The results indicated that the parents who attended the groups forgave their spouse on index transgressions more than initial measures and they also improved relative to waiting-list couples. Besides forgiving an index transgression, parents also reduced their parenting stress, but did not change their dispositional forgivingness.

Conclusion

Over the course of the last 10 years, we have investigated five studies of the full intervention to help people REACH forgiveness, four studies of exceptionally brief attempts to promote forgiveness, and four studies with couples of the REACH or FREE (which includes the REACH) models. In secular samples (all but 2 of the 13 total studies), there is a linear increase in amount of forgiveness depending on time. In its strong version, with at least 5 hours, but preferably 8 to 10 hours of intervention, we have found that the intervention produces substantial forgiveness. The self-enhancement intervention has an immediate effect of inducing a decision to forgive, but that effect is decreased over time. I conclude, tentatively, that the psychoeducational group intervention to promote forgiveness has some empirical evidence supporting its efficacy. It can be considered an evidence-based approach, though the evidence base needs to be broadened.

CHAPTER 14

Promoting Forgiveness and Reconciliation Within Society

Much of the unforgiveness we experience, unfortunately, occurs with people we know the best. It stands to reason. Those are the people with whom we most often interact. So, those are the people we most often offend and are offended by. Living in a family situation that is laced with unforgiveness is stressful for all. People come to therapy in large part because they are having difficulties dealing with family relations, and it is often couples therapy and therapy with alcohol and substance abuse that are the least effective. Because of the prevalence of transgressions within the family and the accompanying pain, parents want not only to heal the wounds in the family, but also to immunize their children from similar wounds. They thus want their childen to develop into forgiving people. I will look first at how to help parents teach forgiveness to their children by considering how forgiveness develops in children and how it often is needed within the family.

However, other forgiveness is needed because we are members of a larger society. When we suffer an injustice at the hands of a person, we feel stressed. We know that grudge-holding and vengeance are not helpful. Those who harmed us are connected to other people. Retaliating can set off a spiral of retribution between our supporters and theirs. The criminal and civil justice systems help resolve injustices, but often leave bitterness and lack of reconciliation in their wake.

Society itself can open wounds as well. We are all members of some groups and might feel tension with out-group members. If that tension rises high, intractible conflict, mass killing, or even genocide can result.

In this chapter, I apply the stress-and-coping model of forgiveness to three societal concerns: raising forgiving children, roles of forgiveness in the justice system, and forgiveness in group differences.

Development of Forgiveness in Children

How children develop forgiveness is more complicated than it sounds. Development of forgiveness proceeds along four parallel tracks, and the train of development does not run at the same speed on each developmental track.

Develop the Capacity to Forgive (Track 1)

On track 1, people must develop the *capacity* to forgive. Preverbal children are not able to grant decisional forgiveness, even if parents socially pressure them to forgive. Yet, even before preschool or elementary school, some children learn to grant decisional forgiveness, and most have the seeds of emotional forgiveness within.

Part of the capacity to forgive is nonrational and depends on emotional and social development. Part of the capacity to forgive is rational and depends on the way people reason about justice (Gilligan, 1994; Kohlberg, 1984) and forgiveness (Enright & the Human Development Study Group, 1994).

Develop the Skills to Forgive (Track 2)

Children must develop the *skills* to forgive. For decisional forgiveness, the child must learn to monitor his or her feelings and recognize the hurt or resentment that can be countered by forgiving. The child must be aware of the situation and able to determine whether forgiveness is appropriate. (For instance, one does not grant forgiveness in the midst of a fight or argument. One does not grant forgiveness to someone who clearly intends to take advantage by continuing to exploit.) Experiencing emotional forgiveness also requires other skills.

Developing reasoning about forgiveness. Enright and his colleagues have studied the development of reasoning about forgiveness. They identified six stages of development about how people reason about forgiveness. Enright's stages, which emphasize mercy, parallel Kohlberg's (1984) six stages of reasoning about justice. The timetables of development of reasoning about justice and mercy are also parallel. In Enright's model, young children think that forgiveness will help them avoid punishment (stage 1) or get rewards (stage 2). As children progress into middle childhood and early adolescence, they learn to grant forgiveness and perhaps experience emotional forgiveness after reasoning that considers social disapproval (stage 3) and approval (stage 4) for their responses to transgressions. Only in adolescence and beyond are children thought to be capable of reasoning abstractly about forgiveness (stages 5 and 6).

Experiencing forgiveness. In some ways, the consideration of how children develop the capacity to reason about forgiveness is less important than whether children actually experience forgiveness after a transgression. One's capacity to forgive (for instance) at stage 5 does not imply that one will ever actually forgive. We all know brilliant adults—cognitively capable of the most complex reasoning about justice and forgiveness—who are spiteful, bitter, unforgiving, and vindictive.

Clearly, the capacity to reason in such a way that a child concludes that one should forgive can be important to whether he or she emotionally forgives. To reason that one should forgive for reasons more socially motivated than motivated by physical rewards and punishments will also affect how children and adolescents think about and try to experience forgiving. So, development of reasoning capacities is not unimportant to actually forgiving. However, by understanding forgiveness as an emotional replacement of negative with positive emotions, we also understand the development of forgiveness as being more complex than mere obedience or cognitive development. Other developmental considerations that are in line with the child's emotional development are important to understanding whether children actually forgive and at which ages. I list six additional considerations affecting the child's development of forgiveness.

Temperament. First, temperament is important. Babies often develop easy, difficult, slow-to-warm-up, or mixed temperaments by 3 months. If emotional forgiveness is seen more as an emotional replacement than as a cognitive decision, we might note that babies with easy temperaments might be considered to be emotionally forgiving. The mother delays a diaper change. No problem. All is quickly "forgiven" by easy babies. In difficult babies, the crankiness persists and may generalize. Obviously, babies do not cognitively understand forgiveness, but emotional unforgiveness (or at least anger) has been replaced with positive emotions toward the mother. Reasoning thusly, even infants emotionally forgive (in a primitive way), and some infants are more temperamentally geared for it than are other infants.

Attachment. Second, childhood attachment to parental love objects should be expected to influence the degree to which children experience emotional forgiveness. Children who develop insecure attachment styles, which do not facilitate close relationships, are expected to not be heavily invested in actually experiencing forgiveness. Those with secure attachment styles are likely to value relationships more as they age. They thus try to preserve and restore them by emotionally (and decisionally) forgiving.

Emotion regulation. Third, from the early months of a child's life, a primitive level of emotion regulation occurs. Even babies at the youngest ages learn to emotionally down-regulate negative emotions by self-soothing, calming, and distracting themselves from their frustrations. As children age, their repertoire of emotion-regulation strategies becomes more varied and sophisticated—and emotion regulation becomes more in line with the way developmental psychologists use the term. Different children develop unique repertoires of emotion-regulation strategies. Those children who develop, even in their preschool years, an early sense of empathy, sympathy, compassion, and unselfish love for others are expected to be able to experience emotional forgiveness more quickly than are children who develop such capacities later or become impaired in those capacities.

Emotion coaching. Fourth, emotion coaching by parents helps children broaden and deepen their emotion-regulation strategies. Through emotion coaching, parents convey their meta-emotional philosophy to children (Gottman, Katz, & Hooven, 1996). They directly and indirectly tell and show children what emotions are acceptable to experience and to express. They train children in how to deal with emotion-provoking experiences—notably (for our purposes) transgressions.

Coping strategies. Fifth, people encounter stress throughout their lives. Stressors demand change. Children appraise the stressors and respond to their appraisals with stress reactions; or they respond to physical stressors, sometimes without appraisal. They try to cope with both situations and their own reactions. Some stress reactions are unpleasant and prompt children to employ problem-focused or emotion-focused coping strategies. Problem-focused coping strategies seek to solve the problem and deal directly with the stressor. Emotion-focused coping strategies seek to manage negative emotions. The development of a repertoire of emotion-focused coping strategies will facilitate or hamper forgiving, depending on what types of coping strategies the child practices.

Spiritual development. Sixth, the religious and spiritual environment in the home will likely also affect the child's development of the experience of emotional forgiveness. Religion and spirituality have been found to be correlated with forgiveness in adults. Adults create most of the environments in which children learn social interactions. Membership in a religious denomination that involves a belief system that values forgiveness more or less strongly will determine some underlying cognitive structures of parents, which they transmit to and teach their children. Spirituality, the personal intensity with which parents adhere to their belief system involving the sacred will affect the ways, frequency, and importance that children are exposed to demonstrations of forgiveness—decisional and emotional.

The importance of parents in developing children's skills oft forgiving. The foregoing six of the child's capabilities affect whether the child forgives. However, the environment within which the child develops also affects a child's development of forgiveness. Parents set that environment in most cases. Children learn to grant decisional forgiveness largely depending on the parents' belief system, their practice of encouraging and rewarding the child's expression of decisional forgiveness after being transgressed against, and their modeling of decisional forgiveness. How children develop experiencing of emotional forgiveness is substantially less due to parental teaching. Instead, it is related to the climate of the parent-child relationship, which affects the child's temperament, emotion-regulation capability, parental meta-emotional philosophy, cognitive development of the ability to reason about justice and forgiveness, repertoire of ways of coping with stress, and religious and spiritual environment.

Intentional skills teaching. Experiencing emotional forgiveness also requires skills. Some of those skills might be learned automatically, and some might be learned and applied intentionally—at least until the child can emotionally forgive easily. Experiencing emotional forgiveness requires the child to recognize that he or she is experiencing unforgiving emotions such as resentment, bitterness, hostility, hatred, anger, and fear. Then, the child must seek to experience more positive emotions toward the person who offended him or her.

Developing the Willingness to Use Skills (Track 3)

Children need to develop a *willingness to use the skills* once they are able to grant decisional forgiveness or experience emotional forgiveness. Being willing to forgive depends on many things—beliefs and values, feedback children receive after they forgive someone, whether a person believes that forgiveness is helpful for his or her mental and physical health or relationship, beliefs that characterize the community within which the child is raised (Sandage & Williamson, 2005), and personal models or heroes.

Developing the Habit of Forgiving (Track 4)

A person could have the capacity to forgive, have developed the skills necessary to grant and experience emotional forgiveness, and be willing to forgive, and not *develop the habit of forgiveness*. Developing the habit of forgiveness is not something that is done merely by willpower. It is a matter of practice and rehearsing forgiveness in a variety of situations and a variety of offenses and hurts.

Social Aspects of the Development of Forgiveness

Preschool Children

In infants, toddlers, and preschoolers, the parental climate often dominates the development of the child. The parent socializes the child into beliefs and values through guiding the child's behavior and enlisting obedience from the child. In addition, infants, toddlers, and preschoolers often have been significantly influenced by other environments such as daycare and church environments. Obviously, traumas that occur in the child's early years of life can strongly affect the child. If the child loses an important person, or experiences some physical abuse, the child can develop difficulties forgiving.

School-Aged Children

As the child reaches school age, authority figures, including parents, teachers, coaches, and perhaps youth-group leaders at church, exert more influence. In addition, the child is strongly influenced by the children that he or she interacts with daily.

Middle-School Children and High School Adolescents

By the middle-school years, the young adolescent attends school as a major task in social development. Parents tend to look at school as an environment that is solely for the purpose of intellectual development. But for children, the social aspect is the centerpiece, and classes can seem like an unpleasant interruption. That means during middle school and high school, an adolescent's interactions with his or her peers are crucial for determining how the adolescent will deal with transgressions. Furthermore, in middle and high schools, transgressions are numerous. Middle- and high-school children are not usually known for being especially socially skilled, so they inflict many transgressions upon each other.

College-Aged Young Adults

In the college years, the young adult is developing an arsenal of coping strategies for managing his or her intimacy and for laying the groundwork for productivity. As the college-aged person becomes more independently in charge of his or her work experiences, he or she deals increasingly with issues of equity in the distribution of resources, punishment for not following rules, and unfairness in the way people are treated. While dealing with these issues of justice, numerous other injustices occur. The college student begins to formulate ways to handle injustices that occur in adult work settings. They will develop important decisions that further shape their propensity to inflict and cope with transgressions. Parental input is largely relegated to consultation when children are in their college years.

Development does not stop at the adolescent years, and the ramifications of that affect the parents.

Adulthood

As adults carry out their work and relationships, establish careers, and interact with friends, communities, and organizations, the damage done by transgressions can be great. As adults try to promote forgiveness in children, they must deal with their own adult developmental issues. These include conflicts at work, relationships with romantic partners, relationships within the extended family, organizational downsizing, and the issues that surround caring for an aging parent—making health care decisions (often in an atmosphere of disagreement among siblings or between the adult and the elderly parent), relocation, and end-of-life issues.

Promoting Forgiveness in Families

In helping family members to forgive, you will want to teach these "rules." If you are counseling someone who is experiencing unforgiveness within his or her family, you can work with the person through individual therapy, as I discussed in chapters 9 through 11, or through couples or family therapy (chapter 12).

Try not to let transgressions happen. It seems obvious, but the most sure-fire way to prevent negative unforgiving feelings from building up within the family is to treat each other with love and respect. Love is being willing to value one's partner or child, and involves treating that person with the respect he or she deserves as a human regardless of how badly the person messes up or disappoints you. People are imperfect and will, in fact, at times mess up. Nevertheless, if people treat each other with mutual respect, those transgressions occur less frequently.

Keep a short list. When the other person messes up, do not allow the hurts to continue to build and fester as if they were an infected wound. Sometimes, it is impossible to discuss wrongs immediately. Sometimes, the anger level is so high that immediate discussion might be counterproductive. But as soon as possible, try to speak respectfully about the transgression and come to a resolution.

Do not keep score. Not keeping score keeps us aimed at loving each other rather than counting relative number of injustices.

Be quicker to say "I'm sorry" than to expect the other person to apologize. When people live in close relationships, they tend to experience as important the things that are done wrong to them more than they are bothered by the things they do wrong to the other person. People therefore naturally tend to look for times when the other person should be apologizing for his or her actions. For a harmonious family, people should be vigilant to detect the times when they themselves might have hurt a family member. The offender should seek out the harmed party to apologize quickly and thoroughly. The offender should take responsibility for his or her own acts and try to assure the offended party that the offender will try not to act hurtfully again.

Begin with the couple, not the children. The foundation for a forgiving family is the relationship between the parents. Although children have a way of turning the family into a child-centered enterprise, the best families have a strong and loving relationship between the partners that flows to the children instead of focusing the love and attention on the children and hoping it flows to the partner. Therefore, encourage family members to keep the parental relationship strong and loving.

Teach children how to forgive early in their lives. When the child is very young, the parents can encourage the child to decide to forgive. Children may not have the capacity for full deliberate emotional forgiveness, but they can learn to grant forgiveness and not hold on to vengeful attitudes or plan paybacks or vengeance. The parents can simply instruct the children to forgive their brother or sister and describe to the children what that means. Children can learn from this instruction how to learn to make decisions to control their behavior.

Parents can use modeling to teach children how to forgive. Parents can teach the children how to forgive by showing them how to forgive. Parents can also demonstrate forgiveness by practicing it with outsiders. Parents are offended or wronged numerous times, as we all are. Instead of railing against the person who wrongs us, the parent can decide to forgive and practice that attitude, keeping grudge-holding, vengeance, and critical comments to a minimum.

Parents can develop family rules. A family rule might be, "We do not hold on to anger toward members of the family," or "We do not act vengefully toward people who have wronged us." Whatever rules that the family agrees upon, it is important that the parents practice those rules and enforce them in their children.

Throughout the lifespan, transgressions occur. When people expect to remain in close personal contact, they must do something to work out their differences and later to heal the painful wounds that transgressions can leave. In close personal relationships, much of this can be worked out in dyadic conversation or in therapy involving the affected parties. But in social units—like family, school, or workplace—it is rare that only two parties are affected.

The family is the primary building block of society, and therapists see many people unhappy with their family. As a result, several interventions have been developed to promote forgiveness and reconciliation in the family.

Few interventions are specifically targeted at other social institutions such as businesses, schools, or courts. Society has become litigious, so how can the justice system be made more open to forgiveness? And should it?

The next generation of interventions may be aimed at systemic interactions. How does an interventionist turn the tide of unforgiveness, which spreads throughout social systems, into forgiveness, which itself can spread throughout the system, bringing peace? In the next section, I examine forgiveness within the justice system.

Forgiveness Within the Justice System

The icon of justice is blindfolded to be fair to everyone. She holds scales in one hand to balance the sides of disputes. She holds a sword in the other hand to defend truth. Transgressions occur frequently in virtually any context. Most people cope with those transgressions and are able to either live with them or arrive at some informal resolution of the differences and perceived inequities. But some transgressions and disputes inevitably will not be reconcilable through negotiation. The perceptions of the disputing parties differ too much. The justice system is aimed at helping people achieve a fair reconciliation by the decision of a fair trier of fact.

Of course, there are two types of courts: criminal and civil courts. Criminal courts deal with violations against the state as represented by the law. The assumption, at least in the United States, is that a crime is committed not merely against a person, but against society. Therefore, society has the responsibility to prosecute the crime. In a murder trial, for example, the case is the State versus the defendant, rather than the estate of a murdered victim versus the defendant. In a civil case, two parties disagree. These people have complaints against one another and are plaintiffs. A judge, court official, or jury is empowered to make a decision about which plaintiff should receive which outcome.

In both cases, attorneys typically argue the case, representing each side. Individuals may represent themselves under certain circumstances. The presiding judge is charged with overseeing procedural justice, ensuring that correct procedures are followed to permit both sides to tell their stories fairly (Blader & Tyler, 2003; Lind, Kanfer, & Earley, 1990). In civil cases, the judge may decide about the case disposition. In criminal cases, the judge may also decide on the sentence based upon the legal code and recommendations of the jury.

The justice system—regardless of whether it is criminal or civil justice—is inherently adversarial. As a result, at the end, both sides will likely believe that to some degree justice was not achieved. Both will be emotionally invested in their points of view. Both will believe that the judge was unfair at some points in the hearing or trial. Both will be dissatisfied with the outcome. Because numerous dissatisfactions are experienced by both sides, and because so many matters of judgment are involved, people will want to appeal. After a final decision, the social issue of justice may be settled, but the individual perceptions of injustice may linger for the rest of people's lives.

Often, much is at stake in trials. Lives are lost. Memories are disrespected. Fortunes change hands. Public humiliations ensue. People live with the consequences of the legal action and might personally hold grudges and communicate their feelings within their family, to friends, and even more publicly.

My purposes below are to consider the experience of an individual going through a criminal and a civil case, examine the sources of possible unforgiveness, and describe ways people may cope with those sources of unforgiveness.

Criminal Justice

To allow ease in discussing the criminal justice system, let us take a particular crime, such as a homicide. Homicides can occur by strangers, but most homicides occur by family members. Some homicides involve murder-suicide, but in all cases, the family of the victim loses a family member. Not only the family, but all members of society are threatened by the commission of a violent crime. A person who was loved, or at least who has blood ties to the family, is lost. Grieving will occur, and the reactions to the justice system need to be seen within the context of grief.

At every stage of a murder—from the discovery to prosecution to sentencing to appeals to carrying out executions (in some states)—there are enormous possibilities for victims to perceive transgressions. The relative of a murder victim will experience shock and trauma that come about because of experiencing the loss and the knowledge that a loved one has been violently taken. Police will usually be vigilant at questioning the whereabouts of family members. Sometimes, insensitive questions have to be asked to establish whether a family member might have motive or opportunity to commit the crime. During the investigation, police do not release all information to the public. That can place the family members of the victim in an emotional bind. Family members are feeling a sense of lack of control. During the height of an active investigation, family members are at peak stress. Victim advocates within the police department inform family members about their rights as victims. The fact is that these rights are minimal. Dealing with the victim's rights advocates is often not satisfactory.

In some cases, investigations do not close quickly. Additional interviews might be undertaken, and family members can feel accused even if that is not the police's intent. Family members are often frustrated by the police's lack of progress in solving the crime. Sometimes, virtually no communication occurs between police and the family members. Police might even solve the crime and catch a suspect but not inform the victim's family.

Victims must often testify in court, suffering under cross-examination but also losing work and other resources. This lack of human process, on one hand, protects the accused from procedural violations, threats, and emotional abuse. It is important to protect the rights of the accused because not all people who are accused of crimes are guilty (LaFave, 2000). The consequences of an abuse of the accused person's rights can be extremely devastating to the accused. He or she could go to jail and suffer indignities for the rest of his or her life. Those possibilities of difficulties far outweigh the inconvenience and emotional upset of the victim. In their calm and thoughtful moments, most people can understand the reason the criminal system is the way it is. Nevertheless, the experience of being the crime victim is one that lots of problems and few solutions attend.

When important cases occur, such as murders, there can be a seemingly never-ending series of appeals. Each appeal awakens painful feelings on both sides of the transgression. Even after the final appeal is exhausted, a capital murder case can involve appeals to the governor for clemency. Often, public awareness is high on capital murder cases because of controversy over capital punishment. The murderer in many states can be sentenced to death by a variety of methods. Family members of victims often expect that such executions will produce a sense of closure. In one way, there is: The seemingly never-ending appeals finally end. Memories, however, continue.

Overall, the problems with the criminal justice system have to do with the inevitable judgments that are made and their perceived fairness. But crimes must be dealt with by society, and victims will likely continue to be wronged by the process.

Restorative Justice

For criminal property cases and smaller offenses, new justice procedures have been employed over the last 20-plus years (Armour & Umbreit, 2005; Brunk, 2001; Zehr, 1995). These have gone under the name of restorative justice. Restorative justice is often contrasted with retributive justice (Darley & Pittman, 2003). Darley and his colleagues (for a review see Darley, 2002) have shown that people perceive the retributive justice model as a method of punishing wrongdoers (for a review, see Exline, Worthington, Hill, & McCullough, 2003), not as rehabilitative or as protection of society. Restorative justice has gained in popularity since its articulation by Howard Zehr (Armour & Umbreit, 2005; Umbreit, 2001; Zehr, 1995). Restorative justice creates fair procedures that protect the rights of the convicted person and allow him or her to be restored to society rather than imprisoned. In prison, people often learn additional criminal skills and are socialized to be better criminals.

Restorative justice procedures also consider the victims. Victim and offender and perhaps supporters of each might meet face to face. There are opportunities to discuss the impact of the crime and to hold the perpetrator accountable to the victims and responsible for the crime. The victim might even receive restitution. Typically, restorative justice occurs after a person has admitted to or has been convicted of a crime. Instead of sentencing, the convicted person is directed to meet with the victim and the victim's supporters and work out mutually agreed-upon outcomes (Galaway, Hudson, Morris, & Maxwell, 1995; Maxwell & Morris, 1993; Roy, 1993; Stuart, 1996; U.S. Department of Justice, 1998). This might involve work for the victim or some sort of restitution to the victim, apologies might be given, and impact statements are listened to and often responded to by the offender so the offender learns of the personal effects his or her crime has had on the victims.

Most outcome research has looked at whether people are satisfied with these restorative justice outcomes (Armour & Umbreit, 2005). Most victims and offenders are more satisfied with them than with criminal punitive justice proceedings. In addition, recidivism in property crimes is often less with restorative justice than when a judge imposes a sentence (Umbreit, 2001).

Laboratory Studies of Restorative Justice

In our lab, we have attempted to set up simulations to find out what people might be experiencing in these restorative justice meetings. Witvliet et al. (2005) measured people's blood pressure, heart rate, skin conductance, and facial musculature while people imagined that they had experienced a crime. Then people imagined that (1) no justice was received by the offender, (2) a restorative justice meeting occurred, (3) or a criminal justice verdict was rendered. All people were asked to imagine that they either had forgiven the person (in one condition) or had not forgiven the person (in the other condition). People were assessed physiologically as they imagined different outcomes occurring and noted their experiences on questionnaires or using a computer joystick to indicate how they were reacting. Based on the 60 people who participated in the study and imagined every condition, most physiological arousal—indicating anger and resentment—occurred with no forgiveness and no justice. Restorative justice reduced physiological arousal more than criminal justice regardless of whether the person imagined forgiving or not forgiving the offender. Forgiveness almost always reduced the physiological arousal. Even in the event of no justice, forgiveness reduced arousal as much as restorative justice without forgiveness or retributive justice without forgiveness.

From these studies, we do not know exactly how real crime victims respond physiologically. Our participants were imagining crimes instead of having actually experienced them. On the other hand, participants rated these imaginations as vivid and lifelike, and people who had really been crime victims responded similarly to those who had not been burglarized.

In another effort in our laboratory, Rebecca Keifer and myself have created role-play simulations of family group conferencing (Galaway et al., 1995; Maxwell & Morris, 1993). In sets of four participants, we randomly assigned two male students to play the roles of victim and offender. We randomly assigned two older female students to play the roles of the offender's and victim's mothers. All four people met with a mediator, who conducted a mediated discussion of the crime. People were prepared for the role-plays by being given information about the crimes and what their feelings might be. The offender was told he must either (1) apologize and offer restitution or (2) not apologize and not offer restitution but merely say that he thinks the judge should decide what should be done.

Overall, 16 sets of four participants had discussions. We found in self-reports of people's experience that all people were affected by these role-plays. They reported that a variety of aspects of their life and experience were affected. In the condition where the offender did not apologize or make restitution, people became less forgiving when they played the victim role and even in both supporter roles. The offender became more contrite and regretful when he apologized and made restitution. Empathy was greater on all sides when the offender apologized and made restitution.

Currently, we are analyzing the behaviors that occurred in these role-plays by coding the videotapes of these sessions. Again, we are not suggesting that this is what actually happens in these family group conferences. People who have experienced an actual crime will be more emotionally invested than are these people who are role playing. However, even in the role-play simulations, students who were playing the role of offender sometimes broke down and cried as they apologized for their "crime." Mothers of the victim reacted in anger. Sometimes, they were almost unreasonable as they listened to the offender explain his side of things. So, people really did get into their roles and participate.

Civil Justice

Civil justice involves disputes over property, reputation, or other valuable aspects of life. These disputes escalate, and negotiation comes to a standstill. The disputes cannot be resolved outside of a court.

Are Civil Lawsuits Necessary?

One of the biggest issues in civil law is the degree to which a civil lawsuit is actually necessary. People are often driven by greed and pride, but they do not always recognize their motivations. Instead, they focus on the reasons that they believe that their perception of the story is correct. They focus on their nobler motives, ignoring their baser motives. They believe they need public vindication, and they see the civil legal system as a way to get such vindication.

Like the criminal system, the civil legal system is inherently adversarial. At least half of the people involved in a lawsuit will not be vindicated. At least half will not get what they would like to have. In truth, far more than half will not emerge from a lawsuit with vindication or with the financial or property settlement that they desire. Logically, then, it makes one wonder why people go through the expense, time, and emotional involvement of a lawsuit. People, of course, are not completely logical. They are emotional. The competitive nature and the justice motive are aroused. Their feelings are hurt, and they can see only their side of the argument. They cannot predict or, if they do, give credence to the arguments that are made on the other side. Therefore, they feel that they will almost certainly win the trial. From outside, it is easy to conclude: Most trials are unnecessary.

Is It Worth It?

A number of studies have been conducted involving people's reactions to civil lawsuits. In two studies on medical malpractice (Hickson, Clayton, Entman, & Miller, 1994; Vincent, Young, and Phillips, 1994), people who have gone through medical malpractice suits later have largely concluded that they would not do so again. The outcomes are rarely worth the emotional involvement, especially if one considers that one may be offered a settlement rather than going through with the case. When one looks at the difference in the amount of the settlement offered and amount of award won, a lawsuit is almost never worth the time, money, and effort.

Even for a wrongdoer, it is often worthwhile to confess, apologize, and make restitution rather than go through the civil proceedings. In the 1980s, the Veterans Administration Medical Center (VAMC) in Lexington, Kentucky, pursued the policy of not settling malpractice claims, but litigating. It lost a malpractice lawsuit for millions of dollars (Cohen, 2000). Afterwards, the VAMC changed its policy. It decided henceforth to settle fairly with people who felt that malpractice had been done rather than contest the malpractice complaints. The VAMC saved millions of dollars over the next 10 years. On both sides of the issue, it seems financially better to pay a little more or to lose a little more than one thinks one deserves to avoid lawsuits. But—

Lawsuits Happen

Because pride, greed, and justice motives demand that wrongdoers be held accountable and punished, lawsuits happen. Over the course of the lawsuit, hurtful things are said, allegations are made, lies may seem to be told, characters may be assassinated, and one's arguments are denigrated. In short, lawsuits will provide many opportunities for even more transgressions. In the course of those lawsuits, resentments can build. Unforgiveness grows. I would hypothesize that all parties finish a lawsuit with more resentments, grudges, and unforgiveness than when they began the lawsuit.

Civil Suits and Conscientiousness-Based Virtues

Victims' motives. When wrongs are done, most people want to act virtuously. If they are the wrongdoer, they want to make things right. If they are the victim, they want to respond with humanity and yet achieve justice. Because virtues tend to be grouped into conscientiousness-based and warmth-based virtues (Berry, Worthington, O'Connor, Parrott, & Wade, 2005; Worthington & Berry, 2005), a value conflict almost always exists. This is especially true for the victim. The victim wants vindication and feels entitled to it. Yet, the victim also wants to be empathic, sympathetic, compassionate, and perhaps altruistically loving to the wrongdoer.

Strong situations. Situations tend to highlight one set of motives and place other motives in relative darkness. A blatantly done wrong highlights the conscientiousness-based virtues that make the person want to pursue justice, bring the truth into the open, hold the other person accountable for what he or she did, and seek to build responsibility into the person. The victim senses failure in the other person's self-control, and in one sense, tries to help the person regain self-control. Warmth-based virtues fade into the background and do not emerge naturally. Only the conscious effort of the victim, or ensuing events, can bring out empathy, sympathy, compassion, or altruistic love for the wrongdoer.

Factors affecting the strength of the justice motive. Several factors affect the strength of the justice motive. If those factors can be mitigated or reduced, then the strength of the justice motive can be weakened. That might allow consideration of both sets of virtues. The first factor that impacts the justice motive is the undeservingness of the victimization. If a person does not see any wrongdoing on his or her own part or any provocation for the wrong, the person feels righteously angry and indignant for the wrongdoing. This makes the justice motive very strong (Feather, 1999). Lerner (1980) and Weiner (1993) have observed that justice is maintained and little sympathy is given to people who are seen as responsible for their own victimization. If people are seen as innocent, undeserving victims, then the justice motive is extremely strong.

The severity of the offense is related to the strength of the justice motive. In a classic study, Walster (1966) showed that people judge even accidental offenses harshly if the offenses violate a sense of distributive justice. Betrayals of trust are judged particularly harshly and provoke severe retaliation (Gabriel, 1988). When injustices are perceived to be committed against a group, rather than an individual, they can be seen as symbolic and can provoke extremely hostile and severe retaliation (Tyler, Boeckmann, Smith, & Huo, 1997).

When an offense is deemed to be intentional, it also can provoke a stronger justice motive. It not only can be more difficult to forgive, but can also lead to greater assessments of blame and responsibility. Intentional offenses can also provoke more anger (Folger & Cropanzano, 1998), lead to harsher punishments (Darly & Huff, 1990), and lead to less forgiveness (Boon & Sulsky, 1997).

When a person feels victimized, it is difficult for the person to suspend judgment, calm the justice motive, and examine these three factors objectivly. If the person is to have a chance of thinking rationally about whether to advance a lawsuit, the person needs to think as objectively as he or she can.

Civil Lawsuits and Warmth-Based Virtues

Some motives advocate for reconciliation. People might be motivated to repair relationships for a variety of reasons. Perhaps they dislike conflicts or have an ongoing relationship with the person in which they have invested time, energy, and emotion and do not wish to lose that relationship. Conciliatory motives are often squelched when the justice motive is aroused. The victim is often well advised to consider the conciliatory motive and to pay special attention to the benefits of the relationship that might be lost if the victim reacts legally.

Mercy and *grace motives* also advocate for conciliation (Worthington, Sharp, Lerner, & Sharp, 2006). Mercy is not exacting justice that one is entitled to. Grace is wishing to bless the person even though the person does not deserve it. Mercy and grace motives are part of our heritage as social creatures. They may be thought to derive from humans' shared history with primates or creation in the image of God. Regardless, people manifest grace and mercy motives.

Self-interested motives can advocate for conciliation as well. People's self-interested motives protect and enhance the self. They are not opposed to virtue. Self-care is necessary for most of the species to survive. However, altruism also dictates that self-interest can at times be put on the back burner for the good of a group. Thus, a victim is advised to examine himself or herself for the presence of greed, entitlement, vindictiveness, and a sense of vindication even to the harm of others. When a person has suffered an injustice, the justice motive advocates for restoring what was taken from the self. This can heighten the negative self-interest and trigger retaliation or retribution. By checking the negative self-interested motives, a person can arrive at a more balanced sense of self-interest.

Empathy. When people suffer an injustice, they tend to focus on themselves. Empathy is thus weakened. If others are considered, it tends to be other people who will experience negative fallout from the injustice. A victim who wishes to possibly avoid lawsuits because he or she thinks this might be in his or her enlightened self-interest will be wise to attempt to see things from the point of view of the other.

Offender Apology and Restitution Affect the Victim

If a wrongdoer apologizes, then empathy is often aroused for the wrongdoer. We understand that apologies are difficult to make, and we see that wrongdoer has undertaken something costly. That is particularly true if the apology contains an offer to make some sort of costly restitution and the person followed through and actually made restitution. Apology and restitution together can promote forgiveness. Witvliet, Wade, Worthington, and Berry (2005) have conducted a series of three laboratory studies in which students were asked to imagine that they had been burglarized. (Even though this uses a criminal justice context, the results are applicable to civil justice, too.) In all studies, participants immediately rated the degree of anger, unforgiveness, and physiological arousal that they experienced. The participants were then given information describing the outcome after the burglary had been committed. In one condition, they were told that the police had discovered no new information. In a second condition, the wrongdoer sent them an apology for having stolen from them. In the third condition, the wrongdoer had returned all of the stolen goods and gave the participant $100 for emotional damages. In the fourth condition, the participant received both the apology and restitution.

In the first study, the participants were given a weak and inadequate apology by the criminal. Those participants tended not to forgive. They stayed emotionally aroused. In the second study, the apology was elaborate, with considerable personal groveling involved. Victims tended to give up revenge and avoidance motivations and express forgiveness. Restitution consistently resulted in forgiveness and reduction in unforgiving motivations. The strong apology (studies 2 and 3) produced equally powerful effects, as did the restitution. When the apology and restitution were both included, the effects were additive. In the third of the Witvliet et al. (2005) studies, the physiological responses of the participants were measured. The physiological responses paralleled people's self-reports, indicating that apology plus restitution produced the most reduction in negative physiological reactions. Restitution produced a slight reduction in arousal. Apology produced a slightly less reduction than restitution. No communication produced an actual increase in unforgiving motivations as time went on.

Apologies do reduce people's tendencies to retaliate. In two studies of medical malpractice, Brennan, Sox, and Burstin (1996) examined people who had sued physicians for medical malpractice. When surveyed later, many said they would not do so if given the chance again. If the physician was apologetic, most people said they would not pursue a lawsuit. Gerber (1987, 1990) conducted two studies of physicians who had actually committed a medical malpractice infraction. When patients were kept in contact with the physician and continued to maintain a relationship, the physician was able to experience less guilt and shame and self-condemnation. The maintenance of the relationship between the patient and the physician also gave the physician more of an opportunity to apologize for the malpractice.

The Justice System as Necessary

Whenever misdeeds or misunderstandings become highly harmful, they often cannot be resolved by simple agreement between the parties. The legal system is a societally proven way to resolve such difficulties while ensuring procedural justice. The goal is to provide a balance of distributive justice and retributive justice with a guarantee of fair procedural justice. Nevertheless, the legal system often produces solutions to the societal issues but simultaneously involves damage to the psychology and mental health functioning of the people operating within the system. The system is designed without any attempt to minimize suffering; rather, it is all about fairness and justice.

Forgiveness in Larger Societal Context

Intervention at the social institution level, such as family or justice system, is difficult. But perhaps more widespread in its effects is this: How does one promote forgiveness and reconciliation among people whose lives are intimately intertwined with each other, who are divided by seemingly irreconcilable basic differences, and who have a history of conflict and transgressions against each other that might stretch back for centuries? How can societal forgiveness and reconciliation be promoted?

Race Relations

In race relations, the central issues revolve around equality, which is seen to differ within the races and ethnicity. In the United States, the conflict has traditionally been between whites and blacks. The recent demographics, however, have shown the white majority has been eliminated, changed into a white plurality. Asian and Hispanic minorities have superceded African-American minorities. Thus, both whites and blacks have experienced a loss of their status—the whites as the majority, and the blacks as the largest minority. Again, power struggles are at the root of conflict.

Religions

For religions, the politics of the 1960s and 1970s embraced a strong doctrine of separation of religion and state. As this doctrine became more widespread, people who were highly religious, especially those conservative in their religion, began to resent that their most important values were not allowed to figure into state policies. Thus, people with strongly held theologically conservative beliefs and values began to bring those values into political decision-making. Conservative principles, such as the sanctity of human life, were applied with religious force in some areas, such as abortion and euthanasia. Conservative religious people became more politically active and better organized through efforts, such as those by Jerry Falwell and Pat Robertson; and they have had more political effect in the last 15 years than have religious moderates or liberals. This has built resistance and has divided religious groups along political lines.

Around the world, the fastest growing religion may be Islam. Many in Islam identify the decadent Western culture with the Christian religion. Worldwide, tensions have heated up between Christians and Muslims. Nor have tensions been confined to Christians versus Muslims. Hindus and Muslims have conflicted in India and Pakistan, and other tensions have arisen between Muslims of different sects. Some strains of Islam are particularly combative, such as Wahhabism. The foundations of Wahhabi theology were put in place by the 18th-century evangelist Muhammad ibn-Abdul Wahhab. It has served as fundamentalist theology for many in the Arabian Peninsula.

Philosophical Reasons for Some Group Differences

Prior to the last 25–50 years throughout the world, groups have operated on the basis of a majority rule, with some respect for minority opinion. Postmodernism and multiculturalism, however, have valued the identity of almost every group that perceives itself as being socially unique. The group is considered to have rights and has demanded those rights. This has created a more contentious atmosphere. The contention is increasing. Because issues of justice and inequity have become more salient, people in different groups have increasingly re-examined the past and discovered instances of discrimination, prejudice, and failure to receive their just rights. This has led each group to construct an argument that emphasizes a need to obtain more of society's resources and respect from other groups. Issues of inequality have generated feelings of unforgiveness in many of the group members. Thus, an emotional core of feelings empowers this sense of social need for each group to assert itself and gain power.

Can We Heal Intractable Intergroup Conflict?

Intergroup tensions are perhaps inevitable, but they sometimes erupt into conflicts. Probably the dream of all sane people is to end conflict and war once and for all and live in peace throughout the world. It is almost impossible to conceive of universal peace, yet it is easy to conceive of world war. Probably, the reason for this is because people are social animals and array themselves into groups. In fact, we each belong to countless groups— political, religious, and socioeconomic groups; people who hold attitudes about eating meat; and so on. When we interact with group members and those who threaten our group boundary, psychological processes are set in motion that powerfully influence behavior and the behavior of one group against another group.

Realizing that conflict is almost inevitable does not mean that we abandon ourselves to it wherever it shows up. Rather, we work to minimize conflict to maintain peaceful conditions as long as we possibly can. In addition, we hope to establish healing from past conflicts and set up just social conditions that will make future conflicts less likely.

Reasons for Intergroup Conflict

Tajfel (1978) identified two criteria for defining intergroup conflict: (1) Two clearly identifiable social groups had to be involved, and (2) each group had to show little variability in the way they treated the other group.

In 1997, Brewer identified three intergroup processes that maintained intergroup conflict. *Intergroup accentuation* is the tendency to see in-group members as being more similar to oneself than are members of the out-group. Males, for instance, see themselves more similar to other males than they do to females. Lower socioeconomic status (SES) individuals see others in the same SES as being more similar to themselves than to those in the middle or upper SES. The accuracy of the principle is doubtable. For example, on average, men are about 4 inches taller than women. However, men and women differ far more within their respective groups than the average man differs from the average woman. Intergroup accentuation, however, tends to minimize the differences within the groups and see the members in terms of what the average member of each group is like. In the second principle, *in-group favoritism,* people tend to selectively feel more positive emotions, such as love, trust, and liking, toward people within their in-group than toward people outside of their in-group. The third principle is *social competition*. Life is seen as a zero-sum game between the two groups. If one group gains, the other must lose. Again, the truth of this principle is doubtable, but group members perceive competition to be the case.

As a result of these three principles, people try to interact with in-group members and avoid out-group members. Social conventions, jobs, and other societal structures throw them into interactions with members of the out-group; but people choose to interact more with others to whom they are similar, attracted, and not in competition. Perception hardens the group boundaries. The more that a person thinks about being a member of a group, concentrates on the differences and competition, and notes the affect associated with the members of the two groups, the more people tend to see the world in terms of those two groups. As a consequence, people identify more or less strongly with one of those two groups. Group identity and the strength of that identity end up being an important aspect of when and how hurts can be healed and memories amended.

Healing Hurts

When conflict has resulted in hurts being inflicted on group members, people need to heal from those hurts in order to move past the hurts and live in peace. This will involve healing at the individual level. People have to deal with the traumas that were inflicted on them. They need to be able to heal from post-traumatic stress disorders, the physical and psychological wounds that were inflicted upon them, and the emotional reactions they had to the sight, sound, and memory of people in the other group. In addition, individuals must grieve over their losses and limitations that come about due to the group conflict and the hurts that were inflicted. Either people will create and respond to symbols and rituals in ways that allow them to heal or in ways that keep the traumas emotional and fresh in their minds.

People need to heal in their personal relationships as well as in their individual psyches. We interact with people in the other group. Sometimes, we interact with very few people in the other groups because we have shaped our environments to involve people who are very similar to us. Often, however, in the various walks of life that we move through, we must engage in relationships with people in the other group.

It is not enough to merely be exposed to members of another group. When a person is a member of a hated group, exposure often can make feelings more salient and more difficult to cope with. Early studies by Sherif and other social psychologists showed that if people worked together on superordinate tasks on which they were cooperating, people tended to minimize group differences. Those studies were done in ad hoc groups that were not important to people. Mere exposure and working together on common goals can help hurts heal, but it is very difficult for this to happen.

Why Is This Difficult?

First, we have a tendency to treat people from a disliked out-group as somehow subhuman. This is subtle and usually not done consciously. Studies, however, have shown that we intend to infrahumanize out-group members. For instance, we treat subtle secondary emotions as characteristic of our in-group but do not attribute many secondary emotions to out-group members. Primary emotions such as fear, anger, and hatred are attributed to out-groups, but not more subtle emotions such as guilt, shame, humiliation, disgust, optimism, elation, nostalgia, adulation, and love. The theoretical explanation behind this that has gained the most popularity is called *psychological essentialism* (Haslam, Rothschild, & Ernst, 2000). Psychological essentialism argues that people define their in-group as being endowed with the prototypical human essence. Because the out-group is seen as different, it is somehow seen as infrahuman. Remember Nazi Germany. Jews, the infirm, Russians, and Gypsies could actually be seen as subhuman and therefore be morally excluded from consideration as a person.

Emotion researchers such as Ekman (1992) and Leyens et al. (2000) have shown that in Northern Ireland, Catholics and Protestants attributed more secondary emotions to their in-group than to their out-group, to which they did not belong. They infrahumanized the members of the group to which they did not belong. Kim et al. (in Cairns et al., 2005) showed that, in Northern Ireland, the level of contact with members of the other community predicted more secondary emotions in the out-group than did lower levels of contact with people in the out-group.

A second reason why it is difficult to heal hurts toward out-group members is the difficulty in trusting a whole group. Individuals are easier to trust than are groups. An individual can be seen as relatively reliable. In a group, however, extremists carry out harmful actions regardless of what the group as a whole decides. It is difficult, therefore, to trust a group because there will be violations of any agreements.

A third reason why it is difficult to heal the hurts with an out-group is because identity with one's in-group affects the amount of bias toward the out-group. Hewstone et al. (2004) gave participants in Northern Ireland several versions of a scenario describing an act of violence. The scenario was manipulated so that the group member of the participant, the group member of the perpetrator, and the intentionality to kill the victim (i.e., intentional versus unintentional) and the motivation (i.e., in retaliation or no apparent motivation) were manipulated. Participants rated their attributions of blame and the forgiveness for the perpetrator in each situation. They also rated whether they would recommend the perpetrator be granted early release or should be required to serve a minimum of two additional years for the murders they committed. Participants rated the importance of religion to them, the amount of contact they had with out-group members, their perspective-taking toward the out-group, and other measures. Both Catholics and Protestants were biased in favor of their own group. Protestants were more forgiving of Protestant perpetrators than Catholic perpetrators, and vice versa. However, interestingly, forgiveness was moderated by the degree to which people identified with their own religious groups. Therefore, people who had a low identification with their religious group showed less in-group versus out-group bias than did people with high identification with their own religious group. People highly identified with their group are likely to find it more difficult to heal the hurts that they have experienced because they have more difficulty perceiving reparative actions and situations.

Mending Memories

Faulkner is known for the quote: "The past is not dead, it is not even past." People involved in intergroup conflict do not easily give up the past. In fact, the past is ever present with them. Shriver (1998) has described the Bittburg controversy in which President Ronald Reagan, in an attempt to honor dead German soldiers and promote reconciliation with Germany, offended Jews by choosing a cemetery in which some Nazi soldiers were buried. The past tensions escalated and created a world incident before Reagan finally gave a talk at the cemetery.

Mona Sue Weissmark (2004), in the book *Justice Matters: Legacies of the Holocaust and World War II,* described groups that she brought together of adult children of Holocaust survivors and of Nazi soldiers. The groups shared their stories. Weissmark was amazed at how different the stories were. Holocaust survivors' children tended to refer to the Holocaust and to the 6 million Jewish deaths that took place. Some of the children would say things like, "I didn't even know there was a war until I was a teenager." On the other hand, the Nazis' adult children would talk about the terrible loss of life as the allies bombed Germany night and day, resulting in the loss of millions of German lives. They would say things like, "I didn't even realize that there were death camps until I was a teenager." Clearly, the stories were derived from those learned as a child. The emotional events at the center of the stories differed. They did not even include the same events in many cases.

As Weissmark (2004) points out, there was not a true story and a false story in the two groups. There were two completely different true stories. The task was not to correct inaccuracies in one story or the other, but rather to somehow forge a common story that could serve as a basis for a different kind of reconstructed memory. This is exceptionally difficult, of course, because the memories that each group began with were emotion-laden and were formed in childhood. They came from trusted sources: their parents. Their parents spoke with emotion and high passion about these issues, and the stories had been practiced and elaborated for a lifetime.

In the groups, each side heard the other side's story. But huge change did not occur. The new other perspective occurred in a group involving both in-group and out-group members. But it had many fewer emotional attachments; the authority level was less; and the time for elaboration was less than the basic in-group story. Mending memories is not an easy task in dealing with intergroup conflict.

Smoothing Stress

We can examine intergroup stress from the point of view of stress-and-coping theory. Stressors have occurred throughout a person's life. The parent's stories—we will call them the *received stories*—have placed demands on the child to perceive events in a particular way. People's perceptions have been shaped by those received stories. Encounters with out-group members provide demands to change. Good interactions with an out-group member make a strong demand for the person to challenge the received story. This is a classic definition of a stressor: an event that makes a demand to change.

These stressors are then appraised. The identity of the person and the degree to which the person identifies with his or her group or family will determine the degree to which the new events are seen as challenges or threats to the received story. If the new events are seen as challenges, they may be dismissed by discounting the new events. Or, they may be assimilated. Perhaps they are treated as a rare exception to the received story. The story, however, is left unchanged. If the event is a sufficiently strong event, then a positive interaction with an out-group member could be perceived as a threat to the person's entire framework.

This will create stress reactions, which will be physical and can provoke emotional reactions such as fear, anger, or depression. A cognitive reaction such as making negative attributions to the out-group member even though the interaction was positive, or blaming the out-group member, or defensive reactions such as denial or projection could also occur.

The person will employ coping mechanisms, which can reflect more or less mental health. People tend to maintain their cognitive framework. So, rationalization and justification will be likely coping mechanisms. Other ways of discounting the negative and positive interaction with an out-group member might occur. As positive interactions with out-group members build up, however, more pressure is placed on the person to cope with the threat in ways that change the cognitive framework.

Atrocities Require Special Healing

Intractable conflict may happen between groups that are fundamentally of equal power, or there may be a power differential. Staub (2005) observes, though, that atrocities happen when there is a vast power differential between groups. This power might involve sheer numbers of people, or might involve a control of the government. Atrocities might be localized. In the massacre at Mai Lai in the Vietnam War, U.S. troops under Lieutenant William Calley massacred men, women, and children in a village. Atrocities might also involve genocide or mass killing.

Atrocities require special attention because the perpetrators in atrocities almost never apologize to the victims. In South Africa, very few Nationalist Party Leaders ever apologized. If perpetrators in atrocities or genocide or mass killing admit to their deeds, they usually do not express regret and remorse, but rather justify and excuse their acts.

In genocide and mass killing, both victim and perpetrator are wounded. However, they are wounded in different ways. Weissmark (2004) notes, "Nazis' children and survivors' are embraced in a symbiotic relationship in part, defining themselves in terms of the other—as opposites of the other.... A chasm of shame and vengeance still divides children from both groups. A similar generational animus is found in the world over from Northern Ireland to tribal Africa ... rather than having internalized the parables of the parent, each of the children is also seeking their own vindication, their own justice, and in some cases their own expiation" (p. 38). Even though victims and perpetrators are wounded in different ways and pass those wounds on to subsequent generations, it is difficult for the perpetrators to admit that they are wounded. Because one group more easily recognizes its wounds and the other does not, it is easier to blame one group totally for the wrongdoing. It is difficult to arrive at mutual empathy and mutual sympathy, compassion, love, and forgiveness.

Fostering Healing

Truth. Injustice has two sides. Both sides think that their story is true. Both pass the truth that they understand along to their children by way of parables, stories, reactions to child sentiments, parental attitudes, and descriptions of their own experiences and experiences they know. Weissmark (2004) points out that these reactions are passed along to children also through stories, books that are chosen for the child to read, family rituals, discussion of events, processing things seen on television, conversation, games children play, and others. The message that is told through these methods is, "They hurt us. Don't trust them. They'll take advantage of you. They'll destroy you if given the opportunity."

Weissmark (2004) observes what she calls the devil-victim. Namely, both sides tell stories of their own hardship and how they were victimized by the other side. The sense is that, in suffering, there is a vindication for what one might do. By being a victim, one has been placed on the moral high ground. Thus, all sides agree that truth will set them free. Truth is looked at as the healer that will vindicate their cause. Both sides want to get truth. The truth that each side wants differs.

Justice. Healing can be promoted by bringing about a sense of social justice. Fair principles could be established. Fair procedures could be followed. Equitable distribution of goods could be implemented. Laws that are disobeyed result in fair penalties regardless of who disobeyed. Fairness sounds great in principle, but in reality it is difficult to achieve.

We experience negative events more strongly than positive events. Roy Baumeister (1997) reviewed the literature in six different areas. He found consistently that the emotional impact of one negative or painful event takes about five or more positive events to offset it. The bad, he argues, is stronger than the good. He suggests that this is consistent with an evolutionary background. If something good happens to us, it can make us feel better, but if something bad happens, it can kill us. We are, therefore, hardwired to respond more strongly to aversive events than to positive events. How does a person ever become optimistic or have a positive frame of mind? The answer, Baumeister says, is that the good outnumber the bad.

Healing from past wounds, then, requires justice. But justice is difficult to come by. People pay attention to the inequities more than to just acts. People also attend to their own inequities more vigilantly than to inequities that others experience. Again, we might suggest that this is consistent with an evolutionary framework in that if we experience inequities, we are in danger of not surviving. If other groups experience inequities, then we worry only if it might affect our survival.

Common history. Healing of past wounds can only take place if the two groups communicate their stories and form a public common history. The public narrative needs to consider positive and negative behaviors of both sides of the conflict. It is naïve to think that each side will consider history in the same way. Each side will perceive events that happen to it as more important than the events that happen to the other side and will discount the truth of the other side.

Contact with out-group members. A healed conflict can result from interpersonal contact with members of the out-group. Hewstone et al. (2004) have found that contact with out-group members leads to heightened forgiveness for transgressions by out-group members. They surveyed a representative sample of the population of Northern Ireland. They measured people's perspective-taking, trust of the community, and an index of participants' exposure to violence. Forgiveness was positively associated with more contact from out-group friends, more positive out-group attitudes, greater ability to take the perspective of people in the out-group, and greater trust of out-group members. For Catholics, the strongest predictor of forgiveness was trust. For Protestants, trust and perspective-taking were equally strong predictors of forgiveness, and strong identification with one's in-group was negatively correlated with forgiveness. People who experienced more violence themselves in turn experienced less forgiveness than did those who experienced less violence themselves. Having more contact in a positive setting with people in the out-group was related to more likelihood that forgiveness would be granted.

Prevent recurrence of atrocities and conflict with the out-group. Staub (2005) reviewed his decades of study of genocide. He reflected on his experience in Rwanda attempting to help two groups reconcile. He suggested that understanding is necessary for preventing the recurrence of violence. People need to understand the impact of the events, be aware of the avenues of healing, understand the origins of genocide, and know what basic human needs must be met to maintain peace. Understanding, he argues, is a way station on the road to forgiveness. Inherent to such understanding is being able to take the other person's role and empathically see things from the other person's perspective.

To understand the impact of the event, people on both sides need to share the events from their perspective. Not only must they tell of the events, but the other side must be willing to listen to those events. The other side must also be able to take in the impact of the events and identify emotionally with them.

Staub (2005) identifies four avenues to healing: truth, justice, creation of a shared history, and contact with out-group members. *Truth*, he argues, is a prerequisite to justice. Truth, in all its complexity, must be understood. *Justice* involves retributive justice, restorative or compensatory justice, and procedural justice. Justice reaffirms the innocence of the survivors, restores the moral order, helps people feel safe, negates the impunity of the perpetrators, and re-creates a social balance between victims and perpetrators. The *shared history* must involve a story of what happened, what caused the events, why each blames the other, why neither wants to consider the side of the other, and why neither wants to be the first to understand the side of the other. *Contact with out-group members* presumes mutually enriching interactions.

Staub (2005) attempts to help people understand why genocide and violence occur. It builds up slowly and has deep roots in social conditions and predictable social processes. Social conditions include economic problems, political disorganization, and group conflict. Psychological frustration attends the failure to meet fundamental psychological needs for esteem, recognition, and respect. Social processes that lead up to violence might include the creation of destructive ideologies and scapegoating, in which the negativity experienced by an in-group is attributed to an out-group. Violence also evolves slowly from verbal violence to suggestions of physical violence to mass participation in violence. This move toward violence parallels a downward trajectory of treating the group as less than human. An overly strong respect for authority develops. Groups that are about to perpetrate violence reach back into their past and identify some victimization and woundedness that they each experienced, which they use to legitimize violence. By recognizing the signs of the origins of genocide and violence, societies can take steps to head off violence before it occurs. These provide recognition signals and give societies guidelines for concrete preventive actions.

Provide basic human needs. Violence is rooted in the inability to have basic human needs met. This not only involves material and economic needs, but also psychological needs. Social justice provides for the basic physical and psychological needs of all groups in society so that perceptions of inequity are minimized.

Staub's (2005) treatment of the causes, origins, and developmental course of genocide is consistent with a stress-and-coping theory of unforgiveness. Stressors accumulate along many routes—political disorganization, privation, past inequities, prejudice, and prominence of conflict with an out-group. These stressors are appraised as threatening and the locus of problems is attributed to the out-group, which gradually is seen more as a threat and enemy and less as humans. Emotional, cognitive, and social stress reactions occur, and the powerful in-group dwells in unforgiveness.

The group begins to cope with the interpersonal stress of unforgiveness and the threat posed by the out-group. Anger, resentment, bitterness, hostility, hatred, and fear empower aggressive coping. Suggestions of violence embolden further verbal taunts, which can lead to isolated and finally to mass acts of violence. Mass violence and perhaps genocide can add guilt to the emotional mix.

Practical Ways for Societies to Promote Healing

Apologies by Heads of State

During the 1990s, a number of political and religious leaders—from Bill Clinton to German President Roman Herzog to Pope John Paul II—publicly asked forgiveness for past wrongs committed by their organizations. These leaders used their legitimate authority to apologize on behalf of a group. That apology can then be a symbol. Heads of state can also verbalize forgiveness for a past wrong, but few have done so.

Truth Commissions

The war crimes trials after World War II and during other outbreaks of violence are one way of holding heads of state accountable for the crimes committed under their leadership. Augusto Pinochet, former president of Chile, has been facing war crime trials, as have Slobodan Milosevic (until his recent death) in Kosovo and Saddam Hussein in Iraq. Many countries, however, are moving more toward Truth Commissions. The most widely known Truth Commission is the Truth and Reconciliation Commission (TRC) in South Africa. The TRC has attempted to give the victims of oppression the chance to tell their story. The second side of the TRC has involved amnesty hearings for perpetrators who agree to tell the full truth and cooperate with the authorities. A third phase of the TRC hearings has been hearings about reparations. These TRC hearings have been criticized for many reasons. The South African TRC, despite its flaws, has been the greatest experiment in national healing yet to occur.

Truth commissions are based on the idea that truth emerges from a collective testimony of people with different points of view. Witnesses of events see things from different perspectives. One witness of an atrocity might see several people murdered, while another witness sees different people murdered, while a third witness might see someone attempting to stop the murders. As witnesses tell their perspectives, they provide a record that feeds the public consciousness and eventually can be put together in a public narrative.

Contact between Groups

Contact, as we have seen, is not always positive, because people harm each other on occasion when they are put into contact with each other. Furthermore, the forced contact between out-group and in-group members can result in worsening attitudes of those who are strongly identified with their group. Helpful contact between groups needs to provide opportunities to interact with the other group to allow a more humanizing perception of the opposing group. This is especially true for a person who is high in group identity. Hewstone et al. (2004) have found that contact increases perspective-taking, trust, positive out-group attitudes, and number of out-group friends. All of those can lead to healing of harms.

Transform a Strong Group Identity

The people with high group identity should not have to worry that their group identity would be weakened through group contact. Having a strong group identity is important to people, but the nature of the acts of the group with which they identify can be changed. This would involve including stories about people in the in-group who helped out-group members. Peacemakers can be seen as heroes. People like Nelson Mandela or Desmond Tutu have been identified in South Africa. Members of the Underground Railroad who assisted runaway slaves during the Civil War, and Germans who helped Jews, such as was popularized in Spielberg's movie, *Schindler's List*, have been lionized as heroes as well. All of these efforts can strengthen group identity yet change the group identity to include more positive relations with out-group members.

Identify Signs of Future Violence and Turn From Them

Leaders of groups need to be aware that violence can occur under predictable conditions. These include political disorganization, economic problems, group conflict, suffering attributed to the out-group, frustration, scapegoating, devaluation of the out-group, and creation of destructive ideologies.

Forging Shared Perceptions

Shared perceptions can be forged through a variety of social interventions. These involve Truth Commissions. In addition, sustained dialogs can be promoted (Saunders, 1999). Sustained dialogs include members from both groups. Membership of the core is constant. Dialogs take place over time and during successive meetings until a relationship is formed. People can begin to see the other side as more human.

Agree On an Educational Curriculum

I recall being at a meeting of peace workers. A man from Bosnia was recounting life in the former Yugoslavia. He talked about Truth Commissions and public statements that attempted to promote healing. Then he said, "However, the children of the Muslims and the children of the Christians go to their home and hear their parents tell stories of abuses by the other side. They go to their segregated schools and hear different histories. It is no mystery what will happen when these 6-, 7-, and 8-year-old children become 16-, 17-, and 18-year-old hormone-flooded youth. These youth will have a lust for violence against the other side. And feel completely justified in perpetrating their own abuses." Without a common educational curriculum, we educate children to repeat the past.

Healing of Both Victim and Perpetrators

Both victims and perpetrators have their own wounds. Victims must engage with their own pain, yet at the same time develop empathy for the other side. They must acknowledge that the perpetrators themselves had suffered. They had what they considered legitimate reasons for violence, often born out of their perception that they were abused or discriminated against. Healing of victims can be promoted if perpetrators acknowledge that they have done wrong and that they recognize that the victims have suffered. Testimonials, memorials, and ceremonies are good ways of publicly acknowledging the suffering of the victims and promoting healing. In those testimonials, memorials, and ceremonies, the focus should not be on the harm and cruelties perpetrated but on helping people grieve. A focus on a better future where healing takes place will help promote the healing.

Perpetrators were also wounded, and their character was further damaged by their own despicable actions. They experience shame and guilt and have adjusted their self-image to incorporate their acts. Their own cruelty is difficult to deal with, so they distance themselves from their victims, devalue the victims further, and justify the suffering they have inflicted on the victims. They continue to exclude victims from the moral universe and think of them as somehow less than human—to rationalize past acts, as they did to justify their acts as they were committing them. Perpetrators need to admit and abandon these acts as means of coping. They need to come to terms with loss of power and status and with their shame and guilt. This is best promoted by understanding how they developed the attitudes that led to atrocious acts and by promoting empathy with the victims.

Coping With Stress

We may liken the social and societal stress and coping process to the process of stress and coping within an individual. Societal problems are stressors. People as a group may individually appraise the stressors and their ability to cope with the stressors. They react with stress reactions of emotional arousal, anger, and fear, and then they attempt to cope with those emotions, appraisals, and stressors.

For healing, positive societal coping is needed. Social problems must be solved in ways that consider and account for the basic needs of all group members. Appraisals must be adjusted so that other groups are not seen as a threat. Rather, incorporating groups together, while maintaining each group's identity, is seen as a challenge that can be met if the proper effort and cooperation can be achieved.

The stress reactions of anger, fear, hatred, resentment, and hostility need to be replaced by emotional forgiveness and motivational transformation to more positive benevolent conciliatory grace- and mercy-filled motivations. Positive other-oriented emotions are needed and are experienced in memorials, contact, and mutual effort toward common goals. The coping mechanisms of providing justice and promoting forgiveness can stimulate different solutions, reduce violence, promote better relationships, and build forgiveness into the members of both groups.

Conclusion

Healing the wounds that can lead to societal violence depends on mutuality across a society. People have to be willing to talk and listen to each other and hear the multiple stories from different perspectives. They must accept that two different perspectives dominate and that it is important to construct a common framework. People must accept that merely understanding and acting rationally alone will not solve societal tensions. Instead, emotional and motivational transformations have to supplement rational understanding. Empathy, sympathy, compassion, and love must be infused across the groups. A framework of the warm virtues must be elevated and brought into the light to balance off the conscientiousness-based virtues that tend to be emphasized in times of injustice.

Society needs a plan. That plan needs to be negotiated by all voices at the table so that relationships can be built and trust can grow. This will occur mostly as the warmth-based virtues and altruistic motives—such as grace, mercy, and conciliation—are emphasized, and tolerance for differences can be brought about even in some of the more extreme members of each group.

Conclusion
Forgiveness Is Not a Panacea

Forgiveness and reconciliation are helpful psychological and social processes that have real benefits to people who participate in them. Yet, they are not a panacea. They will not solve all of the problems of individuals, couples, or societies. They are useful, but not the end-all of peace.

Two Sets of Virtues and Real Vices

As I have suggested in this book, people who seek to pursue virtue tend to pursue either conscientiousness-based virtues or warmth-based virtues (Worthington & Berry, 2005). They tend to orient their life more towards one set of virtues than toward the other. However, some strong situations can cause the conscientiousness-based virtues to accelerate to the foreground, overwhelming people's normal tendencies toward warmth-based virtues and enhancing their normal tendencies toward conscientiousness-based virtues. In the same way, other strong situations can accelerate the warmth-based virtues and cause the conscientiousness-based virtues to recede into the background.

Injustices draw attention to conscientiousness-based virtues. It takes conscious effort and structure of a dyad, community, or society to balance conscientiousness-based virtues once they are aroused. Forgiveness is considered by most people to be a warmth-based virtue, though decisional forgiveness can be granted as one's duty.

Of course, life is not always merely a competition between two sets of virtues. There are real vices. Some people do objective evil. Some people do not aspire to a virtuous life at all. In fact, they aspire to hedonism or even to enjoying harming others. Individual virtue, vice, or hedonistic orientations set the backdrop for real problems.

Problems

At the individual level, one of the most prevalent problems is a pursuit of unbridled self-interest. Given any opportunity, some people will place themselves ahead of all others. Other people pursue power at all costs—personal power over a mate, coworker, or even an acquaintance. They may pursue power for the sake of their in-group. They may sacrifice in the pursuit of such group-based power.

Forgiveness can be entered into for one's own benefit. It can be motivated by maximizing one's own pleasure or health. Or it can be motivated by getting rid of a burden of unforgiveness through quickly forgiving. Or forgiveness can be more oriented toward giving an altruistic gift to a person who has harmed one. Such a gift is costly. It is not easy to forgive unselfishly. It is not easy to loose a transgressor from the bonds of guilt or shame, from having wronged a person.

Throughout this book, I have advocated for altruism and seeking the good of others. I believe that most people pursue their own self-interest naturally, so people do not have to be encouraged to pursue their own self-interest. People do as readily pursue others' interests, especially when the others have harmed them. Clearly, I believe there is some balance required. One should not seek to meet others' needs to the extent that one obliterates oneself. This turns out in reality to be rarely the case.

Decisional forgiveness is an act of the will. It can be an act of self-giving and altruism. It can benefit a wide variety of people. In pairs of people and in wider society, people often become immersed in conflict. That conflict creates a strong situation that generates anger and fear. It brings out a sense of grasping as one feels his or her own influence, power, and desires slipping away. Trying to grasp and hold on to power leads people into power struggles in which people fight about who has the say on an issue, not about the issue. Issues are excuses for demonstrating that one has power. Attempts to gain, maintain, or regain power seem to be at the core of unforgiveness as it plays itself out in a dyadic relationship or in wider society.

Dyads require boundaries between two partners. Justice and truth maintain boundaries. But they can become sledgehammers that are used to pound away the boundaries and squash others. Therefore, a balance is necessary between truth and justice and the sense of empathy, sympathy, compassion, love, and forgiveness that hold dyads together into a partnership that is stronger than either partner alone.

At the group level, power dynamics again rear their heads. Issues in groups revolve around who has the power that he or she thinks he or she is entitled to. People develop self-interested agendas to gain, hold on to, or regain power. People in groups exist across the spectrum—from people who are violent hotheads seeking to impose power on the out-group to those who are Caspar Milquetoasts who would give away all power. The balance among the hotheads, agendas of self-interest, and power orientations of those who have been harmed and feel that they are entitled to more resources comes from peacemakers. Peacemakers act altruistically to help in-group members and to promote peace between in-group and out-group members. They are emissaries of unselfish altruistic love, for in-group as well as out-group members.

Differing Agendas Create a Backdrop for Stress

Pursuit of good, pursuit of evil, mere self-interested pursuit of pleasure, and the headlong rush to obtain and use power motivate people toward different—and often conflicting—ends. Transgressions inevitably happen, and resulting stress is part and parcel of life. Damage must be contained, minimized, dealt with productively, and repaired. Efforts to do so can be arenas for the same motives—pursuit of good, evil, pleasure, or power. I hope that many people wish to pursue virtue as often as possible, especially forgiveness.

In this application of general stress-and-coping theory to form a stress-and-coping theory of forgiveness, I attempt to account for the interplay between justice and forgiveness through the injustice gap. I accept that both willful decision-making and emotional experience are at the center of the meaning-making system. Decision allows self-sacrifice, altruism, and noble purpose. Emotion tells people what is important to them and conveys to others that importance. Thus, decisional forgiveness was suggested as a way people can control their behavior toward others after a hurt or offense. The emotional replacement hypothesis was proposed as the mechanism by which emotional forgiveness is experienced. Both occur in social context, and I described both the dyadic and several societal contexts in which forgiveness is often needed to deal effectively with transgressions and ensuing unforgiveness.

Real Benefits

Practicing forgiveness and reconciliation within a context of fair justice can promote benefits of the spirit. A person is often made nobler through laying down his or her life in forgiving rather than standing up and violently opposing the other person. Opening one's arms in reconciliation seems nobler than shoving a clenched fist beneath someone's nose. Yet this can be taken to extreme. There is little nobility in being a doormat.

Mental health benefits can also attend forgiving and reconciling (for a review, see Toussaint & Webb, 2005). Forgiveness reduces anger, depression, anxiety, and fear. Positive mental health states can also arise from practicing forgiveness and reconciliation. People can feel connected. They can respond to stress through the tend-and-befriend coping mechanism instead of fight or flight. Real relational benefits are available if people forgive. These relational benefits can accrue to couples, families, communities, and societies. Relationships improve when justice, truth, and forgiveness operate hand-in-hand.

Physical benefits can also attend forgiveness (see Harris & Thoresen, 2005; Worthington & Scherer, 2004). Violence can be reduced and thus injuries can be prevented or minimized. People's mental health can be made better, so that physical harm through suicides can be lessened. Depression has been associated with physical health costs (for a review, see Cole & Dendukuri, 2003). Physical improvements can exist when people are no longer depressed. Forgiveness, and certainly reducing unforgiveness, might strengthen the immune system (for a review, see Temoshok & Wald, 2005). In addition, interpersonal conflict and thus stress can be reduced by forgiving. This can cause cardiovascular and immune system benefits (see Harris & Thoresen, 2005).

Conclusion

The interpersonal stressors of transgressions pollute the individual, dyadic, and societal levels of human life. Those stressors demand that people adjust. Through justice, truth, and forgiveness, people can cope more positively with these unforgiving interpersonal stressors. Thus, they can be happier and better adjusted, live in more positive relationships, and experience better health.

Forgiveness is not a panacea. It works in combination with justice, truth, and other prosocial actions. However, forgiveness is a great benefit to individuals, pairs of acquaintances, friends, family members, and the larger society.

Appendix
What Is Forgiveness?

In chapter 1, I posed eight case studies to illustrate the complexities of forgiveness. I did not discuss them because the theory was not yet developed. Now we are ready to discuss each. Before you read my response, you might formulate an answer yourself.

Divorced Diana (Case 1)

Diana might have worked through forgiving her ex-spouse and believes herself to have completely have gotten over the difficulties that resulted in the divorce. Years later, she sees her ex-spouse and negative feelings flood her. She is angry, afraid, and sad. "I thought I'd forgiven him," she thinks, "but obviously I haven't."

Discussion. Yes, she has granted decisional forgiveness and experienced emotional forgiveness, but the sight of her ex-spouse triggers old negative emotions. Like burning one's hand makes one respond in anger and fear when getting one's hand near the heat of a stove, the negative emotions warn Diana of a potentially harmful situation and trigger anger, fear, and sadness.

Teeth-Gritting Gertrude (Case 2)

Gertrude was hurt by a romantic betrayal. She is gritting her teeth, clenching her jaws, crossing her arms, and muttering, "Of course I forgive him," without seeming to move her lips. Do we believe her? Has she really forgiven?

Discussion. She says she has forgiven, and she might sincerely have decided to forgive. The decisional forgiveness might even last the rest of Gertrude's life. But it appears she has not emotionally forgiven the betrayal.

Bible-Responding Bob (Case 3)

What about Bob? He says, "Yesterday my boss fired me. He said I took too much time to go to the doctor to deal with my neck injury that I received in an auto crash. He said the company just did not get enough work from me to make it worthwhile to continue my employment. It's so unfair." Then he continues, "However, I forgive him for that unfair treatment."

Bob showed no hostility in his voice or his manner. So I asked, "What prompted you to forgive him so quickly?"

Bob said, "The Scripture says that if I don't forgive someone who wrongs me, then I won't be forgiven by God. So, by will, I simply chose to forgive him."

Did he really forgive? Is it really so easy? Can one simply choose to forgive and by willpower affect full forgiveness?

Discussion. Yes, Bob seems to have sincerely granted decisional forgiveness, and that might have spread to a change in emotion.

Slandered Sally (Case 4)

Sally lost a promotion to vice president of a corporation because she had an enemy within the management team. "I was the subject of a smear campaign. My enemy told things about me that were true, yet she twisted them. It sounded as if I was not working hard and was doing things that were marginally ethical. I have had the opportunity to get even with her before, but I swore not to take revenge on her. So I never have. I have forgiven her. I no longer feel resentment."

Discussion. Sally says she has forgiven, and she cites as evidence her oath not to seek vengeance. Her emotional forgiveness is supported by her self-report that she feels no resentment, and her nonverbal tone of expression seems consistent with her self-report.

Abused Abigail (Case 5)

Abigail, a middle-aged woman, had struggled for years to forgive her father for his physical abuse of her and her siblings. After 2 years of psychotherapy, she felt that her forgiveness was complete. Finally, she initiated contact with her father after being away from home for over 10 years. "He started right in on me," she said. "It was as if I had never been away. He was insulting, demeaning, and ugly. I think he would have attacked me physically, but I yelled that I would call the police and have him put away. Now, I don't know what to think. Did I forgive him? He was able to push my buttons so easily. Of course, he installed those buttons. Still, if I had really forgiven, I should be above being provoked. Shouldn't I?"

Discussion. Abigail appears to have decisionally and emotionally forgiven, but the new interactions have created new transgressions. Forgiving does not give immunity to being provoked anew.

Swindled Sid (Case 6)

Sid, an elderly man who was embezzled of $10,000, said, "The guy who swindled me was a friend. I trusted him. When he asked me to loan him $10,000, I didn't hesitate. Then he skipped town. It took a while, but I got over it. I don't miss the money now, and I don't really hold any hard feelings toward him. In fact, I hope he gets some use out of that money."

"Have you forgiven him?"

"I suppose so," he said. "Never really thought about it as forgiving him. I sorta accepted it and got a kind of peace. I guess you could say I forgave."

Discussion. Sid probably has not forgiven, but he has accepted and moved on. He is at peace.

Elderly Ellie (Case 7)

Ellie, an elderly woman, was really ill. As she talked to a hospice care worker, the woman said, "I used to have so much resentment of Marie. But as I have gotten nearer to seeing my Maker, I have simply determined in my spirit not to be resentful against Marie for the harm she did to me. It's difficult. I struggle every day. I think about her, but I'm determined not to let resentment cloud my last days on this earth. I think I've succeeded. I still get upset, but I honestly think my resentment and hate are totally gone."

Discussion. Ellie might have granted decisional forgiveness, and she might want to believe that she has emotionally forgiven, but she seems to struggle with resentment. Her emotional forgiveness does not seem complete, though it is improved relative to when she "used to have so much resentment."

Survivor Suzanne (Case 8)

Suzanne, a middle-aged woman, was talking with a reporter. She was reacting to the death of her mother. She said, "I believe I have completely forgiven the youth who killed Mama. I have had peace about this since I was able to forgive. I still remember my mother and miss her. Yet I do not feel that this young man should be sentenced to a death penalty for what he did. I'll testify to that in my victim impact statement next week. Still, I don't believe he should be let off. He is responsible for his crime, and society says that he should pay. It wouldn't be right to simply let him walk scot-free. Forgiveness has nothing to do with whether he is required to pay for his crime under the law."

Discussion. Suzanne appears to have forgiven both decisionally and emotionally. She is right to separate the societal accountability from her personal experience of forgiving.

References

Ainsworth, M. S., & Bell, S. M. (1978). Attachment, exploration, and separation: Illustrated by one-year-olds in a strange situation. *Child Development, 41,* 49-67.

Al-Mabuk, R. H., Enright, R. D., & Cardis, P. A. (1995). Forgiving education with parentally love-deprived late adolescents. *Journal of Moral Education, 24,* 427-444.

Angyal, A. (1952). The convergence of psychotherapy and religion. *Journal of Pastoral Care, 5 (Winter),* 4-14.

Arendt, H. (1963). *Eichmann in Jerusalem: A report on the banality of evil.* New York: Viking Press.

Armour, M. P., & Umbreit, M. S. (2005). The paradox of forgiveness in restorative justice. In E. L. Worthington, Jr. (Ed.), *Handbook of forgiveness* (pp. 491-503). New York: Brunner-Routledge.

Aron, E. N., & Aron, A. (1997). Sensory-processing sensitivity and its relation to introversion and emotionality. *Journal of Personality and Social Psychology, 73,* 345-368.

Aronson, E. (1992). The return of the repressed: Dissonance theory makes a comeback. *Psychological Inquiry, 3,* 303-311.

Aronson, E. (1999). Dissonance, hypocrisy, and the self-concept. In E. Harmon-Jones & J. Mills (Eds.), *Cognitive dissonance: Progress on a pivotal theory in social psychology* (pp. 103-126). Washington, DC: American Psychological Association.

Ashby, F. G., Isen, A. M., & Turken, A. U. (1999). A neuropsychological theory of positive affect and its influence on cognition. *Psychological Review, 106,* 529-550.

Ashton, M. C., Paunonen, S. V., Helmes, E., & Jackson, D. N. (1998). Kin altruism, reciprocal altruism, and the Big Five personality factors. *Evolution and Human Behavior, 19,* 243-255.

Aspinwall, L. G., Richter, L., & Hoffman, R. R., III. (2001). Understanding how optimism works: An examination of optimists' adaptive moderation of belief and behavior. *In E. C. Chang (Ed.), Optimism and pessimism: Implications for theory, research, and practice* (pp. 217-238). Washington, DC: American Psychological Association.

Aspinwall, L. G., & Taylor, S. E. (1997). A stitch in time: Self-regulation and proactive coping. *Psychological Bulletin, 121,* 417-436.

Baider, L., & De-Nour, A. K. (1997). Psychological distress and intrusive thoughts in cancer patients. *Journal of Nervous and Mental Disease, 185,* 346-348.

Baron, R. A. (1976). The reduction of human aggression: A field study of the influence of incompatible reactions. *Journal of Applied Social Psychology, 6,* 260-274.

Bartholomew, K., & Horowitz, L. M. (1991). Attachment styles among young adults: A test of a four-category model. *Journal of Personality and Social Psychology, 61,* 226-244.

Baskin, T. W., & Enright, R. D. (2004). Intervention studies in forgiveness: A meta-analysis. *Journal of Counseling and Development, 82,* 79-90.

Batson, C. D. (1990). How social an animal? The human capacity for caring. *American Psychologist, 45,* 336-346.

Batson, C. D. (1991a). *The altruism question: Toward a social-psychological answer*. Hillsdale, NJ: Lawrence Erlbaum Associates.

Batson, C. D. (1991b). Evidence for altruism: Toward a pluralism of prosocial motives. *Psychological Inquiry, 2*, 107-122.

Batson, C. D., Batson, J. G., & Slingsby, J. K. (1991). Empathic joy and the empathy-altruism hypothesis. *Journal of Personality and Social Psychology, 61*, 413-426.

Batson, C. D., Bolen, M. H., Cross, J. A., & Neuringer-Benefiel, H. E. (1986). Where is the altruism in the altruistic personality? *Journal of Personality & Social Psychology, 50*, 175-181.

Batson, C. D., Bowers, M. J., Leonard, E. A., & Smith, E. C. (2000). Does personal morality exacerbate or restrain retaliation after being harmed? *Personality and Social Psychology Bulletin, 26*, 35-45.

Batson, C. D., Klein, T. R., & Highberger, L. (1995). Immorality from empathy-induced altruism: When compassion and justice conflict. *Journal of Personality and Social Psychology, 68*, 1042-1054.

Batson, C. D., & Oleson, K. C. (1991). *Current status of the empathy-altruism hypothesis*. In M. S. Clark (Ed.), *Prosocial behavior* (pp. 62-85). Thousand Oaks, CA: Sage Publications.

Batson, C. D., O'Quin, K., Fultz, J., Vanderplas, M., & Isen, A. (1983). Self-reported distress and empathy and egoistic versus altruistic motivation for helping. *Journal of Personality and Social Psychology, 45*, 706-718.

Battle, C. L., & Miller, I. W. (2005). Families and forgiveness. In E. L. Worthington, Jr. (Ed.), *Handbook of forgiveness* (pp. 227-241). New York: Brunner-Routledge.

Baumeister, R. F. (1997). *Evil: Inside human violence and cruelty*. New York: W. H. Freeman.

Baumeister, R. F., Bratslavsky, E., & Finkenauer, C. (2001). Bad is stronger than good. *Review of General Psychology, 5*, 323-370.

Baumeister, R. F., Campbell, J. D., Krueger, J. I., & Vohs, K. D. (2003). Does high self-esteem cause better performance, interpersonal success, happiness, or healthier lifestyles? *Psychological Science in the Public Interest, 4* (1), 1-44.

Baumeister, R. F., Exline, J. J., & Sommer, K. L. (1998). The victim role, grudge theory, and two dimensions of forgiveness. In E. L. Worthington, Jr. (Ed.), *Dimensions of forgiveness: Psychological research and theological speculations* (pp. 79-104). Philadelphia: The Templeton Foundation Press.

Baumeister, R. F., Stillwell, A. M., & Wotman, S. R. (1990). Victim and perpetrator accounts of interpersonal conflict: Autobiographical narratives about anger. *Journal of Personality and Social Psychology, 59*, 994-1005.

Bell, R., & Hobson, H. (1994). 5-HT1A receptor influences on rodent social and agonistic behavior: A review and empirical study. *Neuroscience and Biobehavior Review, 19*, 325.

Bem, D. J. (1967). Self-perception: An alternative interpretation of cognitive dissonance phenomena. *Psychological Review, 74*, 183-200.

Benson, H., & Klipper, M. Z. (1975). *The relaxation response*. New York: HarperCollins.

Berkowitz, L. (1993). *Aggression: Its causes, consequences, and control*. New York: McGraw-Hill.

Berry, J. W., & Worthington, E. L., Jr. (2001). Forgivingness, relationship quality, stress while imagining relationship events, and physical and mental health. *Journal of Counseling Psychology, 48*, 447-455.

Berry, J. W., Worthington, E. L., Jr., O'Connor, L. E., Parrott, L. III, & Wade, N. G. (2005). Forgivingness, vengeful rumination, and affective traits. *Journal of Personality, 73*, 183-225.

Berry, J. W., Worthington, E. L., Jr., Parrott, L. III, O'Connor, L., & Wade, N. G. (2001). Dispositional forgivingness: Development and construct validity of the Transgression Narrative Test of Forgivingness (TNTF). *Personality and Social Psychology Bulletin, 27*, 1277-1290.

Berry, J. W., Worthington, E. L., Jr., Wade, N. G., Witvliet, C. v. O., & Kiefer, R. (2005). Forgiveness, moral identity, and perceived justice in crime victims and their supporters. *Humboldt Journal of Social Relations, 29*(2), 136-162.

Blader, S. L., & Tyler, T. R. (2003). A four-component model of procedural justice: Defining the meaning of a "fair" process. *Personality and Social Psychology Bulletin, 29*, 747-758.

Bonson, K. R., & Winter, J. C. (1992). Reversal of testosterone-induced dominance by the serotonergic agonist quipazine. *Pharmacology, Biochemistry and Behavior, 42*, 809-813.

Boon, S. C., & Sulsky, L. M. (1997). Attributions of blame and forgiveness in romantic relationships: A policy-capturing study. *Journal of Social Behavior and Personality, 12*, 19-44.

Boszormenyi-Nagy, I. (1987). *Foundations of contextual therapy: Collected papers of Ivan Boszor-menyi-Nagy, M.D.* New York: Brunner-Routledge.

Boszormenyi-Nagy, I., & Spark, G. M. (1973). *Invisible loyalties.* New York: Harper & Row.

Bowen, M. (1985). *Family therapy in clinical practice.* New York: Jason Aronson.

Bowlby, J. (1969). Disruption of affectional bonds and its effects on behavior. *Canada's Mental Health Supplement, 59,* 12.

Bowlby, J. (1988). *A secure base: Parent-child attachment and healthy human development.* New York: Basic Books.

Brandsma, J. M. (1982). Forgiveness: A dynamic, theological, and therapeutic analysis. *Pastoral Psychology, 31,* 40-50.

Brennan, T. A., Sox, C. M., & Burstin, H. R. (1996). Relation between negligent adverse events and the outcomes of medical malpractice litigation. *New England Journal of Medicine, 335,* 1963-1967.

Brewer, M. B. (1997). The social psychology of intergroup relations: Can research inform practice? *Journal of Social Issues, 53,* 197-211.

Brooks, C. W., & Toussaint, L. (2003). *The relationship between forgiveness and depression: Rumination as a link.* Unpublished manuscript, Idaho State University, Pocatello.

Brosschot, J. F., & Thayer, J. F. (1998). Anger inhibition, cardiovascular recovery, and vagal function: A model of the link between hostility and cardiovascular disease. *Annals of Behavioral Medicine, 20,* 326-332.

Brothers, L. (1989). A biological perspective on empathy. *American Journal of Psychiatry, 146,* 10-19.

Brown, B. R. (1968). The effects of need to maintain face on interpersonal bargaining. *Journal of Experimental Social Psychology, 4,* 107-122.

Brown, S. W., Gorsuch, R., Rosik, C. H., & Ridley, C. R. (2001). The development of a scale to measure forgiveness. *Journal of Psychology and Christianity, 20,* 40-52.

Brownstein, E. J., Worthington, E. L., Jr., Berry, J. W., & Shivy, V. A. (2006). *Transgressions in the workplace: Associations with worker personality, productivity, physical health, and mental health.* Manuscript under editorial review, Virginia Commonwealth University, Richmond.

Brunk, C. G. (2001). Restorative justice and the philosophical theories of criminal punishment. In M. L. Hadley (Ed.), *The spiritual roots of restorative justice* (pp. 31-56). Albany, NY: SUNY Press.

Bryant, W. J. (1998). *The application of cognitive dissonance theory in a forgiveness workshop: Inducing hypocrisy to create a commitment to forgive.* Unpublished doctoral dissertation, Virginia Commonwealth University, Richmond.

Burchard, G. A., Yarhouse, M. A., Worthington, E. L., Jr., Berry, J. W., Killian, M., & Canter, D. E. (2003). A study of two marital enrichment programs and couples' quality of life. *Journal of Psychology and Theology, 31,* 240-252.

Bushman, B. J. (2002). Does venting anger feed or extinguish the flame? Catharsis, rumination, distraction, anger and aggressive responding. *Personality and Social Psychology Bulletin, 28,* 724-731.

Bushman, B. J., & Baumeister, R. F. (1998). Threatened egotism, narcissism, self-esteem, and direct and displaced aggression: Does self-love or self-hate lead to violence? *Journal of Personality and Social Psychology, 75,* 219-229.

Cairns, E., Tam, T., Hewstone, M., & Niens, U. (2005). Intergroup forgiveness and intergroup conflict: Northern Ireland, a case study. In E. L. Worthington, Jr. (Ed.), *Handbook of forgiveness* (pp. 461-475). New York: Brunner-Routledge.

Chapman, G. (1996). *The five love languages: How to express heartfelt commitment to your mate.* New York: Moody Publishers.

Coan, J. A., Allen, J. J. B., & Harmon-Jones, E. (2001). Voluntary facial expression and hemispheric asymmetry over the frontal cortex. *Psychophysiology, 38,* 912-925.

Coccaro, E. F. (1989). Central serotonin and impulsive aggression. *British Journal of Psychiatry, 155* (Suppl. 8), 52-62.

Cohen, J. (2000). Apology and organizations. *Fordham Urban Law Journal, 27,* 1447-1482.

Cole, M. G., & Dendukuri, N. (2003). Risk factors for depression among elderly community subjects: A systematic review and meta-analysis. *American Journal of Psychiatry, 160,* 1147-1156.

Cunningham, B. B. (1985). The will to forgive: A pastoral theological view of forgiving. *Journal of Pastoral Care, 39,* 141-149.

Dabbs, J. M., & Ruback, R. B. (1988). Saliva testosterone and personality of male college students. *Bulletin of the Psychonomic Society, 26,* 244-247.

Damasio, A. R. (1994). *Descartes' error: Emotion, rationality and the human brain.* New York: Putnam.

Damasio, A. R. (1999). *The feeling of what happens: Body and emotion in the making of consciousness.* New York: Harcourt Brace & Co.

Darley, J. (2002). Just punishments: Research on retributional justice. In M. Ross & D. T. Miller (Eds.), *The justice motive in everyday life* (pp. 314-333). New York: Cambridge University Press.

Darley, J. M., & Huff, C. W. (1990). Heightened damage assessment as a result of the intentionality of the damage-causing act. *British Journal of Social Psychology, 29,* 181-188.

Darley, J. M., & Pittman, T. S. (2003). The psychology of compensatory and retributive justice. *Personality and Social Psychology Review, 7,* 324-336.

Davidson, D. L. (1993). Forgiveness and narcissism: Consistency in experience across real and hypothetical hurt situations. *Dissertation Abstracts International, 54,* 2746.

Davis, M. H. (1996). *Empathy: A social psychological approach.* Boulder, CO: Westview Press.

deShazer, S. (1988). *Clues: Investigating solutions in brief therapy.* New York: W.N. Norton.

de Waal, F. B. M., & Pokorny, J. J. (2005). Primate questions about the art and science of forgiving. In E. L. Worthington, Jr. (Ed.), *Handbook of forgiveness* (pp. 17-32). New York: Brunner-Routledge.

Diamond, L. M., & Aspinwall, L. G. (2003). Emotion regulation across the life span: An integrative perspective emphasizing self-regulation, positive affect, and dyadic processes. *Motivation and Emotion, 27,* 125-156.

DiBlasio, F. A. (1998). The use of decision-based forgiveness intervention within intergenerational family therapy. *Journal of Family Therapy, 20,* 77-94.

Dorff, E. N. (1998). The elements of forgiveness: A Jewish approach. In E. L. Worthington, Jr. (Ed.), *Dimensions of forgiveness: Psychological research and theological perspectives* (pp. 29-55). Philadelphia: Templeton Foundation Press.

Drugan, R. C., Paul, S. M., & Crawley, J. N. (1993). Decreased forebrain [-3-5S] TBPS binding and increased [-3H] muscimol binding in rats that do not develop stress-induced behavioral depression. *Brain Research, 631,* 270-276.

Edelman, G. (2004). *Wider than the sky: The phenomenal gift of consciousness.* New Haven, CT: Yale University Press.

Eisenberg, N., & Fabes, R. A. (1990) Empathy: Conceptualization, measurement, and relation to prosocial behavior. *Motivation and Emotion, 14* (2) [Special issue: Empathy], 131-149.

Eisenberg, N., Fabes, R. A., Miller, P. A., Fultz, J., Shell, R., Mathy, R. M., & Reno, R. R. (1989). *Relation of sympathy and personal distress to prosocial behavior: A multimethod study, Journal of Personality and Social Psychology, 57,* 55-66.

Eisenberg, N., & Miller, P. (1997) The development of prosocial behavior versus nonprosocial behavior in children. In M. Lewis & S. Miller (Eds.), *Handbook of developmental psychopathology* (pp. 181-188). New York: Plenum.

Eisenberg, N., Miller, P. A., Schaller, M., Fabes, R. A., Fultz, J., Shell, R., & Shay, C. (1989). The role of sympathy and altruistic personality traits in helping: A re-examination. *Journal of Personality, 57,* 41-67.

Eisenberg, N., Schaller, M., & Fabes, R. A. (1988). Differentiation of personal distress and sympathy in children and adults. *Developmental Psychology, 24,* 766-775.

Ekman, P. (1992). An argument for basic emotions. *Cognition and Emotion, 6,* 169-200.

Ekman, P. (2003). Emotions revealed: Recognizing faces and feelings to improve communication and emotional life. New York: Henry Holt.

Ekman, P., Levenson, R. W. & Friesen, W. V. (1983). Autonomic nervous system activity distinguishes among emotions. *Science, 221,* 1208-1210.

Emmons, R. A. (1992, August). *Revenge: Individual differences and correlates.* Paper presented at the 100th Annual Convention of the American Psychological Association, Washington, DC.

Emmons, R. A. (2000a). Personality and forgiveness. In M. E. McCullough, K. I. Pargament, & C. E. Thoresen (Eds.), *Forgiveness: Theory, research and practice* (pp. 156-175). New York: Guilford Press.

Emmons, R. A. (2000b). *The psychology of ultimate concerns: Motivation and spirituality in personality.* New York: Guilford Press.

Emmons, R. A. & Crumpler, C. A. (2000). Gratitude as human strength: Appraising the evidence. *Journal of Social and Clinical Psychology*, 19, 56-69.

Emmons, R. A. & McCullough, M. E. (2003). Counting blessings versus burdens: An experimental investigation of gratitude and subjective well-being in daily life. *Journal of Personality and Social Psychology*, 84, 377-389.

Emmons, R. A. & McCullough, M. E. (2004). *The psychology of gratitude*. Oxford: Oxford University Press.

Enright R. D. (2001). *Forgiveness is a choice: A step-by-step process for resolving anger and restoring hope*. Washington, DC: American Psychological Association.

Enright, R. D., & Fitzgibbons, R. P. (2000). *Helping clients forgive: An empirical guide for resolving anger and restoring hope*. Washington, DC: American Psychological Association.

Enright, R. D., & the Human Development Study Group (1994). Piaget on the moral development of forgiveness: Identity or reciprocity? *Human Development, 37*, 63-80.

Enright, R. D., & Zell, R. (1989). Problems encountered when we forgive one another. *Journal of Psychology and Christianity, 8*, 52-60.

Esterling, B. A., Kiecolt-Glaser, J. K., Bodnar, J. C., & Glaser, R. (1994). Chronic stress, social support, and persistent alterations in the natural killer cell response to cytokines in older adults. *Health Psychology, 13*, 291-298.

Esterling, B. A., L'Abate, L., Murray, E. J., & Pennebaker, J. W. (1999). Empirical foundations for writing in prevention and psychotherapy: Mental and physical outcomes. *Clinical Psychology Review, 19*, 79-96.

Estrada, C. A., Isen, A. M., & Young, M. J. (1997). Positive affect facilitates integration of information and decreases anchoring in reasoning among physicians. *Organizational Behavior and Human Decision Processes, 72*, 117-135.

Exline, J. J., & Martin, A. (2005). Anger toward God: A new frontier in forgiveness research. In E. L. Worthington, Jr. (Ed.), *Handbook of forgiveness* (pp. 73-88). New York: Brunner-Routledge.

Exline, J. J., Worthington, E. L., Jr., Hill, P. C., & McCullough, M. E. (2003). Forgiveness and justice: A research agenda for social and personality psychology. *Personality and Social Psychology Review, 7*, 337-348.

Fabes, R. A., Eisenberg, N., & Miller, P. A. (1990). Maternal correlates of children's vicarious emotional responsiveness. *Developmental Psychology, 26*, 639-648.

Farrow, T. F. D., & Woodruff, P. W. R. (2005). Neuroimaging of forgivability. In E. L. Worthington, Jr. (Ed.), *Handbook of forgiveness* (pp. 259-272). New York: Brunner-Routledge.

Farrow, T. F. D., Zheng, Y., Wilkinson, I. D., Spence, J. F., Deakin, J. F. W., Tarrier, N., Griffiths, P. D., & Woodruff, P. W. R. (2001). Investigating the functional anatomy of empathy and forgiveness. *NeuroReport, 12*, 2433-2438.

Faulkner, W. (1975). *Requiem for a nun*. New York: Vintage Books.

Feather, N. T. (1999). Judgments of deservingness: Studies in the psychology of justice and achievement. *Personality and Social Psychology Review, 3*, 86-107.

Feeney, P. A., Noller, P., & Callan, V. J. (1994). Attachment style, communication, and satisfaction in the early years of marriage. In K. Bartholomew & D. Perlman (Eds.) *Attachment processes in adulthood: Advances in personal relationships* (pp. 269-308). Philadelphia: Jessica Kingsley Publishers.

Fincham, F. D. (2002). The kiss of the porcupines: From attributing responsibility to forgiving. *Personal Relationships, 7*, 1-23.

Fincham, F. D., & Beach, S. R. H. (2002). Forgiveness in marriage: Implications for psychological aggression and constructive communication. *Personal Relationships, 9*, 239-251.

Fincham, F. D, Beach, S. R. H., & Davila, J. (2004). Forgiveness and conflict resolution in marriage. *Journal of Family Psychology, 18*, 72-81.

Fincham, F. D., Hall, J. H., & Beach, S. R. H. (2005). "'Til lack of forgiveness doth us part": Forgiveness and marriage. In E. L. Worthington, Jr. (Ed.), *Handbook of forgiveness* (pp. 207-225). New York: Brunner-Routledge.

Finkel, E. J., Rusbult, C. E., Kumashiro, M. & Hannon, P. A. (2002). Dealing with betrayal in close relationships: Does commitment promote forgiveness? *Journal of Personality and Social Psychology, 82*, 956-974.

Fitzgibbons, R. P. (1986). The cognitive and emotive use of forgiveness in the treatment of anger. *Psychotherapy, 23*, 629-633.

Flanigan, B. J. (1987). Shame and forgiving in alcoholism. *Alcoholism Treatment Quarterly, 4,* 181-195.

Flanigan, B. (1992). *Forgiving the unforgivable.* New York: Macmillan.

Folger, R., & Cropanzano, R. (1998). *Organizational justice and human resource management.* Thousand Oaks, CA: Sage.

Folkman, S. (1997). Positive psychological states and coping with severe stress. *Social Science and Medicine, 45,* 1207-1221.

Folkman, S., & Moskowitz, J. T. (2000a). Positive affect and the other side of coping. *American Psychologist, 55,* 647-654.

Folkman, S., & Moskowitz, J. T. (2000b). Stress, positive emotion, and coping. *Current Directions in Psychological Science, 9,* 115-118.

Framo, J. (1982). *Explorations in marital and family therapy: Selected papers of James L. Framo.* New York: Springer.

Fredrickson, B. L. (1998). What good are positive emotions? *Review of General Psychology, 2,* 300-319.

Fredrickson, B. L. (2001). The role of positive emotions in positive psychology: The broaden-and-build theory of positive emotions. *American Psychologist, 56,* 218-226.

Fredrickson, B. L., & Levenson, R. W. (1998). Positive emotions speed recovery from the cardiovascular sequelae of negative emotions. *Cognition and Emotion, 12,* 191-220.

Fredrickson, B. L., Mancuso, R. A., Branigan, C., & Tugade, M. M. (2000). The undoing effect of positive emotions. *Motivation and Emotion, 24,* 237-258.

Freedman, S. R. (1998). Forgiveness and reconciliation. The importance of understanding how they differ. *Counseling and Values, 42,* 200-216.

Freedman, S. R., & Enright, R. D. (1996). Forgiveness as an intervention goal with incest survivors. *Journal of Consulting and Clinical Psychology, 64,* 983-992.

Freedman, S. R., Enright, R. D., & Knutson, J. (2005). A progress report on the process model of forgiveness. In E. L. Worthington, Jr. (Ed.), *Handbook of forgiveness* (pp. 393-406). New York: Brunner-Routledge.

Fried, C. B., & Aronson, E. (1995). Hypocrisy, misattribution, and dissonance reduction. *Personality and Social Psychology Bulletin, 21,* 925-933.

Gabriel, Y. (1988). An introduction to the social psychology of insults in organizations. *Human Relations, 51,* 1329-1354.

Gaines, S. O., Reis, H. T., Summers, S., Rusbult, C. E., Cox, C. L., Wexler, M. O., Marelich, W. D., & Kurland, G. J. (1997). Impact of attachment style on reactions to accommodative dilemmas in close relationships. *Personal Relationships, 2,* 93-113.

Galaway, B., Hudson, J., Morris, A., & Maxwell, G. (1995). *Family group conferencing: Perspectives on public policy and practice.* Monsey, NY: Criminal Justice Press.

Gerber L. E. (1987). Experiences of forgiveness in physicians whose medical treatment was not successful. *Psychological Reports, 61,* 236.

Gerber L. E. (1990). Transformations of self-understanding in surgeons whose medical treatment efforts were not successful. *American Journal of Psychotherapy, 44,* 75-84.

Gilbert, P. (Ed.). (2005). *Compassion: Nature and use in psychotherapy* (pp. 168-192). East Sussex, England: Psychology Press.

Gilligan, C. (1994). *In a different voice: Women's conceptions of self and of morality.* New York: Garland Publishing.

Gingrich, F., Worthington, E. L., Jr., Sharp, C. B., Monteforte, M., Lao, E., & Bubod, L. (2005). *Worthington's intervention model to REACH forgiveness adapted to three Christian Filipino contexts.* Unpublished manuscript, Virginia Commonwealth University, Richmond.

Gladwell, M. (2002). *The tipping point: How little things can make a big difference.* Boston: Back Bay Books.

Gobodo-Madikizela, P. (2003). *A human being died that night: A South African story of forgiveness.* Boston: Houghton-Mifflin.

Goffman, E. (1969). *Strategic interaction.* Oxford, England: U. Pennsylvania Press.

Gordon, K. C., & Baucom, D. H. (1998). Understanding betrayals in marriage: A synthesized model of forgiveness. *Family Process, 27,* 425-449.

Gordon, K. C., & Baucom, D. H. (1999). A multitheoretical intervention for promoting recovery from extramarital affairs. *Clinical Psychology: Science and Practice, 6,* 382-399.

Gordon, K. C., & Baucom, D. H. (2003). Forgiveness and marriage: Preliminary support for a synthesized model of recovery from a marital betrayal. *American Journal of Family Therapy, 31,* 179-199.

Gordon, K. C., Baucom, D. H., & Snyder, D. K. (2000). The use of forgiveness in marital therapy. In M. E. McCullough, K. I. Pargament, & C. E. Thoresen (Eds.), *Forgiveness: Theory, research, and practice* (pp. 203-227). New York: Guilford Press.

Gordon, K. C., Baucom, D. H., & Snyder, D. K. (2004). An integrative intervention for promoting recovery from extramarital affairs. *Journal of Marital and Family Therapy, 30,* 213-231.

Gordon, K. C., Baucom, D. H., & Snyder, D. K. (2005). Forgiveness in couples: Divorce, infidelity, and couples therapy. In E. L. Worthington, Jr. (Ed.), *Handbook of forgiveness* (pp. 407-421). New York: Brunner-Routledge.

Gottman, J. M. (1993). A theory of marital dissolution and stability. *Journal of Family Psychology, 7,* 57-75.

Gottman, J. M. (1994). *What predicts divorce? The relationship between marital processes and marital outcomes.* Hillsdale, NJ: Lawrence Erlbaum Associates.

Gottman, J. M., Katz, F. L., & Hooven, C. (1996) *Meta-emotion: How families communicate emotionally.* Hillsdale, NJ: Lawrence Erlbaum Associates.

Gray, J. A. (1982). *The neuropsychology of anxiety: An enquiry into the functions of the septo-hippocampus system.* New York: Oxford University Press.

Gray, J. A. (1994). Personality dimensions and emotion systems. In P. Ekman & R. J. Davidson (Eds.), *The nature of emotion: Fundamental questions* (pp. 329-331). New York: Oxford University Press.

Greenberg, L. S., & Foerster, F. (1996). Resolving unfinished business: The process of change. *Journal of Consulting and Clinical Psychology, 64,* 439-446.

Greenberg, L. S., & Malcolm, W. L. (2002). Resolving unfinished business: Relating process to outcome. *Journal of Consulting and Clinical Psychology, 70,* 406-416.

Greenberg, L. S., Rice, L. N., & Elliott, R. (1993). *Facilitating emotional change: The moment by moment process.* New York: Guilford press.

Greenberg, M. A., Wortman, C. B., & Stone, A. A. (1996). Emotional expression and physical health: Revising traumatic memories or fostering self-regulation? *Journal of Personality and Social Psychology, 71,* 588-602.

Greene, J. D., Sommerville, R. B., Nystrom, L. E., Darley, J. M., & Cohen, J. D. (2001). An fMRI investigation of emotional engagement in moral judgment. *Science, 293,* 2105-2108.

Gross, J. J. (1998). The emerging field of emotion regulation: An integrative review. *Review of General Psychology, 2,* 271-299.

Gross, J. J. (2001). Emotion regulation in adulthood: Timing is everything. *Current Directions in Psychological Research, 10,* 214-219.

Gross, J. J. (2002). Emotion regulation: Affective, cognitive, and social consequences. *Psychophysiology, 39,* 281-291.

Gross, J. J., & John, O. P. (2002). Wise emotion regulation. In L. F. Barrett and P. Salovey (Eds.), *Wisdom in feeling: Psychological processes in emotional intelligence* (pp. 279-319). New York: Guilford Press.

Gross, J. J., & Levenson, R. W. (1997). Hiding feelings: The acute effects of inhibiting negative and positive emotion. *Journal of Abnormal Psychology, 106,* 95-103.

Gruen, R. J., & Mendelsohn, G. (1986). Emotional responses to affective displays in others: The distinction between empathy and sympathy. *Journal of Personality and Social Psychology, 51,* 609-614.

Guerney, B. G. (1978). *Relationship enhancement.* San Francisco: Jossey-Bass.

Hall, J. H., & Fincham, F. D. (2005). Self-forgiveness: The stepchild of forgiveness research. *Journal of Social and Clinical Psychology, 24*(5), 621-637.

Haney, C., Banks, C., & Zimbardo, P. (1973). Interpersonal dynamics in a simulated prison. *International Journal of Criminology and Penology, 1,* 69-97.

Hargrave, T. (2001). *Forgiving the devil: Coming to terms with damaged relationships.* Redding, CT: Zeig, Theisen, & Tucker.

Hargrave, T. D., & Sells, J. N. (1997). The development of a forgiveness scale. *Journal of Marital and Family Therapy, 23,* 41-62.

Harley, W. F., Jr. (1986). *His needs, her needs: Building an affair-proof marriage.* (2nd ed.). Grand Rapids, MI: Fleming H. Revell.

Harley, W. F., Jr. (1992). *Love busters: Overcoming habits that destroy romantic love* (2nd ed.). Grand Rapids, MI: Fleming H. Revell.

Harmon-Jones, E. (2001). The role of affect in cognitive-dissonance processes. In Joseph P. Forgas (Ed.), *Handbook of affect and social cognition* (pp. 237-255). Mahwah, NJ: Lawrence Erlbaum Associates, Publishers.

Harmon-Jones, E., Abramson, L. Y., Sigelman, J., Bohlig, A., Hogan, M. E., & Harmon-Jones, C. (2002). Proneness to hypomania/mania symptoms or depression symptoms and asymmetrical frontal cortical responses to an anger-evoking event. *Journal of Personality and Social Psychology, 82,* 610-618.

Harmon-Jones, E., & Sigelman, J. (2001). State anger and prefrontal brain activity: Evidence that insult-related relative left-prefrontal activation is associated with experienced anger and aggression. *Journal of Personality and Social Psychology, 80,* 797-803.

Harmon-Jones, E., Sigelman, J. D., & Bohlig, A. (2003). Anger, coping, and frontal cortical activity: The effect of coping potential on anger-induced left frontal activity. *Cognition and Emotion, 17,* 1-24.

Harmon-Jones, E., Vaughn, K., Mohr, S., Sigelman, J., & Harmon-Jones, C. (2001). Evidence that sympathy reduces relative left frontal activity associated with anger. *Psychophysiology, 38,* S48.

Harmon-Jones, E., Vaughn-Scott, K., & Mohr, S., Sigelman, J., & Harmon-Jones, C. (2004). The effect of manipulated sympathy and anger on left and right frontal cortical activity. *Emotion, 4,* 95-101.

Harris, A. H. S., & Thoresen, C. E. (2005). Forgiveness, unforgiveness, health, and disease. In E. L. Worthington, Jr. (Ed.), *Handbook of forgiveness* (pp. 321-333). New York: Brunner-Routledge.

Hart, B., & Risley, T. R. (1995). *Meaningful differences in the everyday experience of young American children.* Baltimore: Paul H. Brookes.

Hart, K. E., & Shapiro, D. A. (2002, August). *Secular and spiritual forgiveness interventions for recovering alcoholics harboring grudges.* Paper presented at the annual convention of the American Psychological Association, Chicago.

Haslam, N., Rothschild, L., & Ernst, D. (2000). Essentialist beliefs about social categories. *British Journal of Social Psychology, 39,* 113-127.

Hazan, C., & Shaver, P. R. (1987). Romantic love conceptualized as an attachment process. *Journal of Personality and Social Psychology, 52,* 511-524.

Hebl, J. H., & Enright, R. D. (1993). Forgiveness as a psychotherapeutic goal with elderly females. *Psychotherapy, 30,* 658-667.

Hewstone, M., Cairns, E., Voci, A., McLernon, F., Niens, U., & Noor, M. (2004). Intergroup forgiveness and guilt in Northern Ireland: Social psychological dimensions of "The Troubles." In N. R. Branscombe & B. Doosje (Eds.), *Collective guilt: International perspectives* (pp. 193-215). New York: Cambridge University Press.

Hickson, G. B., Clayton, E. E., Entman, S. S., & Miller, C. S. (1994). Obstetricians' prior malpractice experience and patients' satisfaction with care. *Journal of the American Medical Association, 272,* 1583-1587.

Hope, D. (1988). The healing paradox of forgiveness. *Psychotherapy, 24,* 240-244.

Horowitz, M. J. (1975). Intrusive and repetitive thoughts after experimental stress. *Archives of General Psychiatry, 32,* 1457-1463.

Hoyt, W. T., & McCullough, M. E. (2005). Issues in the multimodal measurement of forgiveness. In E. L. Worthington, Jr. (Ed.), *Handbook of forgiveness* (pp. 109-123). New York: Brunner-Routledge.

Huang, S.-T. T., & Enright, R. D. (2000). Forgiveness and anger-related emotions in Taiwan: Implications for therapy. *Psychotherapy, 37,* 71-79.

Human Development Study Group (1991). Five points on the construct of forgiveness within psychotherapy. *Psychotherapy, 28,* 493-496.

Humphrey, C. W. (1999). *A stress management intervention with forgiveness as the goal.* Unpublished doctoral dissertation, The Union Institute, Cincinnati.

Isen, A. M. (1999). Positive affect. In T. Dalgleish & M. J. Power (Eds.), *Handbook of cognition and emotion* (pp. 521-539). New York: John Wiley & Sons.

Isen, A. M. (2002). A role for neuropsychology in understanding the facilitating influence of positive affect on social behavior and cognitive processes. In C. R. Snyder & S. J. Lopez (Eds.), *Handbook of positive psychology* (pp. 528-540). London: Oxford University Press.

Isen, A. M. (2003). Positive affect as a source of human strength. In L. G. Aspinwall & U. M. Staudinger (Eds.), *A psychology of human strengths: Fundamental questions and future directions for a positive psychology* (pp. 179-195). Washington, DC: American Psychological Association.

Isen, A. M., & Labroo, A. A. (2003). Some ways in which positive affect facilitates decision making and judgment. In S. L. Schneider & J. Shantrau (Eds.), *Emerging perspectives on judgment and decision research* (pp. 365-393). New York: Cambridge University Press.

Izard, C. E. (1990a). Facial expressions and the regulation of emotions. *Journal of Personality and Social Psychology, 58,* 487-498.

Izard, C. E. (1990b). The substrates and functions of emotion feelings: William James and current emotion theory. *Personality and Social Psychology Bulletin, 16,* 626-635. [Special issue: Centennial celebration of The Principles of Psychology.]

Izard, C. E. (1992). Basic emotions, relations among emotions, and emotion-cognition relations. *Psychology Review, 99,* 561-565.

Jacobson, N. S., & Christensen, A. (1996). *Integrative couple therapy: Promoting acceptance and change.* New York: Norton.

Jones, D. R. (2004). *Development of the Ethnic Related African American Stress Evaluation Inventory: Correlates of ethnic forgiveness and health outcomes among African-Americans.* Unpublished dissertation, Virginia Commonwealth University, Richmond.

Kachadourian, L. K., Fincham, F. D., & Davila, J. (2004). The tendency to forgive in dating and married couples: Association with attachment and relationship satisfaction. *Personal Relationships, 11,* 373–393.

Kachadourian, L. K., Fincham, F. D., & Davila, J. (2005). Attitudinal ambivalence, rumination, and forgiveness of partner transgressions in marriage. *Personality and Social Psychology Bulletin, 31,* 334-342.

Karremans, J. C., Van Lange, P. A. M., Ouwerkerk, J. W., & Kluwer, E. S. (2003). When forgiving enhances psychological well-being: The role of interpersonal commitment. *Journal of Personality and Social Psychology, 84,* 1011-1026.

Kelly, G. A. (1991). *The psychology of personal constructs, Vol. 1: A theory of personality; Vol. 2: Clinical diagnosis and psychotherapy.* Florence, KY: Taylor & Francis/Routledge.

Kelley, J. E., Lumley, M. A., & Leisen, J. C. C. (1997). Health effects of emotional disclosure in rheumatoid arthritis patients. *Health Psychology, 16,* 331-340.

Kernis, M. H., Cornell, D. P., Sun, C.-R., Berry, A., & Harlow, T. (1993). There's more to self-esteem than whether it is high or low: The importance of stability of self-esteem. *Journal of Personality and Social Psychology, 65,* 1190-1204.

Kiefer, R. P., Worthington, E. L., Jr., Myers, B., Kliewer, W. L., Kilgour, J., Jr., & Berry, J. W. (2005). *Promoting forgiveness in parents from the community.* Unpublished manuscript, Virginia Commonwealth University, Richmond.

Kohlberg, L. (1981). *Essays on moral development: Vol. 1. The philosophy of moral development.* New York: Harper.

Kohlberg, L. (1984). *Essays on moral development: Vol. 2. The psychology of moral development.* New York: Harper.

Kohlberg, L. (1984). *Kohlberg's original study of moral development* (B. Puka, Ed.). New York: Garland Publishing Inc.

Kopp, S. (1970). The Wizard of Oz behind the couch. *Psychology Today, 3*(10), Mar., 70-73, 84.

Krause, N., & Ellison, C. G. (2003). Forgiveness by God, forgiveness of others, and psychological well-being in late life. *Journal for the Scientific Study of Religion, 42,* 77-93.

Krause, N., & Ingersoll-Dayton, B. (2001). Religion and the process of forgiveness in late life. *Review of Religious Research, 42,* 252-276.

Kreuz, L. E., & Rose, R. M. (1972). Assessment of aggressive behavior and plasma testosterone in a young criminal population. *Psychosomatic Medicine, 34,* 321-332.

Kurusu, T. A. (1997). A brief intervention to ready participants in psychoeducational groups to forgive. Unpublished master's thesis, Virginia Commonwealth University, Richmond.

Kurusu, T. A. (2000). The effectiveness of pretreatment intervention on participants of a forgiveness-promoting psychoeducational group in various stages of change. *Dissertation Abstracts International, 60,* 3270.

LaFave, W. (2000). *Criminal law* (3rd ed.). St. Paul, MN: West Publishers.

Lampton, C., Oliver, G., Worthington, E. L., Jr., & Berry, J. W. (2005). Helping Christian college students become more forgiving: An intervention study to promote forgiveness as part of a program to shape Christian character. *Journal of Psychology and Theology, 33,* 278-290.

Lawler, K. A., Younger, J. W., Piferi, R. L., Billington, E., Jobe, R., Edmondson, K., & Jones, W. H. (2003). A change of heart: Cardiovascular correlates of forgiveness in response to interpersonal conflict. *Journal of Behavioral Medicine, 26,* 373-393.

Lazarus, R. S. (1999). *Stress and emotion: A new synthesis.* New York: Springer.

Lazarus, R. S., & Folkman, S. (1984). *Stress, appraisal, and coping.* New York: Springer.

Lazarus, R. S., Kanner, A. D., & Folkman, S. (1980). Emotions: A cognitive-phenomenological analysis. In R. Plutchik & H. Kellerman (Eds.), *Theories of emotion* (pp. 189-217). New York: Academic Press.

Leary, M. R., & Baumeister, R. F. (2000). The nature and function of self-esteem: Sociometer theory. In M. P. Zanna (Ed.), *Advances in experimental social psychology, Vol. 32* (pp. 1-62). San Diego: Academic Press.

Leary, M. R., Springer, C., Negel, L., Ansell, E., & Evans, K. (1998). The causes, phenomenology, and consequences of hurt feelings. *Journal of Personality and Social Psychology, 74,* 1225-1237.

Lederac, J. P. (2001). Five qualities of practice in support of reconciliation processes. In R. G. Helmick & R. L. Petersen (Eds.), *Forgiveness and reconciliation: Religion, public policy, and conflict transformation* (pp. 183-193). Philadelphia: Templeton Foundation Press.

Lerner, M. J. (1980). *The belief in a just world.* New York: Plenum.

Levenson, R. W., & Ruef, A. M. (1991). Empathy: A physiological substrate. *Journal of Personality and Social Psychology, 63,* 234-246.

Leyens, J. P., Paladino, P. M., Rodriguez-Torres, R. T., Vaes, J., Demoulin, S., Rodriguez-Perez, A. P., & Gaunt, R. (2000). The emotional side of prejudice: The role of secondary emotions. *Personality and Social Psychology Review, 4,* 186-197.

Lind, E. A., Kanfer, R., & Earley, P. C. (1990). Voice, control, and procedural justice: Instrumental and noninstrumental concerns in fairness judgments. *Journal of Personality and Social Psychology, 59,* 952-959.

Lomax, E. (1996). *The railway man.* London: Vintage.

Luskin, F. (2001). *Forgive for good: A proven prescription for health and happiness.* San Francisco: Harper.

Luskin, F., & Bland, B. (2000). *Stanford-Northern Ireland HOPE-1 project.* Unpublished manuscript, Stanford University, Palo Alto, CA.

Luskin, F., & Bland, B. (2001). *Stanford-Northern Ireland HOPE-2 project.* Unpublished manuscript, Stanford University, Palo Alto, CA.

Luskin, F., & Thoresen, C. (1998). *Effectiveness of forgiveness training on psychosocial factors in college-aged adults.* Unpublished manuscript, Stanford University, Palo Alto, CA.

Luskin, F., Thoresen, C, Harris, A., Benisovich, S., Standard, S., Bruning, J., & Evans, S. (2001). *Effects of group forgiveness interventions on perceived stress, state and trait anger, symptoms of stress, self-reported health, and forgiveness.* Unpublished manuscript, Stanford University, Palo Alto, CA.

Macaskill, A., Maltby, J., & Day, L. (2002). Forgiveness of self and others and emotional empathy. *Journal of Social Psychology, 142,* 663-665.

Madanes, C. (1990). *Sex, love, and violence: Strategies for transformation.* New York: W. W. Norton

Main, M., Kaplan, N., & Cassidy, J. (1985). Security in infancy, childhood, and adulthood: A move to the level of representation. In I. Bretherton & E. Waters (Eds.), *Growing points of attachment theory and research.* Monographs of the Society for Research in Child Development.

Malcolm, W. M., & Greenberg, L. S. (2000). Forgiveness as a process of change in individual psychotherapy. In M. E. McCullough, K. I. Pargament, & C. E. Thoresen (Eds.), *Forgiveness: Theory, research, and practice* (pp. 179-202). New York: Guilford Press.

Malcolm, W. M., & Greenberg, L. (2003, October). *Forgiveness in emotion-focused therapy: Preliminary results from studies of psychotherapy and couple therapy.* Paper presented at the conference on Scientific Findings in Forgiveness, Atlanta.

Malcolm, W. M., Warwar, S., & Greenberg, L. (2005). Facilitating forgiveness in individual therapy as an approach to resolving interpersonal injuries. In E. L. Worthington, Jr. (Ed.), *Handbook of forgiveness* (pp. 379-391). New York: Brunner-Routledge.

Marty, M. E. (1998). The ethos of Christian forgiveness. In E. L. Worthington, Jr. (Ed.), *Dimensions of forgiveness: Psychological research and theological perspectives* (pp. 9-28). Philadelphia: Templeton Foundation Press.

Matsumoto, D. (1992). American-Japanese cultural differences in the recognition of universal facial expressions. *Journal of Cross-Cultural Psychology, 23,* 72-84.

Mauger, P. A., Perry, J. E., Freeman, T., Grove, D. C., McBride, A. G., & McKinney, K. E. (1992). The measurement of forgiveness: Preliminary research. *Journal of Psychology and Christianity, 11,* 170-180.

Maxwell, G., & Morris, A. (1993). *Family participation, cultural diversity, and victim involvement in youth justice: A New Zealand experiment.* Wellington, New Zealand: Legal Research Foundation.

McCullough, M. E. (1997). Marriage and forgiveness. *Marriage and Family: A Christian Journal, 1,* 81-96.

McCullough, M. E. (2001a). Forgiveness: Who does it and how do they do it? *Current Directions in Psychological Science, 10,* 194-197.

McCullough, M. E. (2001b). Forgiving. In C. R. Snyder (Ed.), *Coping with stress: Effective people and processes* (pp.93-113). New York: Oxford University Press.

McCullough, M. E., Bellah, C. G., Kilpatrick, S. D., & Johnson, J. L. (2001). Vengefulness: Relationships with forgiveness, rumination, well-being, and the Big Five. *Personality and Social Psychology Bulletin, 27,* 601-610.

McCullough, M. E., & Bono, G. (2004). *How rumination deters forgiveness: Two longitudinal studies.* Unpublished manuscript, University of Miami.

McCullough, M. E., Emmons, R. A., & Tsang, J. (2002). The grateful disposition: A conceptual and empirical topography. *Journal of Personality and Social Psychology, 82,* 112-127.

McCullough, M. E., Fincham, F. D., & Tsang, J. (2003). Forgiveness, forbearance, and time: The temporal unfolding of transgression-related interpersonal motivations. *Journal of Personality and Social Psychology, 84,* 540-557.

McCullough, M. E., & Hoyt, W. T. (2002). Transgression-related motivational dispositions: Personality substrates of forgiveness and their links to the Big Five. *Personality and Social Psychology Bulletin, 28,* 1556-1573.

McCullough, M. E., Hoyt, W. T., & Rachal, K. C. (2000). What we know (and need to know) about assessing forgiveness constructs. In M. E. McCullough, K. I. Pargament, & C. E. Thoresen (Eds.), *Forgiveness: Theory, research, and practice* (pp. 65-88) New York: Guilford Press.

McCullough, M. E., Kilpatrick, S. D., Emmons, R. A., & Larson, D. B. (2001). Is gratitude a moral affect? *Psychological Bulletin, 127,* 249-266.

McCullough, M. E., Rachal, K. C., & Hoyt, W. T. (2000). What we know (and need to know) about assessing forgiveness constructs. In M. E. McCullough, K. I. Pargament, & C. E. Thoresen (Eds.), *Forgiveness: Theory, research, and practice* (pp. 65-88). New York: Guilford Press.

McCullough, M. E., Rachal, K. C., Sandage, S. J., Worthington, E. L., Jr., Brown, S. W., & Hight, T. L. (1998). Interpersonal forgiveness in close relationships II: Theoretical elaboration and measurement. *Journal of Personality and Social Psychology, 75,* 1586-1603.

McCullough, M. E., & Root, L. M. (2005). Forgiveness as change. In E. L. Worthington, Jr. (Ed.), *Handbook of forgiveness* (pp. 91-107). New York: Brunner-Routledge.

McCullough, M. E., Sandage, S. J., & Worthington, E. L., Jr. (1997). *To forgive is human: How to put your past in the past.* Downers Grove, IL: InterVarsity Press.

McCullough, M. E., Tsang, J.-A., & Emmons, R. A. (2004). Gratitude in intermediate affective terrain: Links of grateful moods to individual differences and daily emotional experience. *Journal of Personality and Social Psychology, 86,* 295-309.

McCullough, M. E., & Worthington, E. L., Jr. (1994). Encouraging clients to forgive people who have hurt them: Review, critique, and research prospectus. *Journal of Psychology and Theology, 22,* 3-20.

McCullough, M. E., & Worthington, E. L., Jr. (1995). Promoting forgiveness: A comparison of two brief psycho-educational interventions with a waiting list control. *Counseling and Values, 40,* 55-68.

McCullough, M. E., & Worthington, E. L., Jr. (1999). Religion and the forgiving personality. *Journal of Personality, 67,* 1141-1164.

McCullough, M. E., Worthington, E. L., Jr., & Rachal, K. C. (1997). Interpersonal forgiving in close relationships. *Journal of Personality and Social Psychology, 73,* 321-336.

McEwen, B. S. (2002). *The end of stress as we know it.* Washington, DC: Joseph Henry Press

Meek, K. R., Albright, J. S., & McMinn, M. R. (1995). Religious orientation, guilt, confession, and forgiveness. *Journal of Psychology and Theology, 23,* 190-197.

Meichenbaum, D. (1977). *Cognitive-behavior modification: An integrative approach.* New York: Plenum.

Meier, S. E., Brigham, T. A., Ward, D. A., & Myers, F. (1995). Effects of blood alcohol concentrations on negative punishment: Implications for decision-making. *Journal of Studies on Alcohol, 57,* 85-96.

Mikulincer, M., & Nachshon, O. (1991). Attachment styles and patterns of self-disclosure. *Journal of Personality and Social Psychology, 61,* 321-331.

Mikulincer, M. & Shaver, P. (2005). Attachment theory and emotions in close relationships: Exploring the attachment-related dynamics of emotional reactions to relational events. *Personal Relationships, 12,* 149-168.

Milgram, S. (1974). *Obedience to authority.* New York: Harper & Row.

Miller, N., Pedersen, W. C., Earleywine, M., & Pollock, V. E. (2003). A theoretical model of triggered displaced aggression. *Personality and Social Psychology Review, 7,* 75-97.

Miller, W. R., & C'de Baca, J. (2001). *Quantum change: When epiphanies and sudden insights transform ordinary lives.* New York: Guilford Press.

Millon, T. (1998). DSM narcissistic personality disorder: Historical reflections and future directions. In E. F. Ronningstam (Ed.), *Disorders of narcissism: Diagnostic, clinical, and empirical implications* (pp. 75-101). Washington, DC: American Psychiatric Association.

Mor, N., & Winquist, J. (2002). Self-focused attention and negative affect: A meta-analysis. *Psychological Bulletin, 128,* 638-662.

Mullet, E., Neto, F., & Rivière, S. (2005). Personality and its effects on resentment, revenge, and forgiveness and on self-forgiveness. In E. L. Worthington, Jr. (Ed.), *Handbook of forgiveness* (pp. 159-182). New York: Brunner-Routledge.

Neto, F., & Mullet, E. (2004). Personality, self-esteem, and self-construal as correlates of forgivingness. *European Journal of Personality, 18,* 15-30.

Newberg, A. B., d'Aquili, E. G., Newberg, S. K., & deMarici, V. (2000). The neuropsychological correlates of forgiveness. In M. E. McCullough, K. I. Pargament, & C. E. Thoresen (Eds.), *Forgiveness: Theory, research, and practice* (pp. 91-110). New York: Guilford Press.

Newberry, P. A. (2001). Joseph Butler on forgiveness: A presupposed theory of emotion. *Journal of the History of Ideas, 62,* 233-244.

Nolen-Hoeksema, S. (1987). Sex differences in unipolar depression: Evidence and theory. *Psychological Bulletin, 101,* 259-282.

Nolen-Hoeksema, S. (1991). Responses to depression and their effects on the duration of a depressive episode. *Journal of Abnormal Psychology, 100,* 569-582.

Paleari, F. G., Regalia, C., & Fincham, F. D. (2003). Adolescents' willingness to forgive their parents: An empirical model. *Parenting: Science and Practice, 3,* 155-174.

Paleari, F. G., Regalia, C., & Fincham, F. D. (2005). Marital quality, forgiveness, empathy, and rumination: A longitudinal analysis. *Personality and Social Psychology Bulletin, 31,* 368-378.

Pargament, K. I. (1997). *The psychology of religion and coping: Theory, research, practice.* New York: Guilford Press.

Pargament, K. I., Murray-Swank, N. A., & Magyar, G. M. (2005). Spiritual struggle: A phenomenon of interest to psychology and religion. In William R. Miller & Harold D. Delaney (Eds.), *Judeo-Christian perspectives on psychology: Human nature, motivation, and change* (pp. 245-268). Washington, DC: American Psychological Association.

Pargament, K. I., Zinnbauer, B. J., Scott, A. B., Butter, E. M., Zerowin, J., & Stanik, P. (1998). Red flags and religious coping: Identifying some religious warning signs among people in crisis. *Journal of Clinical Psychology, 54,* 77-89.

Park, C. L., & Folkman, S. (1997). Meaning in the context of stress and coping. *Review of General Psychology, 1,* 115-144.

Park, C. L., Folkman, S., & Bostrom, A. (2001). Appraisals of controllability and coping in caregivers and HIV+ men: Testing the goodness-of-fit hypothesis. *Journal of Consulting and Clinical Psychology, 69,* 481-488.

Pennebaker, J. W. (2004). *Writing to heal: A guided journal for recovering from trauma and emotional upheaval.* Oakland, CA: New Harbinger.

Pennebaker, J. W., Barger, S. D., & Tiebout, J. (1989). Disclosure of traumas and health among holocaust survivors. *Psychosomatic Medicine, 51,* 577-589.

Pennebaker, J. W. & Francis, M. E. (1996). Cognitive, emotional, and language processes in disclosure. *Cognition and Emotion, 10,* 601-626.

Pennebaker, J. W., Kiecolt-Glaser, J., & Glaser, R. (1988). Disclosure of traumas and immune function: Health implications for psychotherapy. *Journal of Consulting and Clinical Psychology, 56,* 239-245.

Pennebaker, J. W., Mayne, T. J., & Francis, M. E. (1997). Linguistic predictors of adaptive bereavement. *Journal of Personality and Social Psychology, 72,* 863-871.

Pennebaker, J. W., & Seagal, J. D. (1999). Forming a story: The health benefits of narrative. *Journal of Clinical Psychology, 55,* 1243-1254.

Pietrini, P., Guazzelli, M., Basso, G., Jaffe, K., & Grafman, J. (2000). Neural correlates of imaginal aggressive behavior assessed by positron emission tomography in healthy subjects. *American Journal of Psychiatry, 157,* 1772-1781.

Plutchik, R. (2002). *Emotions and life: Perspectives from psychology, biology, and evolution.* Washington, DC: American Psychological Association.

Post, S. G., Underwood, L. G., Schloss, J. P., & Hurlbut, W. B. (2002). *Altruism and altruistic love.* Oxford: Oxford University Press.

Rachman, S. (1997). A cognitive theory of obsessions. *Behaviour Research and Therapy, 35,* 793-802.

Raskin, R., & Novacek, J. (1991). Narcissism and the use of fantasy. *Journal of Clinical Psychology, 47,* 490-499.

Ripley, J. S., & Worthington, E. L., Jr. (2002). Hope-focused and forgiveness group interventions to promote marital enrichment. *Journal of Counseling and Development, 80,* 452-463.

Ripley, J. S., Worthington, E. L., Jr., Bromley, D. G., & Kemper, S. D. (2005). Covenantal and contractual values in marriage: Marital Values Orientation toward Wedlock or Self-actualization (Marital VOWS) Scale. *Personal Relationships, 12,* 317-336.

Roberts, R. C. (2005, February). *The philosopher in psychology and pastoral work.* Paper presented at the Geneva Institute lectures of the American Association of Christian Counselors, Dallas, TX.

Rowe, J. O., Halling, S., Davies, E., Leifer, M., Powers, D., & Van Bronkhorst, J. (1989). The psychology of forgiving another: A dialogal research approach. In R. S. Valle & S. Halling (Eds.), *Existential-phenomenological perspective in psychology: Exploring the breadth of human experience* (pp. 233-244). New York: Plenum Press.

Roy, S. (1993). Two types of juvenile restitution programs in two Midwestern counties: A comparative study. Federal Probation, 57, 48-53.

Rusbult, C. E., Hannon, P. A., Stocker, S. L., & Finkel, E. J. (2005). *Forgiveness and relational repair.* In E. L. Worthington, Jr. (Ed.), *Handbook of forgiveness* (pp. 185-206). New York: Brunner-Routledge.

Rusbult, C. E., Verette, J., Whitney, G. A., Slovik, L. F., & Lipkus, I. (1991). Accommodation processes in close relationships: Theory and preliminary empirical evidence. *Journal of Personality and Social Psychology, 60,* 53-78.

Rushton, J. P., Fulker, D. W., Neale, M. C., Nias, D. K. B., & Eysenck, H. J. (1986). Altruism and aggression: The heritability of individual differences. *Journal of Personality and Social Psychology, 50,* 1192-1198.

Russell, J. A., & Carroll, J. M. (1999). On the bipolarity of positive and negative affect. *Psychological Bulletin, 125,* 3-30.

Rusting, C. L., & Nolen-Hoeksema, S. (1998a). Regulating responses to anger: Effects of rumination and distraction on angry mood. *Journal of Personality & Social Psychology, 74,* 790-803.

Rye, M. S., & Pargament, K. I. (2002). Forgiveness and romantic relationships in college: Can it heal the wounded heart? *Journal of Clinical Psychology, 54,* 419-441.

Rye, M. S., Pargament, K. I., Ali, M. A., Beck, G. L., Dorff, E. N., Hallisey, C., Narayanan, V., & Williams, J. G. (2000). Religious perspectives on forgiveness. In M. E. McCullough, K. I. Pargament, & C. E. Thoresen (Eds.), *Forgiveness: Theory, research, and practice* (pp.17-40). New York: Guilford Press.

Rye, M. S., Pargament, K. I., Pan, W., Yingling, D. W., Shogren, K. A., & Ito, M. (2005). Forgiveness and divorce: Evaluation of an intervention to break the cycle of pain. *Journal of Consulting and Clinical Psychology*, in press.

Salovey, P., & Mayer, J. D. (1989–1990). Emotional intelligence. *Imagination, Cognition, and Personality, 9*, 185-211.

Salovey, P., Mayer, J. D., Goldman, S. L., Turvey, C., & Palfai, T. P. (1995). Emotional attention, clarity, and repair: Exploring emotional intelligence using the Trait-Meta-Mood Scale. In J. W. Pennebaker (Ed.), *Emotion, disclosure, and health* (pp. 125-154). Washington, DC: American Psychological Association.

Salovey, P., Rothman, A. J., Detweiler, J. B., & Steward, W. T. (2000). Emotional states and physical health. *American Psychologist, 55*, 110-121.

Sandage, S. J. (1997). *An ego-humility model of forgiveness.* Unpublished doctoral dissertation, Virginia Commonwealth University, Richmond.

Sandage, S. J., & Williamson, I. (2005). Forgiveness in cultural context. In E. L. Worthington, Jr. (Ed.), *Handbook of forgiveness* (pp. 41-56). New York: Brunner-Routledge.

Sandage, S. J., Worthington, E. L., Jr., & Calvert-Minor, S. (2000, August). Promoting forgiveness, shame-proneness, guilt-proneness, and hope. Paper presented at the meeting of the American Psychological Association, Washington, DC.

Sapolsky, R. M. (1994). *Why zebras don't get ulcers: A guide to stress, stress-related diseases, and coping.* New York: Freeman.

Sapolsky, R. M. (2005). The physiology and pathophysiology of unhappiness. In E. L. Worthington, Jr. (Ed.), *Handbook of forgiveness* (pp. 273-303). New York: Brunner-Routledge.

Sapolsky, R. M., & Share, L. J. (2004). A pacific culture among wild baboons: Its emergence and transmission. *PLoS Biology, 2*, 534-541.

Saunders, H. H. (1999). *A public peace process: Sustained dialogue to transform racial and ethnic conflicts.* New York: St. Martin's Press.

Scharfe, E., & Bartholomew, K. (1995) Accommodation and attachment representations in young couples. *Personal Relationships, 12*, 389-401.

Scheier, M. F., & Carver, C. S. (1985). Optimism, coping, and health: Assessment and implications of generalized outcome expectancies. *Health Psychology, 4*, 219-247.

Schönbach, P. (1990). *Account episodes: The management or escalation of conflict.* New York: Cambridge University Press.

Segerstrom, S. C., Tsao, J. C., Alden, L. E., & Craske, M. G. (2000). Worry and rumination: Repetitive thought as a concomitant and predictor of negative mood. *Cognitive Therapy and Research, 24*, 671-688.

Seybold, K. S., Hill, P. C., Neumann, J. K., & Chi, D. S. (2001). Physiological and psychological correlates of forgiveness. *Journal of Psychology and Christianity, 20*, 250-259.

Shaver, P. R., & Hazan, C. (1993). Adult romantic attachment: Theory and evidence. In D. Perlman & W. Jones (Eds.), *Advances in personal relationships* (Vol. 4, pp. 29-70). London: Kingsley.

Shaver, P. R., & Mikulincer, M. (2004). What do self-report attachment measures assess? In W. S. Rholes & J. A. Simpson (Eds.), *Adult attachment: Theory, research, and clinical implications* (pp. 17-54). New York: Guilford Press.

Shi, L. (2003). The association between adult attachment and conflict resolution in romantic relationships. *American Journal of Family Therapy, 31*, 143-157.

Shriver, D. W., Jr. (1998). Is there forgiveness in politics? Germany, Vietnam, and America. In R. D. Enright & J. North (Eds.), *Exploring forgiveness* (pp. 131-149). Madison: University of Wisconsin Press.

Skinner, E. A., Edge, K., Altman, J., & Hayley, S. (2003). Searching for the structure of coping: A review and critique of category systems for classifying ways of coping. *Psychological Bulletin, 129*, 216-269.

Smedes, L.B. (1984). *Forgive and forget: Healing the hurts we don't deserve.* New York: Harper & Row.

Snyder, C. R. (1994). *The psychology of hope: You can get there from here.* New York: The Free Press.

Snyder, D. K., Gordon, K. C., & Baucom, D. H. (2004). Treating affair couples: Extending the written disclosure paradigm to relationship trauma. *Clinical Psychology: Science and Practice, 11*, 155-160.

Soldz, S., & McCullough, L. (Eds.). (2000). *Reconciling empirical knowledge and clinical experience: The art and science of psychotherapy.* Washington, DC: American Psychological Association.

Solomon, R. L., & Corbit, J. D. (1974). An opponent-process theory of motivation: I. Temporal dynamics of affect. *Psychological Review, 81,* 119-145.

Spielberger, C. D., & Moscoso, M. S. (1999). La expression de colera y hostilidad y sus consecuencias en el sistema cardiovascular. *Psicologia Contemporanea, 2* (1), 32-43.

Staub, E. (2005). Constructive rather than harmful forgiveness, reconciliation, and ways to promote them after genocide and mass killing. In E. L. Worthington, Jr. (Ed.), *Handbook of forgiveness* (pp. 443-459). New York: Brunner-Routledge.

Stuart, B. (1996). Circle sentencing in Canada: A partnership of the community and the criminal justice system. *International Journal of Comparative and Applied Criminal Justice, 20,* 291-309.

Subkoviak, M. J., Enright, R. D., Wu, C. R., Gassin, E. A., Freedman, S., Olson, L. M., & Sarinopoulos, I. (1995). Measuring interpersonal forgiveness in late adolescence and middle adulthood. *Journal of Adolescence, 18,* 641-655.

Symington, S. H., Walker, D. F., & Gorsuch, R. L. (2002) The relationship of forgiveness and reconciliation to 5 and 16 factors of personality. *Journal of Psychology and Christianity, 21,*141-150.

Tajfel, H. (1978). *Differentiation between social groups: Studies in the social psychology of intergroup relations.* Oxford, England: Academic Press.

Tangney, J. P. (2000). Humility: Theoretical perspectives, empirical findings, and directions for future research. *Journal of Social and Clinical Psychology, 19,* 70-82.

Tangney, J. P., Boone, A. L., & Dearing, R. (2005). Forgiving the self: Conceptual issues and empirical findings. In E. L. Worthington, Jr. (Ed.), *Handbook of forgiveness* (pp. 143-158). New York: Brunner-Routledge.

Tangney, J. P., Boone, A. L., Dearing, R., & Reinsmith, C. (2002). *Individual differences in the propensity to forgive: Measurement and implications for psychological and social adjustment. Unpublished m*anuscript, George Mason University.

Tangney, J. P., & Dearing, R. (2002). *Shame and guilt.* New York: Guilford Press.

Tangney, J. P., Miller, R., Flicker, L., & Barlow, D. H. (1996). Are shame, guilt, and embarrassment distinct emotions? *Journal of Personality and Social Psychology, 70,* 1256-1269.

Tangney, J. P., Wagner, P. E., & Gramzow, R. (1992). Proneness to shame, proneness to guilt, and psychopathology. *Journal of Abnormal Psychology, 101,* 469-478.

Tangney, J., Wagner, P. E, Hill-Barlow, D., Marschall, D. E., & Gramzow, R. (1996). Relation of shame and guilt to constructive versus destructive responses to anger across the lifespan. *Journal of Personality and Social Psychology, 70,* 797–809.

Taylor, S. E., Klein, L. C., Lewis, B. P., Gruenewald, T. L., Gurung, R. A. R., & Updegraff, J. A. (2000). Biobehavioral responses to stress in females: Tend-and-befriend, not fight-or-flight. *Psychological Review, 107,* 411-429.

Temoshok, L. R., & Wald, R. L. (2005). Forgiveness and health in persons living with HIV/AIDS. In E. L. Worthington, Jr. (Ed.), *Handbook of forgiveness* (pp. 335-348). New York : Brunner-Routledge.

Thayer, J. F., & Lane, R. D. (2000). A model of neurovisceral integration in emotion regulation and dysregulation. *Journal of Affective Disorders, 61,* 201-206.

Thompson, L. Y., Snyder, C. R., Hoffman, L., Michael, S. T., Rasmussen, H. N., Billings, L. S., Heinze, L., Neufeld, J. E., Shorey, H. S., Roberts, J. C., & Roberts, D. E. (2005). Dispositional forgiveness of self, others, and situations. *Journal of Personality, 73,* 313-360.

Thoresen, C. E., Luskin, F., Harris, A. H. S., Benisovich, S. V., Standard, S., Bruning, J., & Evans, S. (2001). Stanford forgiveness project: Effects of forgiveness intervention on perceived stress, state and trait anger, and self-reported health. *Annals of Behavioral Medicine, 23,* SO37.

Toussaint, L., & Webb, J. R. (2005). Theoretical and empirical connections between forgiveness, mental health, and well-being. In E. L. Worthington (Ed.), *Handbook of forgiveness* (pp. 349-362). New York: Brunner-Routledge.

Toussaint, L. L., Williams, D. R., Musick, M. A., & Everson, S. A. (2001). Forgiveness and health: Age differences in a U.S. probability sample. *Journal of Adult Development, 8,* 249-257.

Triandis, H. C. (2005). Issues in individualism and collectivism research. In R. M. Sorrentino and D. Cohen (Eds.), *Cultural and social behavior: The Ontario Symposium, Vol. 10* (pp. 207-225). Hillsdale, NJ: Lawrence Erlbaum Associates.

Tyler, L. E. (1973). Design for a hopeful psychology. *American Psychologist, 28*, 1021-1029.

Tyler, T. R., Boeckmann, R. J., Smith, H. J., & Huo, Y. J. (1997). *Social justice in a diverse society.* Boulder, CO: Westview.

Umbreit, M. S. (2001). *The handbook of victim offender mediation.* San Francisco: Jossey-Bass.

U.S. Department of Justice. (1998). *The restorative justice fact sheet.* Washington, D.C.: Author.

Van Lange, P. A. M., Agnew, C. R., Harinck, F., & Steemers, G. (1997). From game theory to real life: How social value orientation affects willingness to sacrifice in ongoing close relationships. *Journal of Personality and Social Psychology, 73*, 1330-1344.

Van Lange, P. A. M., Rusbult, C. E., Drigotas, S. M., Arriaga, X. B., Witcher, B. S., & Cox, C. L. (1997). Willingness to sacrifice in close relationships. *Journal of Personality and Social Psychology, 72*, 1373-1395.

Vincent, C., Young, M., & Phillips, A. (1994). Why do people sue doctors? A study of patients and relatives taking legal action. *Lancet, 343*, 1609-1613.

Vitz, P. C., & Mango, P. (1997a). Kernbergian psychodynamics and religious aspects of the forgiveness process. *Journal of Psychology and Theology, 25*, 72-80.

Vitz, P. C., & Mango, P. (1997b). Kleinian psychodynamics and religious aspects of hatred and a defense mechanism. *Journal of Psychology and Theology, 25*, 64-71.

Wade, N. G. (2002). Understanding reach: A component analysis of a group intervention to promote forgiveness. *Dissertation Abstracts International: Section B: The Sciences & Engineering, 63*, 2611.

Wade, N. G., & Worthington, E. L., Jr. (2003). Overcoming interpersonal offenses: Is forgiveness the only way to deal with unforgiveness? *Journal of Counseling and Development, 81*, 343-353.

Wade, N. G., Worthington, E. L., Jr., & Meyer, J. (2005). But do they really work? Meta-analysis of group interventions to promote forgiveness. In E. L. Worthington, Jr. (Ed.), *Handbook of forgiveness* (pp. 423-440). New York: Brunner-Routledge.

Wade, S. H. (1989). *The development of a scale to measure forgiveness.* (Doctoral dissertation, Fuller Theological Seminary, 1990). *Dissertation Abstracts International—B, 50*, 5338.

Walker, D. F., & Gorsuch, R. L. (2002). Forgiveness within the Big Five personality model. *Personality and Individual Differences, 32*, 1127-1137.

Walster, E. (1966). Assignment of responsibility for an accident. *Journal of Personality & Social Psychology, 3*, 73-79.

Watson, D., & Clark, L. A. (1997). Measurement and mis-measurement of mood: Recurrent and emergent issues. *Journal of Personality Assessment, 68*, 267-296.

Wegner, D. M. (1994). *White bears and other unwanted thoughts: Suppression, obsession, and the psychology of mental control.* New York: Guilford Press.

Weiger, W. A., & Bear, D. M. (1988). An approach to the neurology of aggression. *Journal of Psychiatric Research, 22*, 85-98.

Weinberg, N. (1994). Self-blame, other blame, and desire for revenge: Factors in recovery from bereavement. *Death Studies, 18*, 583-593.

Weiner, B. (1993). On sin versus sickness: A theory of perceived responsibility and social motivation. *American Psychologist, 48*, 957-965.

Weissmark, M. S. (2004). *Justice matters: Legacies of the Holocaust and World War II.* Oxford: Oxford University Press.

Wispé, L. (1986). The distinction between sympathy and empathy: To call forth a concept, a word is needed. *Journal of Personality and Social Psychology, 50*, 314-321.

Witvliet, C. v. O. (2005). Unforgiveness, forgiveness, and justice: Scientific findings on feelings and physiology. In E. L. Worthington, Jr. (Ed.), *Handbook of forgiveness* (pp. 305-319). New York: Brunner-Routledge.

Witvliet, C. v. O., Ludwig, T. E., & Bauer, D. J. (2002). Please forgive me: Transgressors' emotions and physiology during imagery of seeking forgiveness and victim responses. *Journal of Psychology and Christianity, 21*, 219-233.

Witvliet, C. v. O., Ludwig, T. E., & Vander Laan, K. L. (2001). Granting forgiveness or harboring grudges: Implications for emotion, physiology, and health. *Psychological Science, 121*, 117-123.

Witvliet, C. v. O., & Vrana, S. R. (1995). Psychophysiological responses as indices of affective dimensions. *Psychophysiology, 32*, 436-443.

Witvliet, C. v. O., Wade, N. G., Worthington, E. L., Jr., & Berry, J. W. (2005). *Apology and resti-tution: The effects of each on victims' unforgiveness, empathy, forgiveness, and emotional psychophysiology in the context of crime.* Manuscript under editorial review.

Witvliet, C. v. O., Worthington, E. L., Jr., Root, L. M., Sato, A. F., Ludwig, T. E., & Exline, J. J. (2005). *Forgiveness and emotion: A psychophysiological analysis.* Manuscript under edito-rial review.

Wolpe, J. (1958). *Psychotherapy by reciprocal inhibition.* Stanford, CA: Stanford University Press.

Worthington, E. L., Jr. (1982). *When someone asks for help: A practical guide for counseling.* Downers Grove, IL: InterVarsity Press.

Worthington, E. L., Jr. (1988). Understanding the values of religious clients: A model and its application to counseling. *Journal of Counseling Psychology, 35,* 166-174.

Worthington, E. L., Jr. (1989). *Marriage counseling: A Christian approach to counseling couples.* Downers Grove, IL: InterVarsity Press.

Worthington, E. L., Jr. (1991). A primer for intake interviews with couples. *American Journal of Family Therapy, 19,* 344-350.

Worthington, E. L., Jr. (1998a). An empathy-humility-commitment model of forgiveness applied within family dyads. *Journal of Family Therapy, 20,* 59-76.

Worthington, E. L., Jr. (1998b). The Pyramid Model of Forgiveness: Some interdisciplinary spec-ulations about unforgiveness and the promotion of forgiveness. In Worthington, E. L., Jr. (Ed.), *Dimensions of forgiveness: Psychological research and theological perspectives* (pp. 107-137). Philadelphia: The Templeton Foundation Press.

Worthington, E. L., Jr. (2000). Is there a place for forgiveness in the justice system? *Fordham Urban Law Journal, 27,* 1721-1734.

Worthington, E. L., Jr. (2001). Unforgiveness, forgiveness, and reconciliation in societies. In R. G. Helmick & R. L. Petersen (Eds.), *Forgiveness and reconciliation: Religion, public policy, and conflict transformation* (pp. 161-182). Philadelphia: Templeton Foundation Press.

Worthington, E. L., Jr. (2003). *Forgiving and reconciling: Bridges to wholeness and hope.* Downers Grove, IL: InterVarsity Press.

Worthington, E. L., Jr. (Ed.). (2005a). *Handbook of forgiveness.* New York: Brunner-Routledge.

Worthington, E. L., Jr. (2005b). Initial questions about the art and science of forgiv-ing. In E. L. Worthington, Jr. (Ed.), *Handbook of forgiveness* (pp. 1-13). New York: Brunner-Routledge.

Worthington, E. L., Jr. (2005c). Questions, some answers, and more questions about forgiveness: Research agenda for 2005–2015. In E. L. Worthington, Jr. (Ed.), *Handbook of forgiveness* (pp. 557-574). New York: Brunner-Routledge.

Worthington, E. L., Jr. (2005d). *Hope-focused marriage counseling: A guide to brief therapy* (Rev. ed. with a new introduction). Downers Grove, IL: InterVarsity Press.

Worthington, E. L., Jr., & Berry, J. W. (2005). Virtues, vices, and character education. In W. R. Miller & H. D. Delaney (Eds.), *Judeo-Christian perspectives on psychology: Human nature, motivation, and change* (pp. 145-16). Washington, DC: American Psychological Association.

Worthington, E. L., Jr., Berry, J. W., Canter, D. E., Sharp, C. B., Scherer, M., & Yarhouse, M. (2003, October). *Forgiveness and communication in marital enrichment and with parents.* Paper presented at the Scientific Findings on Forgiveness conference, Atlanta.

Worthington, E. L., Jr., Berry, J. W., & Parrott, L. III. (2001). Unforgiveness, forgiveness, reli-gion, and health. In T. G. Plante & A. Sherman (Eds.), *Faith and health: Psychological perspectives* (pp. 107-138). New York: Guilford Publications.

Worthington, E. L., Jr. & DiBlasio, F. A. (1990). Promoting mutual forgiveness within the frac-tured relationship. *Psychotherapy, 27,* 219-223.

Worthington, E. L., Jr., & Drinkard, D. T. (2000). Promoting reconciliation through psychoedu-cational and therapeutic interventions. *Journal of Marital and Family Therapy, 26,* 93-101.

Worthington, E. L., Jr., Kurusu, T., Collins, W., Berry, J. W., Ripley, J. S., & Baier, S. N. (2000). Forgiving usually takes time: A lesson learned by studying interventions to promote for-giveness. *Journal of Psychology and Theology, 28,* 3-20.

Worthington, E. L., Jr., Kurusu, T., McCullough, M. E., & Sandage, S. J. (1996). Empirical research on religion and psychotherapeutic processes and outcomes: A 10-year review and research prospectus. *Psychological Bulletin, 119,* 448-487.

Worthington, E. L., Jr., Mazzeo, S. E., & Canter, D. E. (2005). Forgiveness-promoting approach: Helping clients REACH forgiveness through using a longer model that teaches reconciliation. In L. Sperry and E. P. Shafranske (Eds.), *Spiritually-oriented psychotherapy* (pp. 235-257). Washington, DC: American Psychological Association.

Worthington, E. L., Jr., O'Connor, L. E., Berry, J. W., Sharp, C. B., Murray, R., & Yi, E. (2005). Compassion and forgiveness: Implications for psychotherapy. In P. Gilbert (Ed.), *Compassion: Nature and use in psychotherapy* (pp. 168-192). East Sussex, England: Psychology Press.

Worthington, E. L., Jr., Sandage, S. J., & Berry, J. W. (2000). Group interventions to promote forgiveness: What researchers and clinicians ought to know. In M. E. McCullough, K. I. Pargament, & C. Thoreson (Eds.), *Forgiveness: Theory, research, and practice* (pp. 228-253). New York: Guilford Press.

Worthington, E. L., Jr., & Scherer, M. (2004). Forgiveness as an emotion-focused coping strategy that can reduce health risks and promote health resilience: Theory, review, and hypotheses. *Psychology and Health, 19*, 385-405.

Worthington, E. L., Jr., Sharp, C. B., Lerner, A. J., & Sharp, J. R. (2006). Interpersonal forgiveness as a consequence of loving one's enemies: Roles of emotions and motivations. *Journal of Psychology and Theology, 34* in press.

Worthington, E. L., Jr., & Wade, N. G. (1999). The social psychology of unforgiveness and forgiveness and implications for clinical practice. *Journal of Social and Clinical Psychology, 18*, 385-418.

Worthington, E. L., Jr., Witvliet, C. v. O., Lerner, A. J., & Scherer, M. (2005). Forgiveness in medical practice and research. *EXPLORE: The Journal of Science and Healing, 1*, 169-176.

Zehr, H. (1995). *Changing lenses: A new focus on crime and justice*. Scottdale, PA: Herald Press.

Index